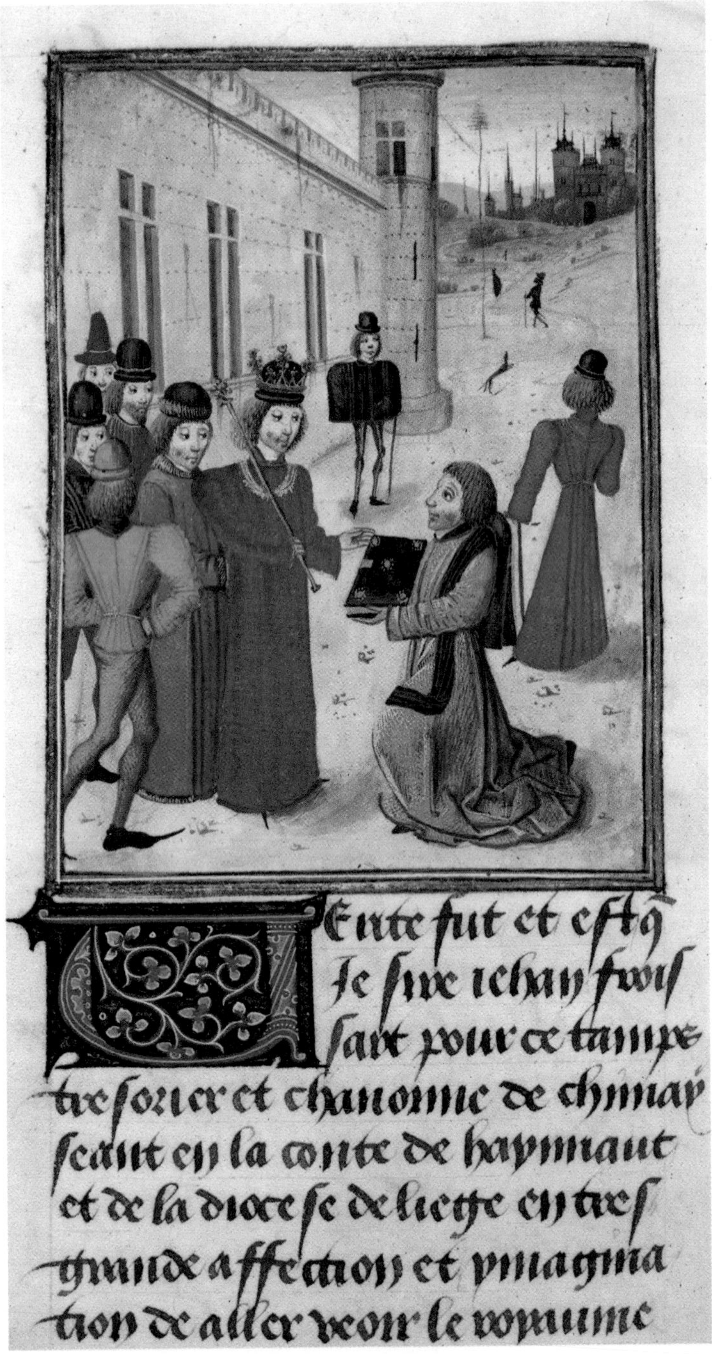
Erite fut et est q
le sire iehan frois
sart pour ce tamps
tresorier et chanonne de chimay
seant en la conte de haynnaut
et de la diocese de liege en tres
grande affection et ymagina
tion de aller veoir le royaume

FROISSART PRESENTS HIS BOOK TO KING RICHARD

CONTEMPORARY CHRONICLES OF

the hundred years war

FROM THE WORKS OF JEAN LE BEL

JEAN FROISSART & ENGUERRAND

DE MONSTRELET · TRANSLATED

& EDITED BY PETER E. THOMPSON

THE FOLIO SOCIETY · LONDON

MCMLXVI

Maps drawn by K. C. Jordan FRGS

PRINTED IN GREAT BRITAIN
Set in 12 point Monotype Poliphilus leaded one point
Printed and bound by W. & J. Mackay & Co Ltd, Chatham, Kent
Illustrations printed by Jarrold & Sons, Norwich

contents

illustrations

maps

endpapers

The arms of England represent the coat assumed in 1340 by Edward III when he quartered France and England in support of his claims to the throne of France; the event is described on page 55. The French arms at that time were covered with fleurs de lys, and known as France Ancient. The arms of France are the modified version of only three fleurs de lys (France Modern) which had been adopted by the fifteenth century. In the picture facing page 32 it can be seen that the illustrator of this fifteenth century manuscript has shown the arms of England quartered with France Modern.

introduction

The span of history covered by the Hundred Years War is one of constant interest for the social as well as the military and political historian. In this volume the story of the war is told by means of passages translated from three French chroniclers who between them cover its whole duration; they are chroniclers rather than historians, yet where questions of social or political interest seem to be passed over the answers can sometimes be gleaned from the text. The extracts here given contain about one-fifteenth part of the original chronicles, and are linked by a connecting narrative which deals also with political issues. With so much to choose from, some criterion of choice had to be established. Since the war was essentially an Anglo-French conflict, I have chosen passages which deal with direct relations between these two countries, or with great occasions in either of them. France never succeeded in invading England, and military encounters therefore took place on French soil; there were various French raids on our coasts and I have included accounts of some of these. The fighting in Spain, Scotland and elsewhere is mentioned only in passing because it is outside the main course of the struggle between England and France.

The story covers the great English victories at Crécy, Poitiers and Agincourt, the episode of the Burghers of Calais, coronations and royal funerals, tournaments and pageantry, abdications and usurpations, popular discontent and royal assassinations, the quarrels of Plantagenet and Lancaster, of Armagnacs and Burgundians, of Lancaster and York, the madness of Charles V, the incredible story of Joan the Maid, and the final liberation from the English of all France except Calais. It is a period which witnessed the true end of the Middle Ages and the decline of chivalry; which saw the rise of nationalism and the virtual resurrection of the English language. The most lively narrator of the three authors whose works are here translated was certainly Jean Froissart; he is also the best known both here and in France, but the others have their own qualities and have suffered through neglect.

I have described the chroniclers as French, but this may well be misleading to English readers. None of them came from the kingdom of France. Le Bel and Froissart were from the county of Hainault, a territory that was allied to England and France in turn; we shall see how Froissart's loyalties changed with events, but both constantly profess their admiration for the chivalrous exploits of Edward III of England. Monstrelet was from Flanders and by loyalty a Burgundian. To be born in what is now France, or to write in French, did not mean that the chronicler was in sympathy with the cause of the French king. It was the remarkable achievement of Joan of Arc that French-speaking France was almost a nation by the end of the war.

JEAN LE BEL must have been a man with considerable panache. A lengthy and eulogistic portrait of him survives from the pen of his friend Jacques de Hemricourt; it is worth quoting in order to get a picture of the man before we come to the scanty details of his life: 'Never in the memory of living man had there been at Saint Lambert's anyone with better qualities than he, more open or of a better ordered life, for I knew him and visited him so often that I can record the truth. He was tall and well built, and dressed in rich stuffs like those of a knight banneret . . . If his squires of honour saw any noble stranger, bishop, knight or squire, they invited him to dinner or supper without consulting their master, and for these invitations his board was always ready; if any prince stayed in the town he had to dine at the canon's house . . . He never went to church on week-days without sixteen or twenty persons to conduct him . . . and on solemn feasts he had forty or fifty followers, all of whom returned to dine with him . . . In his youth he bore arms and fought in the tournaments . . . He was gay and cheerful, and could compose songs and virelays . . . God granted him to live all his life in health and prosperity, and he reached the age of eighty before he died . . . In his latter years he had twin sons by a lady of noble stock named Marie des Prés . . . to them he left great possessions.'

He was himself of noble birth, his family name being Del Cange and his father the first to take the name Le Bel. He was born in Liège about the year 1290, and at least by 1313 he had become Canon of Saint-Lambert de Liège. In 1327 he took part in the Scottish campaign, serving under Jean de Hainault (in Edward III's army), whose men joined the English forces at York about Whitsuntide, pursued the Scots to their own country and returned to France in August of the same year. Apart from some details of wills and law-suits that are irrelevant to our purpose, the only other fact known about him is that he died on the 15th of February 1370.

His aim is to record 'the true history of the noble and valiant King Edward'; with both him and Froissart we come to accept the word noble as a constant epithet in the Homeric tradition. Le Bel is an aristocrat in all his thought and he is always seeking 'fine feats of arms', which are much more important to him than diplomacy, politics and military tactics. War is the field in which knights could achieve glory and renown; Crécy was a glorious victory, notable not only for the deeds performed by valiant knights but also for the fact that Edward gave orders for so many of the conquered to be spared from slaughter, and it is of no concern to him that the victory remained isolated and that its effects were never gathered into any form of national supremacy.

Though Edward remains constantly noble, Le Bel is aiming at the truth and he does not suppress what he believes to be true in the episode of the Countess of Salisbury,* nor does he cover up Edward's cruelty towards the six citizens of Calais. And though he admires the English, he judges them to be envious and xenophobe; the French he finds fickle. The picture we get is a balanced one, never cluttered with detail, but entirely free from historical moralizing. What judgements he makes are the result of his aristocratic outlook, as when he tells us that King Philippe lost his battles because he consulted lawyers and bishops and the masters of his treasury instead of the true professionals, his lords and barons. Froissart, on the other hand, makes it clear that English supremacy was due to the power of her archers.

Like Froissart, he draws the matter for his chronicles from his own experiences and from eyewitnesses. No doubt the open house that he kept in Liège provided him with ample contacts among those who had been present at the events he describes. He sat down to write, he tells us, because of the gross misrepresentations of fact that were to be found in a rhymed chronicle which was popular in his day. This book has been lost, the last trace of it being a mention in an inventory of the library of Charles VI which was drawn up in 1423. Froissart tells us that Le Bel spared neither pains nor money in seeking out the truth about the events he set out to describe. He wrote at the request of Jean de Hainault, Seigneur de Beaumont; to him, and probably to others, he submitted the first part of his work as a check on its historical accuracy. This first part (Chapters 1–39) was written between 1352 and 1356, the year in which his patron died; the remainder between 1358 and 1361.

His style of writing is simple; though he writes in the Picard dialect his language is a purer French than that of Froissart. He does not seek to secure as many viewpoints as Froissart did, and it is easier

* See also p. 13.

to see the lines of history in Le Bel. Froissart copied his work wholesale; the extent of his borrowings was not known to modern scholars until 1861, when the manuscript of Le Bel's chronicles was discovered by Paul Meyer. This manuscript has been carefully edited by J. Viard and E. Déprez for the Société de l'Histoire de France, and it is this edition that has been used in the present work.

What is common to them both is that in a largely illiterate age their chronicles were intended to be recited rather than read. In Chapter LXXVI Le Bel says: 'Now I shall pass on rapidly, so that I may not bore my readers or my listeners.' He shows his concern for a listener in frequent remarks at the start of a new section such as: 'Now I will return to the affairs of the King of France.' The majority of these have been cut in the present edition, prepared in a literate age. It is remarkable that his writing is so entirely free from the rhetorical devices of earlier prose literature, all of which was intended for reciting aloud.

JEAN FROISSART is probably the best known of medieval chroniclers, and in England he owes this position no doubt to the splendidly vigorous translation of 1525 by Lord Berners. He was indefatigable in his search for the material of his chronicles, and there is ample evidence of his methods in the prefaces and narratives here translated. Like Le Bel, he loved, and sought to record before all else, the performance of fine feats of arms, and he revelled in pageantry such as was to be seen when Queen Isabella made her triumphal entry into Paris in 1389.

The date of his birth is variously given as 1335 or 1337, but he was certainly born in Valenciennes, a town in the independent county of Hainault; he was not a Frenchman. Valenciennes was famous for its weaving and its lace-work, and may have given us the English word 'valance';* this connexion with the world of the Flemish weavers no doubt turned Froissart's thoughts and interests as much to England as to France.

If, as seems likely, his poem *L'espinette amoureuse*† (The Thorn-Bush of Love) is largely autobiographical, he began his education in a mixed school, probably in a nunnery. He tells us that he sought the favours of the girls at school with presents of brooches, apples and pears; that he loved the games that children play; that he liked

* Though the OED derives it from O.F. *valer*, to descend or hang down.

† See Bibliography.

ballades and *rondeaux* better than his lessons; and that he fought with his schoolfellows and enjoyed watching others fight.

By 23 he was in minor orders, and in 1361 he went to London, taking with him a manuscript book, telling the story of the battle of Poitiers and the events of the following years, for presentation to Philippa of Hainault, King Edward III's queen. The book has not been preserved and it is not known whether it was in prose or verse, but it is certainly a forerunner of the million words of the Chronicles to which he was to devote his life. The gift achieved the end the author no doubt intended, and he was taken into the service of Queen Philippa; his stay in England lasted for five or six years. During this time, already avid for material for the history he now intended to write, he travelled to Scotland (where he met David Bruce), Flanders and Brittany. At Berkeley he was given a first-hand account of the death of Edward II.

The court in London of those years was a place after Froissart's heart. The queen was from his native county and it was she who had intervened to save the six burghers of Calais; the king was the acknowledged master of the art of war and idolized as the victor of Crécy and Poitiers; the King of France was in London, too, as a prisoner, but like the large number of important French nobles who were captured with him at Poitiers he was trusted on parole, and many of the amenities of English court life were open to him and his nobles. French was the language of the English court and of the nobility, and nothing prevented Froissart from questioning those on both sides who had been in the fighting at Poitiers and elsewhere. He tells us of Chaucer's embassy, and it is said that he later met Petrarch —but he never talks of literature in his chronicles.

In 1366 he was sent to Aquitaine with the Black Prince and was present in Bordeaux when Richard II was born there. He was recalled to England, but soon sent abroad again, this time to Italy in 1368–9 for the wedding of Edward's son the Duke of Clarence. In 1369 his protectress died, and with Edward now dominated by Alice Perrers there was no place for him at the English court. He returned from Italy to his native town and, he says, went into business. But we hear no more of this activity, and soon he has found new patrons for his work on the chronicles.

From internal evidence in the various manuscript versions (there are more than fifty, some incomplete, of the First Book) we can deduce something of the way he worked on the material he had gathered. When he returned to Valenciennes in 1369 it is obvious that he needed the wherewithal to live and to continue his search for material; he must then have begun writing a series of versions each brought slightly more up to date, prepared by different scribes for immediate purchasers. His story starts in 1325, and for the early part he borrows copiously and often without any alteration from Le Bel, augmented here and there by his own researches. These additions are usually quite separate sections. He has undertaken the work, he tells us, at the request—and no doubt with the financial assistance—of Robert de Namur, Seigneur de Beaufort, who had offered his services to Edward III at the siege of Calais. He was the nephew of Robert d'Artois and had married the sister of Queen Philippa. We do not know how long he remained Froissart's patron, but his name does not appear in versions later than about 1373, the year in which Froissart presumably took priest's orders and was given the living of Les Estinnes-au-Mont in Hainault. The story was then continued down to 1378, but in a smaller number of manuscripts.

The texts so far described constitute what is known as the *Première Rédaction*; it is important to consider them separately, because they represent a similar outlook in spite of minor corrections and additions. Froissart is writing under the influence of the hospitality and the information he received while he was in the service of Queen Philippa, and his attitude is markedly pro-English. In this group of manuscripts we find also the greatest zest for living and for the splendour of knighthood.

Probably in 1376 he acquired new patrons. Firstly Gui de Châtillon, Comte de Blois, Seigneur de Chimay et de Beaumont, whose father had been killed at Crécy and whose mother was the daughter of that Jean de Hainault who had led the French king from the battlefield* and had himself been captured, then redeemed only by a ruinous ransom. The other was Wenceslas de Brabant, Duc de Luxembourg, son of the blind King of Bohemia who was killed at Crécy; for him Froissart wrote the romance of *Méliador*. When he died in 1383 Froissart remained in the definitive service of Gui de Blois.

Under their influence an important revision of the chronicles is made. Whole passages are rewritten to give more weight to the French point of view, and at the same time there are a number of additions which make the understanding of events easier for the uninformed reader: some of these have been incorporated in the present translation, and are acknowledged in the index of sources. This revision,

* See p. 70. This Jean de Hainault was the friend and patron of Jean Le Bel.

which is known as the *Seconde Rédaction*, was begun, it would seem in 1376, before he had completed the last years of the first version. It exists in only two manuscripts, the MS d'Amiens and another which is a poor copy of it. Luce suggests that no more copies were made because the author really preferred the earlier version. A clue to the nature of the work may perhaps be discovered when we find that there are numerous additions where the author praises members of the House of Blois who had previously received no mention.

In this version his debt to Le Bel is greatly reduced. One instance of this is of particular interest, and perhaps shows that Froissart lost no regard for truth in rewriting his story from a more French view-point. There was an episode in the Scottish wars when the Earl of Salisbury's castle at Wark was delivered by Edward's forces in 1342. The earl was a prisoner in France and the countess received the king with great hospitality. 'It is true', writes Froissart in the Amiens text, 'that master Jean Le Bel maintains in his Chronicles that the English king treated her most villainously and, according to him, had his will of her by force. But I tell you before God that I have spent a long time in England and made many enquiries in the king's own household and among the chief lords of that country, and have never heard this evil report confirmed.'* The episode, with the delightful account of a game of chess between king and countess in the Amiens text, are not included here, because they do not come within the brief of the Hundred Years War.

This second version ended in 1383 with the death of Wenceslas. Froissart was now made Canon of Chimay and spent much of his time at Chimay, a town in Hainault. Here he wrote Book II of his chronicles, covering the years 1377 to 1385. But it would be as well to mention at this point the *Troisième Rédaction* which Froissart prepared late in his life—from internal evidence it was clearly written after 1400—and which survives in a single manuscript in the Vatican Library, the MS de Rome. It goes no farther than the death of Philippe VI of Valois in 1350, but contains much that was not in any of the previous editions—evidence from his journeys through England and his stay at Berkeley in 1366, from his conversations with Sir John Chandos, and from his visit to Scotland in 1365. He is much less dependent on the work of Jean Le Bel, the pro-French tendency of the Amiens version is intensified, and he is now heavily critical of the English. When he tells us that the Londoners think they rule the country and can get rid of any king they do not like, we

* Luce, t. III, p. 293.

realize that he is showing his personal disgust at the way the English treated Richard II, who had received him with such courtesy in 1395. He still allows that, during the life of Queen Philippa, England was a country 'full of gracious living, prosperity and honour'.*

The Rome manuscript has not been translated into English; one of the passages in which he details the shortcomings of the English is reproduced in Appendix I. The scorn he shows for the common people is echoed in other places in the same version where he describes the *vilains* of Flanders in the grossest terms.

It was in 1386 that Froissart accompanied his patron Gui de Blois to Chimay. With the completion of Book II in 1388 he felt the need to cover new ground and travel in search of further information. In the autumn of that year he set out for Béarn and spent some three months in Orthez at the court of Gaston Phébus, Comte de Foix. He had been provided with letters of introduction by Gui de Blois and his intention was to gather materials for his Third Book on the wars in Spain and Portugal. He fulfilled this object, but there is also a great deal in the book about England and France. On his ride to Orthez in the company of Espan de Lion, he proved an untiring questioner. 'Each night,' he writes, 'when we arrived at our inn, I would write down all that he told me,—either then or in the morning, so that I might have it fixed in my mind for future use, for there is no memory so exact as the written word.' After his stay at Orthez he visited Avignon, Rome and Auvergne, and was in Paris by August of 1389 to witness the triumphal entry of Isabella of Bavaria. Thence to Valenciennes, where he completed the writing of Book III by 1390.

Here, too, he started the writing of the fourth and last book. In 1395 he interrupted his work to satisfy a fancy to revisit the English court, and to see the king, who was born in Bordeaux while he was there in the service of Queen Philippa. His patron Gui de Blois had just died and he seems to have continued his work under the patronage of Albert of Bavaria, uncle of Queen Isabella, with whom he had been on friendly terms since 1384 and who, as a Knight of the Garter, was no doubt glad to make it possible for Froissart to visit England.† On his return he revised the Third Book, and completed Book IV in 1400. We know that the third revision of the First Book was written after 1400, but nothing further is known of his life, though the year 1410 is popularly accepted as the date of his death.

*Ed. Luce, t. 1, p. 286.

† See pp. 235–242.

It will be seen from this that there is considerable difficulty in deciding which version should be used in an English translation, more so in that there is no complete modern edition of any version that is satisfactory. The first two books and part of the third have been admirably and carefully edited by a succession of scholars* between 1869 and 1957 for the Société de l'Histoire de France, and for the extent of its material this edition has been used; for the last part of his work we have used that of Kervyn de Lettenhove, published in Brussels between 1867 and 1877, though it is less accurate from a textual point of view. Siméon Luce, who edited the early volumes, explains in his Introduction why he chose the versions that appear in his edition. As far as the First Book is concerned, if the *Troisième Rédaction* (MS de Rome) had been complete, he would have used that throughout, but it ends as we have said in 1350. The *Deuxième Rédaction* (MS d'Amiens) represents second but not final thoughts, and exists in only one satisfactory manuscript. He therefore chooses the *Première Rédaction*, which was by far the most widely circulated, since it exists in some fifty manuscripts, and it is this which has through the centuries been known as 'Froissart'. Perhaps indeed the profusion of manuscripts shows that it was the author's most favoured version. Luce gives a full table of variants from every existing manuscript, and these have been used where helpful in preparing the present translation. There is no difficulty over Books II and IV of which only one version was written. For Book III the single manuscript of the revised version has been followed.

The Chronicles have been twice translated in full. Firstly in 1525 by John Bourchier, Lord Berners, a version in colourful English which has for the modern reader all the romance of chivalrous language, no doubt because it is not far removed from that of Malory. But it is full of inaccuracies of translation, random abbreviations are made in the texts, and names of places and persons are often sadly distorted and unidentifiable. Secondly we have the version of Thomas Johnes published from 1803 to 1805 on his own press at Hafod. Many of Berners's mistakes are put right, but too many are blindly followed, as are some of his omissions and summarizings; it is quite obvious that he worked with Berners in front of him; his prose, moreover, is as dull as Berners's is lively. Neither had the advantage of a scholarly edition to work from. Johnes also translated Monstrelet.

Vivid and lively as he often is, Froissart has been accused by later critics of wordiness and repetitions. If we remember that his books

* See Bibliography, Appendix II.

were intended for literate as well as illiterate* (or lazy?) patrons, we should not be surprised that he often repeats himself in different words when describing an important event. To take just one example: in his account of the battle of Poitiers he gives two summings-up of the heroic deeds; the second (omitted from this edition)† being merely a variant of the first, no doubt so that it should not fail to catch his listener's ear. This, moreover, is thoroughly in the tradition of French medieval epics, as seen for instance in the *laisses similaires* of the Chanson de Roland. In Book III Froissart tells how during his stay with the Comte de Foix he would read aloud his poem *Méliador*: 'Every night after supper I read to him from this book. As I read no one dared speak a word for he wished that I should be clearly heard, and himself took great delight in listening. When I came to anything that he wished to question or discuss, he loved to ask me, not in his Gascon speech but in good and fair French.'

It is with the same concern for the listener that Froissart is constantly using direct speech, even if it is only an interjection here and there; one thinks of the interchange of invective between Sir John Chandos and Clermont before the battle of Poitiers, and the subtly varied conversation between Sir James Audley and the Black Prince after the same battle. Though the use of direct speech might seem obviously desirable in such literature, Froissart in fact used it more freely and more naturally than his predecessors had done.

He loved detail, too, of the kind that made more vivid the background to the events he describes. To everything he narrates he brings the eyewitness approach, whether he was there in person or not. He collects his material and writes it down at once, sorting it into order later. What he writes is always open to the distortion of contemporary recording: there is no pretension to historical judgement or true perspective. But he has no prejudices other than a passion for knightly behaviour, and where he finds it he does not fail to record and praise it, even if he has scarcely a word of reproach to the noble Black Prince for his behaviour at the sacking of Limoges. Though a priest, he has no commitment to the clerical cause; the few 'pious passages' are rare enough to strike us as both unexpected and sincere. Where the author of the *Grandes Chroniques* attributes the defeat at Crécy to divine interference, Froissart by his analysis of Philippe VI's foolish conduct of affairs appears as a scientifically rational historian.

Is it his regard for knightly valour that leads him at times to ignore

* What fun he makes of Philip Mansel's inability to read. See p. 155.

† Book I, §. 390. *v.* Source References.

the 'common people'? There is little enough about them in his chronicles, but we do here and there get a glimpse of them—complaining at the way they were being bled white to equip a fleet for the invasion that never came off ('If they spoke out they were beaten or killed'); an admiral being told to avoid them for his ships' crews ('See that you take on board no common folk or serving men, for they would do us more harm than good'); fishermen of the two nations fraternizing in mid-Channel and exchanging top-secret information. It is in the third version that he becomes angry with the people who had helped to dethrone Richard II, and his anger spills over on to the populace of Flanders. But in no version has he any praise for their anonymous self-sacrifice in war.

The errors of fact that are the result of Froissart's 'journalistic' approach have been corrected in the present edition. What might be called simple errors of a date or name have been put right without any indication; errors of chronology, or emphasis, or fact have been corrected in footnotes. The errors are visible because Froissart was among the first whose accuracy can be checked by other sources; we do not know how inaccurate are the unchecked chronicles of early medieval times or of antiquity.

ENGUERRAND DE MONSTRELET set out consciously to continue the work of Froissart, and his book begins in 1400. He must therefore have acquired his information for the first decade largely from others, for he was born probably in 1390. His father is described as esquire (there is a village called Montrelet in Picardy, whose lord in 1125 was one Enguerrand de Montrelet). Little is known of the chronicler's life; he was married and had at least two children; one was made a knight of St John of Jerusalem in 1444. There exists a Letter of Grace dated 1424 from Henry IV of England to Enguerrand de Monstrelet, exculpating him from blame for having joined in the robbing of some Armagnac merchants in the course of some sort of affray; such events were very common at the time, and only random incidents can have become the subject of official notice.

In 1436 he was appointed to two posts, open to him by virtue of his noble birth. One was the office of lieutenant du gavenier to the Duke of Burgundy, which authorized him to collect the *gave*, a tax payable by the churches of Flanders in return for the protection of the Duke of Burgundy; the other was that of bailiff of the chapter for the church of Cambrai, a town in which he seems to have spent most of his life. In 1444 he became Provost of Cambrai, an office he held for two years. In 1445 he was appointed bailiff of Walincourt and continued in the office until his death in mid-July 1453. He was buried in the church of the Franciscans in Cambrai.

In the Prologue to his First Book, Monstrelet tells us it 'will begin on Easter Day in the year 1400, the year which sees the end of the last volume of the work of that wise and famous historian Sir Jean Froissart, a native of Valenciennes in Hainault, whose reputation will long survive in his excellent writings. This first book will end with the death of the most Christian King Charles the well-beloved and sixth of his name, who departed this life in his palace of Saint-Pol in Paris, near the Célestins, on the 22nd day of October in the year 1422.'

There is no evidence that Monstrelet engaged in the profession of arms, and in this he is unlike the two other chroniclers we are dealing with. It is true that Froissart, once he was established as 'the chronicler', no longer found time for fighting; Monstrelet devoted the whole of his energies to inquiring into the exact turn of events and is at pains to tell us that his inquiries were always impartially made of those who had fought on either side. Though a Burgundian by office, he can be acquitted of partiality, as a reading of his work will show (for instance in his sympathy with the Armagnacs over the murder of the Duc d'Orléans). 'In particular,' he tells us in the Prologue, 'I inquired of Kings of Arms, and the heralds and poursuivants of several lords and countries, who by virtue of their office should be well informed and able to give a true account of events during the wars in France. Having received their information, often repeated, and putting aside all doubtful reports and those disproved by later accounts, I spent a considerable time in weighing them up and counterchecking them for truth. Then at the end of a year, and not before, I prepared my final version.'

This gives us an interesting clue to Monstrelet's methods as an historian. Though there are many colourful pages in his work, he is a much more diligent historian (as opposed to chronicler) than his predecessors, and his writing is often enough tedious by his very searching for accuracy. He is most thorough in giving us the documents of history—royal letters, treaties, legal proceedings and so forth. Very seldom does he enter into the narrative in the manner of Froissart; indeed, in one of the rare instances where he does so he infuriates the reader by saying that though he was present when the Duke of Burgundy spoke with Joan after her capture at Compiègne, he has forgotten what they said! He is much more political in his outlook, less concerned with 'high feats of arms'. In his work we no longer find the term 'flower of chivalry' for the body of knights in a battle; the great tower by the bridge at Orléans was defended by 'the flower of the best men of war in England', and there is a new term to be found in the word 'combatant', to cover all ranks of fighting men. His sympathies with all these men are wider; in describing the battle of Patay he speaks of the ordinary soldiers as being 'the sort who are always brought from their own country to die in France'—a pattern that continued to 1945.

Book II takes us from 1422 to 1444. In the Prologue there is an interesting comment on the mechanization of war, an opinion which has been echoed with each 'advance' in the techniques of slaughter. 'Without in any way wishing to detract from the prowess of the ancient heroes or to belittle their deeds, I would claim that we find that as many feats of valour have been performed in the time covered by this present book . . . during which many new and cruel instruments of war have been developed which were unknown before. By means of these subtle inventions many different methods of conducting a campaign have come into being.'

This book covers the story of Joan of Arc. Everything Monstrelet has to say about her is translated here, and the length of these extracts must be balanced against the million or so words of the chronicles. Though he tells us that the English 'had never been so much afraid of any captain or commander in war as they had been of the Maid', he is very moderate in his assessment of her worth to Charles VII, whom, unlike most of his contemporaries, including Joan herself, he describes as king, not dauphin, before his coronation. At this deeply significant ceremony in Reims there is no word that Joan wept with joy at the fulfilment of her plan, no mention of her at the ensuing feast. After the relief of Orléans, Monstrelet takes pains to remind us that it was as much the achievement of her wise and experienced captains, and it is only after this moment that he begins to apply the adjective noble to the French. Her trial is described merely in a letter from the King of England to the Duke of Burgundy; in his estimate of Charles VII's achievements at his death, Monstrelet makes no mention of Joan.* There is no mention in the Third Book of her rehabilitation in 1456.

It is probable that the work of Monstrelet ends in 1444, though a Third Book has been repeatedly published as being by him. At the end of the Second Book he had promised to continue his story in a

* See pp. 343–44.

third, but since it covers the years 1444 to 1467 it cannot all have been written by him; in fact, it follows closely enough the *Grandes Chroniques de France*, with borrowings from minor writers. All we can say is that the authorship is unknown, may not be due to only one writer, and that it is now usually attributed to Mathieu de Coucy, a friend of Monstrelet. It has been convenient to use this work to conclude the history of the war.

There are only nine manuscripts of these chronicles, and three black-letter editions. The first two books have been carefully edited in the publications of the Société de l'Histoire de France; my own translation has been made from the handsomely printed edition of 1603 which contains all three books and some 'additional chronicles'.

I have suggested that the period of this war saw the virtual resurrection of the English language, and it is worth while halting to examine the position; the linguistic problem is, of course, closely linked with the general political situation of the country. For two centuries after the conquest, French—mostly in the Anglo-Norman dialect—had remained the language of the court, and was firmly entrenched in the law, in the hierarchy of the Church, and in education (English was indeed forbidden in the schools). Henry I was the only English king until Edward IV who had taken an English wife; Henry Bolingbroke was the first king since the conquest whose mother-tongue was English. Ranulf Higden tells us in his *Polychronicon*: 'a man of Kente, southern, western and northern men speken Frensshe al lyke in soune and speche, but they can not speke their Englyssh so.'* There is a record of an early Parliament of Edward III which resolved that 'all nobles, knights and honest men should instruct their children in the French language so that they be of greater use in the wars'.

In reading of these wars we find English knights conversing freely with the French, and I can find no record of any need for an interpreter until 1418, when John Strecche records that the French sent a Scotsman to parley with the English at Pont-de-l'Arche. But there are suggestions here and there that the French of the English was different and not always clear, as, for instance, when King Jean surrenders at the battle of Poitiers to the man who speaks the best French.† There is an interesting comment in Froissart's MS de Rome concerning the year 1329, when Edward III first paid homage for

* Higden wrote in Latin and died in 1364. This quotation is from the English translation published by Caxton in 1387.

† See p. 118 and footnote.

Aquitaine in Amiens Cathedral. In the *Première Rédaction* the fact is simply recorded that King Edward paid homage 'by word only, without putting his hands between those of the King of France'. King Philippe accepted this willingly, asking only that Edward should consult his sealed documents when he returned home to see what else he should do, in consultation with his Parliament. In the last version, however, Froissart here adds this note: 'The nature of the English is such that they are always afraid of being taken in, and give their reply after an unexpected delay. What they agree to one day, they will deny on another. In this they are encouraged by the fact that they do not fully understand the language of France, and they are not prepared to accept what is said unless it is to their own profit.'* Getting round a treaty on grounds of verbal misunderstanding is no new device.

As early as 1337 Froissart tells us of English being spoken in Parliament, though from the context it is clear that this was unusual. The reference is again to the last revision: 'Then an English clerk got up to speak, a bachelor of laws and well versed in three languages—Latin, French and English . . . He spoke in a moderate manner, and in English, so that he should be better understood by everyone, for a man has a better idea of what he wants to say in the language he has known from childhood than in any other.'† It could, of course, be argued that in this manuscript Froissart is basing his comments on the England he visited in 1395 rather than that of 1337, the year he may well have been born. Yet when Froissart visited England in 1395 he found King Richard's court thoroughly conversant with French, and also remarks on the fact that documents were clearly understood if they were in Latin and French.

The struggle with France served rather to emphasize English insularity than to increase her sense of solidarity with the continent of France, and this became more obvious as the English claim to the French crown began to lose its serious intention, and when with the Black Death the English-speaking serfs began to achieve their emancipation. In 1356 it was ordered that English should be used in all cases tried before the sheriffs' courts in London. In 1362 the same order was extended to the law courts, and the next year Parliament was opened for the first time in English. Henceforward the use of French as an official language decayed steadily—though French was not officially abolished in the courts until 1731!

* Luce, t. 1, p. 306.

† ibid., p. 360.

The use of titles, and the form of proper names and place names, have presented some difficulties. Names of persons and places have wherever possible been recorded in the forms now known. Those who have titles have often acquired a higher rank, and confusion has sometimes been avoided by retaining the best-known title, at the risk of chronological error. Many 'French' knights were fighting in the English cause—whether they came from Aquitaine, Gascony, Hainault or elsewhere—and some of these had earned titles from the English sovereign; it is not always easy to know on which side they were fighting; some, moreover, changed their loyalties for personal or political reasons. This is too complicated a situation to admit of any rule-of-thumb, but as far as possible those French who were fighting for the King of France are given their titles in French; French knights are, for convenience, given the title Sir. The Dukes of Burgundy and Brittany become an exception, particularly in the later part of the war, because their English titles have entered into our own history.

Years have been recorded throughout in 'new style', though in one or two places there was no means of checking the precise day and month and an error may have been perpetuated. The dates in square brackets have been supplied from other sources so that the exact chronology can be followed.

A more complicated problem is found in the indication of time of day. The mechanical clock was being perfected in the course of this war; it took many years to bring it to a point of reasonable accuracy, and no doubt the old and the new methods of telling the time overlapped. The old method, which we find in Le Bel and the greater part of Froissart, is that of the canonical hours. These were the seven hours of monastic prayer, at which the monastery bell was rung: no doubt the sound of this bell was all-important to those who lived and worked within earshot, for the sundial is very rarely mentioned in medieval writings.

The seven hours were *Matins* (immediately followed by Lauds), which was properly a midnight office, but could be said as late as daybreak; *Prime*, sunrise; *Terce* (tertia hora = 6 a.m. to 9 a.m.), mid-morning; *Sext*, midday; *Nones*, mid-afternoon; *Vespers*, late afternoon; *Compline*, evening, end of the day. Each gives some hours' latitude; there were Lenten, summer and winter timings, and they could vary between the monastic orders, so that confusion could reign in any one town. Nones and Vespers are the most uncertain: the former can apply to noon (Sext being much more rarely noticed), but is also sometimes used for the hour when work ended, which is more properly that of Vespers. The day was not divided into twenty-four hours until 1370, and the use of canonical hours continued until the end of the century. Froissart changed from the old system to the new a little earlier; the first mention of clock time in the extracts here translated is when (p. 233) he speaks of 'the stroke of nine o'clock' in describing an event of 1393.

To read in modern English a description of events that took place six hundred years ago requires an effort of the imagination, and the translator is sensitive to the great difficulty that faces him. Berners was near enough to Froissart for the difference in time to appear negligible to the modern reader. When it comes to speech the difficulty is even greater. Where the quoted speech is obviously colloquial it can only lose its effect if it is translated into modern colloquial equivalents; yet the cult of quaintness must be avoided. In the present translation the spoken word has been allowed to retain a tinge of archaism which has been excluded from the rest of the work.

Another problem, most marked in dealing with Froissart, is the medieval habit of giving two nearly synonymous words when one will do—'written and recorded', 'noble and valorous', 'rightly and properly', 'glory and renown', 'fine deeds and noble feats of arms'. This habit becomes tedious to present-day readers, while lending a rhythm and a colour to the prose which cannot easily be put into modern English. Some pairs of words have been left as in the original, two nouns have sometimes been rendered, for instance, by adjective and noun, sometimes one of the pair has been omitted; only in Froissart's Prologue to Book I has the text been left virtually as he wrote it. The present translation aims above all at laying before a modern reader a completely accurate rendering of the original in a form which retains all the life and liveliness of the men who wrote these Chronicles for posterity.

THE CHRONICLES OF JEAN LE BEL

The causes of wars are notoriously complex, and their perspective is often distorted by successive historians. The three chroniclers whose writings are the basis of this volume were concerned firstly with the recordings of facts and events, described fully or from certain angles only according to the nature of the sources to which they had access. Of the three only Froissart was ready to alter and amend his narrative as new sources became open to him. They were concerned only secondarily with causes, and those immediate; the flow of historical causation does not run through their pages.

The immediate cause of the Hundred Years War is seen to be the dynastic question when the Capetian house became extinct on the male side in 1328, but more cogent reasons for war must be sought in the problems aroused by the Duchy of Aquitaine and the nature of the homage to be paid for it by the English crown. Aquitaine or Guienne—the names are virtually synonymous—had been added to Henry Plantagenet's dominions by his marriage to Eleanor of Aquitaine in 1152. Two years later he succeeded to the English throne on the death of Stephen, and the English king now had some sort of control, often remote enough, over Normandy, Brittany, Maine, Anjou, Poitou, Aquitaine—an unbroken area covering more than half of modern France, and the whole western seaboard from the Somme to the Pyrenees. With the changing qualities of successive monarchs the loyalties of these various provinces were continually being revised; in 1259 a Treaty was ratified in Paris by the terms of which King Henry III of England renounced his claim to Normandy and the other lands that had been lost since 1204, retaining only the little county of Ponthieu in the north, and Aquitaine in the south-west. The boundaries of this province were clear enough to the west—the Pyrenees, the coast and the Gironde; inland the limits of the fief were very uncertain, chains of fortified towns were established by both sides and the people lived in constant uncertainty as to which was the better master to serve. There was no such thing at this time as a unified France.

More important than the question of vague frontiers was the fact that the Treaty of Paris required the English king to do personal homage to the King of France for his Duchy of Aquitaine. Was this to be a formality or a vow to support the King of France against his enemies? The matter was never resolved, but English kings showed a reluctance to visit the French king to carry out the feudal ceremony. The fief was successively confiscated and restored as if it had been the plaything of a naughty child. Marriages were arranged to bring about better relations: Edward I in 1299 took as his second

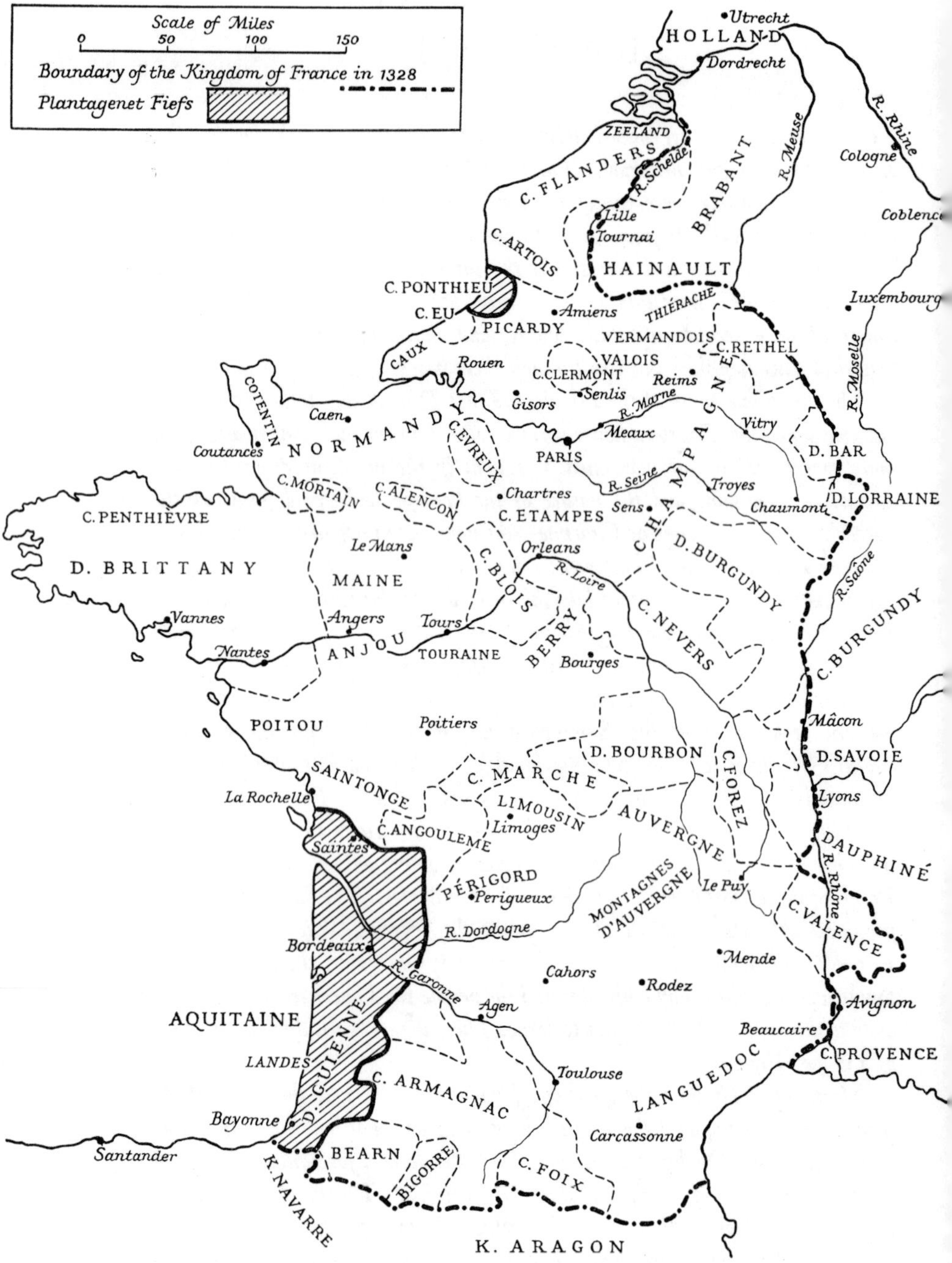

FRANCE AT THE START OF THE HUNDRED YEARS WAR

wife the sister of Philippe le Bel of France; in 1308 Edward II married Isabelle, eldest daughter and second child of the same king. Better relations did not ensue.

In 1314 King Philippe le Bel died leaving three sons and a daughter who was Queen of England. By 1328 the three sons had been crowned in turn and had died. Isabelle, as second child, had never seriously been considered for the throne; the situation, in fact, was new, since previous kings from Hugues Capet at the end of the tenth century had always had the good fortune to leave a male heir, and the succession of this heir could be confirmed on or shortly before the death of the reigning monarch. The practice of female succession was, moreover, universal in feudal France, at least outside the monarchy. When Louis X died in 1316 he left a daughter, Jeanne (later Queen of Navarre), by his first wife, but because of the mother's misconduct her legitimacy could well be called into doubt. The problem was further complicated by the fact that five months after Louis's death the queen gave birth to a son who lived only five days. In the uncertainty that ensued the late king's brother, who had already been granted the regency, claimed the crown as Philippe V and held it without serious opposition, but without the full support of the nobles. He summoned an assembly of notables in 1317 who obligingly decreed that no woman could succeed to the throne of France. Edward II, in spite of his wife's claims, recognized the new king, though he excused himself from attending the coronation.

Early in 1322 Philippe died leaving five daughters, and his younger brother immediately claimed the throne as Charles IV, without any apparent opposition. Six years later he, too, had died, leaving only daughters, one born two months after the king's death. There were two men who could lay some claim to the throne: Philippe of Valois, first cousin of the last three kings, son of the influential Charles, Comte de Valois, who had died in 1325, and Edward III, then aged 16, whose claim appeared to be weakened for two reasons—that his right was transmitted through a female and that he was king of a country whose rights in Aquitaine had put him in the position of a disobedient vassal.

There is every reason to believe that the rhymed chronicle which Jean le Bel refers to at the beginning of his Prologue has been lost.

Prologue

¶ He who would read or hear the true history of the noble and valiant King Edward, who is at this time reigning in England, let him take this short book which I have begun to write, and beware of a large book in rhyme which I have seen and read, and which some fanciful writer has composed full of inventions and errors. Its beginning is entirely false and full of lies up to the start of the war which that king undertook against King Philippe of France. From there on it is a mixture of truth and falsehood, with many passages of pure invention and repetitions to eke out the rhyme, and such a profusion of feats of arms performed by some of the knights and others that they must necessarily appear incredible and impossible. A fanciful rhymed history of this sort must seem in very bad taste to any reasonable person, for from such wild words one might attribute to those knights or squires feats so outrageous that their bravery would be diminished, because the truth would no longer be accepted. This would be a pity for them, and one should therefore always keep as close as one can to the truth.

History, it seems to me, is so full of noble deeds that it deserves to be recorded in writing so that only the true facts may be remembered; I should welcome someone who knew them well and could write them better than I. So many notable and perilous fights, fixed battles and other feats of arms have occurred since the year of grace 1327 when this noble king was crowned in England that he and those who were with him in these engagements or with others when the king was not present . . . should all be counted among the truly valorous, although there are a great number of these who should be held the most valorous of all, such as the Prince of Wales, son of the king in his youth, the Duke of Lancaster, Lord Renaud of Cobham, Sir Walter de Manny, Sir Franck de Halle and others I shall not name. In all the battles in which these took part they were on the side of the victors, whether by land or by sea, and bore themselves so bravely that they must be considered more than usually valorous.

In spite of this the others who fought at their side must not be held less worthy, for indeed we must call brave all those who were daring enough to fight to the end in these cruel and numerous battles, doing their duty throughout. It is enough to say: 'These knights acquitted themselves best in this battle', naming the knights and the battle, and: 'These other knights fought very well, too, and so did these' without attributing to any of them deeds which it is not possible to believe a man could accomplish. One should thus make a record of all the battles and minor engagements one wishes to mention, for we all know that when a fixed battle is in progress fortune swings first to one side then the other, but that some individuals are always doing better than others, so these men must be mentioned by name.*

* From the accounts of all three chroniclers, however, many long lists of names have been omitted, since they would have overburdened the passages in which they occur. Mention has always been retained of 'the most truly valorous'.

Since in these rhymed chronicles one always finds falsehoods in plenty, I wish to devote my leisure to making as exact a history as I can, in prose, of all that I have seen and heard, or learned from those who were present when I was not. I shall use the memory God has given me and write as briefly as I can, but without omitting anyone of importance. If I cannot finish my task, let someone else do so to whom God shall grant such favour.

Edward III and the French Succession

¶ After the severe and hard-fought campaign [against the Scots under Bruce, 1327]* it was not long before the noble king, the queen his mother, Henry Earl of Lancaster (his uncle), Sir Roger Mortimer and the other English barons who had remained in the king's council, made plans for his marriage. They therefore sent to Sir Jean de Hainault a bishop, two knights banneret and two learned clerks, to beg his help in arranging the marriage of the noble king and to use his good offices with Comte Guillaume de Hainault, who was count also of Holland and Zeeland, to send one of his daughters, for they would prefer her to any other because of the esteem in which they held the father.

The noble knight Sir Jean de Hainault entertained these lords ambassador as richly as he could—and he was noted for his hospitality. When he had feasted them well he took them to the earl his brother at Valenciennes, where they were welcomed with great honour and so royally entertained that it would take many pages to tell of it all.

When they had thus been entertained they delivered their message as they had been bidden, and very skilfully they did it. The noble earl replied at once and most courteously, with the counsel of Sir Jean his brother and of the countess the girl's mother, saying that he owed much thanks to the king, to the queen his mother, and to all the lords by whose counsel they had come, since they did him great honour in sending such a distinguished embassy, and that he would willingly accede to their request if it had the approval of his Holiness the Pope

* The campaign against the ageing Robert Bruce was led in person by Edward III, who hoped to efface the shame of Bannockburn. It proved to be entirely inconclusive.

and of Holy Church. This reply was highly satisfactory to them, and they at once sent two knights and two learned men to the pope in Avignon to seek the necessary dispensation for this marriage, for it could not be arranged without the pope, since they are both closely related, though of the third degree, to the royal line of France, their mothers being first cousins, the daughters of two brothers.

Very soon after they had come to Avignon [30 August 1327] they achieved their task, for the pope and the College of Cardinals readily granted their request because of the great nobility of the parties. When the messengers returned from Avignon to Valenciennes with the documents from the pope the marriage was at once confirmed, and the young lady was equipped with everything that was fitting for one who was to become the Queen of England.

When she was fully ready she was married to a proxy duly arranged by the King of England, and then she set out for England, where her husband was waiting to crown her in London.* The noble knight Sir Jean de Hainault her uncle conducted her as far as London, and very magnificently he was received and feasted by the king, the queen mother and all the ladies and barons of England. In London there were great festivities and a great assembly of lords, dukes, earls, barons, knights, ladies, maidens, a great array of fine clothes and accoutrements, much jousting for love of the ladies, and more dancing and feasting every day than can be recounted. These festivities lasted for three weeks . . .

At the end of that time Sir Jean departed with all his train, having received gifts of fine jewels from various persons, and the young queen remained behind with a small company of her own people, notably a young aspirant to knighthood, Gautier de Masny [later Sir Walter de Manny] who remained in her service as esquire trenchant at the queen's table, and who afterwards acquired such favour with the king and the barons that he was accepted by all as one of the king's privy council; he performed deeds of bodily prowess in so many places that their number cannot be told, and was engaged in so many bold enterprises, as you will hear in this book, that he was classed among the bravest in the kingdom. He should be considered among

* This chapter is copied almost word for word by Froissart in his *Première Rédaction*, but both he and Le Bel are factually inaccurate. The Princess Philippa was married by proxy at Valenciennes in 1327; after her arrival in England she was solemnly married in York Minster on the 24th of January 1328. The festivities in London took place after Easter that same year. Her coronation took place on the 25th of February 1330.

the most valiant and worthy, after the noble King Edward and the Duke of Lancaster, who surpass all others in renown.

¶ King Charles IV of France, known as Charles le Bel, who was the uncle of the young King Edward III of England, was thrice married and died without male issue, which was a great pity for the realm of France, as you will hear. His first wife Blanche was one of the most beautiful ladies in France, the daughter of the Comtesse d'Artois; she broke her marriage vows and for this was long imprisoned in the Château Gaillard—a sorry business—before her husband became King of France. When the crown became his the twelve peers and the barons of France did not wish the kingdom to remain without a male heir if it could be avoided, and they held a council and decided that he should take as wife Marie the daughter of the Emperor Henry of Luxembourg and sister of the noble King of Bohemia, for which reason an annulment of his marriage to his first wife, now imprisoned, was obtained from the Holy Father.

By his second wife, who was a most modest and humble woman, he had one son who died young, shortly before his mother, who died at Issoudun in Berry. The deaths of both occurred in suspicious circumstances, certain persons being privately blamed. Later the king took as his third wife Jeanne the daughter of his step-uncle the Comte d'Évreux and sister to the King of Navarre. It so happened that she was with child as the king lay on his deathbed; when he realized that he was dying he declared it his wish that if the queen gave birth to a son Philippe de Valois should be regent of France until this son should be of age to reign, and if she gave birth to a daughter the twelve peers and barons of France should hold a council among themselves and give the kingdom of France to him who had the greatest right. Soon afterwards he died, on the 1st of February 1328.

It was not long before the queen gave birth to a daughter, a source of regret to everyone in the land. When the twelve peers and other lords heard this they assembled in Paris as soon as they could and, by common accord, granted the kingdom to Philippe de Valois, disallowing the claims of the Queen of England, who was the first cousin of the late King Charles, because they said that the kingdom of France is so noble a realm that it should not pass to a female heir . . . They had Philippe crowned at Reims on Trinity Sunday in the year of our Lord 1328, and thence have come great wars and disasters to the kingdom of France, as will be found later in this book if any read that far.

the preliminaries to war

In the year of his accession King Philippe VI, the first of the House of Valois, gained a notable victory over the Flemings at Cassel, putting an end to the revolt that had arisen through their dissatisfaction at being too heavily taxed by the kings of France. The effect of this was twofold: it was now much more difficult for Edward III to entertain thoughts of contesting Philippe's claims to the French crown, and secondly it put the Flemings in a position where they were much more likely to help the English on whom they depended for the wool trade. It is true that the Flemish aristocracy were French in sympathy, but, as we have seen, the loyalties of the nobles in the more powerful provinces could change overnight, and it must not be forgotten that the burgesses would constantly push the claims of a country on whom they were economically dependent, just as the English wool-merchants were among the chief financial supporters of the English war effort throughout the period of the hostilities. The war no doubt did as much harm as good to the wool trade, and among the causes of the war economic reasons are invariably subordinate to political ambition. It is only in the late revision (the Rome manuscript) that Froissart mentions the contribution of the wool trade to the royal treasury.

Shortly after Philippe's coronation two English bishops had gone to Paris to put forward the claims of Edward III and to protest at Philippe's usurpation. The embassy was not taken seriously, and when Philippe returned victorious from Cassel he sent to London to summon Edward to do homage for his fief in Aquitaine. Edward demurred, and Philippe threatened to confiscate the fief once more. This time Edward consented, and the homage was duly paid in Amiens Cathedral in June 1329.

Just a year later he was again summoned to Paris, this time to clarify the nature of his homage and assert in words that it was liege and not simple homage that had been vowed at Amiens. Edward instructed his officials in Aquitaine to resist any encroachment by the King of France; he also invoked the help of Pope John XXII at Avignon. King Philippe withdrew his claims in part, and declared himself satisfied with a written undertaking that the ceremony at Amiens had implied liege homage. The two kings met shortly afterwards, in April 1331, to discuss the difficulties in Aquitaine, and Edward's claims to the French throne were apparently at an end.

After the secret meeting the two kings prepared plans for a joint crusade to the Holy Land, though Edward was the less enthusiastic partner. But events in

Quant le roy anglois ot oui ce
point et la requeste des flamens
il ot grant besoing davoir bon conseil
et advis sur ce car pesante chose lui
estoit de prandre le nom de roy de fran
ce et de ce dont il navoit encores
riens conquis et encores point ne sa
voit quele chose lui en adviendroit
ne se conquerroit le pouvoit Et dautre
part envis le refusoit pour lamour

KING EDWARD QUARTERS THE ARMS OF FRANCE
WITH HIS OWN

Scotland were to prevent the realization of such a project. In 1332 Edward Balliol had himself crowned king in opposition to the established sovereign David Bruce, and had soon secured French support for his cause. In 1333 Edward III recaptured Berwick, and remained in the far north of England to watch events. He withdrew from the crusade, and Philippe made it clear that any hope of a settlement in Aquitaine would depend on Edward's abandoning the Scottish campaign.

This state of uneasiness lasted for three or four years; Pope Benedict XII attempted to bring peace between the two sides, but he seemed to have lost the goodwill of both through the affair of the crusade, which was finally abandoned altogether. Towards the end of 1335 the English Parliament, infuriated by Philippe's open hostility, voted sufficient funds for Edward to face a war if it became necessary. It was at this time, too, that he received the unexpected help of Robert of Artois.

¶ The man who did most to secure for Philippe the crown of France was Robert Comte d'Artois, who was one of the highest barons in France and one of the most closely related to the royal line. He had married the sister of King Philippe and had constantly been his closest companion. For this reason he was held in much respect, before Philippe was crowned king. This Comte Robert was for three years the chief voice in the king's council, everything being done according to his wishes and nothing decided if he were not present. Afterwards, however, the king was seized with hate for him because of a lawsuit which was brought before the king concerning the earldom of Artois, which the said Robert claimed to have won by virtue of a letter, though some said the letter was false.* If he had been caught he would certainly have been hanged, even though he was the nearest to the royal blood of all the barons of France and the king's brother-in-law. He was therefore forced to leave France in 1331, and went to Namur, where he was received by his sister's children the young Comte Jean and his brother.

When the king realized he could not lay hands on him since he had fled from France, he had his wife arrested, though she was his own sister, together with her children, and had them closely guarded in prison for so long that she died there. After the death of their mother and of Robert their father he kept the children guarded for most of his own life, until they were old enough to be knights, and whatever anyone said to him, and in spite of all reasons of kinship, he

* The document was declared to be false and cancelled by decree of the *Parlement*; one of Robert's accomplices was burned at the stake.

would not alter his attitude, but retained their property and kept them as closely guarded as if they were thieves or murderers. He later sent word to the young Comte Jean and his brother that they were not to give any support to their uncle Robert if they valued his love; if they did he would dispossess them of their lands. He wrote similarly to Adolphe de la Marck, Bishop of Liège, that in such circumstances he was not to recognize Jean as comte out of loyalty to the king. As a result Comte Jean and his brother no longer dared to harbour their uncle Robert or allow him to stay in their country, and he was obliged to seek refuge with his powerful cousin the Duc de Brabant, who was so closely related to him that he was bound to receive him. The king learned of this and immediately informed the duke that if he harboured or supported Lord Robert on his lands in any way whatsoever he would consider him to be his enemy and make war on him by any means he could.

The duke no longer dared to keep Lord Robert openly for fear of the king, and sent him secretly to Argenteau-sur-Meuse until he could see what action the king would take. But the king, who had spies everywhere, learned of this, and was very angry; in a short time he had bribed a considerable body of men to make war on the duke; the noble King of Bohemia (who was the duke's cousin), the Bishop of Liège, the Archbishop of Cologne, and a large number of powerful barons were all allied against the duke, and challenged him on the king's persuasion. They quickly entered the duke's territory and went through the land of Hesbaing, burning and laying waste on all sides. Twice they went through these lands, staying as long as they chose, and with them, sent by the king, was the Comte d'Eu, his constable, with a large company of men, to demonstrate that the campaign had the king's support. After further laying waste his lands they granted a truce to the duke at the instigation of the noble Comte de Hainault, and the duke declared that he would be obedient to the king and his council in every dealing he had with them and with those lords who had made war on him. Lord Robert thus dared not remain in France any longer, nor in Germany either openly or secretly, and in 1334 fled as quietly as he could to the noble King of England . . . who most willingly kept him in his service and appointed him to his council, granting him the Earldom of Richmond* in England which had previously belonged to his ancestors.

* The Earldom of Richmond had for many generations belonged to the Dukes of Brittany; Froissart's *Troisième Rédaction* correctly says he was given the Earldom of Bedford.

Then the king discussed with him the attitude he should adopt towards the crown of France, with the result that, partly on Robert's advice, the king declared war on the realm of France, from which war so many evils have come.

Edward seeks alliances

As the prospect of war came closer Edward set about the important business, above all for a small country, of establishing alliances. The obvious place to seek them was in Flanders and the Low Countries, for reasons that have been partly explained. In August 1336 Edward had published a royal decree which forbade wool to be exported outside the kingdom. The decree was directed against Flanders, since the Comte de Flandre—if not the whole of his people—was loyal to the French cause. Brabant, however, was granted an exception, and a wool staple was later established at Antwerp.

¶ After King Edward had . . . reconquered the fair city of Berwick and laid waste the lowlands of Scotland, placing garrisons to guard whatever places he chose, he returned rejoicing to his own country [1337] and was universally loved and honoured by great and small alike for the nobility of his words and deeds, for his great-heartedness and for the fair assemblies of ladies and maidens that he held, so much that one and all said he was King Arthur come again.

On several occasions he held deliberations with those whose counsel was most valuable to him as to how he should act in view of the great wrong done to him in his youth concerning the throne of France, for by right of succession it should have been his, as the Comte Robert d'Artois had not failed to inform him, although the twelve peers of France had awarded it to Philippe de Valois without calling for any other opinions in making their decision. He did not know what to think, for if he could do anything to alter the situation he would be most unwilling to abandon his claim. But if he were to be repulsed in an action to stake his claim, and then sat quiet and did nothing about it, he would be widely blamed for engaging in arms without increasing his dominions. He was moreover fully aware that with the forces of his own kingdom he would find it difficult to overcome the French, unless he bought an alliance with some powerful lords or with some of the twelve peers or other barons of France. He therefore made frequent requests to his intimate counsellors to advise him on this matter, for he would not undertake anything without taking advice.

In the end his council approved the following statement: 'Dear lord, the problem seems to us so great and of such consequence that we would not dare to undertake to counsel you. But, dear sir, we would suggest, if you agree, that you should send ambassadors, with careful instructions of your desires, to the noble Comte de Hainault, whose daughter you have married, and to his brother Jean who has served you so loyally, asking them to give you friendly advice on this matter, for they know better than we what is relevant to the problem. They are moreover bound by their love for the queen your wife to uphold your honour and if they agree to the action you have in mind, they will be able to suggest which lords are most likely to help you and how you could best win them over.' 'With this advice,' replied the noble king, 'I am in full agreement, for it seems sound and wise to me, and it shall be done as you suggest.' He then asked the noble Bishop of Lincoln to undertake this embassy on his behalf [January 1337], requesting two knights banneret—who were present at that time, but whose names I have forgotten—and two legal specialists to join the bishop.

They could not refuse the request of so noble a king and readily consented to go; they got ready as quickly as they could, then left immediately, soon reaching Valenciennes in Hainault. There they found the noble earl, so sick with gout and gravel that he could not move, and also Jean de Hainault his brother. It goes without saying that they were much honoured and feasted during their stay.

When they had been fittingly entertained they revealed to the earl and his brother the reasons why they had been sent on this embassy, and explained all the doubts the king had had. When the earl had heard all this he was in no way put out, saying that the king was not unwise to weigh up all these reasons for and against, for when one wishes to undertake a matter of such weight one must have some idea how it may be successfully concluded and, as far as one can judge, what may be the final outcome. He added: 'If, God helping, the king is successful, I should be overjoyed, and you may well imagine I would rather that victory went to him who has married my daughter than to the King of France who has never lent a hand to me though I have married his sister; for he has secretly turned young Jean de Brabant, Duc de Limbourg, from marrying my other daughter and has kept him for one of his own daughters. For this reason I would not fail my dear and beloved son the King of England if he were to decide in council that he should undertake this matter, but would help him with advice and assistance to the best of my ability, as would Jean my brother who has been of service to him in times past. But you will realize that he will have need of other help than ours, for Hainault is a small country beside the kingdom of France, and England is too far from us to give us help.'

'Truly, sire, you give us good advice and show us much love and goodwill, for which we thank you on behalf of our lord the king,' replied the noble Bishop of Lincoln on behalf of all the others, adding: 'Advise us now, dear sir, which lords our master may most trust to help him so that we can take back your advice to him.' 'Upon my soul,' said the earl, 'I can think of none better to help him in this affair than the Duc de Brabant who is his first cousin, the Bishop of Liège, the Duc de Gueldre, the Archbishop of Cologne, the Marquis de Juliers, the Seigneur de Fauquemont. These lords are more likely to be able to provide an abundance of armed men in a short time than any others I know in any country in the world. They are excellent men at war and if they wish can easily provide eight or ten thousand men—but they must be paid worthily, for they like their money. If my son the king were to come over with the support of the lords I have named, he would be powerful enough to seek battle with King Philippe of France in Paris itself.' This advice was most welcome to the king's ambassadors, and they took leave of the noble prince and Jean his brother, and returned to England with the full report of their council.

When they reached London the king entertained them sumptuously, and they told him all that had been deliberated in Hainault. The king was so delighted with this support for his proposals that he immediately equipped ten knights banneret and forty other young knights bachelor, at great expense, to go across the sea to Valenciennes with the noble Bishop of Lincoln, in order to treat with the lords whom the Comte de Hainault had named and to do whatever else he and his brother Jean should recommend.

When they reached Valenciennes [May 1337] everyone respected them greatly because of the splendid state that they maintained, sparing nothing in their attentions as if the king had been there in person, so that all marvelled at it. Some of the young knights had one eye covered with a piece of cloth so that they could not see with it. It was said they had vowed to the ladies of their own country that they would use only one eye until such time as they had performed some deed of arms on French soil, but this they would not themselves confess to those who asked them. The people thought it a most wonderful vow.

When they had been much entertained in Valenciennes by the noble earl, the other lords, the citizens and the ladies, the Bishop of Lincoln and the greater part of the knights went off on the earl's advice to the Duc de Brabant, who also entertained them worthily. They became on such good terms with him that he promised to support in his own country the king and all the English—as indeed he should do for his first cousin—and they could come and go in Brabant, armed or unarmed, whenever they chose. The duke promised further, for a certain payment in florins, that if King Edward were to challenge the King of France, he also would challenge him and enter into the realm of France with a thousand armed men. This he promised on oath, though he broke his promise shortly afterwards, as you will read. The English lords were very pleased, for they seemed to have performed their office well. They returned to Valenciennes, where by virtue of the messages they carried and the gold and silver they were able to dispense they secured the presence in that city of the Duc de Gueldre, the Marquis de Juliers, who spoke for himself and for his brother Valerant, Archbishop of Cologne, and the Seigneur de Fauquemont. With all these they were able to speak in the presence of the noble Comte de Hainault, who could not move from his quarters, and of Jean his brother, and in the end, by the payment of considerable sums of money among the lords and their men, they persuaded them to challenge the King of France and provide a certain number of trained men with crested helmets.

In those days the great lords thought little of men-at-arms unless they had crested helmets, while today the criterion is how many are armed with swords, how many with cuirasses, with habergeons, with iron helmets. Times have changed from the days I remember, for all the things we used to love to speak of—caparisoned horses, crested helmets, plate armour, and individual coats of arms have all gone by the board, and habergeons which they now call cuirasses, quilted doublets, and iron helmets are all the fashion. The poorest retainer is now as well and as smartly armed as a noble knight.

The assembled nobles further agreed to enlist the support of other barons from beyond the Rhine, who were in a position to bring large numbers of knights provided that they had sufficient reasons for doing so. They then took their leave and set out for their own country. Although the Bishop of Liège, Adolphe de la Marck, had received a pressing invitation, and messengers had been sent with handsome presents, he would not take any step against the King of France, to whom he had sworn faithful allegiance. No request was sent to the noble King of Bohemia, for it was known that he was too closely united to the King of France by the marriage of their two children.

When all these German lords had returned home, having made the promises of which you have heard, the English nobles remained in Valenciennes, where they spent heavily on sumptuous living.

¶ . . . It occurred to them that it would be a great support to their king in what he proposed to undertake if he could secure the help of the Flemings who at that time were at loggerheads both with their own Comte de Flandre and with the King of France. They consulted the Comte de Hainault, who said it would indeed be of the greatest support to them, but he did not see how they could secure this help without first winning the friendship of Jacques d'Arteveld.* The English lords said they would do everything possible to win it, and very soon left for Flanders, dividing into three separate parties to visit Bruges, Ypres and Ghent; they made promises of money on all sides and spent so freely that it seemed as if their money fell from the sky.

The Bishop of Lincoln and his companions, who had gone to Ghent, proved so persuasive that they won the favour and friendship of Jacques d'Arteveld and of the whole town [8 May 1338], in particular a valiant old knight banneret, Sohier de Courtrai, who was much loved by the people; he was considered the bravest and most worthy of all the knights of Flanders, and the one who had always given the most loyal service to the nobles. This valiant knight mixed with the English lords and showed them much honour because men of valour should always show honour to other knights as far as they can. But he was ill rewarded, for accusations were laid against him to the King of France because of his regard for the English, and the king ordered the Comte de Flandre to find some means to have him arrested and executed. The earl dared not go against the king's command and contrived to send for the brave old man, then clap him in prison [6 July 1337, Bruges], and have him executed [21 March 1338]. There was widespread grief at his death, and the earl lost much popularity as a result.

The English lords pursued their activities so vigorously that

* Jacob van Artavelde, a brewer of Ghent who was then leading a Flemish revolt against the Comte de Flandre, the French king's vassal.

Jacques d'Arteveld gathered several assemblies of representatives of the chief cities to discuss matters together. The English offered them generous trading rights in the king's name, without whose liberality they could scarcely have succeeded. After considerable discussions it was agreed by the whole Council of Flanders that the King of England could come and go as often as he chose in their country,

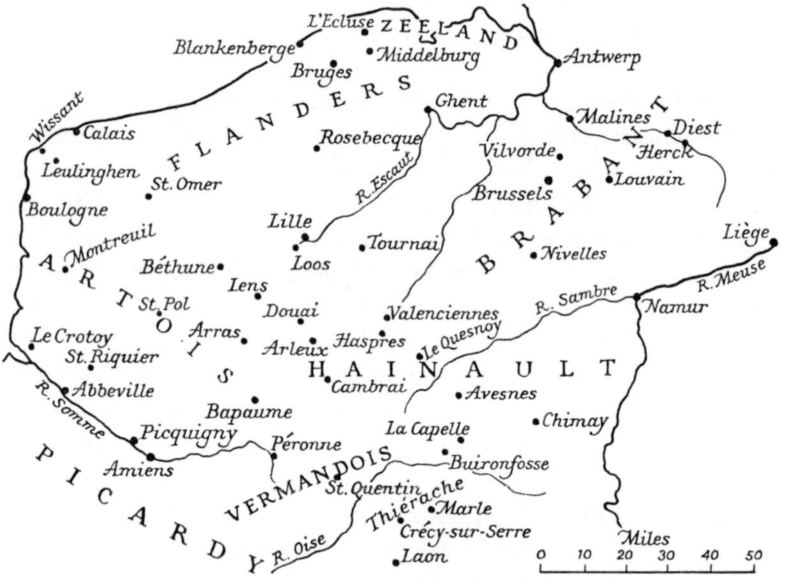

FLANDERS AND HAINAULT

with or without armed men; but they declared themselves so closely beholden to the King of France that they could not cause him offence or enter his lands without incurring a heavy fine in florins which they might only just be able to gather. They therefore hoped this treaty [10 June 1338] would suffice for the time being.

The English were pleased enough with this arrangement and they returned happily to Valenciennes. Frequent messengers were sent to the king in England to inform him of their progress and to ask for large sums of money to be sent, for their own expenses and also for distribution among the German lords,* and an advance of half what had been promised to the Duc de Brabant if he would send men to help them. The money was sent, and the advance was made. But the nobles of Brabant made no haste to leave with the men they had promised, finding reasons to delay joining the good King Edward

* Froissart follows Le Bel completely, but adds here of the Germans that 'they desired nothing more ardently than money'.

after they had once assembled their men—a delay which was to have unhappy consequences for the king.

The war is generally taken to have begun in 1337. On the 24th of May King Philippe had once again ordered the fief of Aquitaine to be confiscated. There were some immediate skirmishes on the border of that province, but for a year or more efforts were still being made to prevent the outbreak of general hostilities. Edward began to speak of Philippe as 'the man who calls himself King of France', and the letters that he sent to Paris by the Bishop of Lincoln on All Saints' Day in the same year were thus addressed; in them he withdrew the homage he had paid at Amiens in 1329. A state of war had occurred.

Philippe in his turn set out building an alliance, but with the Comte de Flandre, Jean de Luxembourg (better known as the King of Bohemia), and some other scattered alliances in the same area, he had a far less satisfactory set of allies than those secured by England. Meanwhile Edward was actively continuing his negotiations in Flanders and Brabant, and finally outbid Philippe for the support of the German emperor.

¶ In the summer of 1338 the King of England decided he would cross to the Continent with a great company of earls, princes, barons and knights and went straight to Antwerp to discover for himself more exactly what his cousin the Duc de Brabant intended to do. When it was known that he had arrived in that city many people came to see him and the great state that he maintained. After he had been most honourably entertained, he decided to discuss matters with the duke his cousin, with the Duc de Gueldre his brother-in-law, with the Marquis de Juliers, with Sir Jean de Hainault, with the Seigneur de Fauquemont and with the other lords with whom he had made agreements, to determine how and when they would be ready to put their undertakings into effect.

They all obeyed the summons and came to Antwerp between Whitsun and St John's Day in the year 1338. After they had been richly entertained according to the manner of England, King Edward called a council in which he very courteously set out his need to know what each of them intended, and begged them to let him know their decision as quickly as possible, because he had come over for that purpose and had his own men ready. It would be a great disadvantage to him if they did not give him their decisions quickly.

These lords held a long council together, for the question vexed them and they could not reach agreement; they had always before them the example of the Duc de Brabant, who kept a long face and would not reveal his plans. When they had discussed things at great length they delivered this reply to the noble King Edward: 'Sire, when we came hither we came chiefly to talk with you, and were therefore not fully prepared to give an answer to the questions you have put to us. We prefer now to return each to his own people, and will meet you again here on a date you shall fix, when we will give you a clear answer, so that no blame shall lie with us.'

The noble king saw that there was nothing else to be done and agreed to the proposal. They fixed a date for the decisions to be announced three weeks after St John's Day. But the king made clear to them the great expense he was put to by each day that he added to his stay, since he had expected they would be as ready to make decisions as he was himself. He told them he would not return to England until he was fully informed of their intentions. The lords then went their ways, and the king settled in the Abbey of St Bernard until the appointed day, some of the English nobles and knights remaining to keep him company in Antwerp and others spending heavily on their pleasures up and down the countryside, where they were well entertained. The Duc de Brabant returned to his own lands, whence he sent frequent gifts and money to the King of France to persuade him not to believe any evil reports he might hear.

As the day approached for the decisions to be announced the lords sent excuses to the king saying that, although they were fully ready as they had promised, he should persuade the Duc de Brabant to move first, for he was the nearest to the king and yet he was making very slow preparations. As soon as they knew that the duke was ready to move they, too, would set off for the meeting and be there as soon as the duke. The noble king accordingly spoke to the duke and told him how the lords had replied; he begged him in the name of friendship and of kin to think carefully and to see that he did not let his sovereign down, for it was obvious that he was dallying over his preparations and that if he did not mend his ways they would most likely lose the encouragement and support of the German lords.

When the duke heard this he did not know what to say and asked for time to think. Later he replied to the king that he would be very quickly ready when the need arose, but not until he had held discussions with those lords on a day to be arranged. From this the king realized that he could obtain no better promise and that there was no advantage in angering the duke; he therefore agreed to request those lords to meet him at Halle on the Feast of Our Lady in mid-August if— they would not come to a nearer rendezvous—in order to discuss their plans; at the same time he asked the duke to be good enough to be ready on that day so that the Germans had no excuse for not coming. This was agreed.

The day approached, and the said lords arrived. But the noble prince the Comte de Hainault was not present, since he had departed from this world the previous winter,* after knighting with his own hand his son, young Comte Guillaume, a thing I had forgotten to mention earlier. This young earl was at the discussions in his father's place, along with others, including his uncle, Sir Jean de Hainault. When they had all assembled they held long deliberations, for there were important issues at stake. They did not want to hold to their undertakings nor to incur dishonour by renouncing them.

Finally, after lengthy discussions, they reported their decisions thus to the King of England: 'Dear lord, we have taken some time to reach any conclusion because what you ask is a matter of great weight, and we can see no cause for defying the king at your instance, unless you can negotiate some agreement with the emperor to order us to defy the King of France on his behalf, for he has every right to do so as we shall explain. If that comes about you will not find that we shall fail you in promptness to do your will in accordance with our promise.

'Now, the cause that the emperor can have to defy the king is this. It is well known that there is a longstanding agreement between the Emperor of Germany and the King of France that no King of France shall occupy any land belonging to the Empire; yet King Philippe has done just this, against his oath, in occupying the fortresses of Crèvecoeur and Arleux and other lands in Cambrésis, which is Empire territory, and these lands he still holds. For this reason the emperor has good cause to defy him and to make his subjects defy him. We therefore beg you to pursue this negotiation vigorously for our honour and our country, and you will find that we also will do our utmost to the same ends.'

Noble King Edward was dumbfounded at this report; he had a good idea that it was designed merely to delay any action and he could sense behind the words the voice of his cousin the Duc de Brabant. Judging, however, that he should not hope for stronger support than this and that he would gain nothing by showing anger, he made the best of the situation and replied in these words: 'My lords, it is a fact that this problem had not been made clear to me, and if I had been informed earlier I should have had a plan ready. Yet I

* He died, in fact, on 7 June 1337.

am willing to do in this matter as you wish, and ask your help and advice, since I am in a foreign land beyond the sea, where I have spent much time at great expense and to no purpose. Give me, then, good counsel for your honour and mine, and know that if I do not risk blame over this, you cannot save your honour.'

¶ It would be a very long business to recount all that was said in their councils. In the end it was agreed among them that the Marquis de Juliers should go and speak to the emperor, taking with him some of the king's advisers* and knights and other men of the Duc de Gueldre, in order to perform his task to the best advantage. . . .

This deputation set off after each of the lords had sworn an oath in the presence of the rest to allow no excuse or delay to their being, from the Feast of St John in the year following, 1339, the enemies of King Philippe of France, nor to their being ready as they had promised. They then all returned home, while the Marquis de Juliers set off with all his company to the emperor, whom he found in Nuremberg.†

Why should I go into great detail concerning all that they had to discuss? I could not give a full account, because I was not there, but the marquis spoke to the emperor with such charm and without regard to what they spent that their purpose was achieved. It was here that the Marquis de Juliers was given his title, having previously been count, and the Duc de Gueldre obtained the title of duke, he, too, having been a count. Further the emperor gave authority to four knights and two noble lawyers, all members of his council, to make King Edward his vicar over the whole Empire, with permission to mint gold and silver coinage in his name. He ordered every one of his subjects to give obedience to the king as vicar as they would to their emperor. When the marquis had completed his duties he and his company set out on their return journey.

¶ When the noble King Edward and the other lords had ended their council . . . the king withdrew to Louvain, where he had the castle prepared for his residence; he sent orders to the queen his wife that he wanted her to cross the sea and join him, for he was not able to return home that year. He sent a considerable force of knights to protect his country, especially on the Scottish border. The other

* These (according to Froissart) included the Bishop of Lincoln.

† In fact, the meetings took place at Koblenz, and the King of England was himself present.

Englishmen who were also over in those parts settled themselves in various parts of Flanders, Brabant and Hainault.

At All Saintstide the Marquis de Juliers returned with all his company and told the king that he thought he had succeeded in his embassy, asking that the other lords should be summoned to an assembly at Martinmas in either Malines, Louvain or Diest in order to hear his report. The noble king was delighted at this news and communicated with his cousin the Duc de Brabant, who readily agreed to the date, though he could not accept that the meeting should take place in his own territory, since he wanted to conceal his intentions from the King of France. He would not therefore go to Utrecht, where the meeting was likely to have been held, but preferred Herck in the county of Looz, not far from his own lands. The noble king was so anxious to pursue his affairs that he had to put up with all the desires and whims of his cousin (the duke), since he had come so far, and agreed that the assembly should be held at Herck.* He notified this decision to his allies, who all obediently assembled on the Feast of St Martin [11 November 1338].

When they were all there the town was packed with lords, knights, squires and other folk. The market-hall, where bread and meat and other commodities were sold, was hung with fine tapestries so that it looked like a king's chamber, and the king sat crowned, a foot higher than all the others, on a butcher's bench, on which meat had been cut and sold. Never was a market-hall so honoured. Here, before the commons and the lords, were read aloud the letters from the emperor by which Edward, the noble King of England, was proclaimed vicar and lieutenant of the Empire, with the right to dispense justice and to mint gold and silver coinage in the name of the emperor; the letters also ordered all princes and subjects of the Empire to obey the king as vicar and give him their fealty as they would to the emperor himself. When the letters had been read each of the lords present took an oath of fealty to obey him as vicar of the Empire, and this oath was sworn and confirmed between the parties as if it had been in the presence of the emperor. They further agreed to revive and confirm an ancient statute by which anyone who wished to make war on or harass another should offer satisfactory challenges three days before he proposed to act; this statute seemed very reasonable to them all, but I do not know whether it has been universally observed.

* Other reports, probably more accurate, say this proclamation took place on 5 September 1338 at Koblenz when both the king and emperor were present.

When all this had been completed the lords left after taking an oath to have their forces ready, three weeks after the feast of St John, for an attack on Cambrai, which though by right a part of the Empire had gone over to the French king. When the lords had departed the noble King Edward returned to his queen, who recently arrived at Louvain in great magnificence, though I had forgotten to tell of her in my desire to pursue the main narrative. They held their court there in great state all that winter, striking great quantities of gold and silver coin in Antwerp, eagle-crowns in the emperor's name like the crowns struck by the French king which had and still have currency.

Meanwhile the Duc de Brabant continued his underhand policy of denying every action he appeared to be taking. He kept sending messengers to the King of France to inform him of the opposite of what he was in fact doing, and though everyone could see the evident deceit, no one dared to speak a word. Finally he ordered Léon de Crainhem, one of his most intimate advisers, to go to the King of France and remain quietly with the court wherever it went, offering the duke's excuses to the king and denying any hostile report that might reach him. Sir Léon dared not disobey his lord's command, and continued to do what was his duty, though it was plain for everyone in France to see that all the excuses he was offering for the duke were so many lies. He was so troubled and ashamed by it all that he resolved never to return to Brabant, but remained quietly in France to remove suspicion from himself, and finally died of grief, after the duke had confiscated his lands because he refused to come back to Brabant at the duke's command. He reported this to the King of France, who excused his behaviour and granted him a pension for his lifetime, which was unhappily to end so soon.

Thus the winter passed and the feast of St John Baptist approached. The German lords began to prepare their forces for their undertakings, and the King of France made counter-preparations, since he knew of the German plans. The noble King Edward caused his forces to be got ready in England and brought over the sea as soon as St John's Day [24 June 1339] had come, himself going to Vilvorde and seeing to his men's lodging. When the town was full he lodged them in tents and pavilions on the open ground below the meadows, and there they remained from St Mary Magdalen's Day [22 July] until after the Feast of the Nativity of our Lady [8 September], waiting week by week for the arrival of the other lords and particularly for the considerable forces of the Duc de Brabant.

When the noble King Edward saw that the duke and the other lords were not coming, he sent fresh messengers ordering them upon the oath they had sworn to meet him in Malines on the Feast of St Giles [1 September] and explain their delay. The noble king remained in Vilvorde, at great expense (as you can imagine), wasting his time in frustration; but he could do nothing about it. He was maintaining at his own expense at least six hundred armed men, chosen men who had been sent from England, and five hundred archers, without counting all their retainers. All this he had to bear to no immediate purpose, quite apart from the great sums he had given to the Germans, who kept putting him off with soft words; moreover, he had to maintain heavy forces at sea against the Genoese, the Normans, the Spaniards and the men of Bayonne whom the King of France was paying to harass the English. They were led by the Admiral Hue Quieret and Barbavera, a great sea warrior, and caused the English much trouble and many losses, both then and later.

When the German lords with the Duc de Brabant and the Comte de Hainault finally came to Malines in response to the king's command, they agreed after much talking that the king could set out in a fortnight's time, for they, too, would be ready then or soon after; they agreed to be at Cambrai on a certain date, and together prepared messages of defiance which were to be delivered to the King of France* on behalf of all of them, except the Duc de Brabant, who was not prepared at that moment to defy France. When this agreement was reached they all left Malines and hastened to complete their preparations. King Edward returned to his men more joyful than when he had left them, and gave orders for them to be ready in a fortnight. The Duc de Brabant now realized that he could delay no longer, and gave orders for his company to be got ready.

the war begins

Edward spared no pains to confirm the alliances he had made, often by financial settlements. Late in 1338 he held courts in Brabant and Hainault at which the vassals of his new vicariate were summoned to do him homage. Only financial difficulties prevented him from opening hostilities against the King of France,

* Froissart tells how it was the Bishop of Lincoln who carried the defiance from the king and the Germans.

in spite of widespread loans and borrowings. The French were strong enough at sea to sack the Isle of Wight and make brief landings on the English coast. Yet when, in September, Edward at last, with disappointing help from his new allies, made a punitive expedition into Cambrésis and Thiérache, Philippe refused his challenge to fight.

In Le Bel's narration of these events there is a reference to the army commanders chosen by King Edward. His six chief men at this time were Lancaster, Warwick, Northampton, Suffolk, Reginald Cobham and Walter de Manny, and in his last campaign twenty-two years later he took with him the same six commanders. This is a remarkable tribute to the king's skill in selecting his leaders and in inspiring their confidence, for, as Burne points out, they were sons of those same nobles who had shown the reverse of loyalty to Edward II.*

¶ Soon after St Lambert's Day, the seventeenth of September 1339, King Edward marched out of Vilvorde in Brabant to burn and lay waste the kingdom of France and to fight with King Philippe de Valois, who held it illegally and by force. With him there went sixteen hundred men-at-arms brought up in the finest traditions of English knighthood. Among these were the Bishop of Lincoln, a valiant man who had long laboured in this cause, and the young Earl of Derby, son of Henry Crouchback, Earl of Lancaster, who later did such deeds of prowess that he was considered among the most valiant of men; after his father's death the noble King Edward gave him the title of Duke of Lancaster, by which name he is always known. The gayest man you could find in all the world was the Earl of Northampton and Gloucester. Also present were the Earl of Warwick and the Earl of Salisbury, marshal of the army; the Earl of Suffolk, Lord Stafford, Jean de Hainault, Seigneur de Beaumont and several others whose names I do not know. But I must not omit Sir Reginald Cobham, who must be considered then and now as one of the most valiant of his countrymen. Nor should I fail to mention Sir Walter de Manny, whom the noble king had retained as one of his inner council, giving him such wide lands in England that he had become a knight banneret; indeed, he now maintained much greater state than the knights banneret who attended the king.

Along with all these were a great company of lords, knights and barons who so loved the king that they were ready to serve him at their own expense, asking neither wages nor their expenses at court until the year was over, if the need for an army should last so long.

* *The Crecy War*, p. 354.

I must tell you, too, that when this noble King Edward first conquered his own kingdom in his youth people thought little of the English in general and never spoke of their valour or their courage, even after the Scottish campaign. They had no plate-armour, no basinets with chin-pieces, no gorgets, no small weapons, only heavy hauberks and large surcoats emblazoned with their arms and gloves of cotton stuff, with a helmet of iron or boiled leather. But since the coming of noble King Edward, who has done much for their training, the English have learnt the arts of war so well that they are the most noble and debonair fighters you can meet . . .

The day came when the noble king was to move towards France, in accordance with the agreement made with the other lords at Malines. He left Vilvorde [20 September 1339] with all his army and passed through Nivelles and Hainault by short marches, so as to wait in Cambrésis for the other lords his allies who were following behind him, except the Duc de Brabant, who arrived six or seven days after the rest.

When the various lords had joined forces they took counsel and decided to march together towards Cambrai, laying waste the country round about because the city of Cambrai refused to welcome or support them, and there to await the Duc de Brabant. This was agreed, and the land of Cambrésis was completely ravaged. The young Comte Guillaume de Hainault agreed with this action, but some of the wiser of his men urged that the land of the King of France should not be laid waste, for when all the others had gone away again his own territory, which bordered the king's lands, would suffer for it and he would not be able to defend or guard it.

The count therefore dispatched important envoys to the King of France his uncle, who had already reached Péronne in Vermandois with the largest army he could muster, to offer whatever excuses they could that these lords had passed through his lands and laid them waste, and at the same time to offer his services with five hundred armed men to defend his kingdom. The King of France listened attentively to the messengers, but he thought it was a pretence and that his nephew was more attached to the other side than his own. However, he did not show this, and told the messengers to inform his nephew that he did not refuse his service, but that when a battle became imminent he should withdraw in the king's direction, for he would be grateful to see him.

¶ With the King of France at Péronne was the noble King of

Bohemia and a thousand men-at-arms, knights and squires of the best that could be had, and the Bishop of Liège with six hundred armed men from his own land to defend the kingdom. Meanwhile the Duc de Brabant arrived in Cambrésis to keep his agreement, with twelve hundred fully equipped companies of men-at-arms. The noble king and all the other lords were delighted at this, and the duke asked them all to rest for the space of two days to await the last comers before sending defiance to the King of France in Péronne . . .

When the duke's defiance had been sent to the King of France, the King of England and his allies left Cambrésis and entered French territory, burning and wasting the land as they passed. They lodged the first night not far from Péronne in the White Friars' Abbey of Mont Saint-Martin,* which they later sacked. The King of France was near Péronne, although he still had a wide river to cross with all his army. The noble King Edward and the other lords here awaited the morrow, thinking that the King of France, who could see his kingdom being burnt and pillaged—a thing never before known—must cross the river to engage them. But he took no such step.

When they saw that the King of France would not come over the river to them they sent to inform him that if he did not come to fight them he would see something else that he had never seen before, for they were not prepared to risk a crossing themselves. Early next morning they decamped, and skirted as close as they could to the river, burning and wasting the land; they camped at Origny on the Oise, from where they took several undefended towns and fortresses. There was an abundance to be pillaged, for it was rich land and the people had not destroyed or hidden anything. A Benedictine Convent was completely burnt and ruined, and many of the nuns were ravished by the English, which was a matter of great shame.

Next day they moved off, the earl-marshal, Salisbury, the Earl of Suffolk and Lord John of Hainault riding with five hundred armed men to Marle, burning the suburbs and the town of Crécy-sur-Serre in Laonnois and all the surrounding countryside. They found it so full of riches that they all took what they wanted, and returned about the time of nones to lodge in the Abbey of Vadencourt-et-Bohéries, where King Edward and all the other lords had preceded them.

The following day they set off from Bohéries and passed through Thiérache, burning and wasting, and finding such abundance of cattle and other things that they did not know what to do with it all.

* Le Bel incorrectly states Mont Saint-Jean.

To those who would buy, an old cow or an ox could be had for fourpence, or two sheep for one penny sterling.*

At that time the King of France left Péronne and lodged in the Abbey of Bohéries which King Edward had recently left, and was following the English with the intention, he said, of engaging them in combat. That night the King of England was camped near to La Capelle and La Flamengrie in Thiérache; there news reached them that the King of France, the most noble King of Bohemia and the Bishop of Liège were following him in the hope of a fight. The English lords therefore held a council and decided to lie low the next day in order to see what the King of France and those other lords wanted to do, for they were very ready to engage them in battle if they could and waited to see what God should will.

Next day the King of France and all his army moved forward, and camped two short leagues from their enemy by a town called Buironfosse, everyone expecting to go into battle the following day. Guillaume the young Comte de Hainault had left the allied lords after he had sent the messengers to the King of France, and had withdrawn to Le Quesnoy in Hainault to see whether his uncle the king was going to offer battle. When he heard that his uncle had left Péronne and was seeking a fight with the English he left Le Quesnoy with four hundred armed men and went to Buironfosse, where he knew his uncle lay. In fact, the king was taking counsel with his men whether or not to engage in combat with the enemy who were burning and wasting his lands. The earl offered suitable greetings to his uncle, who did not receive him as warmly as he had hoped, nor did he like it that the king was, as he thought, taking so long to decide on a point of honour. He therefore left the king and returned to Le Quesnoy, whence he had set out at midnight, allowing his uncle to pursue his deliberations as he chose.

On the day following, when the noble King Edward and the lords who were camped near La Capelle and La Flamengrie knew that the King of France was lodged so near to them, they rose at daybreak and devoutly heard mass, after which they moved into the fields and drew up their foot soldiers in three companies, fairly close to each other, all ready to face the powers of France. They sent their horses and their baggage behind a neighbouring wood, while the lords and their men remained ready on foot until after midday,

* The coins named are the *gros*, which is the equivalent of the groat, and the *estrelin* or easterling (from the name Easterlings given to the Hanseatic merchants) which gives us our word sterling.

awaiting the coming of the King of France and his great army, who were at Buironfosse. Here the king was debating with his princes and barons what to do; there was much dissension in this council among the lords and barons of France, for some said that it would be dishonourable not to fight when the enemy was so near and in their own country and when they had been burning and wasting the king's lands under his very eyes; others said that it would be madness to fight, for he did not know the minds of all his followers, whether some might be intending treason, and moreover that the chances were not equal, since the king was not favoured by fortune and he would be beaten and his kingdom destroyed; and even if by some chance the enemy were beaten, he would have done nothing to conquer the King of England nor to win his lands or the possessions of the other English lords.

The day was spent in these deliberations and disagreements without any settlement being reached, and the hour of nones was reached. Meanwhile the King of England and his allies, who had been standing in the field till nones without drinking or eating, realized that the French had no stomach to fight and would not come forward. They therefore discussed together what should be done; various opinions were listened to, and it was finally agreed by common consent that no reasonable person could blame or reproach them if they now departed, for they had offered battle to the King of France on entering his realm before doing harm to the country, and had then remained there for seven days, burning and wasting the land under the eyes of the king and all his army so that the like of it had never been seen before. There they had awaited the day for battle,* with the French but two short leagues of flat country away, without a river or fortress to impede their progress, and yet they made no move to show themselves or to advance. The English were now short of victuals, wine and bread, and did not know where they could secure replenishments. For all these reasons they were agreed on departure, and accordingly they struck camp and moved away late at night to Avesnes, taking with them all their baggage and their booty.

When the French and their king saw that the English had gone they, too, departed, each to his own town, and maintained that in doing so the honour was theirs, for they had driven away the enemy without any conquest being made even though much of the land had

* Froissart adds that the English had sent a herald to the French king asking for a day of battle to be fixed, and that the herald had been loaded with gifts because of the good news he bore of an impending fight.

been wasted; plenty of his realm still remained to the King of France, and if the English king wanted to conquer France he would have to make many more such incursions. This was how the French reasoned in order to excuse their departure; and the English held the opposite view, so that each attributed the praise to themselves. The reader can weigh these various arguments and give honour where he feels it due, after considering the reasonings and the military achievements.

'Edward, King of England and France'

Edward's next step was to secure a military alliance with Flanders and everything seemed in his favour. The English refusal of wool supplies to the Flemish towns had caused serious hardship among the weavers, and it was in their interests that Jacob van Artavelde had organized opposition to Comte Louis de Nevers, whose attachment to the French cause was held to be responsible for the commercial disasters. Artavelde held Ghent and Bruges against armed attack by the count, who in February 1339 fled to the French court. The whole of Flanders was left in rebel hands. Though Edward was unable to secure their active support before his abortive campaign in Thiérache, he went calmly ahead with his negotiations and by the end of the year had won them over with the promise of unhindered supplies of wool, with help in regaining Lille and the other towns occupied by King Philippe le Bel, and with a financial settlement to help them to organize their military forces. The account that follows is taken from Froissart, who makes the issues clearer than Le Bel.

¶ We will now turn to the King of England and see how his fortunes were progressing. After he had returned to Brabant from La Flamengrie, he set out for Brussels. There he was joined by the Duc de Gueldre, the Comte de Juliers, the Marquis de Blankenberghe, the Comte de Mons, Sir Jean de Hainault, the Seigneur de Fauquemont, and all the barons of the Empire who had allied themselves to him, for they wished to discuss the problem and decide how they might carry on the war in which they had engaged. To speed the decision, they summoned a conference to be held in the city of Brussels [December 1339], to which they called Jacob van Artavelde, who came joyfully and in full state, bringing with him all the councils of the chief towns of Flanders. At this conference in Brussels many things were discussed. It would seem that the King of England was advised by his friends from the Empire to place before the Flemings a request to help him to continue the war and challenge the King of France, and to follow him wherever he should lead them; if they did this he would help them to regain Lille, Douai and Béthune.

The Flemings received this proposal with pleasure, but they asked permission to consult privately about the king's request, and to give their answer speedily, which the king granted. After they had taken counsel at their leisure, they gave their reply thus: 'Beloved lord, you made us this same request on a former occasion, and you know indeed that if we can in any way carry it out, while keeping faith and our own honour, we would do it. But we cannot wage war against the King of France, whoever he may be, for if we take arms against him we are under a solemn oath to pay two million florins to the papal exchequer and to incur sentence of excommunication. But if you are prepared to accept a suggestion we make, you will find a well-advised remedy. This is to adopt the arms of France and quarter them with those of England, assuming the title of King of France, by which we will recognize your right, and obey you as we should the King of France. We shall ask of you exemption from our former bond, which as King of France you will grant to us. In this way we shall be freed from our oath and ready to follow you wherever you may be pleased to order us.'

When the King of England had listened to the arguments of the Flemings he felt the need of receiving sound advice in counsel, for he was unwilling to assume arms and a title which he had in no way yet earned by conquest. He was, however, reluctant to refuse the help and support of the Flemings, who were in a better position to assist him in his task than any others at that time. The king therefore took counsel of the Duc de Brabant and the Duc de Gueldre, the Comte de Juliers, Lord Robert of Artois and Jean de Hainault and of his most intimate and trusted friends, with the result that finally, when all the advantages and disadvantages had been thoroughly weighed, he replied to the Flemings that, on the advice of the lords above mentioned, if they were ready to bind themselves by an oath to help him to pursue the war, he would willingly accept their conditions. He swore, moreover, to restore to them Lille, Douai and Béthune, and they all replied 'Yes'.

A day was accordingly fixed for a meeting at Ghent [6 February 1340], to which came the King of England and the greater part of the barons of the Empire above named who were his allies, and with them all the national and local councils of Flanders. At this assembly all the statements and arguments previously heard were repeated and when agreement had been reached they were recorded in writing, sworn and sealed. Then the King of England assumed the arms of France quarterly with his own, and took from that day the title of King of France, retaining it until he laid it down again by an agreement of which you will hear later where it is recorded for you in this history.*

At this assembly held in Ghent many things were thrashed out. The lords proposed in council and agreed that siege should be laid to the city of Tournai. The Flemings were delighted at this, for they thought they would be strong enough to capture it. And once it was taken, and held by the King of England, they would have no difficulty in recovering Lille, Douai and Béthune, together with their dependencies, which belonged of right to the land of Flanders. It was further proposed and agreed that they would be even better pleased if the province of Hainault were with them in this, so they could take armed refuge there. The count was therefore begged to join the assembly, but he sent such reasonable excuses that the King of England and all the barons declared themselves satisfied.† This, then, was the state of affairs when the lords took their leave and went each to his own country or province, while the King of England bade farewell to his cousin the Duc de Brabant and returned to Antwerp. The queen his wife remained in Ghent with all her household, and was frequently visited and comforted by van Artavelde and the barons, and by the ladies and maidens of Ghent.‡

Shortly after this the king's ship was got ready in the harbour of Antwerp, and he and the greater part of his men embarked for England. He left behind in Flanders two lords, wise and brave men, to cement the friendship with the Flemings and make it clear to them that their interests were one with his own; these were William Montague, Earl of Salisbury, and the Earl of Suffolk, who established a garrison in the town of Ypres, and spent the whole winter in active

* By the Treaty of Calais, 1360. See p. 132.

† A later revision by Froissart puts the matter differently: '. . . but he excused himself, saying that never would he perform any act hostile to the King of France his uncle, unless the French declared war first.'

‡ A later MS adds: 'And at this time the Queen of England gave birth to a fine son in the Abbey of St Pierre de Ghent, and called him John, the Duc de Brabant standing sponsor for him. He later became Duke of Lancaster, through his marriage with the daughter of Henry Duke of Lancaster and Blanche his wife.' This was John of Gaunt (= Ghent), fourth son of Edward III, born March 1340.

harassing of Lille and the surrounding countryside. Meanwhile the King of England was on his way by sea to London, where he arrived on the eve of St Andrew's Day 1340, and was welcomed with much rejoicing by the people, who were eager for his return after so long an absence. Here he received many complaints of the havoc caused to the fair city of Southampton by the Normans and Picards; the king was very angry to learn of the losses suffered by the citizens, but he consoled them as best he could, saying that their turn would come and he would then make these plunderers pay dearly for what they had done. And indeed he carried out his promise within a year, as you will read later in this history.

Edward's immediate hopes were now fulfilled. He assumed the title of King of England and France; the alliance sealed at Ghent was ratified in March 1340 (the year of Chaucer's birth) by the English Parliament, and the Comte de Hainault then agreed at last to send his defiance to the King of France. But serious financial problems weighed him down. His queen had been left in France, not because of the impending birth of a son, but as security for the loans he could not repay to his creditors in the Low Countries. New taxes had to be imposed in Westminster and were received with growing hostility—and the thought of defeating France was still a long way off.

Edward pursued his policy relentlessly, and used the new taxes to equip a fleet with which he set sail in June 1340 to engage the enemy off Sluys. By the 24th he had destroyed the combined French and Castillian navy and so gained command of the sea. In July his army joined the Flemish forces and marched on Tournai. Lacking the equipment and the knowledge of siege tactics, they made no headway; to make things worse the Duc de Brabant and then the Comte de Hainault went over to the French king. Edward was quite happy to accept a year's truce at the instigation of Pope Benedict XII: the alliances he had built up had failed, no doubt partly because England was not wealthy enough to maintain them. The next in defection was Louis of Bavaria, who revoked Edward's office as Vicar of the Empire and so removed his imperial support.

The truce—like so many that were to follow in the next hundred years—was used by both sides to reconstitute their fortunes. Philippe, already helped by the defections among his enemy's allies, set about destroying the power of Artavelde, who was finally killed by the people of Ghent in 1345 after offering the countship of Flanders to Edward's eldest son, the Black Prince. In 1342 the Flemish rebels had been excommunicated by the pope because they had broken their allegiance to the lawful count. Meanwhile Edward was in great financial troubles and was forced to remain in England, where he proceeded to punitive measures against Archbishop Stratford and others who, he said, had failed to raise the money needed for his campaign.

It was at this point that events in Brittany opened the way to Edward for a more advantageous interference in the affairs of France. When the Duke of Brittany died in 1341 the succession was contested by his niece Jeanne de Penthièvre and his half-brother Jean, Comte de Montfort. The latter had seized the ducal treasure and half a dozen of the chief towns in the Duchy, in defiance of the King of France, who was to have acted as arbitrator. In July, Montfort secured the promise of English support in return for acknowledging Edward as King of France; in September the French peers declared Charles de Blois, Jeanne's husband and a nephew of Philippe, to be the rightful Duke of Brittany. The royal army was sent to Nantes, which it captured, taking Montfort prisoner.

Montfort's wife, Jeanne de Flandre, now entered the struggle—which became known as 'la guerre des deux Jeannes'. *Edward himself took an army over, but in January 1343 a further truce was imposed by the papal legates. War soon broke out again; by the end of 1345 Montfort was dead, Jeanne de Flandre had gone mad and their son Jean was declared duke under the protection of the English crown. Edward, in fact, was in control of affairs in Brittany. An effort by the pope in Avignon, late in 1334, to secure agreement had met with failure; in the course of protracted talks it became clear that the real matter of dissension was not the succession to the French crown (though Edward made a token claim for this) but the feudal question of Aquitaine. France was even ready to 'restore' the fief to England, but only if it remained part of the kingdom of France.*

Edward lands in Normandy

When the extended truce expired in March 1345, Edward took the offensive in both Brittany and Aquitaine. In 1346 his forces were resisting the siege of Aiguillon, a key fortress in the latter duchy, when the way was opened for a landing in the north—not in the now suspect land of Flanders, but in Normandy. Philippe had just confiscated the lands of Godefroi de Harcourt in the Cotentin, and Godefroi had promptly offered his services to Edward. All this enabled Edward to make plans for an invasion force and he lost no time in carrying them out.

Before his account of the rapid campaign that led to Crécy, Le Bel inserts a comparison of the two kings which is not copied by Froissart.

¶ No one who reads this history will wonder why I call the King of England the noble King Edward and the other simply King Philippe of France, though they might think I did it out of prejudice. While being just to each of them, I do not use these terms out of any preconceived loyalty, but to honour the man who bore himself the more nobly in this history. This was King Edward, whom it is impossible to honour too highly and who always accepted wise advice in his undertakings, always loved his knights, squires and men, and always did honour to each according to his estate; always defended his kingdom against its enemies and gained conquests from them, always fearlessly risked his own life with the lives of his followers both at home and abroad, and always paid the wages of his armed men and gave generously of his own wealth. For all these things he deserves to be willingly served, and by all acclaimed as a noble king.

King Philippe did not behave in like fashion: he allowed various parts of his kingdom to be laid waste and pillaged while he remained in or around Paris for an easy life and his own safety; he always accepted bad advice from lawyers and bishops, and from those who would say to him: 'Dear lord, have no fear and take no risk for your life, for you do not know whom you can trust and would have difficulty in avoiding betrayal. Let this young King of England waste his time and his wealth in such mad pursuits; all his pride will not dethrone you, and when he is exhausted he will have to go back home. He still has not taken Boulogne, Amiens or Saint-Omer; when he has gone, you can easily recover your losses.' It was these men that King Philippe listened to, not the lords and barons of his realm, some of whom he wickedly put to death, suspecting treason, and disinherited their heirs, though it was they who should have been honoured by all men. Furthermore he burdened the country with heavy and unjust taxes, and the Church with tithes, was constantly minting unbacked currency in various places, minting more to raise funds, and then devaluing it when he chose so that there was no means of setting a true value on merchandise. Nor were his army properly paid, so that they often had to spend from their own purses, or to sell their horses and their arms while waiting for the king's treasury to pay. A prince who rules in this way has little right to be loved by his people, and it is a terrible pity that the kingdom of France, which had been so universally blessed with honour and wisdom, clergy and knights, merchandise and all good things, should be thus stricken by evil counsel and brought to such misfortune by its enemies and its own weakness that he who should be their lord is deceived and almost all the lords and knights of the country are dead or in prison. I believe it is only by a miracle that God can permit such a thing. But I have said enough and shall turn to my account of the noble King Edward, who has so well deserved the love, respect and honour of all men, for which we should give thanks to God.

This noble king was well aware that those of his men who were resisting the siege of Aiguillon had a hard task, and he remembered his promise that he would soon enter the kingdom of France and do more damage to it than had ever before been done.* He therefore spent all that winter and summer in preparing ships of all kinds and issued general orders that everyone should be ready to embark on St John's Day to go wherever he chose to take them. When St John's Day came they were all ready and went on board their vessels, which immediately set sail [1 July 1346, from Portchester harbour]. King Philippe soon had news of this and sent a large body of men-at-arms to guard the coasts, for he did not know where King Edward intended to land. With them he sent the Comte d'Eu, his constable, who had come from the siege of Aiguillon to protect the country round the fair city of Caen in Normandy, with a large number of armed men; the king remained in Paris for reasons of personal security. But King Edward was sailing hard towards France; he had no thought for security or piling up treasure, for riches meant nothing to him unless he could spend them freely.

King Edward had such good fortune at sea that he arrived at the beginning of July off the isle of Guernsey,† in the year of grace 1346, and with him was a most noble knight called Godefroi de Harcourt, brother of the Comte de Harcourt. This Godefroi had been suspected of treason and banished from France; if King Philippe had held him still, he would have done with him as he did with Olivier de Clisson.‡ King Edward had in his army four hundred armed men,

* Froissart adds that when Edward left England he intended to proceed to Aquitaine for the relief of Aiguillon and that the landing in the Cotentin was made at the direct suggestion of Harcourt.

† It was off the Isle of Wight that King Edward assembled his fleet, on the 11th of July, before sailing for France.

‡ Olivier de Clisson had been a prisoner in England, and was exchanged for Lord Stafford. On his return to France he was suspected of having entered into a disloyal treaty with King Edward. Such a treaty did exist and had been entrusted to the Earl of Salisbury; when he heard of the king's conduct towards his wife while he was himself a prisoner, he retired secretly to France and handed the treaty over to King Philippe. Olivier was beheaded on the king's orders and his body displayed on a gibbet. For the affair concerning the Countess of Salisbury, see Introduction, p. 13.

knights and squires—not more, whatever may have been claimed—and fully ten thousand archers and ten thousand foot soldiers.

When he had landed on Guernsey, which is a large island, he spent four or five days there burning and laying waste, and took the island's fortress, which was found to be full of treasure. There he decided to sail for Normandy and on the advice of Godefroi de Harcourt, who knew the country well, to land on that part of it known as Le Cotentin.* He sent a third of his men to burn and waste the coastal lands; it was marvellously rich country, with a large number of fine towns, and the noble king and his son the Prince of Wales, who had not till then borne arms,† were to go by land, burning and laying waste through Normandy, and so reach Paris to greet King Philippe himself. The noble King Edward created Godefroi de Harcourt marshal of the army‡—and gladly he undertook the task—with the Earl of Suffolk to help him.

When King Philippe, who was with his barons in Paris, learned this he sent letters throughout his kingdom bidding all the lords and barons to prepare for war, but it was too late; he would have done better to follow wiser counsel than that of the masters of the exchequer and the treasury. At his bidding, many lords came to Paris, including the King of Bohemia and many other lords of the Empire, with all the forces they could muster. In all they numbered twenty thousand armed men and sixty thousand foot soldiers, including the Genoese.

Meanwhile King Edward continued his march through Normandy, having divided his army into two parts. The Earl of Warwick and Lord Stafford went along the coast, capturing all the vessels large and small that they could lay their hands on, and added them to the English fleet. The archers and foot soldiers followed them along the coast by land, burning, wasting and pillaging everything. Soon they reached the fair port of Barfleur [14 July], and took it, since the men of the town surrendered to save their lives. But their action did not save the whole town from being sacked, its gold, silver and jewels taken; there was so much treasure that even the meanest servants would scorn fur-lined capes and coverlets and such things. All the men of the town were ordered out of their houses on to the ships, for they did not want them to get together again to cause any trouble.

* They landed at Saint-Vaast-la-Hougue, 12 July 1346.

† The Prince of Wales was then 16, and was, in fact, dubbed knight on landing.

‡ Harcourt had come to England early in 1345; like Robert d'Artois, his rise was rapid. In future he will be referred to as Sir Godfrey Harcourt. Some English historians call him Geoffrey.

After Barfleur had been captured and sacked, they spread farther along the coast and did as they pleased with the country, for there were no soldiers of King Philippe to oppose their passage. Thus they arrived at a large and rich port known as Cherbourg, which they took and pillaged as they had done Barfleur. In the same way they dealt with Montebourg, Valognes [18 July], and various other fine towns, in all of which they found great treasure. Then they reached a large walled town, with a fortress, called Carentan, and here there was a considerable force of King Philippe's men. Those lords and armed men who were still in the ships made a landing in order to attack the town; when the citizens saw this they feared for their lives and possessions, and in spite of the garrison that was stationed in the town said they would give themselves up if their lives and belongings were spared. But they offered up their money, because they knew that it was lost in advance. The English lords, however, were not prepared to abandon the fortress thus, and laid siege to it for two days so successfully that the garrison, who could expect no relief, yielded themselves on the same terms as the citizens. The English did as they chose with the town, ordering the menfolk on to the ships, as they had done elsewhere.

Why should I recount what followed at great length? The English lords and their armies went along the whole of the coast, burning and wasting everywhere, from the Cotentin to the eastern confines of Normandy, doing as they chose without any kind of opposition. They sent all their booty to England with a large number of prisoners they had taken; much wealth was gained from their ransoms, and with it King Edward was able to pay his soldiers generously . . .

This last sentence gives the key to Edward's future success: once a successful campaign was under way there would be sufficient wealth from ransoms and booty for the demands on the taxpayer at home to be very considerably eased.

In spite of his disclaimer, Le Bel does, in fact, describe the triumphal progress through Normandy and into the Île de France. Saint-Lô is taken, and a battle fought with the Comte d'Eu to capture Caen. From there the English proceed through Louviers, Mantes and Vernon to the Seine at Poissy.

¶ And so King Edward came to Poissy, a large town, where he found the bridge, as at Vernon, had been destroyed, which annoyed him because it prevented him from crossing the river. He stayed there for four days [13–16 August] and had the bridge repaired as best he could. During this time he sent his marshal, Sir Godfrey Harcourt, to Saint-Cloud to set fire to the place, which is less than a couple of leagues from Paris, so that King Philippe might see the smoke rising.

When the bridge at Poissy was sufficiently repaired for carts and waggons to cross it, King Edward went over with all his army and there was no one to molest them, a most miraculous event in three ways. Firstly that the English could repair the bridge at Poissy in so short a time without having any contrivances ready for the work, and no ship from which to work in midstream; nor had they any materials of a suitable length. And yet it was done in four or five days.

The second miracle is that when the bridge was rebuilt King Philippe—a mere seven leagues away in Paris, where he had all the assembled forces of his lords whom he had summoned for the defence of his kingdom—did not come and attack an enemy who were sending sparks and smoke over his own head, or even attempt to defend the passage of the Seine.

The third is that when he knew the enemy was so close he did not advance upon them along the Seine, knowing that all the bridges were down and that they could neither escape nor cross the river unless they rebuilt one of them. I do not understand. The truth is that he had not the heart or the courage to fight, for his advisers had him in their power and passed information to the effect that if he fought he would be betrayed and destroyed; they whispered in his ear that his betrayers would be some of the highest and most powerful nobles in the land (some of whom were put to a horrible death because of such suspicions . . .) with the result that King Philippe did not dare go into battle. A prince who mistrusts his people will never achieve anything worth while. It should be believed that it was those who advised him thus who wished to betray him, rather than the noble lords who had risked life and limb in battle and who had been falsely suspected. I think I have said enough.*

When the noble King Edward had . . . crossed the Seine . . . he saw clearly by various signs that King Philippe had no desire to come out and fight with him. He therefore continued on his way through Beauvoisis towards Beauvais; in the course of their march Sir

* Le Bel said too much—or too little. There was the fierce engagement with an armed force from Amiens who attempted to prevent the rebuilding of the bridge, but more important King Edward treated the French offer of battle with high scorn, suggesting he would march round Paris to the south, a move that was supported by the action of the Prince of Wales's troops. The king then rapidly directed his troops back and they crossed the rebuilt bridge on 16 August.

Godfrey Harcourt, his marshal, who was riding with the vanguard, met a large body of men of Amiens, mounted and on foot, who were heading for Paris at their king's command. He attacked and routed them, killing or taking prisoner many of them, at which the king was overjoyed, and continued each day to burn and waste the country on all sides, as he had done on his way through Normandy.

I could not name all the towns and villages that they laid waste, nor the extent of each day's march, but he ultimately arrived near the city of Beauvais and lodged for the night in the Abbey of Saint-Lucien.* On the next day, when he had advanced some distance, he was surprised to see the abbey in flames, and was very angry. He passed quickly round Beauvais without stopping to destroy it, for his chief intention was to lay siege to the strong town of Calais, since he could not entice King Philippe to battle as he wished. He went on to Milly [18 August] in Beauvoisis and lodged in the town. The two marshals passed so close to Beauvais that they could not resist attacking the gates on three sides of the city, burning and plundering two fine abbeys as well as suburbs and villages outside the walls. They collected an unbelievable quantity of booty, and then departed in different directions, burning and pillaging on all sides, and continued thus till they rejoined the king at Milly.

The king left Milly the following day and advanced through the country, still plundering and laying waste, and lodged the next night in a town called Grandvilliers, which he left again the next day and passed by the undefended fortress at Dargies, which he burned as he did all the surrounding countryside as far as Poix. Here there were two castles and a fine large town, but the commanders had departed, leaving only two fair maidens, who would soon have been violated had not two knights protected them and brought them before the king, who received them honourably and had them conducted where they wished to go.

That night the army were lodged in the town and the surrounding villages, and the king in the finer of the two castles. The good people of the town parleyed with the commanders and marshals of the army, and secured that the town should be spared from burning on payment of a certain sum in florins, which was to be handed over the next morning. When morning came the king and his army departed, leaving a small party behind to receive the town's ransom. But when

* Le Bel and Froissart both call it Saint-Messien (whose bones were also preserved there). In fact, only a small part of the abbey was burned. Froissart says the king hanged twenty men for their part in this.

the citizens had come together to make the payment, and saw that the army had left and that only a few men remained, they set on these men and began to kill them. Some ran after the army and returned quickly with reinforcements, so that the citizens were killed without mercy and the whole town burned, as it deserved to be. After this the king and his army marched on to Airaines. Here he gave orders that no one, on pain of death, should set fire to the place, because he wanted to stay there and decide how he could most easily cross the River Somme.

In the meantime King Philippe of France had been in Paris with a great multitude of lords and all manner of men while the English were in Poissy burning Saint-Germain and the castle of Montjoie. When he learnt that the enemy had crossed the bridge at Poissy and gone ahead through Beauvoisis towards Ponthieu, he called a council to decide whether he should leave Paris with the lords there assembled, catch up with the English near Amiens and there offer battle whatever the chances should be. As a result he left Paris in a state of great fear, all the lords and their men following him on horse or on foot, and by long marches reached the town called Nampty, three leagues short of Amiens, and there he lodged with all his army. They were now only five leagues from the English . . .

The King of England had spent two nights at Airaines, and from there had sent his marshals to burn and pillage all the valley of the Somme towards the sea, and to see in what place they might effect a crossing. The marshals, in obedience to the king's command, arose

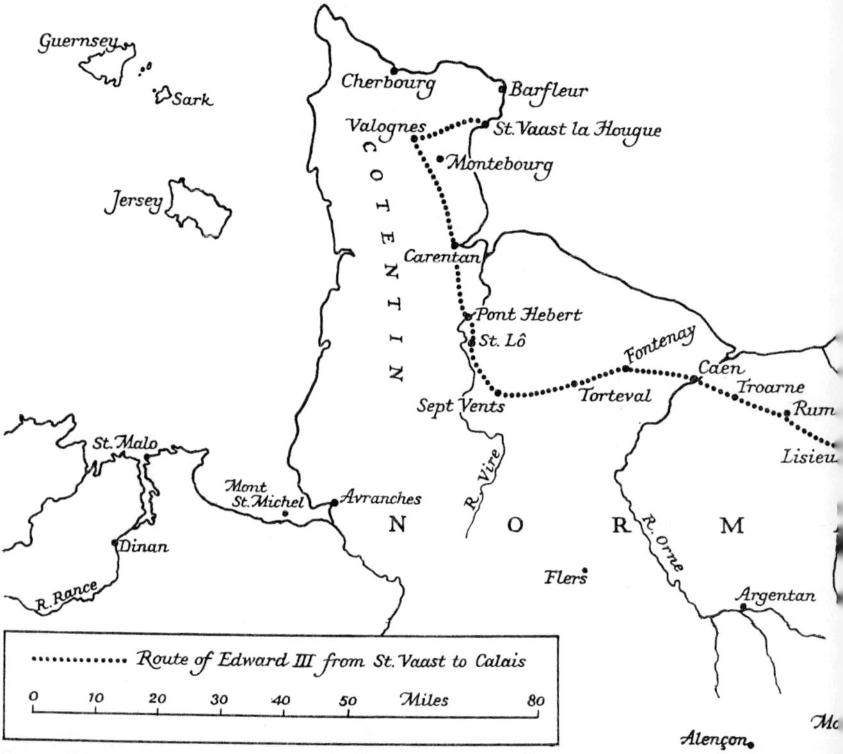

early and with a large company of men and archers passed through Longpré to the bridge at Pont-Remy. Here they found a great many knights from the neighbourhood, with a large company of cross-bowmen and others to defend the bridge. The English started a sharp attack to win the bridge, but without success.

When they saw that these French were so well equipped that they could not force a passage by any means, they withdrew, and marched to a considerable town called Fontaine-sur-Somme, burning and wasting as they went, and from there similarly to Long-en-Ponthieu, but here, too, they were unsuccessful in an attack on the bridge. They continued on their way and reached Longpré-les-Corps-Saints, a fine town with a large collegiate church, to all of which they set fire. They gathered vast quantities of booty, but found the bridge had been destroyed, so that there was no hope of a crossing, and returned to Airaines.

When they came before the king they told him all that had

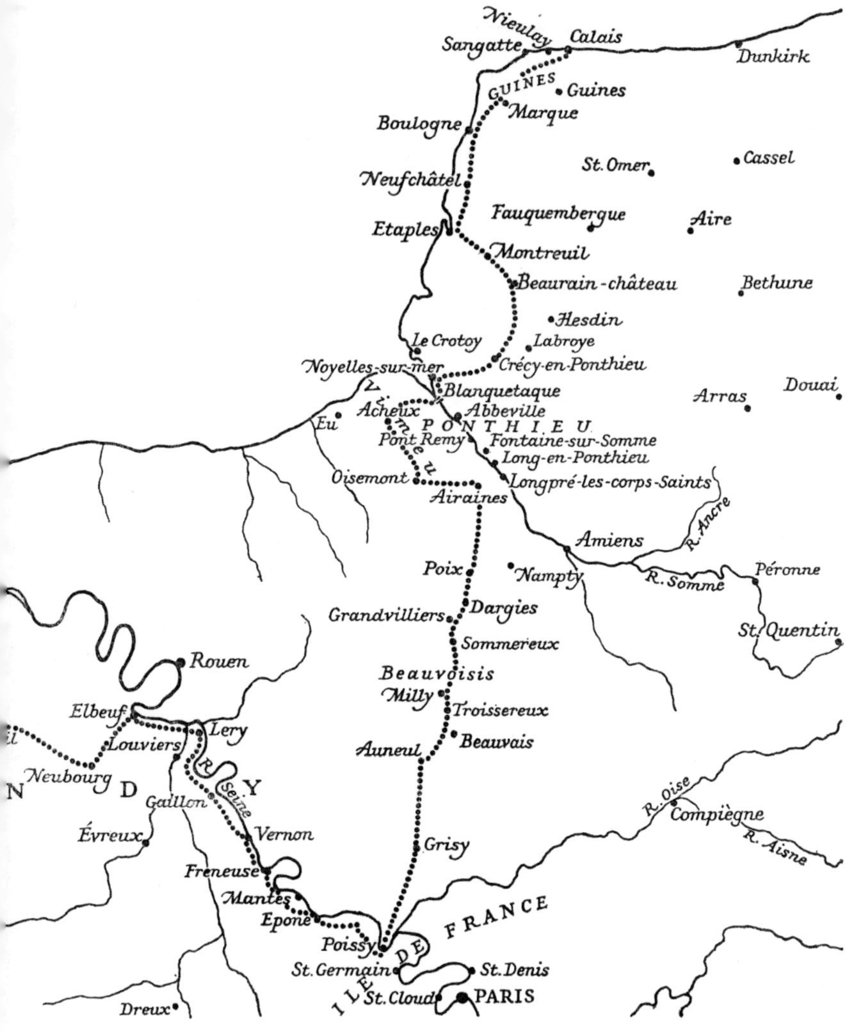

occurred and how they had found no bridge that was not either destroyed or so well guarded that a crossing was impossible—not very comforting news for the king, who after some thought ordered all to be ready to depart in the morning, when he intended to find out how he could continue the journey he planned. On the next day, then, he set out with his whole army and went straight through Vimeu towards Oisemont, and Abbeville in Ponthieu, destroying everything as he passed.

The King of France left Nampty the same day and ordered Godemar du Fay to ride with a large body of armed men through Amiens to guard all the crossings of the Somme and engage in skirmishes to prevent the English from passing. Godemar obeyed the king's orders to the utmost of his power, and the King of France rode with such speed that he arrived by noon at Airaines, which the King of England had left only that morning, and stayed there that day and the next day while his army caught up with him. He was very annoyed not to find the enemy there.

The noble king Edward and his marshals rode on at great speed, destroying all as they passed, to Mareuil, where they burned the town, the fortress and the priory, and so many small towns round about whose names I do not know that the sparks flew as far as the town of Abbeville. From there they rode on to Oisemont, where all the people of Vimeu had collected. When they saw the English approaching through the fields they came forth, thinking to defend themselves, but as soon as they felt the English arrows they preferred to take to flight, in the course of which large numbers were killed, wounded or taken prisoner, and the town was taken and plundered. The king lodged that night in the chief house, still reflecting on how he could cross the river.

The next morning he called some of the prisoners before him, and said that if one of them could tell how he could cross the river he would release him and two or three of his friends, and make him, moreover, a gift of a hundred golden crowns. One of the serving-men who was eager to win this offer replied: 'Yes, by God, if you will keep your promise I will take you tomorrow morning to a spot where your whole army can be across the river before tierce, and you can cut off my head if it is not so. I know a ford which twelve men can go through abreast twice in the day, and the water no higher than their knees, for when the tide comes in the water is so deep that no one can cross, but when it goes out the river is so low that you can easily ford it. This is not so elsewhere, because here there is firm gravel and hard

uant le Roy Dangleterre et ses ges
furent oultre passez ala blanche
tache et quilz orent nue en chace leurs
ennemis et deluwe la place ilz se traistret
bellement et ordonneement ensemble
et avvouterent leur charoy et chevau
chierent ainsi quilz avoient fait on pa
is de bevin et de biuien et devant passe
ala Et ne se effraierent de Roy puis qtz
se sentirent oultre la Riuiere de some et
Retracia et lona dieu le Roy Danglethe

THE FORD OF BLANQUETAQUE

white marl where you can take your waggons across in safety; that's why they call it Blanquetaque.'

The noble king could not have been more pleased if someone had given him twenty thousand crowns, and told the man that if they found everything as he had described it he would set all his companions free to show his pleasure. Then he had it cried abroad among his whole army that everyone should be ready to move off at the sound of the trumpet. He did not sleep at all that night; at midnight he arose and ordered a trumpet to be sounded. When everything was ready, chests and baggage loaded, and riders mounted he set off with that man and some of his fellows as guides. As the sun rose they reached the ford of Blanquetaque, but the tide was too high for them to cross. They waited there, while the remainder of the army joined up with them, until the hour of prime when the ebb-tide was due. But before it had fully come Godemar du Fay arrived on the other side with a large troop of armed men and people of that district, whom he drew up in battle order to defend the passage.

King Edward would not abandon the project and ordered his marshals to advance the men under cover of the archers' fire. Then began a terrible fight, for the French defended the ford most vigorously and the first to cross did not have things their own way, but left many of their number dead or wounded. In the end, however [24 August] the English crossed over and the French were routed. Many dead were left lying on the field.

The last of the English were able to cross over unmolested, with their carts, waggons and beasts of burden. It was only by the grace of God that the noble king learned about the ford, and his men considered it a true miracle, for if he had not crossed the river that very day King Philippe would have cut off the English army and dealt with them as he chose. When all the waggons were across everyone rejoiced and wanted to lodge in a large town called Noyelles-sur-Mer. They discovered, however, that it belonged to the Comtesse d'Aumale, daughter of Robert d'Artois, so they respected the town and the surrounding land for love of the earl. For this the lady gave humble and sincere thanks to the king and his marshals.

On the next day the marshals went off to a fair-sized town called Le Crotoy, well stocked with wine and other treasure—for it is a seaport—and took it easily. After wasting the surrounding countryside they returned with considerable booty of large and small cattle to the main army, which was heading for Crécy. The noble King Edward declared that if the French king were to come—though he had twice as many men—he would await him, for he had the right of inheritance on his side, through his mother, and that King Philippe had cheated him of his rights . . .

the battle of crécy

¶ When the King of France left Airaines the next morning he found that all his land had been burned and plundered. He had not gone far when he was informed the English had crossed the Somme at Blanquetaque and killed the men who were defending it. There is no need to tell how grieved he was at the news. He halted his men and inquired whether there was any place where he could bring his army over; they replied that the only possibility was the bridge at Abbeville.* He therefore marched towards that town, where he awaited the arrival of his men, and passed them over as they came, to be ready for the next day.

Next morning [Saturday, 26 August 1346] they left Abbeville with banners unfurled, and it was a great sight to see these lords finely dressed and nobly mounted, with pennons fluttering in the breeze—an army estimated at twenty thousand men-at-arms on horseback, and more than a hundred thousand on foot, of whom twelve thousand were pikemen or Genoese. The King of England had no more than four thousand horsemen, ten thousand archers and ten thousand Welsh and foot-soldiers.†

King Philippe urged his men on to follow the English, and sent a party of knights and squires to spy out where they were, for he believed they could not be far off. When they had gone four leagues they returned with the report that the English could not be more than another four leagues away. He then gave orders for a valiant and experienced knight to go ahead with four others and find out the disposition of the English forces. These brave knights gladly undertook their mission, and on their return found some of their own banners had advanced to within a league of the English; they made these halt to await the others, then went back to the king and said they had seen the English less than a league away, drawn up in three

* Froissart adds that the tide was now high, making it impossible to use the ford of Blanquetaque. The bridge at Pont Remy was presumably too far west to be useful.

† A consideration of all the various accounts of the battle of Crécy would give the size of the forces as 15,000 for the English and 40,000 for the French.

divisions. The king therefore held a council to decide on their action, and asked this valiant knight, Le Moine de Bazeilles, to give them

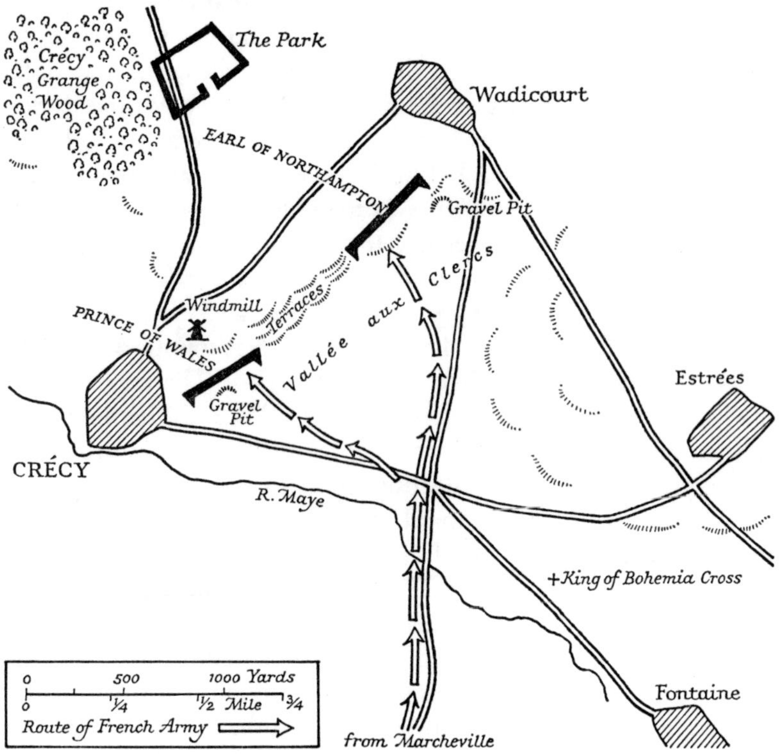

THE BATTLE OF CRÉCY

his opinion. He replied that he was unwilling to speak in front of the great lords, but that it was his duty to do so. 'My lord,' he said, 'your army is widely scattered, and it will be late before it can be all assembled. I would advise you to camp for the night, and then after mass in the morning to draw up your battle array and advance on your enemy in the name of God and Saint Denis, for I am certain from what I have seen that they will not flee but will await your coming.'

The king was pleased with this advice, and would gladly have followed it. But when he gave orders that everyone should retreat with his banner—for the English were arrayed very close to them—none would do so unless those in the van came back first, and those in the van refused to retreat because they thought it shameful to do so; meanwhile those at the rear continued to advance, and thus the valiant knight's advice was wasted through the pride and envy of the lords. They still rode proudly ahead, one in front of the other without any order, and came within sight of the English, who were waiting for them in careful array, and now it was even more shameful to turn back.

Then the commanders of the pikemen and the Genoese cross-bowmen ordered their men forward in front of the companies of the lords so as to shoot first at the English, and they advanced close enough to loose their arrows on the enemy. But very soon pikemen and Genoese were routed by the English archers and would have taken to flight if the companies of the chief lords had not been so fired with envy of each other that they did not wait to make a concerted attack, but rushed forward in such disorder that the pikemen and the Genoese were trapped between them and the English. The weaker horses fell on top of them, and the others trampled them and fell on top of each other like a litter of piglets. The arrows of the English were directed with such marvellous skill at the horsemen that their mounts refused to advance a step; some leapt backwards stung to madness, some reared hideously, some turned their rear quarters towards the enemy, others merely let themselves fall to the ground, and their riders could do nothing about it. The English lords who were on foot advanced among them, striking them at their will, because they could not help themselves or their horses.

The misfortunes of the French lasted until midnight, for it was nearly dark when the battle began, and the King of France and his company never came near to the fighting. At the end it was necessary for the king to withdraw from where he was, and Comte Jean de Hainault, who had been detailed as the king's personal bodyguard, took his bridle, conducted him sadly and unwillingly from the field, and rode with him through the night to Labroye, where the king took some rest, very sick at heart. Next day he continued to Amiens to await those that remained of his men. This sorry remnant of the French—lords, knights and others—who were left behind, withdrew like routed men, uncertain where to go, for it was pitch dark, not knowing of any town or village, and not having eaten all day. They went off in groups of three or four like lost men, and did not know whether their leaders or brothers or cousins were dead or had escaped. Never did a greater disaster befall any Christian men than happened then to King Philippe and his army. It took place in the year of grace 1346, the day after the Feast of Saint Bartholomew, on the evening of a Saturday, at Crécy-en-Ponthieu. The night passed before the French knew that they had lost, but it was spent in the disastrous happenings of which you have just read.

I have recorded the truth as exactly as I could, as I heard it from the mouth of my lord and friend Comte Jean de Hainault, whom may God absolve, and from ten or a dozen knights of his household, who were in the thick of the fight with the valiant and noble King of Bohemia, and who had their horses killed under them. I have also heard similar accounts from several knights of England and Germany who were engaged on the other side.

Having completed the story of the battle as the French knights told it to him, Le Bel now adds further details of what happened on the English side, a break which interrupts the continuity of the story. It is worth noting that Froissart in the Première Rédaction, *against his usual practice, does not copy Le Bel's account of Crécy, but gives a version more closely based on English witnesses; he copies Le Bel for his* Seconde Rédaction, *but reverts to the 'English' version for the third and final one. In the* Seconde Rédaction *there is one notable addition in Froissart (not repeated in the third)—that the English used cannons at Crécy, a claim which is supported by Villani (who says they had three* bombardes*) and by the Chronicle of Saint-Denis. In the* Courrier de la Somme *dated 5 September 1850 it is recorded that a farmer had unearthed a cast-iron cannon ball 9½ inches in diameter while ploughing on the site of the battle.*

Let me now tell you how King Edward had drawn up his array of battle. This valiant king knew on the Friday evening that King Philippe was in Abbeville with his whole army, and was delighted to learn it. He told all his men to take their rest and pray to Our Lord that He should allow them to come out of the trial with honour and joy, for he had the right of inheritance on his side, and he would not move a step forwards or backwards, but wait there for King Philippe if he would come.

Next morning he called his men from their tents and told them to arm. He had an enclosure with only one entrance prepared from all the carts and waggons of the army, and placed all the horses in it. Then he drew up his battalions with great care; he gave the first to his elder son the Prince of Wales, with 1,200 men-at-arms, 3,000 archers and 3,000 Welsh, and he appointed as commanders the Earl of Warwick, the Earl of Stafford, the Earl of Kent, Sir Godfrey Harcourt and several others whose names I do not know. He gave the second to the Earl of Northampton, the Earl of Suffolk and the Bishop of Durham, with 1,200 men-at-arms and 3,000 archers, and kept the third, which was to be in the centre, under his own command with 1,600 men-at-arms and 4,000 archers, who were all English or Welsh, for there were not half a dozen archers from Germany . . .

When the valiant king had thus drawn up his battle array in an open field which had no ditches or trenches, he went among his men exhorting each of them with a laugh to do his duty, and begged and encouraged them so greatly that the cowards became brave men. He gave orders that on pain of death no one should leave his place, and no one should rob or pillage the dead or the living without his permission, for if they won the day there would be plenty of time for pillage, and if fortune turned against them there would be no point in taking booty. This done, he gave permission to all to break off in order to eat and drink until the trumpet was sounded, when all should regain their ranks. Everyone loved and respected him so much that no one would disobey his orders. About the hour of nones, news reached the noble king that King Philippe was close at hand with his army. He immediately had the trumpet sounded and everyone at once drew up in ranks to await the French, in such an orderly fashion that fortune favoured their cause.

When the battle was over and darkness had fallen the king sent round an order that none should chase after the enemy and that none should rob or disturb the dead until he gave permission, so that in the morning they should be able to recognize them. He then ordered all into their tents to take their rest fully armed, but the lords were to come and sup with him; the marshals were to see that the army was well guarded. One can imagine the joy with which the king and his barons supped and spent the night, giving thanks to God for the good fortune that had enabled them to hold the field with so small a number against the might of France.

Next morning there was a thick mist, and a large number of English went with the king's permission to see whether they could find some of the French reassembling. They did indeed find large bodies of militia from the villages and towns who had spent the night in the woods or under a hedge, who were now inquiring of each other what was happening and what they were to do, for they did not know how things stood nor where the king and their leaders were. When they saw the English coming they waited for them, thinking they were their own men; and the English fell on them like wolves upon sheep and killed as many as they chose. Another company of English fell upon a similar body of men also seeking news of where their leaders were. Some were looking for their masters, some for their relatives, some for their companions, and the English killed all whom they came across. About the hour of tierce they returned to camp, just as the king and his barons finished hearing mass, and they told him what they had done. At this the king ordered Lord Reginald Cobham, a most valiant knight, to take a herald with a good knowledge of coats of arms, some of the lords and all the other heralds, and go amongst the dead, making a list of every knight that could be recognized; all the princes and chief lords were to be placed together on one side, each with his name indicated. Lord Reginald did as he was ordered; they found nine princes, some 1,200 knights, and a good fifteen or sixteen thousand squires, Genoese and others. Only three hundred English knights were found dead.*

It is right that I should tell you the names of the princes and chief barons who died in this battle: of the others there would be no ending. I shall begin with the highest and most noble the valiant King of Bohemia, who, blind though he was, wished to be among the first in the battle. He ordered his men, on pain of death, to lead him so far into the front of the battle that he could himself deal blows at the enemy. The next greatest prince was the Comte d'Alençon, own brother to the King of France; then Comte Louis de Blois, son of the king's sister, the Comte de Salm in Saumois, the Comte de Harcourt, and the Comte de Sancerre. It was said that for many a year there had not been so many princes killed in one day—not at Courtrai [1302], at Bénévent [1266] or anywhere else.

On the Sunday that followed the valiant King Edward stayed all day in the field to see whether the King of France would reassemble his men; but he did not come. The valiant king then left with all his army, and had the bodies of his dead carried to an abbey near by. He sent his marshals to burn and waste the surrounding country as he had done before; they found this easy, for there was no one to oppose them. In this way they made towards Saint-Josse and burned Beaurain and all the country round Montreuil-sur-Mer, together with outlying townships of some size; they burned Saint-Josse and left the town, likewise Étaples and Neufchâtel and all the country round Boulogne. On the 4th of September King Edward arrived outside the fair town of Calais, which was considered one of the strongest towns in the world.

* A liberal estimate for the number of French killed; cp. among other sources *Chronographia* and Northburgh. Froissart gives the number of English dead as three knights and twenty archers.

the siege of calais

¶ When the noble king began the siege of Calais he announced that he would not abandon it, winter or summer, until he had succeeded and until King Philippe had come to do battle and been defeated. Since it was such a strong town, with so many able defenders, he would not allow his men to launch an attack on it, for he might have lost more than he gained. He therefore had a lodging built of wood and thatched with straw in which to pass the winter; around the camp he had deep trenches dug so that his army could not be attacked or molested. Each of the lords constructed a lodging for himself as best he could, of wood, saplings and straw, so that in a short time they erected a large and well-defended town. There was merchandise to be bought whenever they wished—butchers' shops, a market for cloth and all commodities as good as at Arras or Amiens, for they had the Flemings on their side and it was from them that the goods came; much, too, was sent from England, for the sea is narrow at that part.

Even more would have arrived if it had not been for the Genoese and other sailors who roamed the seas attacking and robbing all they met. One of these sea-rovers was called Marant, the other Maistrel, and they caused much annoyance to the English and several times destroyed the provisions for their army. There were often fierce skirmishes round the town between the men of Calais and the besiegers. The marshals made frequent forays to see what they would encounter, and brought back cattle and sheep for the army, burning and pillaging everywhere, so that the whole county of Guines with the town and its fortress was burned, as was the town of Marque. All the land indeed was laid waste. There were frequent fine engagements, in which some lost and others won, as often happens in such sieges and such feats of arms. There is not time to tell all that was done, so I shall pass over much . . . but I must not omit an act of great courtesy which King Edward performed on behalf of the poor people during the siege.

When the men of Calais saw that King Edward would not leave that winter and that their provisions were insufficient, they sent out five hundred people and passed them through the English forces.

BOOKMARK

The Folio Society

BOOKMARK

Postage
will be
paid by
Folio Society

No Postage Stamp
necessary
if posted
in Great Britain or
Northern Ireland

BUSINESS REPLY SERVICE
Licence No. S.W.1342

The Folio Society,
6 Stratford Place,
London W1

When the noble king saw these poor people sent out of their town he had them all brought before him and gave food and drink generously to them; when they had eaten and drunk well, he allowed them to pass through his army and gave to each, out of love for God, three old pennies sterling, and had them conducted safely beyond his camp. This must be recorded as the act of a very noble nature.

While Edward and his army were in France, David Bruce, King of Scotland, undertook the invasion of England at the instigation of King Philippe of France. He penetrated as far as Durham, where he was defeated and made prisoner by the English army at the battle of Neville's Cross, which took place on 17 October 1346. King David remained in captivity until 1357, when he was released on a promise to pay ten thousand marks and to sign a truce between the two countries. In a passage found only in the Rome MS, Froissart tells us that in 1365 he spent fifteen weeks at the court of King David and visited a great part of Scotland in his company. From the knights he met there he learned much about the details of the battle of Neville's Cross.

Meanwhile in Brittany the truce of Malestroit (which lasted from January 1343 to Michaelmas 1346) had expired and hostilities were renewed. The English took La Roche Derrien in the name of the Comtesse de Montfort and there resisted an attack by Charles de Blois, whom they took prisoner and sent to England. In Aquitaine the Earl of Derby was in command of a fair-sized army which captured a number of strongholds, including Saint-Jean-d'Angély and Saint-Maixent, and finally took the city of Poitiers on 4 October.

¶ After the capture of King David of Scotland, the noble queen had a great desire to go and see her lord the king. She therefore ordered ships to be got ready, made provision of jewels to give to the knights and of all that was necessary for a journey by sea, and set sail with a body of men-at-arms, in great danger of being captured or lost at sea.* Three days before All Saints' Day she joined the army camped outside Calais. There the king went out to meet her and embraced her with great joy, and took her into his apartment. He gave out that on All Saints' Day he would hold open court for love of the queen. This court was held in great splendour, in the presence of some seven hundred knights and others, so numerous that all who had come to

* Records exist to show that she embarked on or about 10 September; it is also known that on 17 October she was in Ypres with her sister. She may not have joined her husband until the end of the month, but she had certainly left before the battle of Neville's Cross.

see the queen could not be served. The noble lady spoke so graciously with her knights that it was a pleasure to see her, and she gave handsome presents of jewellery to those who most deserved them. She remained for a long time with the king, and had brought with her many ladies and maidens with whom the knights and squires spent their time most pleasantly; the king, too, was glad to see them.

¶ King Edward had been camped outside Calais for the space of six months, when he learned that the King of France had issued a general order throughout France that the nobles and their followers should join him at Arras at Whitsuntide to raise the siege of Calais. He then began to consider how he might do most damage to the French and yet maintain his siege long enough to starve the defenders, since he realized that the town was so well fortified and garrisoned that he could not take it by a direct attack, and it always grieved him to see his men wounded or killed in a fruitless engagement. He therefore ordered the building of a lofty fort, made of heavy timbers, on the edge of the sea, and equipped it with bombards, espringals and other heavy pieces of artillery; there were forty men-at-arms and two hundred archers, and thus they could keep so close a watch on the harbour of Calais that nothing could come in or out without being destroyed by them.

It was by this means that the occupants of the town were most harassed. King Edward's next move was to request the Flemings to move off towards Cassel, Aire and Saint-Omer and burn and waste the land as they went. At this the King of France decided to make for Arras himself, and to send most of his men in the direction of Saint-Omer and Aire, where they had many skirmishes with the Flemings, winning some and losing others. In the end the Flemings were heavily repulsed, and the French laid waste all the country known as Laleu. While King Philippe was in Arras and his men were pursuing the Flemings messages came from his people who were in Calais that he should come and help them at once, because their provisions were running out. The town was defended by Jean de Vienne, a knight appointed captain by the king, and his companion Jean de Surie; also by Arnoul d'Audrehem, a bold and valiant knight who was one of the most respected in France . . .

When King Philippe heard this news he felt both grief and pity; he called his forces together and went to Vieil-Hesdin, announcing that he intended to march against the English army, for he would not attend to any other affair until he had raised the siege of Calais. Next day* he left Hesdin and made for Fauquembergue, whence he moved camp to Guines, where everything was burned and wasted. The day following he camped on the cliffs at Sangatte, close to the English forces, with such a large army that I could not estimate its numbers. When the besieged in Calais saw him on the cliffs at Sangatte they were overjoyed, for they thought the siege would be raised; but when they saw him settling into camp their hopes were a little diminished.

When the noble King Edward saw King Philippe arrive in such strength to fight with him and raise the siege of Calais—which had cost him so much in men and money, and which he could with difficulty sustain much longer—he was very worried as to what might be the outcome. He observed that the French could not come any nearer to him or to the town of Calais except by one of two routes, either following the dunes along the coast, or lower down where there were quicksands and swamps; there was only one bridge, which was at Nieulay. He therefore had all his ships drawn up in front of the dunes, and equipped them plentifully with espringals, bombards and archers, so that the French army did not dare to pass, and he sent his cousin the Earl of Derby with a large body of men-at-arms and archers to guard the bridge at Nieulay, so that the French could not come across except by the marshes, which were anyhow impassable. Overlooking the cliffs at Sangatte was a tower held by thirty-two English to protect the passage of the dunes, and this had been further protected with a double row of deep trenches.

When the French were encamped at Sangatte . . . a band of common soldiers went to this tower; the English archers let fly a rain of arrows, but the soldiers launched an attack with such vigour that they captured the tower and killed all its defenders. Meanwhile King Philippe had sent his marshals, the Seigneur de Beaujeu and the Seigneur de Saint-Venant, to study the land and see how they could best approach the English army. The marshals made a thorough examination of all the possible routes, then returned to the king and told him in few words that there was no way by which his army could approach the English forces, unless he wished to expose his men to heavier losses than those he had suffered in the battle of Crécy.

Next day after mass King Philippe sent important envoys to the King of England, using the bridge at Nieulay by permission of the Earl of Derby, to tell him how unjustified was his siege of Calais and

* In fact, he stayed nearly a month at Hesdin, and arrived at Fauquembergue on 20 July 1347.

beg him in the king's name to allow him to pass where a way was possible and so to let him do battle; if he would not permit this, he would withdraw to more open country and there fight, allowing God to give victory to whom He chose.

When King Edward heard this he thought for a moment and then replied: 'My lords, I have reflected upon what you have said in the name of your master, as you call him—though he has wrongfully usurped my inheritance. Tell him then from me that I have been here for nearly a year, openly and to his knowledge, and that he could have come sooner had he wanted to. But he has allowed me to stay here so long that I have spent much of my own treasure and I believe I have so conducted matters that I shall soon be lord of the fair town of Calais. I am therefore not very ready to do just what he wants, nor to risk losing what I have so nearly won. If he will not come by one way, let him come by the other.' The envoys saw that they would get no other reply by waiting, so they went back to the King of France, who was both surprised and despondent—hardly to be wondered at, seeing that he had with him so great a number of noble lords, some from distant lands, and that he would now have to return home with nothing achieved.

At this point [27 July] there arrived two cardinals who had held long and frequent parleys with the two kings to try to find some ground of agreement between them. They first asked King Philippe to grant a stay of three days only to see whether they might be able to make some arrangement with the King of England, of whom they then asked the same thing. He agreed and sent to this conference the noble Earl of Derby, the Earl of Northampton, Sir Walter de Manny—in whom he placed great trust—and Sir Reginald de Cobham. King Philippe's representatives were the Duc de Bourbon, Jean de Hainault, the Seigneur de Beaujeu and Sir Geoffroi de Chargny. These barons continued their talks throughout the three days, with the two cardinals acting as intermediaries between them; while they parleyed the noble king continued to reinforce his army and strengthen the trench-fortifications along the dunes so that the French could not possibly find a way through. As for the people in Calais, they were not very pleased with all this parleying, for it merely extended their fast.

When King Philippe saw that no agreement had been reached he decided to make for Arras and leave the men of Calais to make terms with the English, and [2 August] he ordered his army to strike camp. No one could refrain from weeping when they heard the lamentations of the citizens of Calais as they watched the army departing without bringing them any help. When the English saw the French leave their camp many of them went out to harass the rear of the army. They found many tents that had been left behind, and gathered quantities of bread, wine and meat that had been brought there by the commissariat, who had fled when they saw the English coming. Everything was either taken or destroyed.

When the citizens of Calais saw that King Philippe had indeed gone, that all their hopes were at an end, and that they were in such dire straits through lack of food that even the richest could scarcely keep themselves alive, they decided in a council that they would do better to place themselves freely in the good graces of the King of England, since they might find a better fate thus than to let themselves die of hunger. All agreed to this advice and asked their captain, Jean de Vienne, to be their spokesman. He accordingly mounted to the battlements and made signs that he wished to parley. The king dispatched for this purpose the Earl of Northampton, Sir Walter de Manny, Sir Reginald de Cobham and Sir Thomas Holland.

When they arrived Sir Jean addressed them thus: 'My lords, you are most noble knights and you know that the King of France whom we regard as our sovereign has sent us here to protect this town and fortress. These orders we have obeyed so that no harm might come to it. We have done our best. Now our help has failed us, and you have so constrained us that we have no food left, and we must die of hunger if the noble king does not take pity on us. Beg him therefore, dear lords, that in the name of pity he may show mercy to us and allow us to go in peace if he can be satisfied to have the town, the fortress and all the wealth we possess.'

Sir Walter de Manny replied saying: 'Sir Jean, we know the mind of our sovereign, for he has instructed us. It is not his intention that you should go in peace as you have asked; you must all submit yourselves entirely to his will, to be killed or ransomed as he chooses, and it is not surprising that he should be angry seeing that you have caused him so much trouble and have cost him so much in men and treasure.' Sir Jean replied: 'It is too hard a thing for us to consent to what you request. We in this town are a handful of knights and squires who have served our lord as loyally as we know how—as you would have served yours in a like situation—and have suffered much distress. But we would rather endure greater torments than man has ever suffered than allow the smallest child in this town to suffer the same fate as the great. Humbly beg the king therefore that he should receive us with mercy, as prisoners if he will, but that he should spare our lives.' Sir Walter said he would gladly bear this message and that they would do their best. They told the king all that had been said, but he would not listen to any prayers or arguments that he should accede to this last request.

'This way, my lord,' said Sir Walter de Manny, 'you might well be in the wrong and set a bad precedent. If you were to send any of us to guard one of your fortresses, by Our Lady we should not go very willingly if you put these people to death as you propose, for they would do the same with us in a similar situation, even though we were merely doing our duty.' This argument softened the king's heart somewhat, and he said: 'My lords and friends, I do not wish to stand alone against you in this. Go back and tell them that for love of you all I will readily receive them as prisoners, except that I will have six of their chief citizens who must come to me in white shirts, a halter round their necks, bringing with them the keys of the city, and with them I shall do as I will.'

The English lords returned with this message and told Sir Jean that they had obtained the concession with great difficulty. Sir Jean said that since no better terms could be obtained, he would be ready to convey them to the citizens and to his fellows. The knight went down from the battlements, and sounded the bell to assemble all the citizens, men and women, who in the misery of their hunger were hoping to hear good news. As the knight announced the terms they began to weep and to wail so that it wrung one's heart to hear them. Then the richest citizen in the town, the Seigneur Eustache de Saint-Pierre, rose to his feet and said in the hearing of them all: 'Masters, it would be a great shame to allow such people as we have in this city to die by hunger or from any other cause, and so it would be a most charitable act in the name of Our Lord if anyone can prevent it. If by my death I can save these people I have such sure confidence in Our Lord that I know I shall have pardon for my sins. I am therefore ready to be the first of the six, and will gladly place myself barefooted, in a white shirt and a halter round my neck, under the mercy of King Edward.'

When this citizen had finished speaking they all gathered round him, praising him for his compassion; several men and women let themselves fall at his feet, and this was not to be wondered at in view of the great distress they had suffered through famine in the last six weeks . . . Soon another citizen, also very rich, stood up similarly and declared that he would be the second. Then a third rose up, afterwards a fourth, then a fifth and a sixth, but I do not know all their names. All said that they offered themselves to King Edward of their own free will, to do as he chose with them, in order to save the rest of the townspeople according to his promise, and that they considered him the most valiant prince living. It was a sad thing for the six, but a wonderful offering to the town.

The capture of Calais

¶ These six citizens, the richest in the town . . . at once got ready [3 August 1347] in the state in which they were to go to King Edward, and spoke thus to the knights: 'It is from our desire to save the people of this town that we array ourselves as you now see us and in accordance with the message you brought back, and we have with us the keys of the fortress and of the town. Lead us out, therefore, and pray for us that he may be ready to spare us.'

The four lords conducted the six citizens towards the king, as the whole army assembled in the camp. There was, as you may imagine, a great crowd of people; some said they should be hanged on the spot, while others wept for pity. The noble king, accompanied by his earls and barons, came out into the field; after him came the queen, who was with child, to see what would happen. The six citizens immediately fell on their knees in front of the king, and spoke thus: 'Noble king, you see before you six citizens of Calais of ancient and honourable stock, merchants of substance. We bring you the keys of the fortress and town of Calais, and yield them to your pleasure. We have done all this in order that you see fit to spare the rest of the citizens who have suffered much distress. Have pity and mercy on us therefore out of your great nobility.' There was not a lord or a knight in that place who did not weep for pity or come near to doing so. Yet the king's heart was so hard with anger that for some time he could not reply; then he gave orders that their heads should be cut off at once.

Every lord and every knight begged him with tears to the best of their ability to show pity on these men, but he would not listen. At this the noble knight Sir Walter de Manny spoke up: 'Noble lord, will you not check your anger? You have a reputation for generous behaviour: do not do something now which would cause you to be spoken of shamefully. If you do not show mercy, everyone will say that your heart is full of cruelty because you killed these good citizens who came to yield themselves up to you of their own free will in order to save the rest of the people.' At this the king stiffened and said: 'Sir Walter, calm yourself, I shall not change my mind. Send for the executioner. The men of Calais have caused the death of so many of my men that these six must die.'

Then the noble Queen of England, who was near the time of her delivery, approached the king in great humility and fell on her knees before him, weeping so pitifully that the sight was hard to bear. 'Noble lord,' she said, 'since I crossed the sea in such peril, as you know, I have asked no favour of you, but now I beseech you on my knees for the love of Our Lady's son to have mercy on these men.' The king said nothing for a time, looking at his wife as she wept bitterly on her knees before him; then his heart began to soften a little and he spoke. 'My lady, I wish you had not been here, but you have made your request so tenderly that I have not the heart to refuse you. And though I do so unwillingly, nevertheless take these men, I give them to you'—and he took the six citizens by their collars and handed them to the queen, and spared the lives of all the people of Calais for her sake, while the noble lady had the six citizens clothed and gave them succour.

Thus was the strong town of Calais besieged by King Edward from the beginning of September in the year of Our Lord 1346 until it surrendered on the 3rd day of August in the year 1347. How strong a desire the king had to conquer the town can easily be imagined, since he maintained the siege for nearly a year and spent freely from his treasury in the expenses of the campaign, the wages of his army, the construction of habitations and the making of engines of war, notwithstanding all his other commitments of war in Scotland, Gascony, Brittany, Poitou and other parts. It is certain that no other Christian king in history ever conducted so many campaigns at one time or incurred such heavy expenses as he did up to that time. I cannot tell how time will deal with all this . . .

When the noble king had given the six citizens to the queen he sent his marshals, Sir Walter de Manny and several others into the town to take possession of it, ordering them to take Jean de Vienne and some of the others and send them to England, and that all the soldiers and townspeople should be turned out of the town in the clothes they had on and nothing else. These orders were carried out. The marshals made all the soldiers bring their military equipment into the market-hall, where it was thrown into a heap. Then they seized the houses of all the chief citizens and ordered that no one, on pain of death, should do any damage to them. When all this was completed the king entered the town in company with the queen, to the sound of trumpets and bugles and in great solemnity. In the castle he held a grand council, and sent home those of his men of whom he had no further need. He remained in the town for the space of three weeks, setting the castle and the town in good order and arranging who should garrison it and who should stay on in the town.

It seems to me a great pity that these worthy citizens and their good wives should be treated in this way, for there were great numbers of them in the town with much wealth and great possessions, all of which they had to abandon. One must be hard of heart not to feel pity for them, and indeed King Philippe never made any restitution for what they had suffered.* At that time the French king had withdrawn to Arras and was in the process of discharging his foreign mercenaries. He also sent large detachments of his own men to guard the coasts and so prevent further invasion by the English. But there was no indication that he intended to undertake any campaign against the English in their own land, as the King of England had done and was still doing against him.

The two cardinals had been at work all this time endeavouring to secure an agreement by visiting each party in turn; by their efforts a truce was arranged [28 September 1347] to last until the Feast of St John Baptist 1348, each side to keep what they had taken. When this truce had been signed King Philippe left his men and went back to Paris. King Edward installed Sir John Montgomery† as keeper of the castle in Calais, and gave him a large body of men-at-arms; he established in the town great numbers of men who would carry on their trades in the houses of the former citizens; to the soldiers and others who remained there he distributed the arms which had been taken at the surrender. Then he left for England with his noble queen, and came to London,‡ where they were welcomed with great joy; one can imagine the great feasts that were held in his honour.

He also went to see his prisoners, and greeted them most courteously, entertaining them to dinner with himself in his own great hall.

* This statement, repeated by Froissart, is quite incorrect; in fact, the king had made considerable grants, material and financial, within a week of the surrender of the town.

† Le Bel and Froissart name Aimeri de Pavie, who was, in fact, appointed a year later.

‡ 14 October. Froissart informs us that before they left Calais the queen gave birth to a daughter, Margaret.

There was a distinguished company at that feast, and the king must have thanked God that he had as prisoners the King of Scotland as well as so many noble Frenchmen, whilst his enemies had not one of his own men as captives.

It seems to me that in the things of this world it must be held for much honour to the king, and as a sign of great favour from God, that he and his men had laid waste the whole of Scotland as far as the city of Aberdeen and the great forest of Jedburgh, and had captured the town of Berwick and all the castles in that region. Others of them had wasted and pillaged the greater part of Gascony nearly as far as Toulouse as well as the whole of Poitou, capturing various castles and strong towns such as Lézignan, Saint-Jean-d'Angély and the city of Poitiers, and had done the same with the great land of Brittany.

Later, at the head of his own troops, he had laid waste all the Cotentin, Normandy, and from the County of Évreux as far as Paris; there he had crossed the Seine at the bridge of Poissy and wasted the Beauvoisis, the country round Amiens and the county of Ponthieu. Then he had remained two whole days with his small army drawn up in battle array, in open country without trenches or fortress, against the whole might of France, and had defeated them, killing or capturing all the great barons of the realm of France, the Empire and Germany. Then without returning to his own country he had laid siege to the fortified town of Calais for nearly a year, and at the end of that time had captured it, as you have heard. I should think that such great and noble undertakings are not achieved without very great honour, and that it is impossible to praise and extol too highly the very noble king to whom God has so manifestly granted His aid.

THE CHRONICLES OF JEAN FROISSART

an uneasy truce

Edward was now a hero to his people and had acquired fame—through bad French generalship at Crécy as well as by the skill of his own archers—as the greatest military leader in Europe. The men who returned with him were no longer disgruntled, having tasted the financial rewards of a successful campaign; it was left to the merchants at home and those who represented them in Parliament to complain about the costs of war. Edward did not reduce the scale of his ambitions, even though he knew that the campaign which ended at Calais had emptied his coffers for the time being, and though he knew, too, that Crécy and Calais had been only a beginning to his hopes of destroying French power.

To glorify and consolidate the prowess of his knights, Edward instituted, on St George's Day 1349, the Order of the Knights of the Blue Garter. Shortly after his accession King Jean le Bon founded in France, in November 1351, the Order of the Star, but the order quickly fell into ruin when twenty-six knights of the Order were killed in one engagement in Brittany the following year.

Now it was the King of France who found it necessary to beg funds of his Parliament, and his recent defeats made his task harder. The Estates were summoned later in 1347 and after remonstrating with the king on the evil counsel he had followed in his conduct of the war they granted meagre advances which were insufficient for the offensive which was contemplated against England.

The truce signed after Calais was, with various interruptions, extended to 1355, though at no time was it observed in all the theatres of war. More likely causes for the absence of major campaigns were the impoverishment of both sides and the Black Death which raged through Italy, France and Britain for over a year. It first showed itself in the south of France late in 1347 and spread rapidly through the country. By the end of 1348 it reached England; on 1 January 1349 the king wrote to the Bishop of Winchester saying that the next session of Parliament was prorogued because 'a sudden visitation of deadly pestilence had broken out at Westminster'; in March it was further adjourned sine die. *It is difficult to provide any accurate figures of the death-roll, but it would seem that about a quarter of the population had died by March 1350, when the plague abated; some towns and villages lost half their inhabitants.*

Taxation registers were upset as families were wiped out and where there was no one to replace the clerk who kept the registers in order. Arable land was turned over to grazing or abandoned; labour was difficult to secure and absurd wages were offered by those who could afford to do so, until the 'Statute of Labourers' in 1351 decreed that no wages were to be offered higher than those in force in 1348, an arrangement which was unsatisfactory to the labourers themselves. Crime increased, and in France we find companies of routiers *indulging in organized brigandage, often led by freelance fighting men from England who covered their greed for booty with a cloak of patriotism and gave dissatisfied peasants the chance of easy money. These companies, and peasant rebellions, were to become more of a threat after Poitiers.*

Philippe VI died in August 1350 and was succeeded by his son Jean, who is known in history as Jean le Bon. He found it no easier than his father to get money from the representatives of the people and was at first unable to provide an army or fleet of any size. Military activity, between or in defiance of the truces, took place in Brittany (the scene of the famous Combat des Trente *in which thirty English knights were defeated by thirty French opponents) and in Aquitaine. Edward meanwhile was collecting trump cards: he still held prisoner the French claimant to the duchy of Brittany, Charles de Blois, and had secured from him a promise to pay homage to Edward for the Breton fief if he were released; he also secured the alliance of King Charles of Navarre—at least for the time being. Negotiations for peace finally broke down at Avignon in the spring of 1355 and both sides had perforce to renew the war.*

Edward made rapid preparations to send his son the Black Prince to Aquitaine with as large an army as he could spare, and himself sailed for Calais. From here he made what was little more than a raid as far as Amiens, avoided (for one reason or another) meeting the forces of King Jean in battle, and set sail for home [9 November 1355] as soon as he received an appeal for help from the people of Berwick which had just been captured by the Scots [6 November]. Within six weeks Berwick had been retaken by Sir Walter de Manny in the presence of the king.

The Black Prince landed at Bordeaux, probably in late July 1355. With an Anglo-Gascon army of about six thousand men he marched towards Toulouse, too strongly defended for him to attack it, took and pillaged or burned Castelnaudary and the towns, but not the fortresses, of Carcassonne and Narbonne. Here he turned back, capturing about twenty towns and fortresses before reaching Bordeaux in late November, when he dismissed the army, who had returned with booty of immense value. They had met with virtually no opposition from the French forces under the Comte d'Armagnac.

Charles of Navarre had been reconciled to the King of France by the Treaty of Mantes in 1354, receiving as the price of his friendship a large estate in the Cotentin. But, by the autumn of the next year he had resumed negotiations with Edward, and was organizing resistance to the gabelle *in*

Normandy. King Jean now acted; he went in person to Rouen and arrested Charles on the 5th of April 1356 while he was at dinner with his own son, the Duke of Normandy, the future Charles V. The result was firstly that Charles of Navarre's two brothers were thrown into active opposition to the French cause, and secondly that Edward sent Henry of Lancaster into Brittany at the head of an army. Lancaster, who had Sir Robert Knollys with him, took and burned several towns and approached Rouen with some three thousand English and supporters of the Navarrese. King Jean managed to assemble an army of thirty thousand and marched towards Rouen. Lancaster promptly withdrew towards Cherbourg after less than a month's campaign; he managed by stratagem to avoid an open battle, but some of his supporters were besieged at Évreux and Breteuil, both of which places fell to King Jean, the latter between the 12th and the 19th of August.

Meanwhile the Black Prince had reassembled his forces in Aquitaine; he left Bordeaux in early July with an army of about eight thousand, and went through Limousin and Auvergne, laying waste as they went, in order to join up with Henry of Lancaster in support of the cause of Navarre. As he approached Berry, King Jean received news of his advance, and here Froissart takes over the story. First, however, comes the chronicler's Prologue to his work, because this interesting passage, with all its rhetorical repetitions, gives us an insight into his whole attitude to the choice of subjects for his Chronicles.

¶ Marvellous deeds and noble feats of arms have been performed in the course of the great wars between France, England and the neighbouring kingdoms, wars which the kings and their counsellors set on foot, and in order that all these may be duly recorded and their details known to present readers and to posterity, I will undertake to set down in order a prose account of it all, according to the true information I have received from valiant men, knights and squires who played a part in the events related, and also from heralds of arms and their marshals, who are, rightly and properly, skilled in seeking out and relating such matters.

You may know that Master Jean le Bel, sometime Canon of Saint Lambert's in Liège, wrote a chronicle in his day of such of these things as he chose to record. I have embellished and augmented this book according to my own choice with the help of the narratives and advice of the persons above mentioned, without taking sides or showing any bias or favour for or against anyone, except only that the noble deeds of the brave, whatever their country, provided they won their lands by their own valour, are fully acknowledged and recounted, for it would be a sin and an impertinence to forget or conceal them. Feats of arms are indeed so dearly purchased and paid for, as those who are concerned well know, that one should never lie in order to please others, thus taking glory and renown from the valorous and giving it to those who are in no way worthy of it.

Now, I stated at the outset of this prologue that I would write of marvellous deeds. Indeed, every man that reads and studies this book may and should marvel at the wonderful happenings that he will find in it. For I believe that, since the world was created and weapons were invented, there is no chapter of history in which, for its length, so many marvellous happenings or feats of arms will be found as were performed both on land and sea in the wars I have referred to; of these I now propose to tell you. But before I begin to write of them, I want to air a few thoughts on the subject of valour, for valour is so noble a virtue and so highly to be encouraged, that it should certainly not be mentioned merely in passing; it is a light both temporal and spiritual for all men of good birth, and just as wood cannot burn without fire, so no man of breeding can attain to perfect honour or glory in the world without valour.

For this reason all men of breeding who wish to advance themselves should desire eagerly to acquire a justified reputation for valour —through which they may be counted among the number of valiant knights—and to reflect and consider how their forebears, whose heirs and successors they are and whose arms perhaps they bear, are held in honour and renown for their noble deeds. I am sure that if they read and study this book, they will find as many fine deeds and noble feats of arms, rough encounters, hard-fought assaults, terrible battles and all other forms of prowess in arms which are works of valour, as they will find in any book of history, ancient or modern, that can be named. For them it will be a source of good examples, to encourage them to act valiantly, for the recorded deeds of brave and noble men will naturally stimulate and inspire young knights who are directing their lives towards achieving perfect honour, of which valour is the basic quality and the sure begetter.

This is why I would not wish that any young knight should be deprived of taking up and following a career of arms for lack of means or fortune, provided he has the health and strength to do so, but rather that he should take up arms willingly and with a good heart. He will soon fall in with great and noble lords who will take him into their care if he is worthy of it, help him to advance, if he deserves it, and provide for him in accordance with his noble deeds. Moreover, in the world of arms there occur so many great marvels and fine adventures that a man could not and durst not imagine or conceive the blows of fortune that are endured, and you will find in this book when you read it how many knights and squires have made their name and advanced themselves more by their own valour than by their birth. The title of valiant knight is so high and noble, and his valour so fine and outstanding that it shines in those halls and other places where great lords are gathered together in assembly; he is noticed above all others, and pointed out, and they say: 'There's the man who led this skirmish or that army, who ordered such and such a battle so successfully and conducted it so wisely, who wielded the blade of his lance with such vigour, who penetrated the enemy's lines two or three times, who fought so valiantly and so boldly undertook this task, and who was found grievously hurt among the dead and the wounded yet scorned to flee from his appointed post.'

Such are the seeds that are sown for the praise and encouragement of brave men, and noble knights are advanced similarly by their valour. Thus one will see a valiant young knight sitting in great honour at the table of a king or a prince, a duke or an earl, where there is never a place for those of higher birth or greater possessions. For just as the four Evangelists and the twelve Apostles are nearer to Our Lord than all others, so are valiant knights nearer to Honour and held in higher esteem than all other men. This is indeed right, for they acquire titles of honour by combat, resting neither night nor day in great labour, sweat and toil, in exertion, stress and constant vigilance. And when their valorous deeds are widely known, they are told and celebrated, as we have said above, and written in the record of books and chronicles. For it is in these writings that we find memorials of such brave and noble men of times past as the nine* valiant knights who rose to fame by their valour, the twelve knights companion who held the pass against Saladin and his power, the twelve peers of France who stayed behind in Roncesvalles and there fought and sold their lives so valiantly, and all the others whom I cannot here name and the record of whose mighty deeds I cannot tell, for it would divert me too much from my chief purpose. From this we can perceive a division of society into various different groups: men of valour labouring in arms to advance themselves and increase their own glory; the common people who spend their time discussing the memorable deeds and fortunes of the valiant; and clerks, who write down and record their rise to fame and the prowess of their youth.

* These are Joshua, David and Judas Maccabeus: Hector, Alexander and Caesar; Arthur, Charlemagne and Godfrey de Bouillon.

Now, I have often reflected upon the question of valour, wondering where and for what reasons it has reigned supreme, being found now in one country now in another. Similarly in my youth I listened to the talk of valiant men and brave knights concerning the rules of valour, and they marvelled as much as I do now, so that I propose to develop the matter further. The truth according to ancient writings is that, after the Flood, when Noah and his family had repeopled the earth and men began to bear arms and fight and pillage among themselves, valour first settled in the kingdom of Chaldaea for the sake of King Ninus, who founded and built the great city of Nineveh which was three days' march in length, and also of Queen Semiramis his wife, who was a most valorous lady. After them, valour changed its abode and came to reign in Jerusalem and Judaea, through the merits of Joshua, David and the Maccabees. When it had reigned there for a time it established its sway in the kingdom of the Medes and Persians, because of the renown of the great King Cyrus, of Ahasuerus and Xerxes. Later again, it moved to Greece, because of Hercules, Theseus, Jason, Achilles and other valiant knights; then to Troy, because of King Priam, Hector and his brothers. Then it settled in Rome and among Romans everywhere, for the sake of the noble senators and consuls, tribunes and centurions. These men and their offspring held all power for a matter of five hundred years, causing almost the whole world to give tribute to them until the time of Julius Caesar, the first Roman Emperor, of whom all the others are heirs and descendants.

In time the Romans tired of valour, which departed to live and rule in France, firstly for the honour of King Pepin and King Charlemagne his son, who was King of France and Germany and Emperor of Rome, and for the other noble kings who followed them. Then later valour reigned a long time in England, for the sake of King Edward [III] and the Prince of Wales his son, for in their time the knights of England and her allies have performed as many brave deeds to prove their knighthood, and been through as many hard-fought encounters, as any knight before, as it will soon be learned from this book.

I cannot tell whether valour will move on from England or retrace its steps, for as has been shown it has made a circuit of the countries I have named, holding greater or lesser sway among their peoples according to its fancy; but I have said enough about these strange migrations. I shall therefore say no more, but pass to the subject with which I began, and show without further delay in what way war first began between the English and the French. And in order that in days to come it may be known who undertook this history and was its author, I give you my name. Those who wish so to honour me call me Sire* Jean Froissart, born in the brave, fair and gracious city of Valenciennes in the County of Hainault.

The Black Prince Pillages France

¶ When King Jean of France had completed his expedition to reconquer all those towns and castles in Lower Normandy which were held by the King of Navarre, whom he had put in prison, he returned to the city of Paris. Scarcely had he settled in when he was informed that the Prince of Wales had already penetrated far into his kingdom and, with his whole army, was making a swift advance on the rich land of Berry. This news was most unwelcome to the king, and he swore an oath that he would go out to attack the prince wherever he might find him.

Being determined to defend the boundaries of his kingdom, the king therefore once more issued a special summons to his nobles and others who held fiefs from him, that they should all, on pain of being declared disloyal, start off to join him on the borders of Touraine and Blésois as soon as they received the letters, for he wished to engage the English in battle. Then all those lords who had been summoned set out on their way, for most of them were equally anxious to fight the English in order to be avenged for the humiliations and ravages they had suffered in the past.

Similarly the king, to hasten the task in hand, left Paris and by hard riding reached the fair city of Chartres, with a large force of armed men whom he had retained in camp. At Chartres [28 August 1356 till early September] they halted so as to find out where the English were. Armed troops continued to arrive from all sides, from Auvergne, from Berry, from Burgundy, from Lorraine, from Hainault, from Artois, from Vermandois, from Picardy, from Brittany and from Normandy. As they arrived they rode out in review formation, and were lodged in the neighbourhood on orders

* The title *sire* was sometimes given honorarily to clerks, though it was of right given only to those of noble birth. Hence Froissart's qualification '*qui tant me voet honnerer*'.

from the marshals, Seigneur Jean de Clermont and Seigneur Arnoul d'Audrehem.

The king sent considerable reinforcements of men and supplies to the fortresses and garrisons of seasoned troops in Anjou, Poitou, Maine and Touraine and everywhere on the border territories where they hoped the English might pass, in order to block their way and prevent them from collecting provisions for themselves or fodder for their horses.

In spite of these precautions, the Prince of Wales and his army, who numbered not less than two thousand armed men and six thousand archers, rode forward at their ease and gathered provisions of all kinds in great profusion, being astonished to find the province of Auvergne, into which they had penetrated, so rich and well provided. But rich as it was, they had no thought of halting there, so anxious were they to come to grips with the enemy. Therefore they burned and pillaged the whole land; when they entered into a town and found it richly stocked with food they refreshed themselves for two or three days and then departed, destroying what remained, staving in barrels of wine and burning fields of wheat and oats so that the enemy might not have the use of them; then they would ride on. Everywhere they found the country rich and fertile, for Berry, Touraine, Anjou and Poitou form one of the richest areas in the world for the needs of an army.

¶ In this way the English reached the outskirts of Bourges, in which city were the archbishop with two knights sent by the King of France to take charge of its defence if need arose, as now indeed it did, for the English had come so close that they were setting fire to the suburbs. At one of the gates there was a heavy skirmish, involving the two knights from within the city, the Seigneur de Gonsant and Sir Hutin de Vermeilles, and many gallant deeds were performed in that action.

The English, however, passed on without doing further damage and came to Issoudun [24–26 August 1356] in Berry, a fortified town on which they made a sudden attack with their whole army, but without success, for the nobles who held the city defended it with skill. From there the English made their way to Vierzon [28 August], a large town with a strong castle, but as the place was poorly fortified and lightly garrisoned, they succeeded in storming it. Within they found more wine and food than they could estimate, and remained there three days to restore their energies.

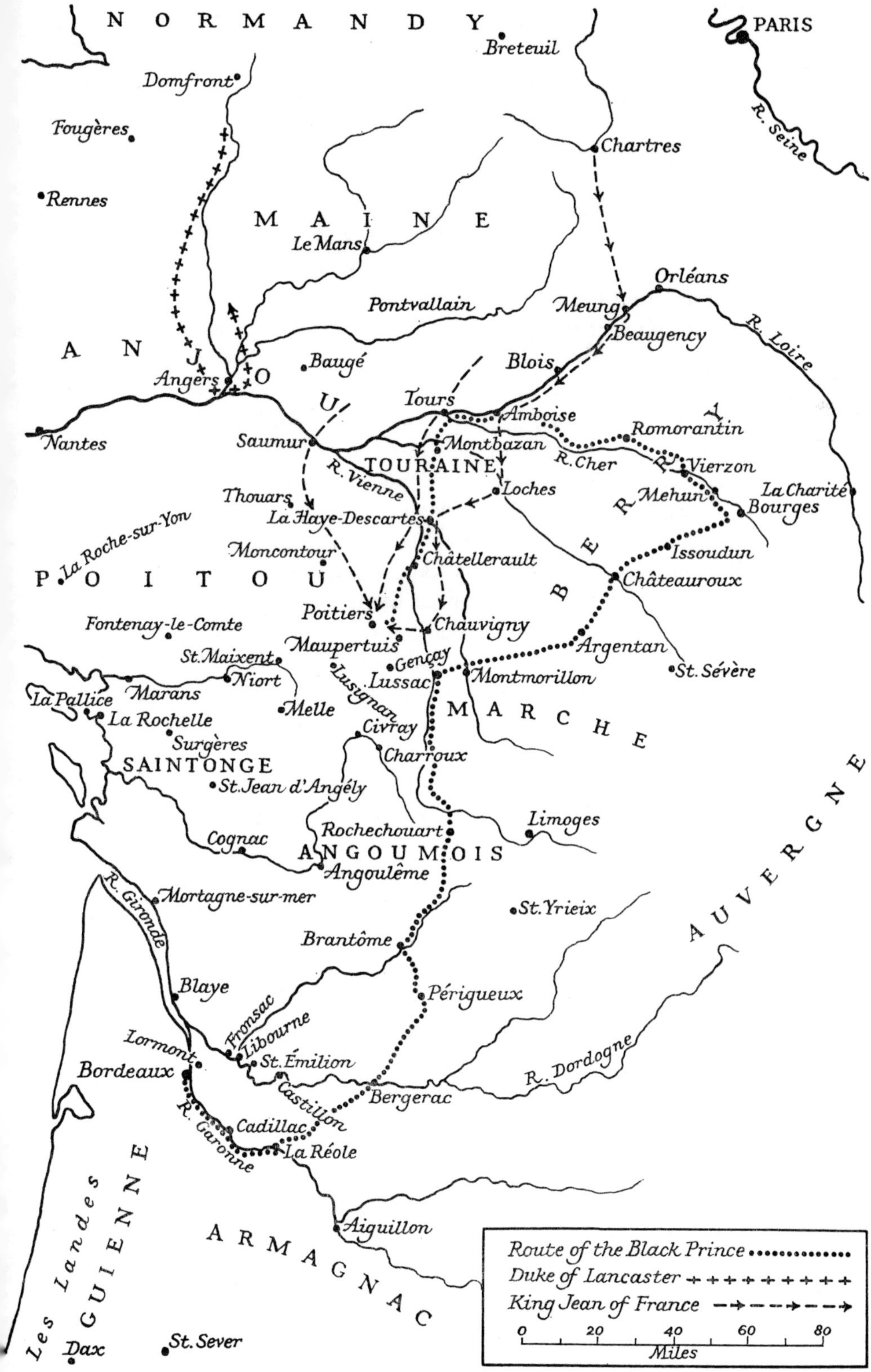

THE BATTLE OF POITIERS
ROUTES OF THE CONVERGING ARMIES

Here news reached the Prince of Wales that the King of France was at Chartres with a large army, and that all the towns on the Loire and all means of crossing the river were so well guarded that he would find no way of getting north of it. The prince therefore took counsel and decided to beat a retreat, through Touraine and Poitou, skirmishing as he went and burning and pillaging the country, to Bordeaux, whence he had set out. When they had had all they wanted from the town he gave orders for Vierzon to be evacuated, for in taking it they had killed the greater part of those they found within. Then they moved on towards Romorantin.

About this time the King of France sent three important noblemen, good warriors, into the province of Berry, to guard its boundaries and to discover the whereabouts of the English troops; these were the Sire de Craon, Boucicault and the Hermite de Chaumont. These three men and their followers, who must have numbered three hundred lance, were riding along the frontier, and had been closely pursuing the English for six days but had found no opportunity of engaging them in a fight, for the English planned their marches and their camps with such skill that no attack on them could be prepared in which they would be at a disadvantage. The French therefore engaged them one day in an ambush near Romorantin, a most suitable spot for the purpose, through which the English were obliged to pass.

That day a detachment including Lord Bartholomew of Burghersh . . . the young Lord Edward Despenser, and Lord Eustace d'Aubrecicourt, all well mounted and with some two hundred followers, had ridden ahead of the prince's forces in order to reach Romorantin, and thus came on the French ambush before they could have any knowledge of it.

As soon as they had ridden past, the French came out of the ambush and put spurs to their horses, for they, too, were mounted on the finest of chargers and swift and lively saddle-horses. The English, by now some way ahead, hearing the thunder of hooves behind them, turned round and realized that it was the enemy who was pursuing them. They therefore halted as if to await the French, who charged ahead in close formation, with lances couched, and launched a fierce attack.

Seeing this, the English opened their ranks and let them pass through, so that they had only five or six horsemen unseated. Then immediately they closed in to attack the enemy. Many a combat, many a lance-thrust followed—all on horseback—and the encounter

ceulx de la ville souffiroient
amedie ou se rendissent —/liii

Les pollee septy du
roy le gentil sire de
mauuy et retdna
a calaix ou mess
jehan de biche latten
doit au quel ilz dist
toutes les post dessy et que cestoit
tout ce quil auoit peu impetrer au
roy silui pra mlt fort les mess jehan
quil conlsist la demourex usqs ace quil
eust ce remonstre ala comunalte li
quel sire de mauuy respondy quil le
feroit conlentiere · lors se pty mess
jehan et vint en marchie et fist soner
la cloche au quel son de cloche vindret

THE BURGHERS OF CALAIS

lasted a long time. Many gallant deeds of arms were performed, many knights and squires on each side were unhorsed and then pushed back into the saddle, and none could say that one party would win the day, so thick was the mêlée and so valiantly did they fight.

Meanwhile the forces of the marshals drew near, and when the French saw them approach along the side of a wood they thought all was lost, as it would have been if they had stayed. Therefore they fled as best they might in the direction of Romorantin, with the English after them full tilt, sparing neither themselves nor their horses. Then followed a terrible rout, with many wounded and felled to the ground.

However, more than half escaped and reached the castle of Romorantin, which was ready to give them a welcome refuge, for otherwise they would all have been captured. Thus there escaped, notably, the three barons above mentioned, along with all other knights and squires who were particularly well mounted. The town of Romorantin was taken at the first onslaught, for at that time it had no real fortifications, and all the French were intent on saving their skins by reaching the castle.

¶ When the prince received the news that his men had been engaged in an encounter he inquired with whom and how they had fared and by what means his men had driven their enemies into the castle of Romorantin. 'Let us ride that way,' said the prince; 'I want to see for myself.' Then the whole army set off to Romorantin, and found the town already full of their own men, studying how best to attack the castle. At their head rode the prince, fully armed and mounted on a black charger, with Sir John Chandos alongside him. They all set to examining the fortress, and decided that it was very pregnable.

Then the prince called Sir John Chandos to him and said: 'John, John, go to the castle gate and speak to the knights therein, to ask them whether they are prepared to surrender quietly, without waiting to be attacked.' Then Sir John left the prince and went to the castle gate, making signs that he wished to parley with them. The men on guard asked his name and by whom he was sent. When he had given his name and said he was sent by his master the Prince of Wales, those to whom he had spoken went to their masters with the information.

Then Boucicault and the Hermite de Chaumont came down and went to the castle gate. As soon as Sir John Chandos saw them he greeted them and said: 'Sirs, I am sent here before you by my lord the prince, who desires, as it seems to me, to behave most courteously towards his enemies. He therefore says that if you will surrender yourselves to him and yield up this castle, which cannot be defended, he will show mercy to you and treat you well.' 'Sir John,' replied Boucicault, 'we thank the lord your prince for the courtesy which he wishes to show us, but we have no mind to accept his terms, and may it never please God that he should take us so easily.' 'How is that, Boucicault,' said Sir John, 'do you consider you are good enough knights to hold this castle against the attack of my lord the prince and his army, and that without hope of reinforcement from anywhere?' 'Chandos, Chandos,' replied Boucicault, 'I do not hold myself to be a good knight. But only folly could make us consider the military conditions you offer, and even greater folly make us accept them when there is no need. Tell your lord the prince, if you will, that he may do as he thinks fit; we are ready to wait for him.'

Thus they parted, and Sir John Chandos returned to the prince and told him as exactly as he could all the words reported above. When the prince heard the reply of Lord Boucicault he thought no less highly of him, and gave orders for citizens of various degrees to lodge his men for that night and the next, for on the morrow he intended to attack the castle to see if they could take it by force. The citizens wisely obeyed the prince's order which was conveyed by the marshals, and the troops were all decently lodged in the town of Romorantin or close by.

¶ On the next morning all the men-at-arms and archers prepared for battle, and each reporting to his own livery troop they made a sudden assault on the castle of Romorantin. The attack was fierce and heavy; the archers, who had been posted on the counterscarps, sent such a continuous rain of arrows that scarcely anyone dared to show himself on the battlements. Some entered into the water up to their necks and came to the walls, others took to the moat, floating on gates and wattles, with pikes and pickaxes, bows and arrows in their hands, to hew and pick at the base of the walls.

Up above them the Seigneur de Craon, Boucicault and the Hermite de Chaumont were eagerly carrying out the task of defence, throwing down rocks and stones and pots full of quicklime with which they harassed and wounded those who were hit. Among the dead on the English side was a gallant squire from Gascony, a most noble man and much lamented, called Raymond de Zedulach, who was in the troop of the Captal de Buch. The attack lasted throughout the day, with little respite, and then the English withdrew to their several lodgings, in order that those who were whole might tend to the wounded, and thus they passed the night.

Next day at sunrise the two marshals of the army caused the trumpets to be sounded, to warn all men to arm and prepare for the assault, and every man who was summoned got ready and took up his station. Then the attack began again, incomparably fiercer than on the previous day, for now the Prince of Wales was there in person, advising them and encouraging them to succeed, saying: 'How much longer will this fortress hold out against us?' His words and his presence greatly encouraged every man-at-arms and every archer engaged in the assault, and they all went furiously into the attack to gain greater renown.

A stone hurled from the walls killed a valiant Gascon squire named Bernard d'Albret, brother of Lord d'Albret, who was standing close by the prince. At this his relations, of whom he had many there present, were very angry, but especially the prince, who swore, aloud so that many heard him, that he would never move from this place until he had taken the castle and captured its occupants. The attack was therefore angrily renewed on all sides to hasten victory, because of the words the prince had spoken for all to hear.

Some of the shrewder knights held that by using lances and arrows in such an attack they were causing unnecessary slaughter and wounding among their own troops and would never take the castle. They therefore ordered cannons to be brought, to hurl cannon shot and fireballs into the lower court of the castle. If these fires took hold they might spread to the roof of the castle towers, which at that time were covered with thatch. If they could not take them by this means, they could not see any way of taking the castle and its defenders.

Fire was brought and shot from cannons and bombards into the lower court, where it quickly spread and caught the thatch roofing of a great tower in which were the three knights who that day and the previous day had performed many feats of arms. When they saw the fire above their heads and that they must either surrender or perish in the flames they were very melancholy and at once came down and surrendered freely to the prince [3 September]. He would not have received them on other terms, because of what he said in the hearing of others.

Thus did the Prince of Wales take the knights we have named, and as his prisoners he made them ride along with him and several other knights and squires who had been in the castle of Romorantin, which they left empty, burned out and despoiled.

¶ After the castle of Romorantin had been taken with its defenders, the Prince of Wales and his men rode towards Anjou and Touraine, burning and wasting the land.

News reached the King of France in Chartres that the Prince of Wales was making great devastation in his country, burning and laying waste all before him, at which the king was much angered and declared that he would take steps against him. He therefore left Chartres and rode towards Blois [10 September], ordering his marshals to send forces of armed men close on his heels; with them he intended to cross the Loire and fight the English. When he reached Blois, he halted there for two days while his orders were carried out; dukes, counts, barons, knights and their troops followed after the king, who then moved on from Blois, halting the first day at Amboise and the next at Loches [13 September], where he stayed to receive news of the English forces, which kept coming in, for the English were being followed and watched by French and Burgundian knights who sent back exact information. Thus the king learned that the English were in Touraine and heading back towards Poitou.

Then the King of France left Loches and came to La Haye [14 September] in Touraine, his armies having crossed the Loire by the bridges at Orléans, Meung, Saumur, Blois and Tours or wherever else they could. There was such a great army that there must have been twenty thousand men-at-arms, without counting the rest, twenty-six dukes and counts and more than seven score banners. The king had with him his four sons, still very young at that time; Charles, Duke of Normandy; Louis, later Duke of Anjou; Jean, later Duke of Berry, and Philippe the youngest, later Duke of Burgundy. So you can well see that since the king and his four sons were there in person, the whole flower of French chivalry was present.

About this time the holy father Pope Innocent VI had sent to France Talleyrand, Cardinal of Périgord, and Nicolas, Cardinal of Urgel, to treat for a peace between the King of France and those with whom he was at enmity, particularly the King of Navarre, whom he kept in prison. They had several times visited and spoken with the king during the siege of Breteuil,* but without obtaining any results.

After the siege and capture of Breteuil the Cardinal of Périgord went to the fair city of Tours in Touraine, where news reached him that the King of France was making all speed to find the English. This news encouraged the cardinal to attempt a settlement and bring

* This siege lasted over a month, and the town capitulated between 12 and 19 August 1356.

peace by some means, if he could, between these two monarchs, or at least to prevent a battle from taking place. He therefore left Tours with speed and rode towards Poitiers, for he gathered that both the armies were making towards that city.

We shall now leave the cardinal for a while, and turn to the King of France, who was putting all his energy into joining battle with the Prince of Wales in order to avenge all the ravages inflicted on his kingdom.

¶ When the King of France learned that the Prince of Wales was making all speed to return to that part of the country from which he had set out, he was afraid the prince might escape from him, a thing he was most anxious to prevent. So keen was he on engaging him in battle that he left La Haye in Touraine with his whole army and rode to Chauvigny [15 September], which he reached on a Thursday evening. A great profusion of barons were lodged in the town of Chauvigny and outside it in a fair meadow stretching down to the River Vienne. After breakfast on Friday the King of France crossed the river by the bridge at Chauvigny, thinking that the English were ahead of him, while in fact they were behind. That Friday there crossed the river sixty thousand horse, apart from others who crossed at Châtellerault, all of them then taking the road to Poitiers.

On his side the Prince of Wales and his men knew nothing of the disposition of the French forces; nor could they, for though they knew that they were on the march they did not know exactly where, but merely that they could not be far off, for their scouts found great difficulty in procuring forage, with the result that the army suffered a serious lack of provisions. They much regretted that they had so thoroughly laid waste the land of Berry, Anjou and Touraine instead of gathering stores.

On the Friday, when the King of France and his great army crossed the river at the bridge of Chauvigny, three of the chief barons of France stayed all that day in the town with a part of their troops because of the size of the crowds on the bridge and in order to be more comfortably housed. They were the Seigneurs de Craon and Raoul de Coucy and the Comte de Joigny; all the others passed over with their equipment, save what they had kept as booty.

On Saturday morning they struck camp, crossed the bridge and followed after the king's forces, which were some three leagues ahead, going through the fields and along heath-roads beside a wood to reach the city of Poitiers.

That same morning the Prince of Wales and his men had left a village close by, sending some of their company to see if anything was brewing and to learn news of the French. These scouts numbered about sixty men-at-arms, all well mounted according to their condition, though their horses were somewhat tired. Among them were two knights from Hainault, Sir Eustace d'Aubrecicourt and Sir Jean de Ghistelles, and they found themselves by chance near to those woods and heaths of which I was just speaking.

The French barons and their men, some two hundred in number, as soon as they saw the English horse, knew at once that it was the enemy, and immediately put on their helmets, unfurled their banners, lowered their lances, and put spurs to their horses.

Sir Eustace d'Aubrecicourt and his companions, who were mounted on the finest chargers, saw coming towards them so great a force of the enemy, and they a mere handful of men by comparison, that they thought it best not to stand, but allow themselves to be pursued, for the prince and his army were not far off. They therefore turned their horses about and took to the edge of the forest, with the French after them, shouting their battle-cries and making a great tumult, in the belief that they would immediately capture them. Thus riding hard in pursuit they got so far forward that they came upon the prince's army where it had halted alongside a wood,* among the heather and bramble, waiting to have news of their fellows. There was great astonishment when they saw them thus pursued.

Seigneur Raoul de Coucy and his troop followed so hard on the English that he came to halt right under the prince's banner. A sharp engagement followed; Raoul de Courcy fought most valiantly, but was nevertheless taken prisoner on parole by the prince's men, and with him the Comte de Joigny, the Vicomte de Breuse, the Seigneur de Chauvigny; nearly all the others were killed or captured, for only a very few escaped. From these prisoners the prince learned that the King of France had gone ahead of them, with a larger army than they had thought possible.

Preliminaries to battle

¶ When the Prince of Wales and his counsellors learned that King Jean and his army were ahead of them, having passed the bridge at

* This was a place marked as La Chaboterie on Cassini's map of France.

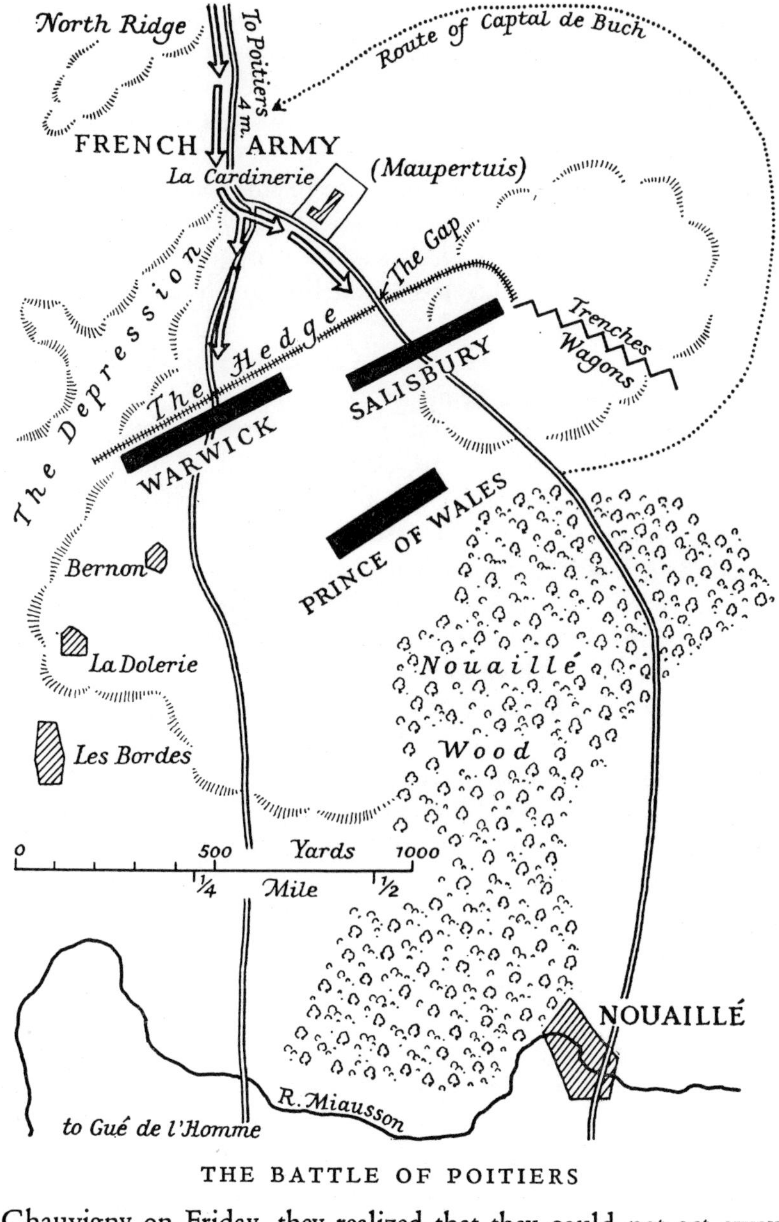

THE BATTLE OF POITIERS

Chauvigny on Friday, they realized that they could not get away without a battle and gathered all their troops together in the camp, where the prince gave orders that none, upon pain of death, should proceed without permission in front of the troop of the marshals. This order was obeyed, and on Saturday [17 September] the English marched forward from prime to vespers, halting at a spot two short leagues from Poitiers,|| in a natural stronghold between hedges and vineyards, with hills on one side. The marshals surveyed the strength of the position and asked the prince what his plans were now. He replied that he intended to remain there and wait for the enemy to seek him out, and trust to the outcome in the name of God and St George. The English camped therefore in this spot, known in the country as the Plains de Maupertuis, which they cunningly fortified with thick hedges of thorn, placing all their baggage vehicles well to the rear. In front they dug several ditches, to prevent any sudden attack on horseback.*||

From here the prince sent out the Captal de Buch, Sir Aymenon de Pommiers, Sir Barthélemy de Burghersh and Sir Eustace d'Aubrecicourt to learn the position of the French army, and with them two hundred men-at-arms, all mounted on the finest chargers. They rode so well, searching on all sides, that they gained exact information concerning the French camp, which was bristling with armed men. These English scouts could not refrain from harassing the rear of the French; some they unhorsed and took prisoner, at which the army began to take alarm. News of this reached the King of France as he was about to enter the city of Poitiers.

When the king learned that the enemy he was so anxious to find was behind him and not ahead of him, he rejoiced at the news and gave orders for all his men to turn about and to pitch camp there. But it was very late on Saturday before the whole army was settled. Meanwhile the English scouts returned to the prince and told him something of the disposition of the French forces, which they declared to be a very big army. The prince was nothing daunted and said: 'By God's grace, so be it. Now must we take counsel how to fight them to our best advantage.'

¶ When Sunday morning came the King of France, impatient to fight the English, ordered a solemn mass to be sung in the royal pavilion, and he and his four sons received communion. After mass he received the visit of the chief barons and those of the blood royal, the Duc d'Orléans his brother, the Duc de Bourbon, with many

* The name Plains de Maupertuis continued in use to the end of the fifteenth century; the spot is now called La Cardinerie. It is situated in the commune of Nouaillé, six miles south-east of Poitiers, on the right bank of the Miausson, between this river and the Roman road from Poitiers to Limoges. The narrow road mentioned is that connecting the hamlets of Les Minières and Bordes.

|| See Appendix p. 348.

other barons of France and of his allies. There they held council and talked for a long time about the best course of action. It was finally agreed that each commander should unfurl his banner and assemble his troops, and prepare for immediate battle in the name of God and St Denis.

The king was more than delighted with this counsel, and caused the trumpets to be sounded throughout the army. Then all his men armed themselves and mounted their chargers and formed up on the field where the king's banners had been planted and were fluttering in the breeze, above them all the oriflamme carried by Sir Geoffroi de Chargny. There you could see a great assemblage of the finest armour, of rich blazonry, banners and pennons, and noble knights and squires, for all the flower of French chivalry was there. No knight or squire remained in his lodging unless he wished to be dishonoured. On the advice of the constable and marshals of France, the army was drawn up in three great battalions, each of sixteen thousand men-at-arms of proved valour. The first was under the command of the Duc d'Orléans, with thirty-six banners and twice as many pennons; the second was commanded by the Duke of Normandy and his two brothers, Louis and Jean;* the third by the king himself. In this last battalion there was a great profusion of noble knights.

Whilst these battalions were forming up the king called to him Sir Eustace de Ribemont, the Seigneurs Jean de Landas, Guichard de Beaujeu and Guichard d'Angle, and said: 'Ride out as near as possible to the English troops, bring me full information about their disposition, their arms and their numbers, and weigh up how we can combat them either on horse or on foot.' They replied: 'Sir, we will gladly do this,' and rode off, coming so close to the English that they were able to survey a fair part of their army. This information they brought back to the king, who was waiting for them mounted on a white charger, watching his troops now and then and praising God that they were present in such great numbers, saying for all to hear: 'All you men, when you were back in Paris or Chartres, Rouen or Orléans, you muttered threats against the English and wished you could meet them in the battlefield. Now the time has come—I will lead you to these English, and you can avenge yourselves for all the wrongs you have suffered at their hands, for we shall not fail to do battle with them.' To which those who heard him replied: 'So be it, God willing; that will we gladly do.'

* These were the three eldest sons of the king.

¶ Whilst the king was exhorting his men with these words the four knights already named came back and, weaving their way through the packed ranks, presented themselves before the king, in the presence of the constables and the two marshals of France and a great body of knights, assembled to learn the plan of attack. The king asked the four scouts what news they had and they replied: 'My lord, our news is good, and today, God willing, you have the advantage over your enemy.' 'Such, by the grace of God, is our hope,' replied the king. 'Now tell us about their disposition and how we might attack them.'

Then Sir Eustace de Ribemont replied, according to what I have been told, on behalf of his companions and at their request. 'Sir, we have had a good look at your enemies, and we estimate their numbers as two thousand men-at-arms, four thousand archers, and fifteen hundred foot-soldiers.' 'How are they placed?' asked the king. 'Sir,' replied Sir Eustace, 'they are in a very strong position; as far as we can judge they are no more than one battalion, but are most skilfully placed. They have chosen a road strongly fortified with hedges and undergrowth, and have posted their archers along this hedge on both sides of the road, so that one cannot approach to attack the army save between these rows of archers. This road has no other entry or issue, and is only wide enough for perhaps four men-at-arms to ride abreast. Where the hedge ends, among vines and thorn-bushes, it is impossible to proceed on foot or horseback, and here are their armed foot-soldiers with their archers in "herce" formation in front.* All this, it seems to us, is most skilfully planned, for if we could fight our way to that point we could not penetrate further without coming up against the archers, whom it would be no light task to dislodge.'

Then the king said: 'Sir Eustace, how then would you advise us to conduct our attack?' To which the knight replied: 'Sir, we should do it on foot, except for three hundred horsemen of the boldest, strongest, toughest and most enterprising of your whole army, well armed and mounted on the finest chargers, who will break through the lines of archers for your own battalions to follow in quickly and fight hand-to-hand with their men-at-arms and overcome them by the

* 'Herse' is the French for harrow (also portcullis). As a military formation there seems some doubt whether it represented a square block of archers placed chequerwise, each archer being as it were a prong of the harrow, or whether it was a hollow wedge of archers, placed between the divisions to cover their flanks. The word itself would support the first interpretation; Colonel Burne, in *The Crecy War*, favours the latter on the grounds of military probability.

fierceness of their attack. I can think of no other advice to give you: if any one has a better plan, let him declare it.'

The king was much pleased with this plan, and gave orders for it to be carried out. At his command the two marshals rode off, visiting each battalion in turn to make an impartial choice of three hundred knights and squires, the swiftest and bravest of the whole army, all mounted on the finest chargers and armed from head to foot.

Immediately afterwards the German troops were drawn up in battle order to act as mounted reinforcements to the marshals, under the command of the Counts of Saarbruck, Nido and Nassau. King John of France was there in his royal armour, with nineteen others similarly clad, || so that one could not tell which of them was the king unless one knew him well; || he had recommended his eldest son to the charge of the Seigneur de Saint-Venant, Sir Jean de Landas and Sir Thibaud de Vaudenay, his three younger sons, Louis, Jean and Philippe, to the care of other noble knights and squires. The royal banner was borne by Sir Geoffroi de Chargny, as being the wisest and most valiant knight of the army . . .

¶ When the battalions of the King of France were ready and in battle order, each lord with his own men under his banner and instructed as to what he was to do, the royal command was given that all should proceed on foot save those who had been bidden by the marshals to open a passage through the English archers, that all those who had lances should shorten them to a length of five feet so that they could be more easily wielded, and that they should also remove their spurs. This order was carried out, for it seemed wise to them all.

As they were thus moving off with great ardour to attack the enemy, up rode the Cardinal of Périgord at full gallop to the king, having left Poitiers early that morning. He bowed low before the king in sign of humility and begged him with uplifted hands to halt a moment for the love of God until he had spoken with him.

The King of France, who was a man always open to reason, granted him his request and asked him what he wished to say. 'Most dear sir,' said the cardinal, 'you have here the flower of French chivalry assembled to attack the mere handful of men that the English are by comparison with yourselves. If you can take them and they put themselves at your mercy without a battle, it would be more honourable and more profitable than if you were to risk the many noble knights you have here. I therefore humbly pray you in

God's name that I may go to the prince and show him how much more powerful you are.' Again the king granted him his request, saying: 'Sir, we are agreeable, but return with haste.'

Upon this the cardinal left the King of France and rode with speed to the prince, whom he found surrounded by his men, all on foot, in the middle of a vineyard, resolutely awaiting the coming of the French army. As soon as he arrived the cardinal dismounted and was warmly received by the prince. After he had bowed in greeting, he said: 'Fair son, if you have given due consideration to the mighty army of France, you will allow me to attempt a settlement between you if I can.' The prince, who was then a young man, replied: 'Sir, if my honour and the honour of my men is preserved, I am ready to fall in with any reasonable suggestion.' To this the cardinal replied: 'Fair son, you speak wisely, and I will make peace between you if I can, for it would be a great pity if so many brave men as there are here on one side and the other came together in battle, with all the slaughter that would ensue.'

With these words, and no more, the cardinal left the prince and rode back to the King of France, with whom he began to discuss terms of treaty and to make proposals in order to bring him to his way of thinking. 'Sir,' he said, 'you have no need to be impatient for battle, for they are all yours without a blow being struck, and they cannot escape or flee from you. I therefore entreat you to grant a truce for today and until sunrise tomorrow.'

At this the king began to weigh the situation in his mind, and was unwilling to grant this respite at the cardinal's first request, or even at the second, for a section of his council would not hear of it, notably Sir Eustace de Ribemont and Sir Jean de Landas, who were the king's intimate advisers. But in the end the cardinal put so much effort into his good work and spoke so eloquently that the king consented to grant a truce to last all that Sunday and until dawn on the following day. The cardinal immediately reported this to the prince and his men, who were not angry at the proposal, because they were still trying to reach a plan of action.

Then the King of France caused a very rich and handsome pavilion of scarlet samite to be erected on the spot where he had granted the truce, and gave leave for all his men to retire to their quarters, except for the troops of the constable and the marshals. There remained with him his sons and others of the blood royal with whom he was wont to take counsel concerning his plans.

Throughout Sunday the cardinal rode from one camp to the other and did all in his power to bring about an agreement; but he found the King of France and his advisers so unbending that they would not stoop to making an agreement, unless they had four-fifths of the English knights as prisoners, and the prince and his men surrendered unconditionally—something they would never have done. And so various offers and proposals continued to be made.

I have been told by the cardinal's men who were present at this time and who reckoned to know something about it, that the prince offered to give back to the King of France all the towns and strongholds that he had captured on this expedition, to hand over all the prisoners that they had taken, and to swear not to take up arms against the King of France for seven years, || for the English were afraid that the French might block them in their present position without making any attack. || But the King of France and his advisers would hear none of it, remaining obdurate unless the prince and a hundred of his knights came and surrendered to the King of France.* On no other terms would they give them a safe passage, but the prince and his counsellors would never have accepted such a treaty.

¶ Whilst the cardinal of Périgord was riding from one camp to the other in the good cause of peacemaker during the time of the truce certain bold young knights from each side rode forth alongside the opposing army to study the disposition of their troops, and some incidents occurred.

Thus it happened that Sir John Chandos, a brave and noble knight of proved skill, had been skirting the French army, and had taken pleasure in beholding such a great assembly of knights, with shining arms and armour. He was saying to himself: 'Please God we may not part without a battle, for if we are taken or beaten by such a great and valiant army as I now see before me, there would be no shame for us; and if through good fortune we win the day, we should be the most highly honoured men in the world.'

Whilst Sir John Chandos was riding and musing thus as he studied the French troops he came up with Seigneur Jean de Clermont, one of the marshals of France, and many violent words of reproach were exchanged. I will tell you why. These two knights (one should perhaps explain it by the rashness of youth) each wore the same device—a Virgin azure, with a sunbeam on the sinister side—embroidered on the surcoats they were wearing. Jean de Clermont

* It is safe to presume that this represents the four-fifths mentioned earlier, and that there were about 125 knights in the English army.

was much displeased to see Sir John Chandos bearing his device, and immediately drew rein, shouting: 'Chandos, I was hoping to meet you. Since when have you taken to bearing my arms?' 'And you mine,' replied Sir John Chandos, 'for they are as much mine as yours?' 'I forbid you to do so,' said the marshal, 'and if it weren't for the truce between our two armies I'd soon show you you'd no right to them.' 'Ha!' replied Chandos, 'tomorrow morning you'll find me ready armed to prove I've as much right to them as you have.'

With these words they parted, but Seigneur Jean de Clermont continued to shout after Sir John Chandos: 'Chandos, Chandos, this is just like your English presumption—you can't invent anything new, but borrow whatever you find good elsewhere.' No blows and no further words were exchanged, and each rode back to his army, leaving the matter at that.

the battle of poitiers

You have already heard tell how the Cardinal of Périgord laboured all Sunday, riding from one camp to the other, to bring the king and the prince to terms, but without success. It was nearly the hour of vespers when he withdrew to Poitiers. All that Sunday the French remained on the field, and in the evening withdrew to their camps, where they refreshed themselves from the abundance of their provisions. The English, however, were beginning to feel great want of stores, which was a cause of great concern to them, for they did not know where to go to forage, so closely were their exits blocked; they could not leave their camp without danger from the French. Indeed, they did not fear a battle so much as that they would be blockaded where they stood. All Sunday they worked at the completion of their defences, and spent it as well as they could in strengthening their position with ditches, round which they posted their archers.

On Monday morning [19 September 1356] the prince and his army were soon arrayed in battle order as on the previous day without any sign of fear or disorder; and the French likewise. About sunrise the cardinal renewed his journeyings from one camp to the other, and thought that by his negotiations he could bring them to terms, but he could not, for the French angrily told him to go to Poitiers or anywhere else he chose and give up acting as peacemaker, for he was likely to bring disaster on himself.

The cardinal, who was seeking only to do good, did not wish to run into further danger and took his leave of the King of France, for he saw that he was labouring in vain. He therefore went to the prince and said: 'Fair son, do what you can, for a battle there must be. I can obtain no terms of peace from the King of France.' This final word from the cardinal put fire into the prince's heart and he replied: 'That is indeed my intention and the intention of all my men. May God help the right!' whereupon the cardinal left the prince and returned to Poitiers.

In the cardinal's company there were brave knights and squires who favoured the French cause more than that of the prince. When they saw that a battle was inevitable, they stole away from their master and joined the French army, placing themselves under the command of the Castellan d'Amposta, a valiant warrior who was at that time of the cardinal's household. The cardinal was quite unaware of this as he rode back towards Poitiers, and had he known he would not have allowed it . . .

¶ The prince's army was drawn up more or less as the four French knights had reported to their king, except that he had ordered a body of wise and brave knights to remain on horseback between his battalions, to withstand the battalion of the French marshals. They had, moreover, on their right flank placed three hundred men and as many archers, all mounted, on a hill which was neither very high nor very steep, to move round under cover of this hill and strike at the Duke of Normandy's battalion which was drawn up on foot below it. All this had been done since the report. The prince was with the main body of his army among the vineyards, all on foot, but with their horses close by so that they could mount without delay if need arose. On their most exposed side they had placed their carts and other tackle as fortifications, so that they could not be attacked from this quarter.

With the prince were some of the most renowned knights of England, Gascony and Hainault . . .; in truth he had with him the very flower of those countries' knights, even if their numbers were not very great, for all told they were no more than eight thousand men, while the French were a full fifty thousand combatant troops, of whom more than three thousand were knights.

¶ When that young man the Prince of Wales saw that battle was certain, that the Cardinal of Périgord was departing with his mission unfulfilled and that the king his enemy professed open scorn for him, he took heart within himself and encouraged his men, saying: 'Fair lords, we are but few compared with the might of our enemies, but let us not be dismayed, for victory lies not with greater numbers but where God chooses to send it. If it happens that we win the day, we shall be held in the greatest honour throughout the world; if we are slain, I have still my father and my noble brothers, and you have true friends who will avenge us. I therefore beseech you to fight today with all your might, for with the help of God and Saint George you will see me act this day like a true knight.'

The prince's men were greatly encouraged by these and many other fine words which he spoke to them and which were repeated by the marshals. With the prince, to guard and advise him, was Sir John Chandos, and whatever was happening he did not leave him throughout the day. Lord James Audley was also with the prince for a great part of the time; it was he who had advised on the drawing up of their battle order on Sunday, for he was a most wise and valiant knight, and well he proved it on the day of battle, as I shall relate.

When Lord James saw that battle was imminent he was glad, for he wished to fulfil a vow he had made; he therefore approached the prince and said: 'My lord, I have always loyally served your father and yourself, and I shall always do so as long as I live. Now, dear sir, I must tell you of a vow I once made, that any time your father or one of his sons should be in action I would be the first into the fray. I therefore most earnestly beg that, as reward for any services I may have done to the king your father or to you, you will grant me permission to leave you for my honour and so be in a position to carry out my vow.'

The prince, in appreciation of his nobility and of his determination to seek out his enemies, gladly granted this, and, taking him by the hand, said: 'Sir James, may God grant you grace and strength this day to be the most valorous of all my knights.' Thus he left the prince and placed himself in the front of all the battalions, accompanied only by four squires from among the most valiant, whom he had retained as his personal bodyguard. He rode off ahead of the other knights to engage with the battalion of the marshals of France, falling in with Sir Arnoul d'Audrehem and his company, and in the encounter which followed he performed wonderful feats of arms, as you will hear when I come to tell of the battle. Likewise on the other side Sir Eustace d'Aubrecicourt, who was a young knight most anxious to acquire prowess in arms, had taken great pains to be among the first in the attack, where indeed he was at the very moment when Lord James was advancing to seek his enemies. How it fell out between them I shall now tell.

You have already heard that the German troops remained on horseback alongside the battalion of the marshals. Sir Eustace d'Aubrecicourt, who was mounted, couched his lance, buckled on his shield and putting spurs to his horse galloped up between the two armies. A German knight, Ludwig von Recombes, who bore arms argent five roses gules, saw Sir Eustace approach, he bearing ermine two bars couped gules; he therefore left his company, which was among the troops under the command of the Count Johann von Nassau, couched his lance and rode at him. They met with such a shock that both were unhorsed, and the German knight wounded in the shoulder.

Sir Eustace rose first, and taking his lance stood over the knight where he lay, ready to attack him again; but he had no time to do so, for there came upon him five German men-at-arms, who felled him and with the help of their comrades carried him off prisoner to the Count of Nassau, who took no notice of him. I do not know whether they put him on oath, but they bound him to a cart which contained their baggage.

Very soon after Sir Eustace had been taken the battle began on all fronts, firstly where the battalion of the marshals, riding ahead of those whose task was to destroy the English archers, entered on horseback into the lane between its two thick hedges. Immediately they penetrated between the hedges the archers began to shoot in quick succession, so effectively from both sides of the lane, sending their barbed arrows deep into the horses' sides that the beasts, smarting under the pain, were too frightened to advance farther. They turned about, some sideways and some the way they had come, falling under their riders, who were unable to prevent it or to rise again, so that the battalion of the marshals was quite unable to reach the prince's army. There were some well-mounted knights and squires who managed to ride their horses through the hedge, thinking thus to get near to the English troops, but they were unable to do so.

Sir James Audley, with his guard of four squires and his sword in his hand, was in the forefront of this engagement, and performed many deeds of arms, as a result of which he came up with the banner of Seigneur Arnoul d'Audrehem, marshal of France, a most brave and valiant knight; after these two had fought together for a long time, Arnoul was seriously wounded, for by now the marshals' battalion was being harried and put to rout by the archers, with the help of the men-at-arms, who came between them as they fell, capturing or killing as they chose. There the wounded Arnoul d'Audrehem was taken prisoner, but by other hands than those of Sir James Audley and his four squires, for he took no prisoner all day, nor did he intend to, so keen was he to be in the front of the attack.

¶ In another part of the field Seigneur Jean de Clermont, the valiant marshal of France, was fighting bravely under his banner as long as he could, but he was felled, never to rise or be ransomed, for he was slain on this field in the service of his master. Some maintain that he owed his fate to the words he had exchanged with Sir John Chandos the previous day. Hardly ever had seasoned troops been routed in so short a time as were those of the marshals, for they fell one upon another and could make no headway.

Those behind, who could not proceed when the rout began, fell back towards the Duke of Normandy's battalion, which was closely packed in front, but which quickly thinned out behind when they heard that the marshals had been routed, for many of them mounted their horses and rode off when they saw a mounted company of English, headed by a host of archers also mounted, coming down round the hill alongside the battlefield. Indeed, the English archers were an inestimable advantage to their comrades, and struck terror into the hearts of the French, for the rain of arrows was so continuous and so thick that the French did not know where to turn to avoid them, with the result that the English kept gaining ground.

¶ When the English men-at-arms saw that the first battalion of the enemy was routed and that the Duke of Normandy's battalion was giving ground and its ranks opening, their strength and their courage were wonderfully renewed, and they immediately leapt on their horses, which were all ready near by. Then they assembled in a body and began shouting, to dismay the enemy: 'Saint George! Guyenne!'* It was here that Sir John Chandos spoke those worthy and memorable words to the prince: 'Ride forward, sir, the day is yours. God will be with you today. Let us make straight for your adversary the King of

* Guyenne lies to the north of Gascony, but the two names are more or less synonymous in the chroniclers of the period, who use the term Gascon for the inhabitants of both provinces. It is taken to include the whole of Aquitaine, and as such was the symbol of English rights in France.

France, for it is there that the battle will be decided. I am certain that his valour will not allow him to flee, and if it please God and Saint George, he will still be there for us—but let it be a good fight, and you have said just now that we should today see you bear yourself like a true knight.'

These words so fired the prince that he said for all to hear: 'Come, John, you will not see me turn back today, for I shall be always among the foremost.' Then turning to his bannerer he said: 'Ride on, bannerer, in the name of God and Saint George!' and the knight immediately obeyed his prince's order. The press and the rout were most perilous; many a man was unhorsed and anyone who fell was quite unable to rise again unless there was someone at hand to help him. As the prince and those under his banner rode into the ranks of the enemy he saw Seigneur Robert de Duras lying dead under a small bush on his right, and beside him his banner, which was 'of France, a saltire gules'. He called two of his squires and three archers and said: 'Place the body of this knight on a shield and carry it to Poitiers, and there present it to the Cardinal of Périgord with my compliments and say that I salute him by these tokens', which order the men carried out without delay.

Now let me tell you what moved the prince to act thus, for some might think he did it by way of mockery. He had already been informed that some of the cardinal's men had remained in the field and taken arms against him, which was not right or proper in military procedure. Ecclesiastics who are negotiating in the cause of peace ought not to take up arms or fight on either side. Because these men had done so the prince was angry with the cardinal and did not hesitate to send him the body of his nephew Robert de Duras. He wished also to cut off the head of the Castellan d'Amposta, who had been taken prisoner, and in his anger would have done so, because he was a member of the cardinal's household, if Sir John Chandos had not checked him with reason, saying: 'My lord, stay your hand and turn your attention to more important things. Maybe the cardinal will have such excuses for his men that you will all be satisfied.' So the prince pushed forward, having given orders that the castellan should be well guarded.

¶ When the marshals' battalion was hopelessly routed, the Duke of Normandy's was breaking up, and most of those who ought to have been fighting were taking to horse and fleeing; the English advanced ready mounted and struck first at the battalion of the Duke of Athens,

Constable of France. Here was a fierce encounter, with many blows struck and many men laid low. The French, who fought by companies, cried: 'Montjoie! Saint Denis!' and the English: 'Saint George! Guyenne!' Between them great prowess was displayed, for the least of them was worth a good man-at-arms.

Then the prince and his men turned their attack to the German battalion, under the Count of Saarbruck, Count Johann von Nassau, and the Count of Nido, but this encounter did not last long, for they soon repulsed the Germans and had them on the run. The English archers shot with speed and skill, and so continuously that no one dared to come within bowshot of them; they killed and wounded very many who could not offer a ransom. The three counts were taken prisoner on proper terms, and numerous knights and squires of their followers were killed or captured.

As the Germans retreated Sir Eustace d'Aubrecicourt was rescued by his men, who were seeking him out, since they knew he was a prisoner of the Germans, a task which Sir Jean de Ghistelles performed under great difficulty. Sir Eustace was remounted, and during the rest of that day performed many excellent feats of arms, taking many important prisoners, from whom he later received large sums which greatly helped him to advance his own interests.

When the Duke of Normandy's men saw the prince's army approaching in such strength after it had overcome and put to flight the marshals and the Germans they were seized with fear. Nearly all of them sought to save both themselves and the king's sons, the Duke of Normandy, the Comte de Poitiers and the Comte de Touraine, who were at that time very young and so easily influenced that they unquestioningly followed the advice of their counsellors. The king's three sons therefore left the field by order, and took the road to Chauvigny, and with them went more than eight hundred lance, fit and sound, who had not been engaged in the battle. However, Sir Guichard d'Angle and Sir Jean de Saintré, who were with the Comte de Poitiers, refused to turn back, and rushed into the thick of the combat.

When Sir Jean de Landas and Sir Thibaud de Vaudenay, who with the Seigneur de Saint-Venant had charge of Duke Charles of Normandy, had ridden a league or more with the duke, they took leave of him and begged Saint-Venant not to leave him until he was in a safe place, assuring him that he would gain as much honour by protecting the duke as he would have done by remaining on the field of battle; then they turned back and came upon the Duc d'Orléans'

le royaume asses en paw. ꝟ

Comment le roy de france mist
sur vne grosse armee pour aller
sur les frontieres de calays et dan
tleterre. Chappie. iiij.ᵛ.xʲ.

⟨D⟩uant ce vint sur le
pie que on compta
lan mille quatre cent
le roy de france son frere leure-
oncles et leure consaulx enten
dirent que les anglois yene dar

THE KING OF FRANCE AT THE HEAD OF HIS ARMY

battalion, complete and unhurt, who had left the field and were then in the rear of the king's own battalion. It is equally true that there were many good knights and squires who, though their commanders had left the field, refused to retreat, preferring to die rather than to be reproached with having fled.

¶ You have earlier in these Chronicles heard at some length of the battle of Crécy, and how extraordinary was the fortune of the French; at the battle of Poitiers, fortune rather similarly proved to be most contrary and most cruel for France, who had an advantage of at least seven to one in numbers. Was it not therefore a great blow of fortune for them that they could not triumph over their enemies? In fact, this battle at Poitiers was much better fought than that at Crécy, for the men-at-arms had much more time in which to size up the position of their enemies: Crécy began after vespers, with a disordered and confused army, while Poitiers began at prime, with troops in good order: . . . if only fortune had favoured the French! Incomparably more fine deeds of arms were performed here than at Crécy, although fewer rulers of countries were killed.

All the French who remained on the field at Poitiers, whether killed or captured, acquitted themselves so loyally towards their sovereign that their heirs are still held in great honour, and their deeds in great esteem. Nor can it be said that King Jean of France was afraid because of anything he heard or saw, but stayed on the field a good knight and a lusty fighter, showing no sign of flight or withdrawal, since he said to his men: 'On foot! On foot!' and caused all his cavalry to dismount. He dismounted himself in front of all his men, a battle-axe in his hands, and sent his banners ahead in the name of God and Saint Denis, Sir Geoffroi de Chargny bearing the king's personal standard, and thus they advanced against the English in good order. The shock was rude and fierce; many blows were dealt with battle-axes, swords and other weapons of war.

The King of France and Philippe his youngest son attacked the battalion of the marshals of England, the Earls of Warwick and Suffolk, with whom were several lords from Gascony . . . King Jean was fully aware that his men were in great danger, for he kept seeing his ranks open and crack, his banners and pennons totter and retreat, repulsed by the might of the enemy, but he thought he could restore his fortunes by force of arms. The French were shouting their battle-cry: 'Montjoie! Saint Denis!' and the English replied with: 'Saint George! Guyenne!'

The two knights who had left the Duke of Normandy's company, Sir Jean de Landas and Sir Thibaud de Vaudenay, returned at a useful moment, and dismounted to join the king's troops, where they proceeded to fight most valiantly. In one place the Duke of Athens was engaged, with his men, and a little higher up the Duke of Bourbon, surrounded by brave knights from Picardy and from his own Bourbonnais.

On the flank were the barons and men of Poitou . . . There were many deeds of knighthood performed and much skill in arms displayed, for you must surely know that all the flower of chivalry was present on each side. Elsewhere were barons and knights from Burgundy and Auvergne, from Limousin and Picardy . . . In the king's battalion was Earl Douglas of Scotland, who fought most bravely for a time; but when he saw the utter rout of the French he fled as swiftly as he could, for on no account did he wish to fall into the hands of the English. He would rather have been killed on the spot.

¶ There is no room to tell of all that happened, or to say: 'This man fought well, and that one better', for I should need too many words. All the same, one should never pass lightly over the subject of arms, and there were present a multitude of noble knights and squires on both sides. Well did they prove themselves, for of the dukes, counts, barons, knights and squires who were killed or captured of the King of France's army, none deigned to flee, but all remained bravely by the side of their lord and acquitted themselves nobly. On the other side you could see knights of England and Gascony advancing so boldly into the fight to seek out their enemies, yet retaining their exact order of battle, that it was a wonder to behold how they risked their lives in so doing. They had much to suffer and endure before they gained the upper hand and were able to penetrate the King of France's lines.

There beside the prince to hold his bridle were Sir John Chandos and Sir Peter Audley, the brother of Lord James Audley; Lord James, of whom we have already spoken, was always in the forefront of the fighting, as he had vowed he would be, and with the help of his four squires had performed such deeds of arms that his courage must ever be remembered. For, brave knight that he was, he had entered into the thick of the battle and fought so valiantly that he was wounded in the body, in the head and on the face, and so long as his strength and his breath lasted he continued to advance fighting, until he fell from loss of blood. Then, with the battle drawing to its close, his four squires took him up and carried him away from the fighting, laying him down alongside a hedge to refresh him. There they removed his armour as gently as they could and tended his wounds, stitching the worst of them and binding up the others . . .

¶ Among the fights and encounters and pursuits that took place in the field that day I shall tell of one that concerned Sir Oudart de Renty. Sir Oudart had left the field of battle, for he saw that the day was lost beyond hope. Not wishing to fall into the hands of the English, if he could avoid it, he had withdrawn a good league, where he found himself pursued for a time by an English knight, with his lance couched, who called out to him: 'Sir knight, turn back, for it is shameful to flee thus.'

Sir Oudart was ashamed to find himself pursued, and halted, with his sword at the rest, resolving to await the English knight, who advanced with the intention of striking Sir Oudart's shield with his sword; but without success, for the Frenchman turned the blow aside and did not miss with his own stroke, dealing the knight such a blow on the helmet that he stunned him and knocked him from his horse, so that he lay on the ground for some time without stirring.

Then Sir Oudart dismounted and coming to where the knight lay, placed the point of his sword on his breast and said he would kill him if he did not surrender as his prisoner, whether he were rescued or not. The knight saw that there was nothing for it but to surrender and go with Sir Oudart, who later ransomed him for a considerable sum . . .

¶ In war and love it often happens that fortune is more wonderfully favourable than one had dared to hope, whether in battle, single combat or fierce pursuit. Indeed, this battle which was fought near Poitiers in the plains of Beauvoir and Maupertuis was a great battle and full of many perils; in it were performed many feats of arms which never came to be known. It was well planned and well fought and in the end the English had the better of the day, but there was great suffering among the combatants on both sides.

King Jean performed many fine deeds, and wielded his battle-axe with great effect. In their efforts to break a way through the press the Comte de Tancarville and several lords and knights were taken prisoner close by the king, and elsewhere, higher up the field, Sir

Charles d'Artois and many knights were captured by the troop of the Captal de Buch.

The rout was continued to the very walls of Poitiers, where the citizens had closed the gates and would allow no one to enter because of the danger to themselves, so that unbelievable numbers of men-at-arms and horses were wounded or killed on the road and before the gates. The French were surrendering as soon as they could find an Englishman to take them, and indeed several English, archers and others, had four, five or even six prisoners; I have never heard of such misfortunes as happened there that day . . .

Sir Geoffroi de Chargny fought most bravely as bearer of the king's standard, and bore the brunt of the thickest fighting around the king; he had his own banner there, too—gules three escutcheons argent. So many English and Gascons came up from all sides that they forced open the ranks of the king's battalion, and the French became so entangled with their enemies that at times and in places there might be five men attacking one of their knights . . . and Sir Geoffroi de Chargny was slain with the king's banner in his hands. Around the king himself there was constant pressure from those who were disputing his capture, and those who knew him and were nearest to him kept crying: 'Surrender yourself, surrender yourself, or you are a dead man.'

There was also present a knight called Denis de Morbecque, a native of Saint-Omer, who had for five years served the King of England in return for a salary, since in his youth he had outlawed himself from the kingdom of France because of a murder he had committed at Saint-Omer in the course of a private quarrel. This knight was fortunate enough to be the nearest of all those around the King of France when his capture became imminent; he accordingly jostled his way through the throng by means of his great strength, and said to the king in good French, to which the king listened more readily than to that of the others,* 'My lord, my lord, surrender yourself.'

The king, finding himself in dire straits and much harassed by his enemies and realizing that there was no longer any use in defence, looked at the knight and asked: 'To whom shall I surrender? To whom? Where is my cousin the Prince of Wales? If I might see him, I would speak with him.' 'My lord,' replied Sir Denis de Morbecque, 'he is not here. But surrender to me and I will take you

* The clause preceeding the asterisk is omitted by both Berners and Johnes. Did they resent the implication that the English in general spoke bad French?

to him.' 'Who are you?' asked the king. 'My lord, I am Denis de Morbecque, a knight from Artois, but I serve the King of England because I was banished from the kingdom of France and have forfeited all my possessions there.'

Then the King of France replied, or must have replied according to what I have since been told: 'Then I surrender to you,' and he gave him his right glove. The knight took it with great joy. All round the king there was a great throng and much jostling, for everyone was trying to claim: 'I have taken him, I have taken him', and neither the king nor his youngest son Philippe could move a step. But now let us leave the throng around the King of France and tell something of the Prince of Wales and the end of the battle.

¶ The Prince of Wales, a most brave and courageous man, who with his helmet on his head was as fierce and cruel as a lion, had taken great delight that day in fighting and pursuing his enemies, so that by the end of the battle he was very hot and tired. Sir John Chandos, who had remained close to him all the time therefore said to him: 'My lord, it is good that you should halt here, and place your banner high above this bush. Then your men, who are widely scattered, will rally to it, for God be praised the day is yours. I can no longer see any banners or pennons of the French, nor any order of battle that could be re-formed. Therefore rest a little, for I see you are much heated.'

The prince consented to the suggestion of Sir John Chandos, and caused his banner to be placed on a high bush to rally all his troops, ordered his trumpets to be sounded, and removed his helmet. Very soon the knights of his bodyguard and of his chamber had prepared and pitched a small pavilion, scarlet in colour. When the prince had entered into it they brought drink to him and to the knights who were with him. These kept increasing in number as they returned from pursuing the enemy. There and all around they halted, and busied themselves with their prisoners.

As soon as the two marshals, the Earl of Warwick and the Earl of Suffolk, had returned the prince asked them if they had any news of the King of France. They replied: 'Nothing definite, my lord. We believe that he is dead or captured, for he has certainly not left the field.' Then the prince, with great urgency, said to the Earl of Warwick and Lord Reginald of Cobham: 'Go and ride far enough out to give me exact news on your return.'

The two lords mounted their horses once more and left the prince. They went to the top of a small hill to survey the land around them, and saw a great crowd of men-at-arms approaching very slowly on foot. With them was the King of France, in great peril because the English and the Gascons had taken possession of him from Sir Denis de Morbecque, who was now some distance away. The strongest were saying: 'I have taken him, I have taken him'; the king, however, anxious to avoid danger from this keen rivalry to capture him, said: 'Gentlemen, gentlemen, lead me courteously to my cousin the prince, and my son with me. Do not quarrel among yourselves over my capture, for I am a great enough lord to make each one of you rich.'

These words and others that the king spoke to them quietened them a little, but their disputes were nevertheless renewed; not a step forward did they take without further quarrels arising. The two lords therefore, when from their hill they saw this crowd of jostling men-at-arms, decided to go towards them, and setting spurs to their horses came up to them and asked: 'What is the matter? What is the matter?' They were told: 'The King of France has been captured, and there are a dozen knights and squires disputing who has taken him.'

Then the two barons, without further words, rode their horses through the press and made everyone stand back, ordering them all, in the name of the prince and on pain of death, to stay where they were and not to approach unless commanded or required to do so. Then all withdrew well behind the king and the two barons, for they dared not disobey the order. The barons dismounted and bowed low to the king, who was overjoyed at their arrival, for they delivered him from great danger.

¶ As soon as the Earl of Warwick and Lord Reginald of Cobham had left the prince, as is above narrated, the prince asked the knights around him: 'Is there anyone who knows aught of Lord James Audley?' 'Yes sir,' replied some knights who were present and who had recently seen him, 'he is grievously wounded and lying on a litter not far from here.' 'By my troth,' said the prince, 'I am grieved to hear of his wounds, and I would gladly see him. Find out, I pray you, whether he can bear being carried here, for if he cannot I will go and see him.'

Then two knights left the prince and came to where Lord James Audley lay, telling him what the prince had asked of them and how much he wished to see him. 'A thousand thanks to my lord the prince,' said Lord James, 'that he is pleased to remember so insignificant a knight as myself.' Then he called eight of his attendants, and had himself carried to where the prince was.

When the Prince of Wales saw Lord James he bent low over him and bade him welcome, receiving him gently and gladly, saying: 'My Lord James, I am much bound to honour you, for by your brave and valiant conduct you have today poured grace and fame on us all, and our judgement holds you to be the noblest knight.' 'My lord,' replied Lord James, 'I would that it were so, though you may say what you please. If today I have offered myself in the forefront of your service to accomplish a vow which I had made, that should be accounted to me for folly rather than prowess.'

Then the prince spoke in reply: 'Lord James, I and all my men consider that you have been the most valiant of our knights this day. In order to increase your renown and to enable you to equip yourself better for the pursuit of arms, I retain your service for ever in my personal suite, with a payment of five hundred marks a year, which I will assign to you from my heritage in England.' 'My lord,' replied Lord James Audley, 'may God grant I shall deserve the great favours you bestow on me.'

With these words he took leave of the prince, for he was very weak, and his attendants carried him back to his tent. He could not have been far off when the Earl of Warwick and Lord Reginald of Cobham came into the prince's pavilion and presented to him the King of France. The prince accepted him as a great and noble gift, bowing low to the king, whom he received handsomely and with dignity as was natural to him. He had wine and spices brought, and himself gave them to the king as a token of deep affection.

¶ Thus was this battle decided in the plains of Maupertuis, two leagues from the city of Poitiers, on the 19th of September in the year of Our Lord 1356. It began about the hour of prime and was all over by nones, but by then the English who had gone in pursuit of the enemy had not all returned, and for this reason the prince had had his banner raised on a bush to rally all his men. Yet it was after the hour of vespers before they were all back from the chase.

It was then reported that all the flower of French knighthood had died, by which the great land of France was seriously weakened and cast into great sorrow and wretchedness, as you will hear later. With the king and his young son the Lord Philippe there were taken seventeen counts, apart from barons, knights and squires; the dead numbered between 5,700 and 6,000, of all ranks. When the English had all or nearly all returned from the pursuit and gathered on the field where the prince was awaiting them they found that they had twice as many prisoners as their own number. They therefore consulted among themselves whether, in view of the large body of prisoners, they should ransom most of them on the spot, and this they decided to do.

The knights and squires who were prisoners found the English and the Gascons most courteous. Great numbers of them were ransomed that day, or released on their honour to return to Bordeaux on the Gironde the following Christmas in order to pay their ransoms. When all the English had returned they retired to their own camps, close to where the battle had been fought; some took off their armour, and then disarmed their prisoners, each honouring his own as much as he could. For the prisoners a man had taken in battle were his own, to ransom or release as he chose.

It can well be imagined that all those who were with the Prince of Wales in this victorious battle became rich in honour and possessions, as much by the ransoms of their prisoners as by the gold and silver, plate and rich jewels, and chests stuffed full of heavily ornamented belts and fine mantles. Of armour, jambes and basinets they took no notice, for the French had come there so plentifully equipped as if they had thought the day would be theirs. Now we shall turn to Lord James Audley, and tell what he did with the five hundred silver marks that the Prince of Wales gave him.

¶ When Lord James Audley had thanked the prince sincerely for his gift, and had been carried back to his tent on the litter, he had scarcely rested before he sent for Sir Peter Audley his brother, Sir Barthélemy de Burghersh, Sir Stephen Gonsenton, Lord Willoughby and Lord Ralph Ferrers, who were all his blood relations. As soon as they had come into his presence he endeavoured to speak as best he could, for he was very weak from the wounds he had received. He called forward the four esquires who had been his personal bodyguard that day, and spoke then to the knights who were present: 'Gentlemen, my lord the prince has been pleased to give five hundred marks a year to me and my heirs, for which gift I have done him a small service, as much as my bodily strength would allow. Here you see four squires* who have always served me loyally; and in parti-

* These four squires were Cheshire men, Delves of Doddington, Foulshurst of Crewe, Hawkstone of Wrinehill and Dutton of Dutton. Lord Audley's title was Lord Audley of Newhall by Wrenbury in Cheshire. Sir Hugh Calveley and Sir Robert Knollys were from the same county.

cular, what honour I have earned today is due to their enterprise and boldness. Because of this, in the presence of you who are of my blood, I now wish to reward the great and welcome services they have done me. It is my intention to give and bequeath to them the gift of five hundred marks which my lord the prince has granted to me, in the same form and manner as he has granted it. I disinherit myself of this gift and transfer the inheritance to them, freely and irrevocably.'

Then the knights who were present, looking at each other, said: 'It is a very worthy deed for Lord James to make this gift.' And together they added: 'By God's grace, so be it. We will bear witness to this whenever need shall arise.' Then they forthwith left him, some going to join the prince, who was to give a supper to the King of France and his son, with most of the counts and barons who had been taken prisoner; their own provisions were to be used, for the French had brought great stores with them which had fallen into the hands of the English and the Gascons, many of whom had not tasted bread for the past three days.

¶ When the evening had come the Prince of Wales gave a supper in his pavilion* to the King of France, Lord Philippe his son, Seigneur Jacques de Bourbon and the greater part of the counts and barons who had been taken prisoner. At an upper table, sumptuously laid, the prince placed King John, Seigneur Jacques de Bourbon, Seigneur Jean d'Artois, the Comte de Tancarville, the Comte d'Étampes, the Comte de Dammartin, the Comte de Joinville, and Baron Parthenay; all the others, barons and knights, he placed at the other tables.

Throughout the evening the prince served at the king's table, and at the others, with great humility. Nor, in spite of the king's entreaties, would he consent to sit with him at table, saying that he was not yet worthy to sit at the table of so great a prince and valiant a man as the king had shown himself to be that day. And kneeling in front of the king he said: 'My dear lord, do not, I pray you, be downcast because God has not granted your wishes today. For my father will surely show you all the honour and friendship he can, and will make such a reasonable settlement that you and he will remain good friends for ever. Indeed, it seems to me that you have great cause to rejoice that the day did not turn out to be yours, for you have this day won a high name for valour, above all those who fought on your side.

* A register in the *Hôtel de ville* in Poitiers says that the supper was offered in the Château de Savigny-L'Evesquault, which belonged to the Bishop of Poitiers.

Know, beloved sire, that I am not mocking when I say this, for all those of my men who have seen the whole battle are fully in agreement with me, and award you the prize and the crown, if you will consent to wear it.'

At this there was a general murmur of assent, and both French and English said how nobly and pertinently the prince had spoken. For this they esteemed him highly and all said that in him they had a worthy lord, and would continue to have if he could live long in such fortune.

the black prince returns to bordeaux

¶ When they had supped and held such festivity as became their position, all returned to their tents with their prisoners in order to sleep. That night many prisoners, both knights and squires, paid over the sums required by their captors, who allowed them to settle their ransoms with more courtesy than had ever before been shown, putting no more constraint upon them than to ask on their honour how much they could pay without too much burden, and readily accepting what they said. They let it be widely known that they would not require so severe a ransom from knight or squire that he would not have enough left for his needs or be unable to follow his lord according to his condition and engage in expeditions to his honour and advancement.

The custom of the Germans in courtesy is quite otherwise, for they hold no pity or mercy towards noble knights if they fall into their hands as prisoners, but demand the last farthing and more in ransom, and put them in chains, irons and fetters, in the narrowest cells they have, in order to extort a greater ransom.

Next morning when these lords had heard mass, and eaten and drunk, the servants packed and loaded their possessions and prepared their baggage train. Then they left the camp and rode towards the city of Poitiers.

On the Monday night after the battle Seigneur Mathieu de Roye entered the city of Poitiers with a hundred lance. He had not been at the battle, but in the field near Chauvigny had met the Duke of Normandy, who was returning to France, as has been related, and who told him to make for Poitiers with his men and guard that city until he should receive further orders. De Roye had therefore entered Poitiers, and knowing the English to be so close had all that night superintended the watch on the gates, towers and battlements of the town, and in the morning had distributed arms to all sorts and conditions of men and posted them in defence of the town.

The English, however, passed by without ever approaching the city, for they were so laden with gold and silver and jewels and with prisoners of note that they had neither the time nor the intention to attack any fortress on their route. They thought it was a great achievement if they could bring the King of France and all their other captives to Bordeaux in safety. They therefore travelled by short marches, being unable to advance fast because of their heavily laden horses and their great train of baggage; they covered no more than four or five leagues each day, and pitched camp at a late hour. They rode together in a close body, except only for the Earls of Warwick and Suffolk, who rode ahead with five hundred men-at-arms, to survey the country and open a route. But they encountered no resistance anywhere, for the whole country was so scared by the great disaster of Poitiers and the slaughter or capture of the nobles of France and the taking of their king that no one made any attempt to engage the English in action, preferring quietly to guard their fortresses.

During this journey it came to the ears of the Prince of Wales how Lord James Audley had made over to his four squires the pension of five hundred marks which he had given to him. He was much amazed at this, and as soon as they were encamped he sent for him. When Lord James heard he was summoned to the prince he had a good idea why, and asked to be taken to him on his litter, for he could neither walk nor ride. He immediately greeted the prince, who received him with great courtesy and said, 'Lord James, it has been brought to our knowledge that the pension which we* authorized and granted to you when you left our presence and returned to your camp has been given and made over by you to four squires; we would therefore gladly know why you did this and whether our gift was not agreeable to you.'

'My lord,' replied the knight, 'indeed it was mightily agreeable, and I will tell you the reasons which prompted my act. These four squires who are with me here have long served me well and loyally

* Here the French uses *nous* and this has been kept in translation: the prince is obviously 'being official'. He uses *je* in his reply to Audley's words, and had used *je* when speaking to the King of France. Berners follows the French, but Johnes ignores this subtlety.

in many moments of dire need, and yet till the day when I made the gift I had never in any way rewarded their services. And if they had never in their lives served me elsewhere than in the battle of Poitiers I yet owe them as much and more. For, dear sire, I am but one man and have but the strength of one, yet with their support I was able to accomplish the vow I had long made, and with their valiant help I was declared chief among the assailants. If they had not been there I should have been slain in the fray. When I remembered the kindness and love they had shown me, I should have been lacking in courtesy and consideration if I had not rewarded them. For I give thanks to God, sire, that I have always had enough for my needs and shall have to my life's end, so that I never have had nor ever shall have pecuniary worries. If in this, my lord, I have transgressed your desire, I beg you to pardon me and to rest assured that you will receive as devoted service as in the past from myself and the squires to whom I made the gift.'

The prince weighed the words that the knight had spoken, and thought them both honourable and reasonable; then he said: 'Lord James, I shall not blame you for this thing that you have done, but rather am grateful to you for it. For the devotion of these squires and because you speak so highly of them, I confirm your gift to them, and make to you a grant of six hundred marks, on the same terms and conditions as before.' Lord James Audley thanked the prince graciously, and with good reason, and after taking his leave was carried back to his camp. This, as I was informed at the time, is what happened between the prince, Lord James Audley and his four squires.

¶ The Prince of Wales and his army advanced so successfully that they passed through Poitou and Saintonge without harm or danger and reached Blaye, where they crossed the Gironde and so arrived in the fair city of Bordeaux. It would not be possible to tell of all the feastings and celebrations that all the townsfolk and clergy of Bordeaux held in honour of the prince, nor to record how nobly he and the King of France were received. The prince brought the King of France and his son to the Abbey of St Andrew, and there they made their abode, the King of France on one side and the prince on the other. The prince purchased from the barons, knights and squires of England and Gascony the greater part of those earls of the kingdom of France who, as you have heard, had been taken prisoner, and paid for them in ready money. Among the knights and squires of Gascony and other parts there were many meetings to discuss who had captured the King of France.

Sir Denis de Morbecque laid claim to him by right of arms and said he had authentic evidence. Another Gascon squire, Bernard de Truttes, claimed the right was his. Because these two could not agree, the prince decided to withhold judgement until they had returned to England, saying that no declaration would be made before they were in the presence of the king his father. But since the King of France lent his support to Sir Denis de Morbecque rather than to any of the others, the prince gave secret orders that two thousand nobles were to be paid to Sir Denis, to help him to maintain his estate.

Soon after the prince's arrival in Bordeaux the Cardinal of Périgord came there also, having been sent, as we have already seen, on a papal legation, but a fortnight passed before the prince was willing to speak to him, because of the affair of the Castellan d'Amposta's company, who, according to information received by the prince, has been sent by the cardinal to fight in the battle of Poitiers. But Cardinal Talleyrand of Périgord, through the successful intermediary of the lords of Chaumont and Montferrand and the Captal de Buch, his cousins, gave such good reasons to the prince that he was admitted to audience. When he was in his presence he exculpated himself so wisely and effectively that the prince and his council considered he was completely excused and restored to the prince's favour. All his men were released on payment of suitably moderate ransoms, the Castellan d'Amposta himself being set at liberty after he had paid ten thousand francs.

Then the cardinal began to negotiate for the liberation of the king and to suggest various arrangements, but I shall pass briefly over this, because nothing came of it. The Prince of Wales, the Gascons and the English stayed on in the city of Bordeaux, and continued there in great feasting and revelry until Lent [22 February—7 April 1357], spending with reckless prodigality the gold and silver they had got from plunder or ransoms.

I have not so far told you of the joy and revelry there was in England, too, when reports of the battle of Poitiers were confirmed, including the capture of the King of France, and the happy outcome of that day's fighting. The King of England and Philippa his wife were naturally overjoyed; solemn thanksgivings were held in all the churches, so splendidly ordered that it is wonderful to think of them. Certain knights and squires who had been at the battle had returned to England, and they were held in supreme honour. . . .

Henry of Lancaster, now appointed the king's lieutenant in Brittany, had attempted to march with his army to join that of the Black Prince, but had found the bridges over the Loire too well guarded to do so. He had contented himself with the capture of certain fortresses in Normandy, including Domfront and Condé, all of which were shortly afterwards sold to the French for a considerable sum. When he heard of the victory at Poitiers he returned to London with Philippe de Navarre, who had been named King Edward's lieutenant in Normandy, leaving Sir Godfrey Harcourt in charge of the English forces.

¶ . . . All that winter the Prince of Wales and the greater part of the English nobles who had been at the battle of Poitiers remained at Bordeaux on the Gironde, spending their time in revelry and festivities. They were also busy procuring ships and ordering their affairs so that they could conduct the King of France and his son to England, together with most of the barons who were there.

When all the preparations were nearly complete and the time for his departure approached, the prince summoned all the chief barons of Gascony . . . showing them every sign of friendship and giving or promising financial reward, which is just what the Gascons love and desire. Finally he told them that he now wished to leave for England and would take some of them with him; the others he would leave in the Bordelais and in Gascony, to protect the frontiers against the French; to this effect he would hand over to them the cities, towns and castles, recommending them to guard them as if they were their own.

When the Gascons heard that the Prince of Wales, eldest son of the king their master, wished to take out of their power the King of France, whom they had helped him to capture, they were at first unwilling to consent, and said: 'Dear lord, we owe you all obedience and loyal service, and we are glad to grant this to the utmost of our ability, but we do not intend that you should thus remove from us the King of France whom we have laboured to bring to his present condition, for, God be thanked, he is well and in a fortified city, and we have strength and numbers to protect him against the French if they tried to take him from you by force.'

To this the prince replied: 'Dear lords, I grant you that readily. But the lord my father desires to have him and to see him; for the services that you have rendered to him and to me we are deeply grateful, and you will be well rewarded.'

These words, however, could not win the Gascons over to the

prince's intention of taking the King of France away, until Lord Reginald of Cobham and Sir John Chandos, sensing the covetousness of the Gascons, suggested a method: 'My lord, offer them a sum of florins, and you'll see them come round to your demands.' Then the prince offered them sixty thousand florins, but they would not accept. Finally, after much negotiation between one and another, a settlement was made for a hundred thousand francs which the prince had to pay over to the Gascon barons to secure his departure from among them, the sum being handed over in florins before the prince left; he then appointed four barons of Gascony to protect the whole territory until his return.

As soon as this was done the prince set sail [Tuesday, 11 April 1357], with a fine fleet and a large body of men-at-arms and archers; he took with him many Gascons, including the Captal de Buch. The King of France was put in a separate ship by himself, in order that he might be more at ease. In the ships there were quite five hundred men-at-arms and two thousand archers, to be prepared for any dangers or encounters at sea. For they had been informed before leaving Bordeaux that the Three Estates, by whom the kingdom of France was governed, had raised two large armies of mercenaries in Normandy and at Le Crotoy in Picardy to meet the English and take the King of France from them, but they never saw any trace of these forces. They spent eleven days and eleven nights at sea, and on the twelfth day they arrived in the harbour at Sandwich.* Here all the lords disembarked, and took lodging in the town of Sandwich and the surrounding villages, staying there two days to refresh themselves and their horses. On the third day they departed and came to Saint Thomas of Canterbury.

When news reached the King and Queen of England that their son the prince had arrived and had brought with him the King of France, they were overjoyed, which was very understandable. They ordered the citizens of London to make suitable preparations to receive the King of France with all the honour that was due to him. In obedience to this order, the men of the city of London put on the livery of their companies and gave orders for the king to be welcomed at all points; the guilds similarly dressed themselves in their different uniforms.

When the King of France and the prince and their followers came to the shrine of Saint Thomas of Canterbury they made offerings and

* According to the English chroniclers he arrived at Plymouth (not Sandwich), on the 4th of May. They entered London on the 24th of May.

rested for a day. The next day they rode to Rochester and spent the night there. On the third day they reached Dartford, and on the fourth London, where they were received with much honour, as indeed they had been in every town through which they passed. As they rode through London the King of France was mounted on a white charger, well trained and richly caparisoned, with the Prince of Wales on a small black hackney by his side. Thus was he accompanied through all the city of London, as far as the Palace of the Savoy,* which is part of the inheritance of the Dukes of Lancaster. There for a time the King of France made his abode, and there the King and Queen of England came to visit him, receiving him with great ceremony, which they well knew how to do. Many times after that they visited him and consoled him as best they could.

Soon afterwards there came to England by command of Pope Innocent VI the two cardinals beforementioned, Talleyrand, Cardinal of Périgord, and Nicole, Cardinal of Urgel. They began to negotiate for a treaty of peace between the two kings, but in spite of their efforts they could achieve nothing. However, they did secure, by their good offices, a truce between the two kings and their supporters, to last until the feast of Saint John the Baptist in the year thirteen hundred and fifty-nine. Lord Philippe de Navarre and his allies, the Comte de Montfort and the duchy of Brittany were excluded from the truce.† Shortly afterwards the King of France was transferred from the Palace of the Savoy and placed in Windsor Castle with all his household. He was allowed to hunt and to pursue his pleasures as he chose in the neighbourhood of Windsor, as was his son Philippe. All his remaining lords, both earls and barons, remained in London, but could go to see the king as often as they wished, and were trusted on their parole.

* In 1246 Henry III made a gift of land between the Strand and the river to Pierre de Savoie, his wife's uncle, who built a palace there. It was destroyed by fire in Wat Tyler's rebellion of 1381, and restored as a hospital in Henry VII's reign. Now only the rebuilt Savoy Chapel remains.

† This truce was, in fact, arranged on 23 March 1357, before the Black Prince left Bordeaux; it was to last from Easter 1357 to Easter 1359 and not St John Baptist's Day; Philippe de Navarre and the heirs of the Comte de Montfort were expressly included in the truce. That they took no notice of it may have induced Froissart's error.

the death of king jean and the renewal of war

It was England's misfortune that her king showed no powers of statesmanship comparable to his success in arms. The French had suffered a crushing defeat at Poitiers, their king was a captive in England, and the dauphin Charles, as lieutenant of the king, was the tool of bad counsellors, but this situation was not turned to profit by Edward. Both countries were again financially exhausted, and popular discontent became serious. In England it was to come to a head later with Wat Tyler; in France there was an immediate threat of triple rebellion, the various sectors only loosely related.

In the first place the dauphin appeared at 18 too weak a person to rule the country. The merchant representatives in the Estates (the men on whom the brunt of taxation fell) were anxious to remove from office those who were enriching themselves by tax-gathering (as William of Wykeham was to be removed in England in 1371) and to elect a council, on which they as well as the nobles would be represented, to guide (or was it to dictate?) the decisions of the dauphin. Their leader was Étienne Marcel, an ardent and sincere reformer.

Secondly there were the followers of the King of Navarre who felt that he should be regent. Étienne Marcel joined them in a demand for the release of the King of Navarre—perhaps because of the popularity of this ineffectual man—but the demand was refused. While the relations of Charles and his council were growing worse the King of Navarre escaped. In 1358 the Estates imposed on Charles a humiliating reconciliation with his brother-in-law, and Étienne Marcel forced his way into the dauphin's own rooms with a band of armed men, who killed Charles's two chief supporters before his eyes.

Charles reacted by assuming the title of regent and fleeing from Paris. Meanwhile the third threat had been realized—a peasant revolt known as the Jacquerie *(from the name Jacques Bonhomme, applied to any peasant) broke out in May. They had reason enough in the depression that followed the plague, the absence of many nobles (their employers) who had been captured at Poitiers, heavy taxation often irregularly and unjustly gathered, and the widespread ravages of the* routiers *already mentioned. The bands of crudely armed peasants were at first successful in sporadic raids on the nobility; the King of Navarre then added to his popularity by placing himself as their leader, and Étienne Marcel sent them material help. In August, Marcel was killed in a Paris street, and this was the end of the rebellion in Paris. With it the* Jacquerie *faded out, Charles returned to Paris, and the Anglo-Navarrese offensive against him was switched to Normandy.*

Edward had meanwhile been more concerned with the terms of a treaty than with following up his advantage. A first draft was prepared in January 1358 in London, and a succession of meetings were held over the months, the bargaining depending to some extent on the rival fortunes of Navarre and the dauphin. Nothing was concluded, and in October 1359 Edward decided the only way to bring the dauphin to terms was to invade France once more.

He landed at Calais, ravaged the country as far as Reims, threatened Paris and then turned to Beauce. By now winter had brought campaigning to a halt, and Charles had been astute enough to avoid a battle. In the spring of 1360 a treaty was drawn up at Brétigny, near Chartres, and though this last campaign had reduced Edward's bargaining power, he achieved terms that were still a blow to French prestige. This treaty was ratified in person by the two kings at Calais on the 24th of October. The geographical settlement is shown in the accompanying map: the boundaries of English Aquitaine were defined, and in the north Edward was confirmed in possession of Calais, Ponthieu and Guines. Elsewhere he would lay no claim to French territory and evacuate any fortresses held by the English. The French king's ransom was fixed at three million crowns (half a million pounds—eight times the annual revenue of the English crown in times of peace), the king to be released on the payment of the first instalment and important hostages to be held in London until the rest was paid. Then came the significant clauses of renunciation: Edward renounced his claim to the crown, title and arms of France; Jean renounced his right to claim homage for the duchy of Aquitaine and other ceded territories, but these renunciations were not to take effect until after the exchanges of territory had been completed. The renunciations were, in fact, never confirmed, and in spite of Crécy and Poitiers, Edward remained in theory a vassal of the French king in Aquitaine.*

The carrying out of the treaty was beset with difficulties. The payments of the ransom fell behind, many English fighting-men were concerned in the activities of the routiers *and would not accept the truce, King Jean was becoming more interested in a crusade suggested by the pope than in the affairs of his own kingdom, and the Estates were again objecting to the raising of new taxes. Then one of the hostages, the king's second son Louis, Duc d'Anjou, absented himself while on parole. King Jean's honour was stained, and he returned voluntarily to apologize to Edward in London, where he was received with great honour. Three months later he died, on the 8th of April 1364. The*

* It is recorded that Geoffrey Chaucer was taken prisoner by the French during this campaign, and released on payment of a ransom in March 1360.

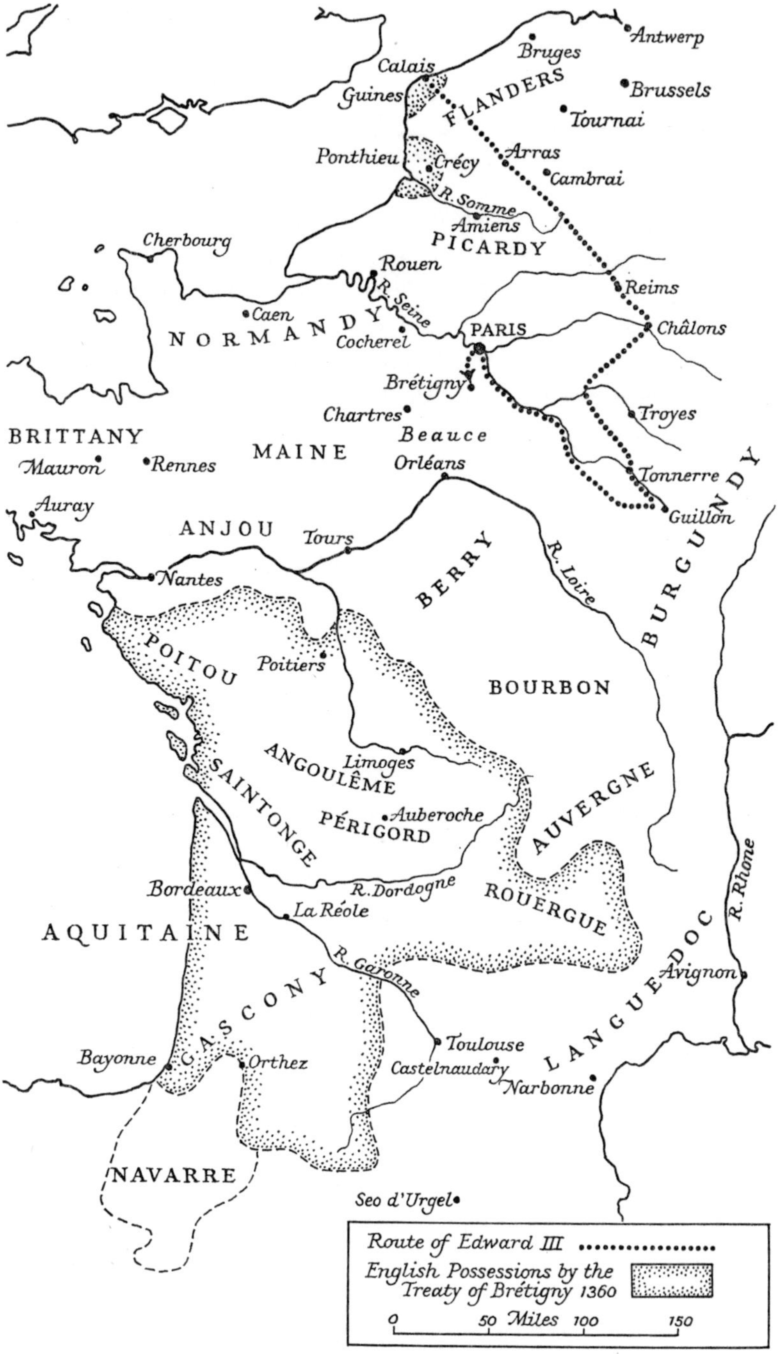
Antwerp
Bruges
Calais
Guines
FLANDERS
Brussels
Tournai
Ponthieu
Arras
Crécy
Cambrai
R. Somme
Amiens
PICARDY
Cherbourg
Rouen
R. Seine
Reims
Caen
NORMANDY
PARIS
Châlons
Cocherel
Brétigny
Troyes
Chartres
Beauce
BRITTANY
MAINE
Mauron
Rennes
Orléans
Tonnerre
Guillon
Auray
ANJOU
Tours
BERRY
R. Loire
BURGUNDY
Nantes
POITOU
Poitiers
BOURBON
ANGOULÊME
Limoges
AUVERGNE
SAINTONGE
PÉRIGORD
Auberoche
R. Rhone
Bordeaux
R. Dordogne
ROUERGUE
La Réole
AQUITAINE
LANGUEDOC
R. Garonne
Avignon
GASCONY
Toulouse
Bayonne
Orthez
Castelnaudary
Narbonne
NAVARRE
Seo d'Urgel
Route of Edward III
English Possessions by the Treaty of Brétigny 1360
0 50 Miles 100 150

FRANCE: THE TREATY OF CALAIS 1360

dauphin was now King Charles V of France, to be known in history as Charles le Sage.

During the hard years of the regency and those that followed the Treaty of 1360 he had unexpectedly grown in stature and on his accession he started methodically to improve the government and the laws of his kingdom. He was clever, cultured, a lover of the arts; he was also lacking in physical strength and in a taste for warfare, and, alone of French kings until Louis XVI, he never commanded his armies in the field. Fortunately he had in Bertrand du Guesclin a military leader who achieved constant successes and acquired a renown that was scarcely deserved, but which itself put heart into his followers.

His reign opened with a notable success against the King of Navarre, who was once again in revolt, this time because he had been turned aside in his claim to the duchy of Burgundy. Du Guesclin had been placed in charge of an army that was to oppose the combined forces of Navarre and the Captal de Buch, which constituted a serious threat to Paris. Three days before Charles's coronation at Reims the French under du Guesclin won a resounding victory at Cocherel (16 May 1364); by the resulting treaty the threat of Navarre was removed. In September of the same year, however, du Guesclin was taken prisoner at the battle of Auray in Brittany; here Sir John Chandos defeated and killed Charles de Blois, leaving Jean de Montfort undisputed in the title of Duke of Brittany, though by the Treaty of Guérande in 1365 he was to pay homage to Charles for his duchy.

In Flanders there was a different situation, though here, too, Charles had secured some advantage. The new count, Louis de Mâle, felt it wise to draw nearer to England because of the importance of the cloth trade. In 1363 Edward set up a wool staple in Calais, whence the wool was taken to Bruges; he further proposed a marriage between Marguerite, Louis's only heir, and one of his own sons, but the pope prevented this on the grounds of consanguinity, though he later agreed to her marriage to the Duke of Burgundy, brother to Charles V, and this took place in 1369. Flanders, it seemed, would now come under French influence, though Louis repeatedly showed his independence, and no one at this stage could foresee the future rise of the Burgundian faction.

The free companies of routiers *were still active; their members were of many countries and their leaders obscure adventurers, often of some military skill, and the various bands worked in isolation except in 1361, when they had converged on Avignon and held the pope to ransom. They owed no higher loyalty than to their leader, and they were popularly, and often unjustly, spoken of as 'les Anglais'. After the various truces of 1365 their numbers and their activities were increased. Edward was often asked to stop their exploits, and there are records showing he attempted to do so. But booty was their pay and he had no hold over them, though the Black Prince successfully forbade them to enter Aquitaine, so that they operated chiefly in Languedoc, Auvergne and Burgundy. The pope even tried to enlist them for a crusade.*

The Spanish problems provided a means of using them. The conflict there was marginal to the main issues of the war and can be dealt with briefly. Don Pedro the Cruel, King of Castille, had made himself violently unpopular and his crown was claimed by his bastard brother Henry of Trastamara. The claim received French support in the form of an expeditionary force, made up mostly of members of the free companies (many, in fact, English), under the leadership of du Guesclin (ransomed after his recent capture). Pedro appealed to the Black Prince, who secured once more the assistance of Charles the Bad of Navarre, and du Guesclin was defeated and captured at the battle of Nájera in 1367, though it was not long before his ransom was paid.

The events in Spain were considered to have nothing to do with the treaty of 1360, the fulfilment of which was still delayed. By 1367 Charles had paid little more than half the late king's ransom, and geographical commissions were still at work defining the ceded territories. The repercussions in Aquitaine were more serious. There the Black Prince found himself embarrassed by the presence of routiers *returned from Spain and by the cost of the Spanish campaign to which Pedro had not contributed the promised sums. His authority was sufficient to dismiss the former; in the raising of money he found greater difficulty. In January 1368 the Estates of Aquitaine granted him the proceeds of a hearth-tax for five years. Some of the vassals in the marginal areas protested; by careful nursing of their grievances Charles had by December persuaded over eight hundred nobles and towns to protest to him as their king, notably the Seigneur d'Albret, who had that year married King Charles's sister-in-law.*

On 15 January 1369 Charles sent a letter summoning the Black Prince to Paris to explain himself. Froissart records his reply: 'We shall gladly go to Paris on the day appointed, since it is commanded by the King of France, but it will be with our helmet on our head and sixty thousand men at our side.' The importance of the 'exchanges of renunciation' now becomes clear. In November of the following year Edward III abolished 'all the hearth-taxes unjustly levied by his son' and granted an amnesty to any who had complained to the French king.

In June 1369 Charles declared war on the Black Prince; in November he declared Aquitaine confiscated from its English overlord—a return to the situation at the start of the war. After some years in which to reorganize his tax-gathering, Charles was more ready than any French king for some time; he had used his resources to encourage French archers and to improve the fortifications of his chief strongholds.

An English raid in Picardy and Normandy under John of Lancaster proved unsuccessful, while the Duc d'Anjou threatened the frontiers of Aquitaine, and was joined by du Guesclin in an attack on Limoges.

¶ When Sir Bertrand du Guesclin arrived at the siege of Limoges there was great rejoicing among the French, and the news was welcomed in both the city and the whole neighbourhood. He immediately began to concern himself with the negotiations for a treaty which had been opened between the Bishop of Limoges, the men of that city and the Duc de Berry, and followed them through with such care and wisdom that the bishop and citizens of Limoges turned to the side of the French. Then the Duc de Berry, the Duc de Bourbon, Guy de Blois and other French lords entered the city with great rejoicing and received its homage, staying there three days to rest.

Within the city the lords above named held council [21–24 August 1370] and decided that they would conclude their campaign for that season, as the Duc d'Anjou had done, and withdraw to their lands to protect their towns and castles against Sir Robert Knollys, who was continuing his campaign in France; they had done very well by taking a city of such importance as Limoges. This decision was strictly carried out. Then the lords departed by their various ways, and Sir Bertrand remained in Limousin with two hundred lance, and took up quarters in the castle of the Seigneur de Melval, who had joined the French.

When the Duc de Berry left Limoges he gave orders, at the request of the bishop, that Jean de Villemur, Hugues de la Roche and Roger de Beaufort should remain in the city with a hundred men-at-arms; then he withdrew to Berry and the Duc de Bourbon to Bourbonnais; the lords from more distant provinces retired to their own lands.

¶ When news reached the Prince of Wales that the city of Limoges had turned to the French side and that the bishop, who was godfather to one of his children and in whom he had in the past placed great trust, had been present at all the negotiations and helped in the surrender, he was very angry, and thought much less well of ecclesiastics, in whom he had previously had great faith. He therefore swore by his father's soul that he would make the men of Limoges pay dearly for this outrage, and that he would undertake no other business until he had recaptured the city and taken vengeance upon it as he chose for this treachery. When most of his forces were assembled they were found to number twelve hundred lance, both knights and squires, a thousand archers and three thousand foot-soldiers. They then left Cognac, the prince being accompanied by his two brothers the Duke of Lancaster and the Earl of Cambridge, and the Earl of Pembroke who called himself their brother.* Sir Thomas Felton and the Captal de Buch remained in Bergerac, there to guard the frontiers against the French and the free companies who were ranging about the country . . .

Then all these armed men set off in great array to start their campaign, and all the country began to tremble before them. From about this time the prince was unable to ride,† and had himself carried in a litter in great state. They took the road through Limousin to Limoges, and by hard riding arrived before that city, to which they immediately laid siege [14 September 1370], the prince swearing he would not leave until he had the place reduced to his will. The bishop and the citizens knew well they had failed in their duty and given the prince great cause for anger; for this they repented sincerely, but could do nothing to put things right, for they were no longer masters of their own city. Jean de Villemur, Hugues de la Roche and Roger de Beaufort, who were guardians and captains of the town, comforted the frightened townsmen by saying: 'Gentlemen, have no fear, we are strong and numerous enough to hold the city against the might of the prince's army. He cannot take us by assault, for we are well provided with artillery.'

Indeed, when the prince and his marshals had made a careful reconnaissance of the circuit of defences around Limoges and knew the number of knights that were within, they declared they could never take it by assault. Thereupon they adopted another plan, and whenever he went out to reconnoitre the prince took with him a large body of miners. These men were soon set to work, and began to mine with great vigour. The knights who were inside the city immediately realized that they were being mined and began to dig in the direction of the mine in order to destroy its effect. . . .

¶ While the Prince of Wales and his two brothers and their army were encamped before the city of Limoges, Sir Bertrand du Guesclin, with a company of some two hundred lance, was riding towards one of the farther parts of Limousin, not daring to camp in the fields for fear of meeting the English, but lodging in the fortresses of Louis de

* John Hastings, Earl of Pembroke, had married Margaret, tenth child of Edward III and the Black Prince's youngest sister. She did not long survive her marriage.

† He suffered from dropsy.

Melval, Raymond de Mareuil and of others who had espoused the French cause. Every day they rode through the land and spared no effort to capture towns and fortresses. The prince was well aware of this, and complaints reached him daily, but he did not now wish to interrupt the siege, for the success of this affair was very dear to his heart.

Sir Bertrand then entered the viscounty of Limoges, a dependency of Jean de Montfort, Duc de Bretagne, and not of the English, and began to attack it in the name of the widow of Charles de Blois, to whom the territory had formerly belonged.* Here he made a successful and unimpeded campaign—for the Duc de Bretagne had never anticipated that Sir Bertrand would make war on him—and arrived before Saint-Yrieix, where he made a heavy assault on the town. There were in Saint-Yrieix no knights capable of conducting its defence; the townsfolk were so frightened when they learned of Bertrand du Guesclin's approach, and even more when a heavy siege was laid to the town, strong though it was, that all immediately surrendered, and placed themselves under obedience to the Duchesse de Bretagne, in whose name the war was being conducted. The Bretons established a large garrison in Saint-Yrieix, repairing and considerably strengthening its fortifications, so that later it was a centre of much trouble to the district and served as a base for the taking of several other towns and castles in the viscounty of Limoges.

¶ For about a month,† not longer, the Prince of Wales remained before the city of Limoges, without attacking or skirmishing, but concerned only with the progress of the miners. The knights and townsmen within the citadel, well aware that the walls were being mined, started countermining in order to reach and kill the English, but their work was unsuccessful. When the prince's miners, who were underpropping their work as fast as they advanced, had reached the end of their task, they said to the prince: 'My lord, whenever you please, we will cause a large section of the walls to fall into the ditch, so that you can enter the town at your leisure and without danger.' The prince was very pleased at these words and said: 'Let the results

* In 1369 Jeanne de Penthièvre, Vicomtesse de Limoges, had donated the viscounty to Charles V, in name only, so that he could fight for its return to France. A counter-donation exists in which Charles V had declared the gift invalid and restored it to Jeanne and her heirs. Charles de Blois, nephew of Philippe VI, was killed in 1364 at the battle of Auray.

† In fact, the siege lasted only six days, from 14 to 19 September 1370.

of your work be seen tomorrow morning at prime.' The next day, when they knew the moment had come, they set fire to the mine, || so as to burn the props on which it was supported, || and, as the prince had ordered, felled a great portion of the wall which filled the ditch, where it collapsed. The English watched this with great pleasure, as they waited ready armed and drawn up in order for the entry into the town.

Those on foot were easily able to enter, and they ran to the gate, which they knocked down by cutting the beam, destroying the wickets at the same time. All this was done so quickly that the inhabitants of the town could take no steps to prevent it. Then the prince, the Duke of Lancaster, the Earl of Cambridge, the Earl of Pembroke and Sir Guichard d'Angle and all the others, with their men entered the city at the same time as the pillagers on foot, who were all ready to damage property and to run through the town killing men, women and children according to orders they had received. Here was a most pitiful business; for men, women and children would throw themselves on their knees before the prince crying, 'Mercy, noble lord, mercy.' But he was so incensed with anger that he would not listen, either to man or to woman, but put every one of them to the sword as soon as they were encountered, without distinction of sex and guiltless as they were. I do not know how they could be so pitiless towards poor folk who were in no position to perform acts of treason; but these people indeed paid more dearly than the great lords who had acted treasonably.

There can be no one so hard-hearted who was that day at Limoges and thought of God, who would not weep for the great evil that was done, for more than three thousand persons—men, women and children—were slain or beheaded there that day. May God receive their souls, for they were indeed martyrs. As they entered the city a troop of English went to the bishop's palace, and finding him there, seized him and carried him off without ceremony to the prince, who looked fiercely on him, only deigning to say that his head should be cut off, by the faith that he owed to God and Saint George. Then he ordered him out of his sight.*

* This bishop was Jean de Cros de Calmefort, cousin of the Cardinal de Beaufort who was elected pope as Gregory XI that same year, an election which may be considered as a sort of protest throughout Christendom at the prince's barbarous behaviour at Limoges. The bishop's life was spared, but a heavy ransom exacted; he was made a cardinal by his cousin in 1371. Roger de Beaufort, mentioned in the next paragraph, was the brother of the cardinal and brother-in-law of Hugues de la Roche.

Sir Jean de Villemur, Sir Hugues de la Roche and Roger de Beaufort, who were in military command of the city, when they saw the miserable calamity that was coming upon them and their people, said: 'Our death is certain: let us sell our lives dearly, as knights should.' Then Sir Jean de Villemur said to Roger de Beaufort: 'Roger, you must be knighted,' to which Roger replied: 'I am not valiant enough to be a knight, but I thank you much for having suggested it.' No more was said, for they had no time to speak at length, but gathering in one spot in front of an old wall, Sir Jean de Villemur and Sir Hugues de la Roche unfurled their banners and they all stationed themselves in good order; they and their men were about eighty in number. On seeing the enemy thus drawn up, the Duke of Lancaster, the Earl of Cambridge and their men drew rein, dismounted and attacked the enemy fiercely. Naturally so small a band of soldiers could not long withstand the English; their ranks were broken and they were all killed or captured.

The Duke of Lancaster was for long engaged in single combat with Sir Jean de Villemur, who was a brave knight, strong and very well built, while the Earl of Cambridge was engaged with Sir Hugues de la Roche, and the Earl of Pembroke with Roger de Beaufort. These three Frenchmen performed many fine deeds of arms against their three adversaries, and the others did not interfere; it would have been fatal for them if they had left their wall. Just at this moment the prince came that way in his carriage, and watched the fighting with pleasure, greatly softening his anger at what he saw. They fought until the three Frenchmen, with common consent, yielded their swords, saying: 'My lords, we are yours, you have conquered us. Do with us according to the laws of combat.' 'By God, Sir John,' said the Duke of Lancaster 'we would not do otherwise, and we shall hold you as our prisoners.' Thus were these three taken, as I have since been informed.

¶ Things did not end there, for Limoges was mercilessly pillaged and looted, and the whole city burnt and destroyed. Then the English departed with their booty and their prisoners and withdrew to Cognac, where the princess had remained. There the prince dismissed all his men-at-arms, taking on nothing further for that season, because he no longer felt in good enough health to do so. Moreover, he was getting worse each day, and this greatly disturbed his brothers and his men.

Now let me tell of the fate of the Bishop of Limoges, who was in great danger of losing his life. The Duke of Lancaster asked to have him from the prince, who consented and handed him over for the duke to do what he would with him. The bishop had friends in the right place, and information was sent to Pope Urban, who had recently returned from Rome to Avignon; this was fortunate for the bishop, because otherwise his life would not have been spared. The pope sent such reasonable and gently worded entreaties to the Duke of Lancaster that the duke could not refuse them, and sent his prisoner to the pope, who was very grateful.

du guesclin made constable

¶ When the King of France was informed of the recapture and destruction of Limoges, and of how the prince and his men had left it completely devastated, he was very angry and felt great pity for the inhabitants who had suffered such losses and distress. It was at this time widely held in France, both in the council of the nobles and prelates and in the general opinion of the whole kingdom, that the French needed a new military commander as constable, since Sir Moreau de Fiennes wished to resign from the office, having proved himself a valiant man of honour, skilful in arms and beloved of all his knights and squires. Therefore, after due deliberation and by common consent, they unanimously elected Sir Bertrand du Guesclin to that office if he would accept it, as being the most valiant, the strongest and wisest to undertake its duties, as well as the most successful in his undertakings. The king therefore wrote letters which he sent to him, asking him to come and speak with him in Paris. The messengers found him in the viscounty of Limoges, where he was capturing castles and strongholds and making them yield in the name of Madame de Bretagne, the widow of Lord Charles de Blois; he had just recently captured the town known as Brantôme, whose people had surrendered to him, and he was then riding towards another.

When the King of France's messengers reached him he received them joyfully and as suited their position, according to his traditional hospitality. They handed over the king's letters and delivered their message clearly and briefly. When Sir Bertrand found that he was given so special a summons he did not seek any excuses for attending on the King of France in order to learn what he wanted. He therefore left as soon as he could and sent the greater part of his men to garrison the towns he had captured, appointing Sir Olivier de Mauny his nephew as their responsible commander. Then by long riding each day he reached the city of Paris, where he found the king and a great number of lords of the council who welcomed him with joy and pomp. There the king told him personally how he had been selected for the position of Constable of France. Sir Bertrand excused himself very humbly, saying he was not worthy of the honour, that he was a poor knight and a mere novice in arms by comparison with the noble and valiant lords of France, and that he had simply been aided a little by good fortune. To this the king replied that his excuses were of no weight, that he must accept the office because it had been thus decided and ordained by the whole council of France, a decision which he could not disobey.

Then Sir Bertrand offered other excuses: 'Dear lord and noble king, I neither wish, nor can, nor dare to go against your good pleasure, but it is very true that I am a poor man of low birth; the office of constable is so great and noble a charge that he who would acquit himself well of its duties should be able to command, and to get the best out of, the great rather than the humble. There are my lords your brothers, your nephews and your cousins, who have their own commands over armies and expeditions, and how shall I dare to give orders to them? And indeed, my lord, jealousy is so rife that I have every cause to fear it. I therefore pray you from my heart to relieve me of this appointment and to give it to another who will be more ready to undertake it and will perform it better.' Then the king replied and said: 'Sir Bertrand, Sir Bertrand, that line of excuse carries no weight either, for I have neither brother nor nephew, earl nor baron, in the whole of my kingdom who will not be ready to obey you, and if any were of a different mind I should be so angry that he would have cause to feel my wrath. I therefore pray that you will accept the office with a good will.' Sir Bertrand knew then that any excuses he might offer would be of no avail and finally agreed to the king's order, though it was much against his will. There was great rejoicing when Sir Bertrand was invested with the office of Constable of France [2 October 1370], and to show the honour due to him the king set him beside him at his own table and showed him every possible sign of affection. He gave him that day, along with his office, an income of more than four thousand francs, as an inheritance for him and his heirs.

¶ Immediately after Sir Bertrand had been invested he told the king he wished to make an expedition against the enemy forces under Sir Robert Knollys, who was at that time on the borders of Anjou and Maine. The king was pleased at this, and said: 'Do what you wish, and take whatever men-at-arms you need; they will all obey you.' Then the constable made his preparations and equipped an expedition of armed men, and left the king in order to ride towards Maine, taking with him Seigneur Olivier de Clisson. When he arrived at the city of Le Mans the constable there set up his garrison, with Lord de Clisson in another town close by;* there were some five hundred lances. Sir Robert Knollys and his men were still in that part of the country, but there was dissension among them, for there was an English knight by the name of Sir John of Menstreworth, who was never of the same mind as the others, but opposed their plans whenever he could and had been against the whole expedition, saying they were wasting their time and their energy in vain, with little achievement to show for it.

This knight, who commanded a considerable force of armed men, then left the others. Sir Robert Knollys and Sir Alan Buxhill continued on their way and camped close to the city of Le Mans. Sir Thomas Grantson, Sir Gilbert Giffard, Sir Geoffrey Worsley and Sir William Neville were quartered a day's march in the rear. When Sir Robert Knollys and Sir Alan learned that the Constable of France and Olivier de Clisson had arrived in the area they were very pleased and said: 'It would be as well to bring our various forces together so that we can retain our advantage in this region. It can only be that Sir Bertrand in fulfilment of his new office has come to have a look at us, and he would not have been satisfied if he had not made this expedition. We have already ridden through the whole kingdom of France without meeting any untoward adventure. Let us notify our intention to Sir Hugh Calveley, who is quartered at Saint-Mor-sur-Loire, Sir Robert Briquet, Sir Robert Cheyne, John Cresswell and the other captains of companies in this district, who will readily join us here. If we can make an attack upon this new constable and the Seigneur de Clisson, who is so great an enemy of ours, we shall have done an excellent thing.' Between Sir Robert, Sir Alan and Sir John Seton there was no disagreement, for they always took counsel in common. They therefore sent letters secretly to Sir Hugh Calveley, Sir Robert Briquet and the others, to inform them of their decision

* Du Guesclin arrived at Le Mans on the 3rd of December, and made a halt there before moving on the next day. Neither he nor Clisson established a garrison in that part.

and to tell them to join with them in order to attack the French. They also sent to Sir Thomas Grantson, Sir Gilbert Giffard, Sir Geoffrey Worsley and the others with them, requesting that they should march to a certain spot which they indicated, for they hoped that the French, who were already on the move, would be engaged in battle. These various knights were very ready to obey their instructions, prepared themselves in order as requested, and set off to join their companions; they were in all some two hundred lance.

Secretly as the English sent the messages to their companions, Sir Bertrand and Olivier de Clisson discovered all that they intended to do. When the information reached them they armed by night and set off with their troops into open country. That same night Sir Thomas Grantson and the others had set off from their quarters and were approaching a place where they expected to find Sir Robert Knollys and Sir Alan. But their route was cut, for just at a place known in the district as Pontvallain they were met by the French, who, being four hundred lance to the English two hundred, rushed upon them and attacked them. Then ensued a fierce and well-fought battle, which lasted for a long time, with as many noble deeds of arms performed on one side as on the other. As soon as they met they all dismounted and advanced upon each other in good order, fighting most valiantly with sword and lance. In the end the French won the day, killing or capturing all the English; not a man fled from the field, except the servants and followers. Many English knights and squires were taken prisoner and carried off to the city of Le Mans [4 December 1370].

News of this defeat rapidly spread to the camp of Sir Robert Knollys and also to that of Sir Hugh Calveley and his companions; they were very angry to learn of it and abandoned their plan because of this mischance. The party at Saint-Mor-sur-Loire advanced no farther, but remained peacefully in their quarters, while Sir Robert Knollys and Sir Alan Buxhill beat a hasty retreat into Brittany, which was not far off. Sir Robert withdrew to his castle at Derval, and dismissed a great number of his men-at-arms and archers to seek any other opportunity that might be open to them. The greater part went back to England, where they had come from, while Sir Alan Buxhill retired to spend the winter in the town of Saint-Sauveur-le-Vicomte, which the King of England had presented to him.

¶ After the defeat of Pontvallain, in which a section of the English were put to rout and their whole expedition thereby frustrated, Sir

Bertrand du Guesclin, who by his first actions in his new office of Constable of France had received great honour and renown, returned into France with the Seigneur de Clisson, taking the majority of their prisoners to the city of Paris, and there kept them without restraint or threats, simply accepting their parole of honour. None were put in chains or fetters, as the Germans do with their prisoners in order to extract a higher ransom. May they be cursed for so doing: they are a people without pity and without honour, and no one should ever give them quarter. The French behaved well towards their prisoners, asking for courteous ransoms that were never extortionate. The prince, the Duke of Lancaster and others of their party who had remained at Cognac after the recapture of Limoges were horrified to hear of the misfortune of Pontvallain and of the losses suffered by the English.

About Christmas of this year Pope Urban V died in Avignon; he was a noble scholar, an upright man, and a good Frenchman. The cardinals then met in conclave and unanimously elected from among themselves the Cardinal de Beaufort as the new pope; he assumed the name of Gregory XI. The King of France was very pleased with this election under divine guidance, for he knew that the new pope was a wise man and a good Frenchman. At the time of the conclave the Duc d'Anjou was with him in Avignon, and he did much to forward his election. . . .

¶ About this time the eldest son of the Prince and Princess of Wales died in the city of Bordeaux, and they were understandably sorrowful. About this time, too, the Prince of Wales and Aquitaine was advised by his doctors and surgeons, who understood the nature of his malady, to return to his own country of England, in the hope of recovering better health than he had been enjoying. The prince willingly consented and said he would gladly return. He therefore gave orders concerning all his affairs, and I believe that the Earl of Cambridge his brother, and John, Earl of Pembroke, and all their men were told to return with him to bear him company.

When the prince was about to leave Aquitaine and his ships were waiting in the harbour of Bordeaux on the Garonne for him, his wife and young Richard their son, he issued a special summons from that city to all the barons and knights of Gascony and Poitou and to all those whose liege-lord he was. When they had all arrived and were assembled in a room in his presence, he reminded them how while he had been their overlord he had always protected them against their enemies, in peace, prosperity and power, so far as he had been able, and that he was now intending to return to England in the hope of recovering his health. He therefore begged them earnestly to give trusting and obedient service to his brother the Duke of Lancaster as in times past they had to him, for they would find in the duke a courteous and accommodating lord, and should therefore give him counsel and help in all his undertakings. Then the barons of Aquitaine and Gascony, Poitou and Saintonge promised and swore on their oath that they would never fail in service to the duke and did homage to him, acknowledging all love, service and obedience to him and sealed their promise in the presence of the prince with a kiss on the mouth.

When this ceremony had been completed the prince did not stay long in the city of Bordeaux, but went on board ship with the princess his wife, their son, the Earl of Cambridge* and the Earl of Pembroke, together with five hundred men-at-arms, without counting the archers. The ships made good speed and arrived safely in the harbour of Southampton [January 1371], where they disembarked and rested for three days before taking horse, with the prince in his litter. At Windsor the king received his children very kindly and asked them about the affairs of Guyenne. When the prince felt he had been long enough with the king he took his leave and went to his castle at Berkhamsted, twenty-six miles from the city of London.

english losses in france

When the Black Prince sailed for home English affairs in France had begun to deteriorate. The armies commanded by the Duc d'Anjou and by du Guesclin were having repeated successes on the borders of Aquitaine. Anjou had occupied Rouergue with scarcely any resistance and had then won over the provinces of Quercy, Limousin and Périgord; in the north the French had retaken Ponthieu. John of Gaunt, Duke of Lancaster, had, it is true, captured Moncontour in Poitou and certain other fortresses, but his successes were of no great significance. His wife Blanche of Derby (through whom he inherited the dukedom of Lancaster) had died of the plague in 1369; she had befriended Froissart, who wrote some verses to her in one of his longer poems. Early in

* The monk of St Albans, in the *Chronicon Angliae*, says that Cambridge remained in Aquitaine; he also says that the Black Prince's party landed at Plymouth, not Southampton.

1372 Lancaster married again, taking as his wife Constance the elder daughter of don Pedro, lately King of Castille, and shortly afterwards he, too, had returned to England. In January of the same year Walter de Manny had died and been buried in the Charterhouse which he founded.

In June the English fleet was defeated off La Rochelle by a fleet sent by Henry of Trastamara, King of Castille. Among the prisoners was the Earl of Pembroke, Edward's son-in-law, who was acting as the king's lieutenant in Aquitaine. An Anglo-Gascon force under Lord Percy and the Captal de Buch reached Rochelle, strengthened the garrison there, and set off in the direction of Soubise. Meanwhile Charles V had reinforced the army under du Guesclin; they captured Montmorillon and Lussac and laid siege to Moncontour.

¶ . . . The knights of England and Gascony who had come into La Rochelle . . . held council together to decide what action they should take, for already they had doubts about the loyalty of the Rochellois. They therefore appointed Sir John Devereux to be seneschal of the city, with three hundred men-at-arms to guard the castle, for as long as they were masters of the castle the citizens would not dare to rebel. . . .

About this time the Constable of France, with many dukes and barons of France under his command, more than three thousand lance in all, was marching through Anjou, Auvergne and Berry, and then entered Poitou according to plan, where they laid siege to the castle of Montmorillon. When they arrived they immediately made a fierce onslaught on it and took it by force. They slew all the men within, and replaced the garrison from their own troops. They next came to Chauvigny on the River Vienne and laid siege to it for two days; on the third day the inhabitants surrendered and were spared. Thence they rode on to the fortified town of Lussac, which surrendered without any need for a siege. From there they went to Poitiers, and lay for a night in the vineyards, which caused great distress among the citizens, for they feared a siege. But for the time they were saved, since the army moved on the next morning and approached the handsome castle of Moncontour, six leagues from Poitiers, which was commanded by John Cresswell and David Holegrave, with sixty bold and valiant companions, who between them had severely harassed the surrounding territories of Anjou and Touraine, and all the French garrisons there. For this reason the constable said he would undertake nothing else until he had captured this fortress.

¶ . . . They immediately laid siege to the town, launching several well-ordered attacks. Since the ditches round the walls were both wide and deep and since they could not easily approach the fortifications, they sent the local peasants to cut great quantities of timber and faggots and drag them thither with ropes; they then threw these into the ditches and spread a lot of straw and earth over them. After four days of this labour they could approach the walls at their leisure, and then they began their attack in earnest, while those within set about their defence—as indeed they were forced to; they withstood the attack for a whole day, suffering many hardships and in constant danger of being captured, but the defenders were of such a hardy nature that on this fifth day they were saved. On the sixth the constable and his Bretons advanced in close formation to make a stronger assault than any so far; they went forward under a cover of shields, carrying pick-axes in their hands, and reached the foot of the walls, where they at once battered away with their picks, removing stones and opening up gaps in several places, so much so that those within began to be alarmed, though they continued their defence as valiantly as ever men fought. John Cresswell and David Holegrave, the commanders, saw the danger from Sir Bertrand's method of attack; they also realized that he would not depart until he had captured the place, and that if he took it by force they would all be killed. Seeing, moreover, that no reinforcements were likely to reach them, they opened negotiations for surrender on condition that their lives and possessions were spared. The constable, who did not wish to overburden his own men, nor to harass overmuch those of the garrison, seeing that they were true men-at-arms, entered into the negotiations and accepted the terms, granting that they should leave the castle unharmed, but could take no other possessions than gold and silver. He had them escorted to Poitiers and took possession of the castle, which he then put in a state of good repair. He and his men remained there to rest, for he could not yet tell where he would march next, whether towards Poitiers or elsewhere.

¶ When it became known in Poitiers that the constable and his Bretons had retaken the castle of Moncontour the men of that city were more alarmed than before, and immediately sent messengers to Lord Thomas Percy their seneschal, who was engaged on the expedition led by the Captal de Buch.* Before this, however, Sir John

* Jean de Grailly, Captal de Buch, Constable of Aquitaine, was at this time engaged on an expedition to Soubise, where he was captured by the forces of Evan of Wales on 23 August 1372. He was kept prisoner in Paris, where he died in September 1376.

Devereux, who commanded the fortress at La Rochelle, had been told how the Constable of France had lain for a night before Poitiers and reconnoitred the place, and how the inhabitants of Poitiers feared they would be besieged in the absence of their seneschal. Sir John did not receive the news with unconcern, but set off with fifty lance to help and advise the men of Poitiers, appointing on his departure a squire by the name of Philip Mansel to be in charge of the castle until his return. When Lord Thomas Percy, on the captal's expedition, heard news that the good people of Poitiers begged him to hasten back to that city with a strong force because they feared a siege from the French who were gathered in some numbers, he told the captal of the request in order to receive his advice. The captal, after consideration, told him that he was not prepared to interrupt his plans, but would give Lord Thomas leave to go to Poitiers with fifty lance. Lord Thomas left at once and hastened to Poitiers, where he was welcomed with joy by the citizens, who were very glad to see him. There he found Sir John Devereux, and together they celebrated the occasion.

The constable, who was still at Moncontour, learned of these movements by which the garrison at Poitiers had been strengthened with men-at-arms. He then received word from the Duc de Berry, who with a considerable army was marching through Auvergne, Berry, Burgundy and the marches of Limousin, that he wanted to lay siege to Saint-Sévère in Limousin, which was garrisoned, under Sir John Devereux, by Sir William Percy, Richard Gill and Richard Holmes, with a large body of trusted companions. For some time they had been overrunning the provinces of Auvergne and Limousin, where they had done much mischief and damage; for this reason the Duc de Berry was anxious to make a sortie towards that town, and begged the constable, if it was any way possible, to join up with him to attack the castle. The constable, who was a man of much forethought, realized that he would do no good just now by marching to Poitiers with his men, and therefore decided to join the Duc de Berry and left Moncontour with his whole army after making arrangements for the guarding of its fortress. He made good speed to the Duc de Berry, who was most grateful for his coming with so many barons and knights. Together they marched to Saint-Sévère, a good four thousand men-at-arms. There they immediately laid siege to the fortified town, attacking it in careful formation, firmly resolved not to leave until they had taken it. Sir William Percy and his men similarly set to defending it.

When news reached Sir John Devereux in the city of Poitiers that the Constable of France and the Duc de Berry, with many barons and knights and a good four thousand men-at-arms were attacking his fortress in Limousin, he was even more worried and spoke about it to Lord Thomas Percy, who was there when the news was brought: 'Lord Thomas, you are seneschal of this region, and you have much power and influence; I beg you to do something to help your cousin and my men, who will be taken by force if we do not help them.' 'By my troth,' answered Lord Thomas, 'I am very willing to, and for love of you I will set out with you and we will go together to my lord the Captal de Buch, who is not far off, and use every endeavour to move him to go and relieve the castle and engage the French.' Then they both left Poitiers, commending the city to the keeping of the mayor, Jean Renaud, a good and loyal man, and by hard riding came to the Captal de Buch, who was campaigning in the direction of Saint-Jean-d'Angély. The two knights then pointed out that the French had taken Montmorillon, not far from Poitiers, as well as the strong fortress of Moncontour, and were now laying siege to Saint-Sévère, which belonged to Sir John Devereux, to whom they owed every service they could give. There were, moreover, within the fortress Sir William Percy, Richard Gill and Richard Holmes, who were too valuable to be lost. The captal reflected a little on these words, and then replied: 'My lords, what does it seem good to you that I should do?' Some knights who had been called to this council replied: 'My lord, for long now we have heard that you are very anxious to fight with the French; you will never have a better occasion than if you now make for Saint-Sévère, and issue a summons throughout Poitou and Saintonge, where we have enough men to combat the French, given the great desire to do so that we have ourselves.' 'By my troth,' replied the captal, 'I will do so. I spoke truth when I said that I desired to fight, and with the help of God and Saint George we shall shortly be doing so.' The captal immediately sent letters from his camp to those barons, knights and squires of Poitou and Saintonge who were not with him, giving them polite orders to hasten with all speed to join him, indicating the position of his camp. All the barons, knights and squires to whom this summons was sent set off without delay to join the captal, each equipped to the best of his ability. When they had all met together, English, Poitevins, Gascons, Saintongeois, they all lodged in the Abbey of Charroux on the borders of Limousin; they numbered a good nine hundred lance and five hundred archers.

¶ When intelligence reached Sir Bertrand and his fellows before Saint-Sévère that the English and the Poitevins and their allies were approaching with speed in order to raise the siege, he was not the least alarmed, but ordered all his men to arm and advance to the assault, an order which every man obeyed. French and Bretons went fiercely into the attack on the fortress, fully armed and each with his shield over his head, every lord with his own banner in the middle of his own men. I can assure you it was a beautiful sight to see these lords of France in rich array, for in this assault there were forty-nine banners and a great profusion of pennons. Among them were the constable and the Seigneur Louis de Sancerre, Marshal of France, each in his proper station, working hard to encourage their men to greater efforts. Knights and squires of all nations advanced to increase their honour and secure their advancement by performing deeds of great valour. Many of them went right through the moat which was full of water and advanced with shields over their heads to the foot of the walls, never retreating because of what was thrown down on them by the defenders. The Duc de Berry, the Duc de Bourbon, the Comte d'Alençon, the Dauphin d'Auvergne and other lords had advanced to the moat and were encouraging their men to fight well, and because of the presence of their lords the men advanced more willingly, fearing neither death nor danger.

Sir William Percy and the two squires of honour, who commanded the castle, watched the vigour of this onslaught which never ceased or slackened, and realized that if it continued they could not hold out, especially as the hoped-for reinforcements were not in sight. Had they known that their friends were only ten leagues off they would have taken new heart, for if this information had reached them they could have held out till help arrived; but they knew nothing of it. They therefore opened negotiations with the constable to avoid greater danger, and the constable, who knew of the approach of the English and Poitevins and that they would be there by evening, willingly accepted their overtures and spared their lives on taking possession of the castle, which he did with great celebration [end of July 1372]. This done, he drew up his whole army in battle order on the field as for an immediate engagement, and addressed them thus: 'My lords, prepare yourselves, for the enemy is approaching, and we hope to fight before nightfall.' The army remained in battle order in the fields outside Saint-Sévère from mid-morning until late evening, awaiting attack from the English and Poitevins, which would indeed have come if news had not reached the captal and his companions that Saint-Sévère had surrendered. He, and those with him, were very angry to hear this news, and swore an oath among themselves that they would never retire to a fortress in Poitou until they had fought and routed the French.

¶ At the time of this expedition there was great dissension among the citizens of Poitiers; for the common people, the prelates and some of the rich men of the town wanted to turn to the French, while Jean Renaud, the mayor, the rest of the rich citizens and all the prince's officers would not hear of it. As a result there was very nearly strife between the two parties. Those of the first party sent secret messages to the constable begging him to advance quickly and take possession of the city, which would then yield to him. When the constable received these messages he told their content to the Dukes of Berry and Bourbon, and said: 'My lords, thus do the citizens of Poitiers write to me. With God's help I'll go there with three hundred lance and see what they want with me. You wait here and keep a check on the English. If I succeed, they will not join with you before I return.' The two dukes readily agreed to this decision, and the constable left secretly, taking with him fifty chosen lance. All were well mounted, and they needed to be so, for in half a day and a night they had to ride fully thirty leagues, since they could not travel by the straight route for fear of being seen. They rode hard, through woods, over heaths, by side-roads in uninhabited country, and if one of their horses became exhausted its rider had to fall out.

The mayor of Poitiers, who had shrewd suspicions of this business, sent a secret messenger to Lord Thomas Percy his master, who was with the captal, and this was the message he delivered: 'Sir, my master bids you take care, for there is good reason, and to return at once to Poitiers where there is great dissension in the city. Five-sixths of the city want to go over to the French, and the mayor your servant has been in great peril of his life. Even now he is afraid you may not be able to arrive in time, for he fears they have sent for the constable.' When the governor of Poitou heard this he was very surprised, but he believed the man's every word, for he knew the fellow and he knew, too, the feelings of the citizens of Poitiers. He therefore told it all to the captal, who said to him: 'Lord Thomas, you shall not leave me, for you are one of the leaders of my army in whom I have the greatest trust. Nevertheless we will send to them.' Lord Thomas replied: 'It shall be according to your wish.' Then Sir Jean d'Angle and some others were called, and were thus addressed: 'Sir Jean, take a hundred lance from our company and ride with haste to Poitiers, enter the city and do not leave it until you receive further official orders from us.' Sir Jean d'Angle immediately obeyed, and a hundred lance were handed over to him from among the company. They rode secretly to Poitiers, but in spite of all speed they could not reach the city before the Constable of France had got there and, finding the gates open, had been welcomed with great rejoicing by his party within the city [7 August 1372].* Sir Jean d'Angle and his troop were but a short league from Poitiers when news of the surrender reached them; they could not advance farther without being destroyed, for the constable was in Poitiers with fully three hundred lance. Sir Jean was very angry at the news, as might be expected, but there was nothing he could do now, so he and his men turned and rode back to the captal, and told him of their misfortune, and of the taking of Poitiers by the constable.

¶ When news of this reached the Gascons, the English and the Poitevins who were united in a common cause they were more amazed and frightened than before, and every baron and knight among them was lost in black and angry thoughts, as they had good reason to be, for things were going hard against them. Then the men of Poitou offered help to the English and Gascons in these terms: 'My lords, know that of a truth we are much displeased at the way things are going in this country, and if there is any help we can bring, consider what you would like us to do, and we will do it, nor will you ever find us failing in courage.' 'We are indeed very ready to believe you,' replied the English, 'and we have no doubts about your willingness. It is only our misfortune that troubles us, for everything is going the wrong way. We must therefore decide how we can best preserve our honour.' Then they entered into lengthy deliberations and decided it would be best for the Poitevins, the English and the Gascons to withdraw each to their own garrisons, and when they found occasion to make a further expedition they would consider where it was to be, would notify each other, and each would find the others ready. This decision was upheld, and they parted on the friendliest of terms, the Poitevins going to Thouars, the Gascons to Saint-Jean-d'Angély and the English to Niort, thus bringing that expedition to an end.

Just as the English, riding in a body, were about to enter the town

* Froissart is wrong in attributing the capture only to the constable; the Duc de Berry played the leading part in it.

of Niort, the gates were shut in their faces, and the men of the town shouted out that they should not enter, but must go somewhere else. At this the English were beside themselves with rage, and said that such rebelliousness could not be tolerated from men of this sort. They at once drew up in order and got ready to attack the town, launching their assault with great courage, while those inside the town defended it to the best of their ability. The assault was long and arduous, but in the end the men of Niort were unable to resist, since there was no knight among them to advise and encourage them. If they had been able to hold out until evening they would have received help from the constable, who was close behind the English. But the English attack was so fierce and effective that they broke through the walls and entered the town, killing the greater part of the townsmen. Then they ransacked and pillaged the whole place, remaining there until fresh information reached them.

¶ You will have read earlier how Evan of Wales went to Spain at the instigation of the King of France to talk to Henry of Trastamara King of Castille and ask him for a part of his navy.* King Henry would never have refused him or sent him back to the King of France, but was very pleased to grant the request. He therefore ordered his admiral-in-chief, Don Ruy Diaz de Rojas, to take command, with Evan, of this whole fleet, which sailed from the port of Santander in Galicia in forty heavy ships, eight galleys and thirteen barges, all well equipped and laden with men-at-arms. They made good headway, with no contrary winds, and arrived as intended before La Rochelle, where they anchored in siege formation. When they saw this large Spanish fleet arrive the people of La Rochelle were in great fear, for they were not used to being besieged either from the sea or by the Spaniards. In spite of the attitude they had for so long shown to the English, they were thoroughly French at heart, and did their best to conceal that they would have turned over to the French if they had dared. But so long as the fortress was in the hands of the English they could not do so without risk of being destroyed to a man. When the men of La Rochelle saw that they were well and truly besieged they took counsel secretly to decide on a plan of action, and came to an amicable arrangement with Evan of Wales and Don Ruy Diaz de Rojas whereby they would be ready to bear the

* Evan (or Owen) of Wales was a member of the family of Welsh princes dispossessed by Edward I, and had put himself at the disposal of France. Charles V sent him to Santander in July 1372 to ask Henry to lay siege to La Rochelle from the sea.

blockade, but that neither side should indulge in hostilities towards the other, and this agreement was kept for some time. . . .

¶ When Sir John Devereux had gone off to strengthen the garrison at Poitiers he had left in charge a squire named Philip Mansel, who was not a very intelligent man, and with him some sixty companions. The mayor of La Rochelle at this time was Jean Chauderier,* a man of great intelligence and cunning in all his dealings and thoroughly French at heart, for when he saw that the time was ripe he revealed to several like-minded citizens a cunning plan that he had conceived. The mayor was well aware that this Philip who commanded the fortress, though a good man-at-arms, was not particularly intelligent or perceptive. One day therefore he invited him to dinner, together with certain citizens of the town, and Philip, suspecting no evil intention, accepted the invitation. Before they sat down to dinner Sir Jean Chauderier, who had his plan all prepared and had informed his fellows of its nature, said to Philip Mansel: 'Commander of the castle, I have yesterday received letters from our dear lord the King of England which closely concern you.' 'And what is in them?' he asked, to which the mayor replied: 'I will show them to you and have them read in your presence, as is your right.'

He then went to a chest and took out an open letter sealed with the great seal of King Edward of England, but an old one which had nothing to do with the present matter. 'Here it is,' he said to Philip and wisely held it out for him to inspect. Philip recognized it at once and was fully reassured; but he could not read, and this was the cause of his downfall. Sir Jean Chauderier called a clerk, who was fully acquainted with the plan, and said: 'Read us this letter.' The clerk took it and read out what was not written in the letter, saying the King of England commanded the mayor to hold a review of all the armed men within La Rochelle, and to send by the bearer of these letters full details of the armed men both in the town and in the fortress, for he hoped very soon to be there and needed this information beforehand. When all this had been said as if it had been read from a letter, the mayor thus addressed Philip: 'Commander of the castle, you hear what the king your master orders me to do. I therefore bid you in his name to assemble your troops tomorrow for a review in the square before the castle. And immediately after yours I will review my own troops in the same place so that you can see them, too, if you wish. Then we can each write an exact account of this to our

* The mayor in 1372 was Pierre de Boudré.

beloved lord the King of England. And, moreover, if your men need money—as I believe they do—I will lend you some as soon as the review is finished, so that you can pay them their wages, for the King of England our master has sent a sealed letter bidding me pay them by virtue of my office.' Philip placed complete trust in these words and replied: 'My lord mayor, since it is tomorrow that I must have this review, by God I will do it willingly, and my men will be much pleased that they are to be paid, for they are in need of money.'

They finished their discussion with these words and sat down to dinner with easy minds. After dinner Philip withdrew to the fortress of La Rochelle and told his men all that you have heard: 'Gentlemen, be of good cheer, for tomorrow immediately after the review you will have your pay, for the king has given orders to the mayor to this effect, and I have seen the letters.' The soldiers, who were very eager for pay, having received none for three months or more, replied: 'This is precious news.' Then they began to burnish their helmets, to rub up their breastplates, and to polish their swords or such other arms as they possessed. That evening Sir Jean made his preparations and communicated his plans to the greater part of those citizens he felt to be of his mind, giving them instructions how they were to act the next day.

Near the fortress of La Rochelle, around the open place where the review was to be held, there were some old houses in which no one lived. The mayor told them that in these houses they would establish an ambush of four hundred armed men, the most able-bodied in the town, and when the garrison had all come out they would place themselves between the English and the castle and cut them off. The citizens could see no better way in which to capture the garrison, and the plan was therefore adopted; men from the town were chosen for the ambush and they took up their station fully armed, with exact instructions what to do. Soon after dawn the mayor of La Rochelle, together with only those officials who were in the plot, came out unarmed to deceive the garrison and to draw them more readily out of the castle. They came forward to the place where the review was to be held, mounted on good stout nags for a quick escape when the skirmish began. When the governor of the fortress saw the mayor and his companions appear he shouted to his men to hurry up: 'Come on, come on! They are waiting for us in the square.'

Then all the men marched unsuspecting out of the castle for the review and in expectation of their pay. Within the castle they left only pages and servant-girls, who were powerless to defend it. As they came out of the gates they left them wide open, since they expected to be returning very shortly, and advanced on to the square to be reviewed by the mayor and his companions, who were parading up and down. When they were assembled in close order the mayor addressed them, first one and then the other in order to gain time, saying: 'You haven't got your full equipment. If you want your full wages you must put that right', and each replied: 'Sir, we will do that willingly.' Thus chatting and jesting he held them until the ambush had come out, all fully armed, and had drawn up between the review troops and the castle and had seized the gate. When the English saw this they knew they were betrayed and done for, and they were panic-stricken—with good reason. At this the mayor and his companions left the square and allowed their men to carry out the plan, so that they soon had the upper hand of the English, who allowed themselves to be taken without resistance, for they saw that there was no good in defending themselves. Then the men of La Rochelle disarmed them all one by one in the square before the castle, and led them off to prison in various places in the town—in towers and gatehouses—so that there were nowhere more than two together.

Soon afterwards the mayor arrived in the square fully armed, with more than a thousand men, and rode at once towards the castle, which immediately surrendered, for there was merely a handful of servants within who could offer no defence. They were very glad to be allowed to surrender, and were left in peace. Thus was the fortress of La Rochelle retaken by the French [8 September 1372].

¶ When the Dukes of Berry, Bourbon and Burgundy . . . who had with them more than two thousand lance, learned that the men of La Rochelle had turned out the English from the castle and taken possession of it themselves, they decided to march to that city in order to know what further action was to be taken. They therefore left their quarters and rode by the shortest route through Poitou to join up with the Constable of France in Poitiers. On their way they came to a town in Poitou known as Saint-Maixent, which was considered to be English because the castle outside the town was held by the English. As soon as the French lords and their army arrived before the town the citizens of Saint-Maixent surrendered on condition that their lives and property were spared, but the castle refused to surrender. The French lords then laid a heavy siege to the castle for a whole day without success; they renewed the assault on the next day so vigorously that they were able to capture it; all its defenders were slain.

After appointing some of their number to guard the town, they rode on and came before Melle, which they captured and transferred to the allegiance of the King of France, then passing on to the town of Civray, which held out for two days before the inhabitants surrendered, their lives and possessions being spared. Thus these lords conquered towns and strongholds on their way to Poitiers, leaving no place behind them that did not divert its allegiance to the King of France. Finally they arrived in that city, where they were received with great rejoicing by the constable and his men, and by all the citizens.

¶ When the three dukes had arrived in Poitiers with their armed followers they lodged them either there or in the flat country round about to be more at ease. The Duc de Berry then took counsel to send to the people of La Rochelle to find out their present intentions, for they kept the town so closely guarded that no one was entering or leaving it. The duke therefore sent certain messengers to parley with the townsfolk and discover their plans; these men were hospitably received and informed that the city was sending certain demands to the King of France and if these were met they would remain loyal to the French cause, but they begged the Duc de Berry and the constable not to send their forces with any hostile intent against the city until they had held further talks. This was the sum of the message that was brought back and it was generally satisfactory to the duke and the constable, who remained peacefully in Poitiers and the neighbourhood without undertaking any expedition against the Rochellois, whilst Evan of Wales blockaded them by sea, though without any assault on the city.

Meanwhile there had been sent to the king in Paris twelve of the foremost citizens of La Rochelle, who had obtained a promise of safe-conduct in both directions before they left the city. The king desired to have them as loyal friends and received them joyfully, willingly listening to their requests, which were as follows: firstly, that the fortress of La Rochelle should be razed to the ground before they would promise allegiance to the king; secondly, that the King of France and his heirs for ever should hold the city as the personal domain of the crown, and that it should not be alienated from the crown by any treaty of peace, agreement, alliance of marriage, or any alliance whatsoever that he might make with the King of England or any other lord; thirdly, they required that the King of France should allow them to mint florins and other coins of the same value and alloy as are minted in Paris, without any exception; fourthly, that no King of France, his heirs or successors, should impose on any householder of theirs any tax, levy, salt-tax, hearth-tax, fine or other like imposition unless they gave their free consent to it; fifthly, they required that the king should absolve them from their oath of fealty to the King of England, which was a great burden to their consciences, and for this they wished the king to secure from their Holy Father the pope a complete absolution for the renunciation of their oath.

When the King of France heard the articles of their request he replied most courteously that he would consider them, whereupon he took counsel several times with the wisest men in his kingdom, and retained the Rochellois in Paris for a considerable time. In the end he was unable to reduce any of their demands and agreed to accept, sign and seal them in perpetuity. They then left Paris well contented, with sealed charters and documents which granted them exactly what they had requested, for the King of France was very anxious to receive their loyalty, and praised La Rochelle as the most famous city he possessed outside Paris. On their departure he moreover gave them fine gifts of jewels and rich presents to be offered to their wives, and thus laden the Rochellois left Paris and set out on their return journey.

¶ When the citizens of La Rochelle were back in their own city, after two months spent on the journey and in Paris, they revealed to those who had sent them and to the people of the city that they had obtained all their demands without any exception. All were very satisfied at this, and pleased with the consent of the king and his council. Within three days they had instructed workmen to destroy the castle and raze it to the ground so that not one stone remained upon another; the rubble was all collected in one heap, and men were sent to use it for the needs of the town and to pave those streets which were in greatest need of it. When this was done they sent to the Duc de Berry inviting him to come to the city if he wished, for they would gladly welcome him in the name of the King of France and perform any duties that were required of them. The duke sent Sir Bertrand du Guesclin in his place to take possession in the king's name. On the duke's instructions the constable left Poitiers, taking with him a hundred lance, and rode to La Rochelle, where he was welcomed with great joy, and he showed them the commission he had to act in the name of the king his master. By right of this he accepted the fealty and homage of the citizens and stayed there three days, receiving all the revenues due to the King of France and being presented with many fine gifts. He for his part gave generously to the ladies and maidens of the city, and after much feasting and revelry, took his leave and returned to Poitiers.

Not long after this the King of France sent messengers to Evan of Wales giving instructions that he would be glad to see him, along with his prisoner the Captal de Buch. By the same messengers he sent orders to Don Ruy Diaz de Rojas, the admiral of the brave King Henry of Castille, to return to Spain with his fleet, since he had no further work for them for the present. The fleet therefore set sail, and before they left they were paid their wages in ready money, with the result that they were all highly pleased with what the King of France had done for them. Meanwhile Evan of Wales took the road to Paris at the king's command, and with him the Captal de Buch. The king was glad to see the captal, for he knew him from former days, entertained him lavishly, and gave him courteous treatment as a prisoner; he offered him handsome presents of money and lands to win his affection so that he would return to the French side. But the captal would hear none of it, and told the barons and knights of France, who visited him to put forward these suggestions, that he would set his ransom at five or six times as much as the yearly income of his estates. This the king was in no way inclined to accept. Matters remained thus, and he was put in the prison of the Louvre and very carefully guarded, receiving frequent visits from the knights and barons of France.

¶ When the Constable of France had taken possession of the fair city of La Rochelle and withdrawn to Poitiers, the lords agreed in council to set forth again and attack any castles in the neighbourhood whose capture would allow that city to be in greater safety, for Marans, Surgères and Fontenay-le-Comte were still held by the English, and every day men from these garrisons were skirmishing as far as the gates of La Rochelle and causing much trouble. The Duc de Berry left Poitiers in great array with the Dukes of Burgundy and Bourbon, the Constable of France and other lords and upward of two thousand lance, and came first before the castle of Benon. One Guillonet de Pau, an esquire of honour of the Comte de Foix, had been appointed commander of this place by the captal, together with a Neapolitan knight known as Sir James, two experienced men of arms. With them in the fortress were a body of trusted companions who were in no way afraid when these lords and the constable laid

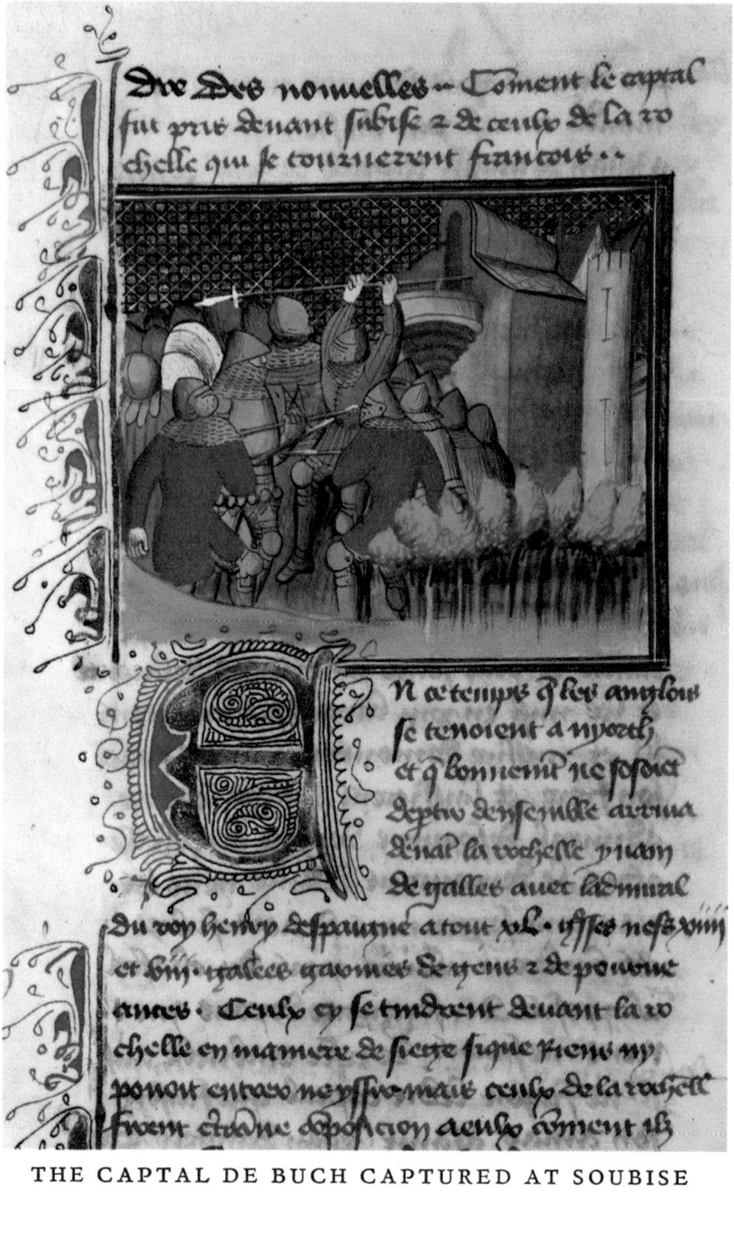

THE CAPTAL DE BUCH CAPTURED AT SOUBISE

siege to the place, for they took strength from their good fortune in being well stocked with provisions and artillery. Two or three attacks were launched, but they were all successfully repulsed by the defenders.

Not far away was the fortress of Surgères, where there were a good sixty English lance, all trusted fighting men. They decided one day that they would set out by night and rouse the French army to see if they could conduct a successful skirmish. When dusk fell they left the fortress and rode out towards Benon, coming up with the French about midnight, when they halted just before the camp of the constable. There they fell to killing and wounding an enemy quite unprepared for attack. Many were caught unawares and wounded; in the constable's own camp one of his squires of honour whom he loved beyond measure was slain. The enemy roused and armed themselves, but the English withdrew when they judged they had done what they set out to do, and retired without loss to their garrison.

When the constable learned of the death of the squire he so loved he fell into an uncontrollable rage and swore that he would not depart until he had taken the castle of Benon, to whose defenders he would show no mercy. On the next day, after he had buried his squire, he ordered all his men to arm and prepare for the assault, going with them armed himself in order to encourage them. The assault was long and arduous, but the Bretons and others fought so valiantly that the castle of Benon was taken, and all those within were put to the sword, not a single one being spared [15 September 1372].

¶ The constable . . . then gave orders to move on to the castle of Marans, four leagues from La Rochelle. The commander of this garrison was a German named Wiesebar, a very brave soldier, who had with him a large body of Germans. But when they saw that these lords of France were coming in such strength and no one holding out against them, that the city of La Rochelle had turned to the French and that the constable had slaughtered the whole garrison of Benon, they were so frightened that they lost all heart to resist, and yielded themselves and their fortress, swearing to remain loyal to the French cause from that day; this oath they made to the Seigneur de Pons, whom the constable sent to negotiate with them and to receive possession of the town. They added only one condition, that they should continue to receive their wages with the same courtesy and regularity as the English had shown, and that if this were not done they should be free to go where they wished. These terms were accepted, so that the Germans remained in the fortress to guard it as before, while the French passed on and came before the castle of Surgères. There they found the castle empty and the gates open, for those who had been guarding it had left for fear of the constable and gone to other fortresses in Poitou. The French therefore entered in and re-established the garrison from their own men [19 September], then rode on to Fontenay-le-Comte, which was held by the wife of Sir John Harpenden with many good knights who were at the outset in no way afraid to hold the fortress against the French.

¶ When the . . . constable and his army reached Fontenay-le-Comte they launched a well-ordered assault on the town and on the castle and its defenders, bringing in siege-engines to aid the attack. Several assaults were made, but no advantage gained, for they found that the defenders were highly skilled in repulsing the attacks. Many further assaults and skirmishes followed, in which great feats of arms were performed and many men were wounded, for almost every day there was some kind of engagement. If the defenders of Fontenay had had any hope that it might be reinforced within three or four months, from any source by land or sea, they would have held out, for they had abundance of provisions and the castle was strongly fortified. But when they thought of the danger they ran by being cut off in that place, with daily renewed threats that if they were captured they would all be killed without mercy, and saw that there was no hope of reinforcements from anywhere, they accepted negotiations with the constable, the outcome of which was that they would be allowed to leave Fontenay with all their possessions and be escorted to the town of Thouars, where all the English knights in Poitou had gathered. This treaty was accepted and ratified, and all the English left Fontenay, taking with them Lady Harpenden, and under the constable's safe-conduct withdrew to Thouars, where they were warmly welcomed. The French thus gained the fortress and town of Fontenay-le-Comte, and appointed a knight to guard it with twenty lance, his name being Renaud de Lazi; they then returned to the city of Poitiers, where they were received with great rejoicing [9–10 October].

¶ When the French lords had rested themselves and their horses for four days in Poitiers, they held a council and decided to march against Thouars, where all the knights of Poitou who supported the

English cause were assembled to the number of about a hundred, and to besiege the town and not to leave until it were decided whether it was to remain entirely for the English or for the French. They departed in good order from Poitiers, a good three thousand lance, knights and squires, and four thousand foot-soldiers, including the Genoese, and arrived before the town of Thouars. There they established everything for a well-ordered siege all round the town and castle, for at this they were adept. They allowed no one to go in or out, nor did they commence any assault, since they knew that they would never take the place by that means, since there were too many excellent knights to defend it; they intended to starve them out unless the King of England or his sons came to raise the siege. When the barons and knights within the town saw the strength of the French forces which were encamped round the town and increasing in number every day, they took counsel, realizing that the besiegers would not leave until they had wholly or in part achieved their aim.

Sir Perceval de Coulonges, an intelligent knight and a good speaker, said one day when they were assembled in council: 'Lords, there is no time to lose. You know that we have maintained our loyalty to the King of England by every means in our power, and that he should indeed be grateful to us, for we have risked our lives in his service to help him to guard and defend his lands, putting aside all personal considerations. Here we are surrounded, unable to leave the town without great danger, and I have been thinking much of how we can escape with our honour, for leave we must, and if you will hear me I will tell you how, without prejudice to any better advice you may offer.' The knights present answered: 'Sir, we would hear your counsel.' Then said Sir Perceval: 'The King of England, whose servants we are in this cause, cannot but know of the peril in which we are by these French, and of the way in which his lands are being daily lost to him. If he wants to lose them, we cannot guard or save them for him, for we are not strong enough of ourselves to withstand or vie with the power of the King of France. In this country we see cities, towns, fortresses and castles, with their bishops, barons, knights, ladies and the common people turning every day to the French cause and making war upon us, a state of affairs we cannot suffer any longer. For this reason I would advise that we enter into negotiations with these French lords who have besieged us here for a truce of two or three months. During this truce, and as soon as we possibly can, let us notify the King of England bluntly of the danger we are in and how his lands are being lost, and if the King of England or one of his sons, or the king with one of his sons, can come to this town in sufficient strength to raise the siege within a limit of time to be agreed between us and them, let us obtain permission from these French lords that we can remain loyal to the English cause for all time; and if not, that we shall be equally loyal to the French from that day. Now tell me if you think I have spoken wisely.' They replied with one voice: 'This is the best way in which we can get out with our loyalty and honour safe.'

No objection was made to this plan, which was confirmed and accepted, and negotiations were set on foot with the Duc de Berry and the Constable of France. These parleyings lasted more than a fortnight, for the French would do nothing without the knowledge of the King of France. The final result of the journeyings and conversations was that a truce was signed by which the knights of Poitou who were defending Thouars, as well as the besiegers, would remain in safety until the feast of Saint Michael.* If within that time the King of England or one of his sons, or the king with one of his sons, came into Poitou with sufficient forces to hold Thouars against the French, they and their lands would remain loyally English for all time, but if the King of England or his sons did not come by that day all those lords and barons of Poitou who were within Thouars would become French and place themselves and their lands under obedience to the King of France. This solution seemed very reasonable to all who heard it. Nevertheless so long as the truce lasted and both sides remained safe from attack, the siege was in no way raised, but the party of the besiegers was reinforced every day that God sent. After careful consultation, the King of France daily sent chosen men from among the thousands of his subjects to help win the day against the King of England, when the period of the truce should be completed.

¶ As soon as they were able, the defenders of Thouars sent messengers with persuasive letters to the King of England concerning the state of the province and the danger they were in, begging him in God's name and for pity's sake to come to their aid, for it concerned him more closely than anyone else in the world. When the King of England read these messages from his barons in Poitou, he said that if God willed he would go in person, with all his sons, to Thouars and would be there by the appointed day. Even his son the Prince of Wales, although he was not yet fully recovered, said he would go

* Froissart is in error. A treaty to this effect was signed at Surgères (not Thouars) on 18 September, and the truce was to expire on St Andrew's Day, 30 November.

and would remain below on the voyage. Then in great haste the King issued a special summons to all his knights and squires throughout his kingdom and outside it, and communicated also to the King of Scotland, by which means he obtained three hundred Scottish lance. It happened by good fortune that provisions were then being collected for an expedition to Calais by his son the Duke of Lancaster, so that these provisions could be diverted to the king's purposes and the Duke of Lancaster's voyage postponed. Never did the King of England have so many skilled men-at-arms or such profusion of archers for any expedition into Normandy or Brittany, or anywhere else.

Before he left England the king gave orders, in the presence of all the peers of the kingdom, bishops, earls, barons and knights and the mayors of all the chief towns and cities, that if he were to die on this voyage, he willed that Richard, the son of the Prince of Wales, should be king in his place of the whole realm of England, and that neither the Duke of Lancaster and his sons, nor his own other sons Edmund and Thomas could claim any right to it. All this he made them solemnly swear and agree to in the presence of all the bishops, earls and barons summoned for this purpose. When the ceremony was over he left London with his three sons, and joined the rest of his men, who were already waiting at Southampton* or near by, where they were to take ship and where their provisions were ready. Then the king, his sons and all their men embarked in due order. When they saw that all was in order they weighed anchor and set sail for La Rochelle. There were altogether some four hundred ships in this fleet, carrying four thousand men-at-arms and ten thousand archers. . . .

The king did not much mind whether he landed in Poitou or the Bordelais: it was all one to him provided he reached France. The king and his huge fleet were becalmed at sea for the whole of nine weeks, with neither contrary nor favourable winds, and were unable to make land in Poitou, Saintonge or Rochellois or the neighbouring territories, and this both astonished and angered them. They set their sails to any wind that was blowing, but they lost as much distance in one day as they had gained in three. They were so long in this unhappy situation that Michaelmas came and went, and the king realized he could not keep to the appointed date for relieving his

* Edward III embarked at Sandwich (not Southampton) on 30 August 1372. The original purpose of the expedition had been to raise the blockade of La Rochelle. It cost the English treasury £900,000.

garrison at Thouars. He therefore decided after such misfortune at sea to return to England, considering Poitou lost for the present. The king was very irate when he ordered the return, and said: 'God and Saint George help us! There was never so evil a king in France as there is now, nor ever one who gave me such trouble as the present one.' Thus without being able to do anything further the king and his sons with all their men returned to England. And as soon as they were back the wind became so favourable for a journey such as they had intended that nine hundred merchant ships from England, Wales and Scotland sailed together into Bordeaux harbour for shipments of wine. From which it was widely claimed that God was on the side of the French.

¶ Sir Thomas Felton, seneschal of Bordeaux, knew that the barons and knights who were defending Thouars had fixed a date when they would go over to the French, and that their lord the King of England had been informed of it. He had therefore given this information directly to all those barons of Gascony who supported the English, with the result that by his activity and their desire to do their duty, many barons, with the largest number of men they could muster, had come to Bordeaux, whence they set out with the seneschal and crossed into Poitou. At Niort they joined up with certain English knights from that garrison, among them Sir Hugh Calveley and Sir John Cresswell, together with certain Poitevins who had preferred to leave Thouars rather than submit to the treaty made by the other lords of Poitou and so had joined the English at Niort. More than twelve hundred lance in all, they made their way to Thouars, and as soon as they knew the time limit had expired without their hearing any news of the King of England they camped round the town.

You will know that to keep to the day appointed by the constable the King of France had sent to Thouars all the flower of his kingdom, for he had a firm report that the King of England and his sons would be there in the greatest strength they could muster. He wanted his own men to be in sufficient force to sustain the day honourably, and with the constable therefore were the king's two brothers the Duc de Berry and the Duc de Bourgogne, a great body of knights and squires, and so many lords and barons that it would delay the story to list them all; there, too, were the flower of arms of all Brittany, Normandy, Burgundy, Auvergne, Berry, Touraine, Blésis, Anjou, Limousin and Maine, together with a considerable number of foreigners, Germans, Flemings and Hainaulters—fifteen thousand men-at-arms and thirty thousand others. In spite of their assembled strength, they were glad to see the feast of Michaelmas come round and that neither the King of England nor his sons appeared to raise the siege. They immediately sent word to the King of France, who was much relieved when he saw that all the knights of Poitou and their lands would revert to France by agreement and without the dangers of a battle.

¶ When the English and the Gascons assembled in strength at Niort* . . . saw that no reinforcements had arrived from the King of England, they held a council to find some honourable way in which these knights of Poitou, who had made an undertaking to the French, might yet be kept on the side of the English, in accordance with the desire of the Gascons. Finally, after long consultation, they sent sealed letters by a herald signifying their plans to the defenders of Thouars. After the customary greeting they said that it had been for the best that they should have sworn an agreement with the French to go over to the French side if the King of England . . . did not send help by Michaelmas, but that the defection was due to the fortunes of navigation and to no other cause. They, however, had come to Niort, some four leagues away, and were twelve hundred or more lance, all tried men. If the men of Poitou would come out of Thouars and offer battle to the French, the Gascons and English would risk their own lives to defend the lands of their lord the King of England.

These letters were eagerly read by the Poitevins, and many were grateful for the offer of the English and Gascons; they deliberated at length about this, taking into consideration their present state and the promise they had sworn to the French, but they could not see any right course of action other than to surrender, since neither the King of England nor his sons would be at the battle which the Gascons proposed. During these deliberations the Seigneur de Parthenay had much to say in favour of accepting the engagement proposed by the Gascons, showing good cause on two counts why it would be right to do so. Firstly, they knew for a truth, and indeed it was generally known, that their lord the King of England had set sail with the major part of his armed power, and that luck had been so much against him that he had been unable to land in Poitou; for this misfortune he should be excused, since there is no remedy against the

* They must have withdrawn to Niort from Thouars, where Froissart says they had camped.

power of nature. Secondly, in spite of the undertaking they had given to the French, they could not give away the lands of the King of England or enter into any alliance with the French without his permission.

What the Seigneur de Parthenay had to say was examined in detail, but soon other reasons were advanced which weakened his argument. Thus it was that one day at the end of a council session the Seigneur de Parthenay said as he left that he would remain loyal to the English and withdrew to his lodging. But the lords of Poyanne and Tonnay-Boutonne came and sought him out because he had ceased to support them, and they brought him back to the council room. There they put forward so many arguments between them that in the end he agreed to all their decisions, and they sent letters politely excusing themselves to the English and Gascon lords who were waiting for a reply at Niort. These the herald took back, together with a copy of the agreement they had made with the French, to make their excuses more valid. When the English and Gascons saw that this decision was final they were very annoyed. They did not yet leave Niort, but remained there another month, so that they could see more clearly what course of action they should adopt. As soon as the deliberations in Thouars were completed the barons and knights of Poitou there assembled sent word to the Dukes of Berry and Burgundy and to the Constable of France that they were all ready to carry out the oath they had sworn and sealed. The French lords were overjoyed at this news and rode triumphantly into Thouars, where [1 December 1372] they received the Poitevins and their lands into the obedience of the King of France.

¶ Thus did all or nearly all of the lords of Poitou turn over to the French; Niort remained to the English cause, together with the towns of Chizé, Gençay, Mortemer, Lusignan, Château-Larcher, Dienné, la Roche-sur-Yon, Mortagne-sur-mer, la Tour de Broue and Merpins. When the French lords had completed taking possession of the town of Thouars, the Duc de Berry, the Duc de Bourgogne and the greater part of the French barons returned to France, while the constable withdrew to Poitiers . . . where he remained all that winter.

By the end of March 1373 the English had suffered further losses at the hands of du Guesclin; of the fortresses named by Froissart only the last four remained in English hands.

Poitou, Angoumois and Saintonge were virtually emptied of all English power, and the whole of Edward's gains had been lost. Only Aquitaine was left, and even her borders were being nibbled by French conquests.

truce by exhaustion

In February 1373 Edward sent a maritime expedition to Brittany under the Earl of Salisbury, who took and burned St Malo; the chief result of the expedition was, however, to cause the French king to send his constable to Brittany and subjugate a great part of the duchy to the French cause. Jean de Montfort, Duke of Brittany, fled to England and sought the help of Edward.

Late in July the Dukes of Lancaster and Brittany landed in Calais with some eleven thousand men. They went through Artois, Picardy, Champagne, Burgundy, Auvergne and Limousin. They pillaged and burned as they went and were in their turn harassed by various enemy bands. It was the declared policy of du Guesclin not to engage with them in battle unless he had the advantage of both position and numbers; the lessons of Crécy and Poitiers seemed to have been learned. By the time Lancaster (who had by now quarrelled with Montfort) reached the mountains, winter had set in. He had already lost much of his baggage and equipment; he now lost many of his troops through cold and privation.

When he reached Bordeaux at the turn of the year he was very ready to sign a truce with du Guesclin—a purely local one, unknown to his sovereign. It was, however, the first of a series of truces which were to check major operations for three years or more. Charles V wisely used the breathing-space to rebuild his navy, which had been virtually inoperative since Sluys; by the resumption of hostilities the French fleet under its admiral, Jean de Vienne, was a serious threat to English communications.

Repeated attempts were made by Pope Gregory XI to turn the truce into a lasting peace. Both sides were exhausted; both made wildly impossible claims which they could not expect to be fulfilled. Each year from 1372 there was at least one major conference attended by highly placed representatives on each side and by an important papal legate. Territorial problems could have reached a solution; a remission of part of the late King Jean's ransom would have been accepted; but there was continued disagreement over the old question of sovereignty in Aquitaine. Pope Gregory, peace-loving but anxious for a reconciliation also because a united Christendom in the west would be of great support for the return to Rome which he desired, could achieve no more than a truce which lasted until 1377.

The physical exhaustion of both sides was increased by the death of the

Black Prince in 1376 and of Edward in 1377, though both had ceased to be more than a legend in the military field, and of Bertrand du Guesclin in 1380, followed in the same year by that of Charles V.

¶ . . . About this time there died Edward, Prince of Wales and of Aquitaine, eldest son of Edward the Third of England, the flower of all the world's knighthood at that time, and one to whom there had been granted the greatest deeds of arms and valorous achievements. This valiant man the noble Prince of Wales departed this life in the Palace of Westminster, outside the city of London. His death was everywhere lamented and there was much mourning over his knightly qualities, for which the noble princes at his death expressed their gratitude to God; never did the great lords show greater faith and penitence. He died on Trinity Sunday [8 June] in the year of Our Lord thirteen hundred and seventy-six. In order to show the true honour and reverence due to him for the knightly virtues he had shown in his life, he was embalmed and put in a leaden coffin and covered over except for the face; he was left thus until the feast of Michaelmas, so that all the bishops, lords and knights of England might be present at his funeral in Westminster.

¶ As soon as the King of France received news of the death of his cousin the prince he caused a funeral service to be sung for him with the greatest pomp in the Sainte-Chapelle in his palace; it was attended by his three brothers and a great number of bishops, lords and knights of the kingdom of France, and the king declared that the Prince of Wales had led a life of magnificent valour.

At All Saints' tide a conference was held in Bruges; the King of England sent, in accordance with his agreement, Sir John Montagu, Lord Cobham, the Bishop of Hereford and the Dean of Saint Paul's; from the King of France there came the Comte de Saarbruck, the Lord of Chatillon and Lord Philibert de l'Espinasse. Both parties had with them their legal advisers. These lords and their advisers remained a long time in Bruges without achieving much, for nothing could come of it when the English and French merely stated their demands. During this time the Duke of Brittany was in Flanders with his cousin the Earl Louis of Flanders, whom he found most pleasant and tractable, but he did not concern himself with these negotiations.

At the beginning of Lent a secret treaty was prepared between the French and English representatives, and each party was to take the treaty back to his king and then return, they or others whom the king might send, to Montreuil, and thus the truce was extended till the first day of May. Then the English returned to England and the French to France with their treaties and reported on the state of affairs when they had separated, after which further envoys were sent to Montreuil—from the French, the Seigneur de Coucy, Bureau de la Rivière, Sir Nicolas Braque and Sir Jean le Mercier; from the English, Sir Guichard d'Angle, Sir Richard Sturry and Geoffrey Chaucer. These knights and legates negotiated for some time concerning the marriage of the young Richard, son of the late Prince of Wales, and Marie, daughter of the King of France, taking treaties back to their own kingdoms, after prolonging the truce for a further month.*

¶ We have neglected to record how the King of England, on the Feast of the Nativity of Our Lord in the year 1376, held a solemn assembly in his Palace of Westminster, which he ordered all the bishops, dukes, earls, barons and knights of England to attend. There Prince Richard was brought before the king and, in the presence of all the above-named, declared to be heir to the lands and crown of England after his father's decease; the king set him beside his throne and caused all the bishops, earls, barons, knights, mayors of the cities and chief ports and harbours of England to swear to acknowledge him as their lord and sovereign. Soon afterwards the king fell into a decline, from which he died within a year, as you will read . . .

¶ When the negotiations were resumed at Montreuil the French were represented by the Lord de Coucy and Guillaume de Dormans, Chancellor of France, and the English sent back to Calais the Earl of Salisbury, Sir Guichard d'Angle, the Bishop of Hereford and the Bishop of Saint David's, Chancellor of England. With them as intermediaries were the two papal legates, the Archbishop of Ravenna and the Bishop of Carpentras. Their negotiations still concerned the

* This brief extension of the truce was the only result of the negotiations, for the young princess died in May of the same year. She was only 7 years old, the same age as Isabelle whom Richard married in 1396. The negotiations were secret and are not mentioned in official chronicles; Froissart, however, was on terms of friendship with all three of the English commissioners, and there is confirmation of his account in the record, dated 17 February 1377, of a treasury payment to the poet: 'Galfrido Chaucer, armigero regis, misso in nuncium in secretis negotiis domini regis versus partes Flandriae.'

marriage already mentioned, and the French offered, along with their princess, twelve cities of Aquitaine in the kingdom of France, but they required that Calais should be razed. The negotiations were, however, broken off without anything being achieved, because in spite of any reasons that the negotiators might advance, the two parties could not, or dared not, agree on a place between Montreuil and Calais where they might come together. Things therefore remained as before; the truce was not further prolonged, and war was renewed when the French returned to France [24 June 1377].

During this time the Duke of Brittany was with his cousin the Earl of Flanders in Bruges, where the papal legates had withdrawn, saying that they had not been able to achieve anything; when the duke learned this he wrote to the Earl of Salisbury and Sir Guichard d'Angle, who were at Calais, asking them to meet him on a given date with a body of archers and men-at-arms, for he wished to return to England and was afraid of being ambushed on the frontier of Flanders and Artois. The Earl of Salisbury and Sir Guichard d'Angle therefore left Calais with a hundred men-at-arms and two hundred archers and went some distance into Flanders for the Duke of Brittany, whom they brought back safely to Calais.

¶ When our Holy Father Pope Gregory XI heard that there had proved to be no means of securing peace between the Kings of France and England, he was much displeased, and he told his brother cardinals that he intended to leave Avignon and that they should make the necessary arrangements, for he intended to transfer his seat to Rome. The cardinals were not very pleased with this decision, and they reasoned with him in various ways to point out that if he went there he would bring confusion into the Church. In spite of their pleadings the Holy Father said that his mind was made up and that he would go, whatever might be the outcome. He therefore got ready and compelled them to accompany him. When they saw that there was no other choice they went along with him, and setting sail from Marseilles [2 October 1376] they reached Genoa, where they rested; after re-embarking in their ships they sailed on to Rome, where they were joyfully received by the inhabitants of Rome and the Romagna [17 January 1377]. By this action of the pope's, great troubles were to ensue in the Church, as I shall tell you later if it is granted to me to continue this history to that point.

The Conflict is Resumed

¶ During all the time that the abortive negotiations were being conducted in Bruges the King of France was making preparations for a large-scale operation at sea with the intention of burning and plundering the coast of England. His men were provided with galleys and large vessels sent by Henry of Trastamara, King of Castille, under the command of his chief admiral, Don Ferrand Sanchez de Tovar. The French ships were commanded at that time by Jean de Vienne, Admiral of France; with him were Jean de Rye and a certain number of experienced knights and squires from Burgundy, Picardy, Champagne and other parts. These armed ships were cruising at sea, awaiting only the signal that the war had been renewed. The English were well aware of the situation, since the commanders of the English islands of Guernsey, Jersey and Wight had sent information to the Council of the King of England. At this time the king was very ill and his doctors despaired of his recovery; the business of the realm was discussed not with him but with his son, the Duke of Lancaster. By him Sir John Arundel was sent to Southampton with two hundred men-at-arms and three hundred archers to guard the harbour, the town and that part of the coast against the French.

When the Duke of Brittany . . . was brought back to Calais by the Earl of Salisbury . . . he received news that the king his lord was seriously ill and very weak. He left Calais as soon as he could, while the Earl of Salisbury and Sir Guichard d'Angle remained there. He landed at Dover, rode thence to London, and asked where the king was. They told him that he lay very sick in the little royal palace of Sheen, on the Thames, five English leagues from London. When the duke . . . arrived he found there the Duke of Lancaster, the Earl of Cambridge, Thomas the king's youngest son, and the Earl of March, who were awaiting the moment when God should require the king's soul; there, too, was his daughter, the Dame de Coucy, who was sad at heart to see her lord and father in these straits.

Three days before St John Baptist's day, in the year of Our Lord thirteen seventy-seven, the valiant and noble King Edward the Third of England departed this life; at his death the whole country and realm of England were cast into grief, and with good reason, for he had been an excellent king. Never had there been the like since the days of Arthur, who was also King of England—in his day known as Great Britain.* His body was embalmed and reverently placed upon a bier, which was carried, with the face uncovered, at a slow march through the length of the city of London by twenty-four knights clad in black, and followed by his three sons, the Duke of Brittany and the Earl of March. Anyone who on that day heard the lamentations of the people, their cries and weeping, and the regrets that were expressed on all sides must have been struck with pity and compassion. Thus was the noble king borne through the streets of London to Westminster, where, as it had been decreed in their life, he was buried beside his wife, Philippa of Hainault, Queen of England. The obsequies were conducted with a nobility and reverence that were worthy of him, in the presence of all the bishops, earls, barons and knights of England at that time.

After the funeral, it was realized that the kingdom of England could not be long without a sovereign, and that it would be good for the whole kingdom that they should as soon as possible have him crowned whom the late king had decreed to succeed him while he was alive. The bishops, earls, barons, knights and representatives of the people of England therefore met and appointed a day by common consent when the young Prince Richard could be crowned without undue delay.

The same week that the king died the Earl of Salisbury and Sir Guichard d'Angle returned from Calais, very sad at the death of the valiant king, but they had to bear their loss because it was God's will. Then all the ports of the country were closed and no one could leave from any of them, because they wanted to set the affairs of the country on a sound footing before the king's death was known.

¶ On the Feast of SS. Peter and Paul the French landed at Rye, a port in the county of Sussex, near the borders of Kent, a fair-sized town of fishermen and sailors. They pillaged and burnt the whole town, then took to their ships and sailed off towards Southampton, without, however, approaching it on this occasion.†

* A very early reference to the title 'Great Britain'.

† The chronology of these maritime raids on England is confusing, because Froissart has telescoped two separate campaigns. From Thomas Walsingham and other sources the order of events can be established as follows:

First Campaign: The French fleet must have left Harfleur immediately the truce ended on 24 June 1377; it was composed of about a hundred galleys. They sacked and

When this news reached London, where all the country was assembled to crown the young King Richard, everyone was horror-struck and they all said: 'We must hasten to crown our king, and then set off against these French before they do further damage.' Thus was the young Richard crowned King of England in the palace and chapel of Westminster on the sixteenth day of July in the same year, the eleventh of his age. On this day King Richard created nine knights and five earls; I do not know the names of the knights, but the earls were Prince Thomas, his uncle, Earl of Buckingham; the Lord Henry Percy, Earl of Northumberland; Sir Thomas Holland, his half-brother, Earl of Kent; Sir Guichard d'Angle, his tutor, Earl of Huntingdon; and Lord Thomas Mowbray, Earl of Nottingham.

Immediately after the ceremony orders were made for some to go to Dover to guard the straits, and some to other parts; the Earl of Cambridge and his brother the Earl of Buckingham were to go to Dover, with a good four hundred men-at-arms and six hundred archers, whilst the Earl of Salisbury and Sir John Montagu his brother went to another port known as Poole with two hundred men-at-arms and three hundred archers.

Whilst the coronation and these other dispositions were proceeding, over a period of ten to twelve days, the reinforcements had not yet reached their destination, with the exception of Sir John Arundel, who had arrived safely with his men at Southampton. His party did good work, for if he had not been well established there, as has been mentioned, the town would have been destroyed by the French, who had landed in the Isle of Wight and set up camp there with their cavalry to launch attacks on the coast. They had succeeded in burning and pillaging the towns of Portsmouth, Dartmouth, Plymouth and Weymouth, which were considerable places, taking several rich men prisoner, and then returned to their ships with their booty and their horses, and weighing anchor set sail for Southampton. They calculated to arrive there on the next tide, and reached the harbour,

---

burned Rye on 29 June, dealt similarly with Rottingdean and were at Lewes by early July, though this incident is placed much later by Froissart. On 20 July they sacked Folkestone, and then proceeded against Portsmouth, Dartmouth and Plymouth. We know that Jean de Vienne was back in Harfleur in early August.

Second Campaign: Embarking in mid-August, the French captured and occupied the Isle of Wight on the 21st, only the castle of Carisbrooke holding out. After attacks on Southampton and Winchelsea, and the burning of Poole, the campaign ended on 10 September after the threat to Dover.

where they gave signs of making a large landing. But Sir John Arundel and his men were informed of their arrival, having watched them at sea making for the harbour, and were drawn up in armed array to meet them. There was a small skirmish, and the French, realizing that they would make little advance, withdrew to their ships, and sailed along the coast of England towards Dover.

Their course brought them, however, to Poole, which is an important town, and there they tried to make a landing; but William Montagu, Earl of Salisbury, and his brother John, had drawn their men up in battle order and were ready for them. Another small skirmish ensued, of no great importance, and the French took to sea again and sailed back along the coast towards Dover. Several coastal villages in these parts would have been burnt and despoiled, had the Earl of Salisbury not followed them along the coast with his cavalry; for whenever they made a show of landing, the earl was there beforehand to defend the coast, showing the French that he had valiant and disciplined men-at-arms to preserve the honour of their country.

¶ As they sailed along the coast of England, Jean de Vienne and Jean de Rye, the French admirals, and the Spanish admiral harried the land and made every effort to force a landing for their own advantage. They came shortly before a considerable town near the sea called Lewes, where there is a very rich priory. The people of the surrounding country had taken refuge there with the prior and two knights, Sir Thomas Cheyne and Sir John Fallesley. The Earl of Salisbury and his brother were unable to get there in time, because of the rough roads and difficult going between Lewes and the country they were in.

The French reached the port [of Newhaven], which they entered in formation, bringing their ships as close to the land as they could; they effected their landing in spite of the English defenders, who did what they could. As they entered Lewes there was a deal of fighting, and many French were wounded by arrows; but they were so numerous that they drove back their enemies, who gathered in a convenient square in front of the monastery to await the foe approaching in close order for a hand-to-hand fight. Many noble feats of arms were performed on both sides, and the English defended themselves very well considering their numbers, for they were very few in comparison with the French. For this reason they exerted themselves all the more, while the French were all the more eager to inflict losses on them. Finally the French conquered the town and dislodged the English; two hundred of them were killed and a large number of the more important men taken prisoner, rich men from the surrounding parts who had come there to win honour; the prior and the two knights were also taken. The whole town of Lewes was ransacked and burnt or destroyed, together with some small villages round about. By high tide the French were already back in their ships, and they set sail with their booty and their prisoners, from whom they learned of the death of King Edward and the coronation of King Richard.*

The Admiral, Jean de Vienne, hastened to send this news to the King of France [Charles V]. He sent one of his knights and three squires with letters of credence in a large Spanish barge which crossed the channel and arrived at Le Crotoy below Abbeville; there they landed, and taking horse, rode towards Amiens without entering Abbeville and by hard riding soon reached Paris. Here they found the king, surrounded by the Dukes of Berry, Burgundy and Bourbon and a great many other nobles, and presented their letters of credence in support of the news which they had to declare.

When the King of France learned the death of his adversary the King of England, and the coronation of King Richard, he was much concerned; not only because he was genuinely grieved, but also because he wanted to perform fitting rites for the dead king, whom in time of peace he called his brother. He ordered the obsequies to be celebrated in the Sainte-Chapelle in Paris with as much ceremony as if the King of England had been his own cousin, by which as King of France he showed that he was not lacking in honour, for he could have done much less had he wished . . .

¶ . . . All the English from round about were assembled at Dover, where the two uncles of the king, the Earls of Cambridge and Buckingham, were stationed with a good four hundred lance and eight hundred archers, and they would gladly have seen the French come in to make a landing there. They had agreed not to oppose a landing, so that they could more readily engage battle, for they considered themselves strong enough to deal with the French; they therefore remained quietly in battle order within the town, from where they saw Jean de Vienne's fleet coming straight towards Dover with the tide. All the English were overjoyed to see them approach and to know there would be a fight; but when the French had come close to

* That they learned of Edward III's death from the Lewes prisoners argues in favour of the chronology of the footnote to p. 174.

the entrance of the harbour they decided not to make a landing there and turned and sailed on the tide to Calais, where they anchored.

The garrison at Calais were astonished to see them arrive so suddenly and hastened to arm and prepare themselves, for they thought an assault was imminent; they closed the gates and barriers and were in a state of great fear because Sir Hugh Calveley, at that time commander of Calais, was absent, although he returned the same evening from St-Omer, where he had ridden with two other knights . . . to whom he had been showing the various garrisons in that neighbourhood. When on his return he saw this huge fleet of French and Spanish ships lying off Calais he ordered a close watch to be kept that night and the following day, during which time they remained constantly armed, for they expected an assault at any moment. It was thought in France, as it was by the English in Calais, that this navy was intending to besiege Calais, but when they had lain off the town for eight days a contrary wind arose which took them unawares and was so strong that it forced them to depart. Such are the dangers of navigation. They therefore weighed anchor and set sail with the wind [*c.* 10 September 1377]. They were soon a considerable distance away, and their course brought them to the harbour of Harfleur in Normandy, where they landed. After this the French king's fleet was disbanded, and I have not heard that they did much more for some time.

A further period of stalemate followed. In both countries a very young king had succeeded to the throne and great difficulties were experienced by rival regents in gathering taxes to continue the war. Though there were other causes, too, we may see in these two difficult regencies the threatening rise of the houses of Lancaster and Burgundy.

Affairs in Aquitaine became quiescent and English prestige was somewhat restored by the sending to Bordeaux in 1378 of a new lieutenant in that city, John Neville. In the same year the English had a fortunate acquisition when Charles of Navarre by his last perfidy sold the town and fortress of Cherbourg. Du Guesclin withdrew from Aquitaine to continue his suppression of the routiers *in Auvergne, and it was at a siege during this campaign that he met his death in 1380.*

After much uncertainty in Brittany, King Charles V had secured the allegiance on oath of the duke, following the death of Richard II. But this had unexpected repercussions, in that the ever-separatist Bretons felt it to be something of a threat to their independence and, as a result, their duke, Jean de

Montfort, soon realigned himself with the English crown. With English help he regained control of Brest and the western parts of the duchy.

The problems of the papacy now prepared the way for a dramatic change in European alignments. France had fiercely opposed the return to Rome of the Avignon pope, Gregory XI; when in 1378 he was succeeded by an Italian, Urban VI, her anger was fully aroused. Later the same year France elected her own candidate, the Genevan Clement VII, who returned to reside in Avignon; only Naples and Scotland joined France to support him. With rival popes each favouring his own supporters there was now no peacemaker pope. When in 1380 Charles V made an effort to secure English support for the Avignon pope by offering lands, and his daughter in marriage, to Richard II, Urban saw to it that Richard should marry Anne of Bohemia.

Military activity was sporadic and unimportant. Edward III's youngest son, the Earl of Buckingham (later Duke of Gloucester), led a raid through northern France in 1380 which did much damage but had no political consequences. There were risings in Languedoc against the royal taxes; in England the vast sums received on account of the ransom of King Jean le Bon—never paid in full—had all been frittered away and new demands for taxes were made. Popular resentment was directed at the Duke of Lancaster, and two of the chief tax-gatherers were dismissed. Lack of money made campaigning impossible.

Richard II began his reign at an inauspicious time, and his troubles were increased by doubts over the regency. The poll-tax that was instituted hit the peasants hardest. In May 1381 they rose in revolt in the south-eastern counties, sacked monasteries, invaded London, burned the houses of foreign merchants, destroyed John of Gaunt's Palace of the Savoy, captured the Tower and murdered the Archbishop of Canterbury. The story of how Richard II, then fourteen years old, quelled the rioting peasants under Wat Tyler is well known.

France prepares to invade England

The problems of the minority in France were perhaps even greater than they were in England. The king's three uncles sought their own advancement at the expense of the royal taxes by projected expeditions to Naples, Flanders and elsewhere. There were risings against the taxes, as in England. In November 1382 the Duke of Burgundy, Philippe le Hardi, routed the pro-English insurgents of Ghent at Rosebecque; as a result Flanders became for the time once more under French influence, and the Burgundian party was greatly strengthened. An invasion of Flanders under the unexpected leadership of the Bishop of Norwich was repulsed. It had, of course, become clear to the English that any war on France was a war on a schismatic country.

At this point the Duke of Burgundy proposed an invasion of England as the surest means of quelling English interference in the affairs of greater France. In early 1386 John of Gaunt, Duke of Lancaster, had set sail for Spain, vainly dreaming of the crown of Castille, which he considered to be his by right. The problems of the regency in England were simplified by his departure, and Burgundy no doubt thought an invasion would be easier in his absence.

The preparations for invasion are described in detail by Froissart; before he takes over the story we catch an entertaining sidelight on the English and the people of Aquitaine, whom Froissart here and elsewhere calls Gascons.

¶ Men from other countries may well marvel how the noble realm of France possesses such a profusion of towns, cities and fortresses that they can scarcely be counted, as many being found in the outlying districts as there are in the very centre of the country. If you travel from Toulouse along the Garonne to Bordeaux, where it is renamed the Gironde, you will pass twenty-five fortified places, and another dozen if you go up the Dordogne, which is a tributary of the Garonne. Some of these castles are English and some French, and they have always been at war with each other, never wishing that it should be otherwise. For thirty years the Gascons have never been constant in the service of one lord.

It is true that the Gascons placed the overlordship of Gascony in the hands of King Edward III of England and of his son the Prince of Wales, but later they withdrew it, as has already been clearly unfolded in this History, at the instigation of King Charles V of France . . . who won back the friendship of the chief Gascons, the Comte d'Armagnac and the Seigneur d'Albret, by his gentleness and his great gifts, while the Prince of Wales lost their support through his impetuosity. For I who have written this History was at Bordeaux when the prince left for Spain, and can affirm that the pride of the English was so great in the entourage of the prince that they had no consideration for any nation but their own, and the nobles of Gascogne and Aquitaine, who had lost their lands in these wars, could not attain any office in their own country. The English said they were not worthy of office, which made them so indignant that they showed it at the first opportunity; because of the prince's

they were wrong to be afraid, because their lord the Duke of Burgundy wished them only well . . .

¶ Meanwhile preparations were being continued at Bruges, Damme and Sluys, the like of which were never known in the memory of man or recorded history. Money was no more spared than if it had rained from the skies or been drawn up from the sea. The chief barons of France had sent their men to Sluys to prepare and load their ships and provide them with everything that was needed, for they all wanted to go across with the army. The king, young as he was, was more anxious to do so than all the others and showed his keenness to the very end. All the great lords made a common effort to stock their ships well and to have them painted and coloured, emblazoning them each with his own arms and devices. The painters had a fine time of it; they were paid whatever they asked, and even then there were not enough of them for the work. They made pennons and flags of silk that were marvels to behold. The masts were painted from top to bottom, and some, in a display of magnificence, were covered with gold leaf, the arms of the owner being fixed at the head. I was particularly informed that Sir Guy de la Tremouille had so richly ornamented the ship in which his men were to cross that the decorations and paintings had cost him two thousand francs. Everything that could be imagined to decorate the ships was, in fact, carried out by the great lords. And all this was paid for by the poor people of France, for the taxes were so great that the richest complained and the poorest went into hiding.

Everything that was being done in France and Flanders for this expedition was known in England. In the cities and large towns, processions of bishops and congregations were ordered to be held three times a week in a spirit of devout contrition; prayers were offered to God to deliver the country from this peril. Yet more than a hundred thousand Englishmen desired nothing better than that the French should land in England, saying cheerfully, as much to reassure themselves as the faint-hearted: 'Let the Frenchmen come. Not a man jack of them will ever get back to France.' Those who were in debt and had neither mind nor means to pay, were delighted, and said to their creditors: 'Hold your tongues. We'll pay you with the florins they are minting in France!' Trusting in this, they went on drinking and spending freely and credit was never refused them, for when they were not offered credit they would say: 'Why do you want money? Isn't it better that we should use up everything in the land than that the French should come and make free with it?' In this way thousands of pounds sterling were wastefully consumed in England.*

At this time the King of England was on the Welsh border with the Earl of Oxford, who controlled everything in the country and without whom no decisions could be taken. The chief members of the king's council were Sir Simon Burley, Sir Nicolas Bramber, Sir Robert Tresilian, Sir John Beauchamp, John de Montagu Earl of Salisbury, Michel de la Pole Archbishop of York, and Sir William Neville the brother of Lord Neville. All these men could do as they willed with the king and led him by the nose; neither the Earl of Cambridge nor the Earl of Buckingham had any power at all unless it pleased these gentlemen. All these discords were well known in France, and because of them they pressed on with their preparations; they were, moreover, most anxious to make the Duke of Lancaster break off his expedition to Castille.

When the lords, bishops and municipalities of England received exact information that the French were all ready to invade and ravage the country, they held a common council to study what measures should now be taken. The king was summoned by his uncles and the whole kingdom to come to London, and was informed that the country in general was dissatisfied with both him and his council. They and he together dared not refuse, and left the Welsh marches, where he had been for a considerable time. He came with the queen to Windsor, where he halted a few days. Leaving the queen there, he moved on to London and took up residence in his Palace of Westminster. There he was visited by those who had business with him, and a council was summoned to decide how to meet this terrible threat to England. At this assembly the Earl of Salisbury, a very wise and brave man, spoke thus in the presence of the king, his uncles and all the bishops and barons of England there assembled:

'My lord and king, good people all, you should not wonder that our enemies in France wish to invade and attack us, for ever since the death of the noble and mighty sovereign our master, King Edward of happy memory, this realm of ours has been in great danger of being destroyed from within by the actions of the common people. They are well aware in France that we are rent by disunity and discord, which is why this great danger is now facing us, and we should be foolish not to fear it. So long as the kingdom of England remained united, the king with his people and the people with their king, we

* Walsingham tells us there were large numbers of unpaid troops roaming the country round London in search of food and plunder.

ruled in power and victory and there was none who did us any harm. It is therefore our urgent duty, more pressing than at any time in the past history of England, to resolve our differences in love and fellowship if we wish to come out of our troubles with honour. Let us look to the ports and harbours of England, that they may be so well equipped and guarded that the country can suffer no harm through our neglect. For a long time now this realm of ours has been in full bloom, and you well know that a tree in flower has greater need of protection than when the fruit has set. Let us remind ourselves that it is indeed in full bloom, for the knights and squires who have gone forth from this land in the last sixty years have had more honour in deeds of arms than those of any other nation you can name. Let us therefore exert every fibre to see that our honour is preserved so long as we live.' And all the lords present cried: 'That would be good.'

The Earl of Salisbury was given a good hearing and his words were accepted as those of a wise and valiant man. I shall not record all that was then said by those present, for I cannot know everything. But I do know that since the defences of Calais were prepared as has been already stated, orders were now given for the protection of all English ports where it was thought the French might attempt a landing. The Earl of Salisbury, because his lands stretched to that part of the coast opposite the Isle of Wight, which faces out to Normandy and the Pays de Caux, was ordered to that island with men and archers from the county of Chester. The Earl of Devon was to guard the haven of Southampton with two hundred men-at-arms and six hundred archers. The Earl of Northumberland was to guard the port of Rye with the same numbers; the Earl of Cambridge was sent to Dover with five hundred men-at-arms and twelve hundred archers, while his brother the Earl of Buckingham went to Sandwich with six hundred men-at-arms and twelve hundred archers. The Earls of Stafford and Pembroke were to guard the port of Orwell* with five hundred men-at-arms and twelve hundred archers. Sir Henry Percy and his brother Sir Raoul Percy were ordered to Yarmouth with three hundred men-at-arms and six hundred archers. At Dover Sir Simon Burley was put in charge of the castle only. Every harbour from Humber to Cornwall was garrisoned with men-at-arms and archers or their garrisons increased.

Guards were posted on all the hills overlooking the coasts opposite France and Flanders. They had Gascony wine-casks filled with sand and fastened one on top of the other, and on the topmost was

* Ipswich.

constructed a platform where there were men looking out to sea by day and by night; from this position they could command a view of seven or more leagues. These guards had orders that if they saw the French navy approaching the coast of England they were to light a fire and torches on the spot, and large beacon fires on the hill-tops to warn the people to assemble in the place where the fires were lit. Orders were also given that the King of France and his men should be allowed to land unmolested and to remain on English soil for three or four days; then, before any attack was to be made, they were to go and destroy all the French ships and their provisions. After which they would still not engage the French in battle, but harass their army so that they could not go foraging and dared not try. All the productive land would first have been laid waste, and England is anyhow difficult country for horsemen. In this way the French would be starved, and destroyed without battle. This was the plan of the Council of England. The bridge at Rochester was ordered to be destroyed; a broad river flows through that town, coming from the county of Sussex and Arundel, and enters the estuary of the Thames opposite the Isle of Sheppey. This bridge was destroyed by men from London for their own greater safety. I have told you that men in the towns of France had burdensome taxes to pay; similar taxes were imposed in England and the people complained of them long afterwards. But at the time they paid up gladly so that they might be better protected. There were gathered in England at that time a hundred thousand archers and five thousand men-at-arms in spite of the great army that had been taken to Castille by the Duke of Lancaster . . .

¶ There were at this time so many ships, galleys, barges and other kinds of vessel being prepared to transport the King of France and his men to England that the oldest then alive had never seen or heard of the like. Lords with their men poured in from every side; every knight and squire held himself fortunate to be going on this invasion of England with the King of France, and they said: 'Let us now invade these miserable English folk who have caused such mischief and destruction in France, and so avenge ourselves for our fathers and mothers and friends whom they have killed.' Others said: 'The day of reckoning always comes in the end. We are lucky to be alive now when this long-desired invasion is about to take place.' It needed twelve weeks to make all the magnificent preparations of these lords and to load their vessels; meanwhile throughout Flanders they kept repeating: 'The king will come tomorrow, the king will come tomorrow.' Men were constantly arriving from Savoy, Burgundy, Barrois, Lorraine, France and Champagne; from Gascony, Armagnac, Comminges, Toulousain, Bigorre, Auvergne, Berry, Limousin, Poitou, Anjou, Maine, Brittany, Touraine, Blésis, Orléanais, Gâtinais, Beauce, Normandy, Picardy and from every other province in France; all came and quartered themselves in Flanders or Artois.

Around the middle of August, when the invasion should have been imminent and men were still arriving from the more distant provinces, the king resolved to set an example to all and show that he was firmly resolved upon the invasion, so as to hasten the late-comers. [At the beginning of September 1386] he took leave of Queen Blanche, the Duchesse d'Orléans, and the other ladies of the Court, and set out after attending a solemn mass in the church of Notre-Dame in Paris. It was his intention not to return to Paris until he had set foot in England, an intention which was believed in all the cities and chief towns of France. The king was accompanied to Senlis by his wife, and there he halted before . . . going on to Compiègne, Noyon, Péronne, Bapaume and Arras. All along the route the countryside was so pillaged by men coming from all parts that the whole land was devastated and not a sou paid for anything. The poor peasants who had harvested their grain had only the straw left; if they spoke out they were beaten or killed. The fishponds were emptied of fish, and houses were knocked down for firewood. If the English had been there they couldn't have made more havoc than these French, who said: 'We've no money now, but we shall have plenty when we come back and then we'll pay you at once.' The poor folk cursed them as they saw the soldiers take the food intended for their own children, but dared not utter a word. They could only mutter under their breath: 'Off with you, dirty rascals, and may never a man of you come back.'

The King of France reached Lille in company with his uncles the Duke of Burgundy and the Duke of Bourbon, the Duke of Berry being still in his own country making his preparations. With the king, too, were so many lords that I should never finish telling you their names. There were, it was said, twenty thousand knights and squires ready to cross over to England, indeed a fine company, together with the same number of crossbowmen, including the Genoese, and a good twenty thousand other stout fellows.

Meanwhile Sir Olivier de Clisson was still in Brittany, ordering the preparation of his fleet at Tréguier, and especially the portable fortifications in wood . . . of which we have already spoken. All the chief knights and squires of Brittany were to go with the Constable of France, accompanied by at least five hundred Breton lances, all chosen men, for it had always been the Constable's firm intention that only men of proved worth should go to England. To the admiral he had said: 'See that you take on board no common folk or serving men, for they would do us more harm than good.' Several of the chief knights, other than the great lords who had equipped ships at their own expense, were able to take with them one other knight and one servant. Here indeed plans were carefully laid and well organized, and it is the opinion of many that if all the French had been able to reach England together and land at an appointed spot, they would have thrown the whole of that country into confusion. There is little doubt they would indeed have done so, for the great lords, the bishops, the abbots and the chief towns were in a state of panic, though the common folk who would risk their lives were not much worried. Those knights and squires of little wealth who had all to win or lose, said to each other: 'The times, thank God, are ripe for us when the King of France comes to invade the land; he's a brave and resolute king, and there's been no king in France like him for three hundred years. He will make his people into good fighters and they will make him a worthy king. A blessing on him for coming to invade us. We shall all be slain or win great riches: there is no other possibility.' . . .

¶ . . . Sir Simon Burley, as governor of Dover Castle, was in a position to receive news from France through the men in Calais or through English fishermen who had often to go as far as Boulogne or Wissant to get good fishing. They brought information back to Sir Simon at his request, for French fishermen they met at sea would readily tell them all they knew—and even more than they knew; whatever war may be afoot between the two countries, fishermen would not engage in any hostilities, but would help each other if need arose and sell fish to the other at sea if one had a better catch. If they attacked each other they would have no catch at all, and no one would dare to go and fish unless they were protected by an armed escort.

From the Dover fishermen Sir Simon Burley learned that the King of France was certain to come and that the French would indeed make landings, one at Dover and the other at Sandwich, in great numbers. Sir Simon believed all these reports, which were also accepted throughout England. One day he went to Canterbury to the Abbey of Saint Thomas,* a fine large building near the Abbey of Saint Vincent, very rich and powerful; both are directed by the Black Friars. When asked for news he told them what he knew, and by his words he showed that the shrine of Saint Thomas, which is particularly rich and splendid, was not very safe in Canterbury, for the town was not well defended. 'And if the French come,' said Sir Simon, 'as they soon will, thieves and robbers will come to this town in the hope of riches and will pillage your church. They will particularly want to know what has become of the shrine of Saint Thomas. If they find it they'll carry it off, and you will have lost it. For this reason I advise you to have it conveyed inside the castle at Dover, where it will be quite safe if the whole of England should be subdued.' The Abbot of Saint Thomas of Canterbury and all his house were so disgusted at these words, kindly though they were meant, that they replied: 'What, Sir Simon, would you deprive our church of its pride and jewel? If you are scared, go and shut yourself up in safety in Dover Castle, for the French will never dare to come as far as here.' They spread the news of Sir Simon's request and the reply they had made, with the result that the people of England became annoyed with him, holding him suspect of unpatriotic activity. Sir Simon left soon after, and returned to his castle at Dover.

¶ [In early October] the King of France arrived at Sluys to show his personal desire for the invasion, to hasten its launching and also to encourage those who had not yet reached Sluys to come as quickly as possible. In Flanders and Artois they kept saying: 'The king will embark on Saturday, or Thursday, or Wednesday.' Every day of the week it was reported: 'He will sail tomorrow, or the day after that.' His brother the Duc de Touraine,† the Bishop of Beauvais, Chancellor of France, and several others of the chief lords of France and of the Parlement had taken leave of the king at Lille in Flanders and returned to Paris. I believe—and indeed I was personally assured—that the government of the country had been entrusted to the Duc de Touraine until the king's return, with the assistance of several French lords, among them the Duc de Blois, who were not ordered to England with the invasion. The Duc de Berry was still far away and making very slow progress, for he did not much want to go over

* The Cathedral Priory at Canterbury had no abbot: perhaps Froissart is confusing it with St Augustine's Abbey.

† This is Philippe le hardi, Duke of Burgundy.

to England. The King of France and the Duke of Burgundy, with the other lords, were disgusted with him for this delay and wished he would come. All the time the provisioning of the ships went ahead, at great cost to the lords, for because of the heavy demand for such things in Flanders they had to pay four francs for what was worth only one. All who were there at that time did not hesitate to spend gold or silver in equipping their ships, even rivalling each other in splendour. If the great lords were well paid for their service, it was at the expense of the ordinary people, who were a month's pay in arrears; the Keeper of the War Chest and the clerks of the Treasury repeatedly said to them: 'Wait till next week, and your troubles will be over.'

Thus they were kept waiting from one week to another, and when they were paid it was only for a month when six weeks' pay was due to them. Some of them, seeing how badly affairs were ordered and how they were being underpaid, became disheartened and said the expedition could never succeed. Some, as soon as they had received a small sum of money, wisely went off home, for the poorer knights and squires who were not in the service of one of the great lords were spending their last florins. Things were so dear in Flanders that they had difficulty in procuring bread and wine; if they wanted to pawn their wages or their arms (which had cost them vast sums) they could not get a sou advanced to them. There were so many people at Bruges, Damme and Aardenbourg, and especially at Sluys since the king's arrival, that it was impossible to find any lodgings. The Comte de St Pol, the Seigneur de Coucy, the Dauphin d'Auvergne and the Seigneur d'Antoing and several other great lords of France stayed in Bruges in order to have better lodgings, and went now and then to Sluys to find out from the king when they should embark. They were told: 'In three, or four, days; or when the Duc de Berry has arrived; or when the wind is favourable.' There was always some excuse, and all the time the weather was getting worse: the days grew shorter and colder, the nights longer, and many lords grew discontented at the delay in embarking, for provisions were running short.

¶ Meanwhile the Duc de Berry arrived in Paris and after hearing mass in the Church of Notre-Dame he set forth, having let it be known that he would not return until he had set foot in England. But his thoughts were very different, for he had no desire for an invasion at this advanced season of the year. Each day while he was

N ce tampz se fist
vne grande assam
blee de seigneurs
en la cite de rains tant de lem
pire dallemaigne comme Ou
royaume de france Et fut la
cause telle comme pour remet
tre leglise en vne vnion. Et fist

A GREAT ASSEMBLY IN RHEIMS

journeying he had letters from the king and the Duke of Burgundy urging him to hurry, for they were now waiting only for his arrival. The duke continued his journey, but in short marches.

About this time the Constable of France left Tréguier, a seaboard town in Brittany, with a great force of armed men and adequate provisions, in all seventy-two heavily laden vessels. In the constable's navy were the ships carrying the portable fortifications to be set up in England when they landed. They had a favourable wind when they set off, but as they approached England it reached too strong a force, and the more they advanced the stronger it blew. When they came off Margate at the mouth of the Thames the wind was so great that in spite of the efforts of the crews the ships were all scattered so that the main body consisted of only twenty vessels. Some were blown up the Thames and there taken by the English, in particular one or two ships carrying a part of the wooden fortifications together with the carpenters who had made them. These were all brought up the Thames to London [29 September 1386], to the great joy of the king and the citizens. A further seven of the constable's ships were blown despite their efforts to Zeeland and there perished with all their equipment, but the constable himself and the chief lords managed to reach Sluys after great difficulty and considerable danger.

The king rejoiced at the arrival of the constable and his barons, and as soon as he saw him he said: 'What do you say, constable? When shall we start? I'm impatient to see England, and I pray you to complete your preparations with speed so that we can set out at once. My uncle of Berry will be here in a couple of days, for he is now at Lille.' 'My lord,' replied the constable, 'we cannot set sail unless the wind is for us. This contrary south wind has been blowing for such a time that the sailors say they've never known a wind keep on so long as it has these two months.' 'By my faith, constable,' said the king, 'I've been on board my ship and this nautical business pleases me much. I think I shall be a good sailor, for the sea doesn't trouble me at all.' 'In God's name it troubles me, my lord,' said the constable, 'for we've been through every danger in coming from Brittany.' The king wanted to know how they had been endangered, and the constable continued: 'By ill fortune, my lord, and the heavy winds which surprised us as we came off the coast of England, we have lost some of our ships and some of our men. I am much distressed at this, and would make good the loss if I could, but for the present that is not possible.'

While the king and the constable were thus discussing the

situation the weather was worsening with the approach of winter, and the lords had heavy expenses to meet. They were also in considerable danger, for the Flemings were not very glad to see them in Flanders, especially the common sort, and muttered among themselves: 'Why the devil doesn't the King of France make up his mind to embark for England, if he must go there? Why does he remain in our country? Aren't we poor enough without the French coming to impoverish us still further?' Others spoke thus: 'You won't see them off to England this year: how should they? The French are bragging and boasting that they will soon conquer England, but they never will. She's not so easy to conquer; the English are of different metal from the French. What will they do in England? When the English went to France and overran the country they fled like larks from the sparrow-hawk and shut themselves up in their fortresses.'

In Bruges particularly, where the French were to be found in the greatest numbers, there was much discontent and people were looking for some trifle to start a riot. At length something very serious was on the point of breaking out, all because of a French youth who had beaten and injured a Fleming; the working people collected arms and began to make for the great market-place. If they had all assembled there as a body, not a baron, knight or squire of France would have escaped a merciless death, for most of these evil folk still rankled under the memory of the battle of Rosebecque* in which fathers, brothers and friends had been killed. But God intervened in favour of the French; when the Seigneur de Ghistelles, who was then in Bruges, heard that the common folk were arming themselves and that others were going to their houses to do likewise, he realized at once that the outcome might be disastrous. With four or five others, he mounted his horse and went through the streets saying to all those he saw going in armed groups towards the market-place: 'Where are you going, good people? Are you not being prevented from earning your livelihood? Get back to your homes; there is nothing amiss. You could easily raise such a riot that you and the city of Bruges would be utterly destroyed. Don't you know that the King of France is hereabouts with all his armed power?' In this way the Seigneur de Ghistelles succeeded in quietening them on that day, and by his soft words make them all go home, which they would not have done had

* At the battle of Rosebecque, on 27 November 1382, the Flemish forces under the command of Philip van Artavelde (who had continued the guerrilla warfare started by his father) were routed by the French under the command of the king, then aged 14, but led by the Duke of Burgundy.

he not been present. The barons and knights of France were so frightened that they shut themselves in their houses and their lodgings, and there awaited further events.

At last the Duc de Berry arrived at Sluys. 'Ha, fair uncle,' said the King of France, 'I have been eagerly awaiting you and you have taken a mighty long time a-coming. Why have you dallied so long? We ought now to be in England and to have fought with our foes.' The duke began to laugh apologetically, and did not at once say what he had in his mind, but expressed a desire to go and see about the equipping of his ship and to look at the fleet which was such a fine sight to behold out to sea. For the next seven days they said in Sluys: 'We shall sail on tomorrow's tide.' The fact was that the wind was so contrary for the crossing to England that they could do nothing, and St Andrew's Day was fast approaching. Was it indeed a fit moment for so many noble lords to put to sea, even though they wanted nothing better than to cross the Channel and though all their ships were ready equipped and provisioned? Many of the highest nobles of the blood royal had nosed their ships out to sea as if to say: 'I shall be among the first to land in England even if the others don't come'—knights such as Robert and Philippe d'Artois, Henry de Bar, Pierre de Navarre, Charles d'Albret, Bernard d'Armagnac and a great number besides. Having set themselves in the forefront, these young nobles did not want the expedition to be abandoned, and a royal council was therefore called to decide what should be done. It was told to me at this time—for I who am writing this history was at Sluys to watch the events and to gather news—by reliable informers, and confirmed by my own observations, that the Duc de Berry caused the whole expedition to be abandoned, against the wishes of his brother the Duke of Burgundy, who consequently nursed a grievance against him for some three months . . .

The Duc de Berry was the senior prince of France and the nearest to the king, being his uncle; moreover, he had lived five years in England as a hostage after the ransoming of his father King Jean. He thus had a good knowledge of England and of her strength, and spoke his thoughts to the inner council of nobles of France on whom the government of the kingdom depended for the time: 'We must first be certain of our desire to vanquish and overcome our enemies, for which reason we are assembled here at Sluys for the crossing to England.' Then turning to his brother, the Duke of Burgundy, he addressed himself only to him and said: 'Thus, dear brother, I cannot deny that I have been present in France at most of the councils at which this expedition has been decided upon, but I have since given much thought to these problems, for they concern a greater and more important undertaking than any that a King of France has attempted before. In view of everything, and considering the dangers and unexpected consequences that could damage the kingdom of France, I should not dare to advise that we should send the king to sea as late in the year as December, when the sea is cold and hostile; for if any harm came of it people everywhere would say we who have the responsibility for government had advised this step and embarked him to his own peril. Moreover, you will certainly have heard it said by the wisest sailors of our coasts that it is beyond their power, at this season and with a contrary wind, to ensure that a fleet of two hundred sail keep together—and England is a very difficult country on which to make a landing. Even supposing we made such a landing, it is a sea-girt country which presents serious hazards for the conduct of a military campaign, with the risk that our fleet and all our provisions could be destroyed in a single night, for we cannot defend ourselves on both sea and land. For these reasons I claim that this expedition is useless, for if it turned out that we were beaten and the king slain or captured, the kingdom of France would be lost to us without hope of recovery, since the whole flower of our knighthood is here. If you would wish to make such an expedition as this for which we are here assembled, it should be done not in winter but in the summer, when the sea is calm and the weather fair, and when the horses can have the grass of the fields for fodder—although again in England you will find little but meadows, woods and heathland. My advice is that we should go no further with our plans at this late season, but reassemble the fleet and all our men here or at Harfleur next summer, and then complete the undertaking we have begun.'

No one offered any opposition to these words of the Duc de Berry, for they considered he was so highly placed as a prince that his advice must be accepted, except only the Duke of Burgundy, who spoke thus: 'The longest and most useful part of our work has already been completed, but if we accept this counsel we shall be held much to blame, since the kingdom of France has already spent such vast sums of gold and silver that our people are still complaining, and if we go home with nothing achieved, the good folk who have provided the funds with which all this has been paid for will say—and with very good cause—that we have deceived them, and that we have assembled this expedition only to drain their purses of gold and silver.' 'Fair brother,' replied the Duc de Berry, 'if we and our men can afford it, the greater part will go back to France. It is all a question of money, and it is better to risk money than the lives of men.' 'By my faith,' replied the Duke of Burgundy, 'if we leave without achieving anything at all, we shall have more blame than honour, and I am anxious that the best should be done.' I was told (while I was at Sluys) that the discussions went on for a very long time before any decision was reached.

When the King of France realized that the undertaking to invade England was to be abandoned he was furious, and had much to say to his uncles. The Duke of Burgundy made it clear that he would prefer setting sail to returning home, but the Duc de Berry and the more sober part of the council would not consent to this. For this reason and to pacify the people the chief lords, such as the Duc de Lorraine, the Comte d'Armagnac, the Dauphin d'Auvergne and those from the furthest provinces, were informed that the departure would be held over until April, and that of the vast stores of provisions those that would keep, such as biscuit and salt meat, would be kept, and the rest would be sold for what they could get. Those barons and their followers who were anxious to cross over to England had to accept the decision. And so the expedition was abandoned; it had cost the kingdom of France three million francs or more in the way of taxes and levies.

It was pitiful to see the great lords and barons of France . . . especially those from distant parts, who had spent all their energies and wealth in the hope of fair weather, taking their departure, incensed at never having seen the coasts of England. The King of France continued his efforts, but after all had been considered it was thought best to postpone their departure until the summer. Then all classes of men set out on their various return journeys, some joyfully, some regretfully. Such is the way of life. Officers were left behind to sell off the provisions and stores, for the lords were well aware that although there was talk of sailing in April nothing of the sort would happen, for there would be plenty to do on another front. When the stores were put up for sale in Damme and Sluys and Bruges there was no one to buy: what had cost a hundred francs was sold for ten. The dauphin d'Auvergne told me himself on his word of honour that his men had embarked stores to the value of seven thousand francs and they were sold for less than seven hundred. It was the same with all the rest, except for those barons who lived near Flanders—in Artois, Hainault and Picardy. The Seigneur de Coucy suffered no loss, because he had all his provisions transported across the River

Schelt to Mortagne, near Tournay, whose seigneury he then held. He had borrowed four thousand bushels of wheat and oats from the Abbot of Saint-Pierre de Gand, and as much from the Abbot of Saint-Bavon, which was collected from their houses in the province of Tournay and in France. I was frequently informed of the steps taken by the abbots to recover their loss, but I never heard that a penny was paid to them and nothing further was done about it. The greater the sums that had been expended, the greater was the loss of those that had paid, and not a man received just payment.

¶ News of the abandonment of the expedition soon reached England; some were much relieved, for they had feared the coming of the French, others were annoyed that they would not be able to make themselves rich by the occasion. In the city of London great festivities were arranged, to which were invited all the lords who had been in charge of the defences at the harbours and coasts. At the solemn feast which was held on Christmas Day, King Richard of England made three of his earls dukes. The Earl of Cambridge became the Duke of York; his brother, the Earl of Buckingham, became Duke of Gloucester; and the Earl of Oxford became Duke of Ireland. The feasting continued with great revelry, for all the people of England believed they had been saved from great danger, according to reports that were current. Many, however, declared that they would never fear the vainglory of the French, and that the whole assembly at Sluys was designed only to make the Duke of Lancaster withdraw from Castille.*

Thus was disbanded the fleet which had cost so much labour and money to the realm of France. The sailors of Holland and Zeeland and Flanders, who had hired out their ships for a very high figure, did not give back anything of what they had received, but exacted the last sou in payment, and returned to their homes.

* Indeed, before the end of November the Archdeacon of Cordova had come to seek French aid in the name of the King of Castille, because of the Duke of Lancaster's initial successes.

the earl of arundel's expedition and the treaty of leulinghen

It is not easy to see why such elaborate plans for invasion should have been abandoned, and one hesitates to think that the whole thing had been put up as a threat and nothing more. As a result the English were inclined to mistrust peace negotiations when they saw the kind of offensive France had been preparing; the war with France was, moreover, a part of life for King Richard's two uncles.

The French had been strengthening their influence in the Low Countries and Germany; Charles VI's marriage to Isabelle of Bavaria (in 1385) had been followed by careful diplomacy among the Flemish barons on the part of Philippe le hardi, Duke of Burgundy. English alliance-seeking was for the moment at a low ebb, and she decided instead on a maritime expedition against the French.

¶ In the year of Our Lord 1388, on the eighth day of April, it was decreed in council by King Richard of England and his two uncles the Dukes of York and Gloucester, that Richard Earl of Arundel should be put in command of a fleet in which he would have a thousand men-at-arms and three thousand archers, and that they should be ready in Southampton, fully equipped and provisioned, by the fifteenth day of May. On St George's Day the King of England held a great feast in his castle of Windsor, to which were invited many of the chief lords who were to accompany the Earl of Arundel on his expedition. There they took leave of the king and his uncles, of the queen and the ladies.

On the appointed day they all arrived at Southampton or near by and went on board their ships on the 20th of May, a day of bright sunshine. With the Earl of Arundel were many of the chief lords and knights of England, and of men-at-arms a thousand lance and about three thousand archers. They took no horses with them, since they hoped that, if things went as they intended, they would land in Brittany and there buy horses cheaply. On the day they left Southampton the sea was so calm that there was scarcely a ripple; next day they reached the Isle of Wight, where they landed and amused themselves until the wind freshened. Then they re-embarked and set sail towards Normandy, not intending to make a landing, but to sail along the coast of Normandy and Brittany until other instructions reached them. Among their ships they had some of shallow draught which are known as fast whalers, and these went ahead to seek adventure, just as on land some knights and squires on the best horses ride ahead to see if there are any ambushes.

¶ For the remainder of that summer the English fleet under the Earl of Arundel wandered back and forth along the coast as the wind carried them, always with the intention of seeking some encounter. You must know (and if you do not you ought to) that from the beginning of October until All Saints' Day it is customary for the weather to be fierce and windy. This year it was particularly so, and the gales hit the English fleet so badly that their ships were widely scattered and even the hardiest sailors on board were frightened by the strength of the wind, which was so great that the Earl of Arundel was forced to make for port for fear of worse damage. Twenty-seven of his vessels reached the harbour of La Pallice, two short leagues from La Rochelle. Here they had no choice but to anchor, since the wind was too strong for them to take to sea again.

When news of this reached La Rochelle, the people of that town at first feared that the English had come to attack them, and so shut their gates and remained within the walls for two days, allowing no one to leave the town. Then further news reached them from La Pallice that the English had no more than twenty-seven ships and had been driven there by the tempestuous state of the seas, and that they did not intend to make any further move, though the Earl of Arundel and more than thirty English knights were present. The men of La Rochelle therefore held a council as to what they should do, and eventually decided that they would not be doing their duty if they did not launch some kind of an attack on these English.

At this time Louis de Sancerre, Marshal of France, was laying siege to the castle of Bouteville with a large force of knights from Poitou, Saintonge, La Rochelle, Pierregord and the Marches; the castle was defended by a Gascon named Guillonet de Sainte-Foy. For not all the French had gone into Germany with their king,* and Lord Louis was in command of all the territory from Montpellier to La Rochelle until the Seigneur de Coucy should return from the

* A small expedition had been sent to punish the Duke of Gueldre for an insulting challenge he had issued to the King of France.

German expedition. The men of La Rochelle therefore decided that they would inform Lord Louis of their position. As soon as he heard it he was glad of the news and ordered the men of La Rochelle to equip six or eight galleys at once and set out from their harbour, for he wanted to fight the English. For this reason Lord Louis raised the siege of Bouteville, since he considered it would bring greater honour and advantage to attack the Earl of Arundel and the knights of England where they lay at anchor than to continue the siege, to which he could always return. He therefore went to La Rochelle, with a large following of knights, squires and men.

I do not know how he received the news, but the Earl of Arundel at La Pallice had been told that the Marshal of France with a large army of knights was coming to attack him, and he was none too glad to learn it. It so happened that the wind had dropped considerably and the sea was much calmer; the earl immediately gave orders for his ships to weigh anchor and make for the open sea—just in time, for if he had delayed one hour he would have been cut off and all his ships taken inside the harbour, so that not a man could have escaped. As they left, the galleys from La Rochelle came up, fully armed and equipped with cannons and artillery, making all possible speed for La Pallice; when they found the English had already gone they gave chase, following them for two leagues out to sea, firing their cannon at the enemy. But they did not dare follow them much farther for fear of an ambush at sea, and so returned home. The Marshal of France was very annoyed with the Rochellois for informing him so late that the English had arrived.

¶ The fleet under the Earl of Arundel spent the rest of the year at sea, wandering along the coasts of Brittany, La Rochelle, Saintonge and the Bordelais; about Christmas-time it advanced on Lower Normandy and a landing was made at Cherbourg, where the earl had wished to launch an attack on that part of the country. Then he moved to Carentan, where the fortress was garrisoned by a large body of knights and squires from Normandy under the Seigneurs de Hambre and de Coucy.

When the Earl of Arundel and his men learned that the town of Carentan was strongly fortified by men-at-arms they passed on, because they realized that in attacking it they stood to lose more than they would gain. They continued on their way and shortly reached a town called Torigni, which they took by storm, pillaging the whole place and gaining much booty as well as many valuable prisoners.

They then moved on to the fair city of Bayeux; though they advanced to the gates of the city they launched no attack, merely engaging in one sharp skirmish. After crossing the ford known as Saint Clement's they did much harm to the country for about a fortnight, without being hindered by anyone. It is true that the Marshal de Blainville was in Normandy, but he had not been informed of the presence of the English. Had he known he would certainly have done something.

When the English had accomplished all they intended, doing damage in Normandy to the extent of a hundred thousand francs, they withdrew in good order across the ford and regained Cherbourg, where they put all their booty on board ship. When their ships were loaded and the wind was favourable they embarked and sailed to England, where they landed at Southampton.

Late in 1388 Charles VI was declared to be of age (he was then 20) and assumed the government of his country. The occasion was created in Reims by the Cardinal of Laon, acting perhaps on the persuasion of Queen Isabelle and of the king's brother Louis, best known by the title he was shortly to acquire, Duc d'Orléans. The uncles were dismissed; and when the cardinal died before the king had left Reims it was widely rumoured that he had been poisoned.

The king's new government was formed largely from the very capable administrators of his father's reign. These men were, on the whole, honestly out to establish a just order of things in France, though some, like Clisson, may have been greedy for personal gain; because they were not of the nobility they were scornfully called 'marmosets'. But though in part they reduced the taxes imposed on the people, their government turned out to be no more popular than that of the uncles.

Charles's own weaknesses were becoming more evident. His love of childish frolics and expensive festivities were giving the court a bad name, and he was unable to control his council by any signs of leadership. The arrival of the Marmosets in power, with the dismissal in England of the king's favourites, produced a situation in which a peace was more likely to be reached than it had been for some time. The negotiations took place at Leulinghen.

¶ You have heard how a truce was concluded between all the English and French garrisons in the land between the Loire, the Dordogne and the Gironde, which was to last until St John the Baptist's Day [1389]. While this truce was in force some of the wiser lords both French and English started negotiations for a general truce between their countries to last three years on land and sea. They intended this treaty to apply in the name of France to all who were fighting in the French cause, including the Kings of Castille and Scotland in all their undertakings by sea or land, and in the name of England to all the allies of her king, including the King of Portugal and several barons of Upper Gascony.

The negotiators had a great deal of work to do before they could achieve their aim, principally because the Scots would not give any kind of approval. When the proposal was communicated to King Robert of Scotland by the King of France he was for his own part ready to accept, for he did not want a war; but he would do nothing without the consent of the bishops and barons of Scotland, and indeed had he made a truce they would not have considered themselves bound by it. He therefore summoned all the bishops and barons who were entitled to be heard on this question, and in their presence had the King of France's letter read aloud, with its request that a three years' truce should be agreed by them.

The request was not acceptable to them, and they said: 'The King of France is proposing a truce at the very moment when the war should be intensified. It is only a short time since we crushed the English,* and the time of the year is such that we can well do so a second and a third time.' A long discussion was held, but none of them could see their way to accept a truce. Finally it was agreed that they would send a bishop and three knights to the court of the King of France to urge the abandonment of such a treaty and to show the goodwill of the kingdom of Scotland. Their appointed envoys were the Bishop of Saint Andrews, Sir Archibald Douglas, Sir William Lindsay and Sir John Sinclair, who left as speedily as they could and arrived by sea at the port of Sluys.

By long days of riding they soon reached Paris, where they presented to the king and his council their letters of credit from the barons and bishops of the kingdom of Scotland. They were given a ready hearing because of their keen desire to continue the war against the English. The matter of the treaty was, however, so far advanced that the French were neither able nor willing to go back on the arrangements; courteous answers were given to the Scots, but it was agreed that events should pursue their course. The truce was therefore concluded, through the intermediary of those lords and bishops of

* Troubles in Scotland, fomented by the French, had caused Richard II to lead a large army against the Scots. Misfortunes of one kind or another dogged this costly expedition, and the army returned to England without having engaged the enemy in battle. 'Crushed', however, is wishful thinking on the part of the Scots.

both kingdoms who had made it their responsibility. Several days of negotiation were spent at Leulinghen between Boulogne and Calais, and a treaty was finally drawn up and signed in the name of England and France, and of all their allies on land and sea, to keep peace for three years without any trickery or shadow of dissimulation.

The signing of this truce (on 18 June 1389) concludes the Third Book of Froissart's Chronicles; the short prologue to his last Book tells us something of the ways in which he worked to collect his information.

¶ At the request and pleasure of the high and noble prince, my dear lord and master Guy de Chatillon, Comte de Blois, and lord of Avesnes, of Chimay and Beaumont, of Schoenhoven and Gouda, I John Froissart, priest and chaplain to the said lord and at that time treasurer and canon of Chimay and of Lille, roused myself again and entered into my forge in order to work on the matter that has been my concern in the past so that from it may be wrought the story of the happenings in the wars of England and France and of all their allies and associates as are shown in the treaties newly concluded at the moment I start on this fresh work.

Consider now, you who read this book, have read it or intend to read it, how I can have learned and gathered together so many facts concerning the many persons about whom I write. The truth is that I started young, at the age of 20; I was born in a world of great events and I have always taken more pleasure in them than in anything else. Moreover, God has so favoured me that I have been well received in kings' palaces and elsewhere, more particularly by King Edward and his noble wife Philippa of Hainault, Queen of England and mistress of Ireland and of Aquitaine, to whom I was clerk in my youth, serving her with literary works and treatises of love. Out of respect for my service to this noble and valiant lady, all the great lords—dukes, earls and barons, knights and others of the nobility, of whatever nation they were—welcomed me with open arms and were of great assistance to me.

Thus by virtue of my connexion with this noble lady, and at her expense or at the expense of the great lords, I have visited in my time the greater part of Christendom, or at least that part which is worthy of being visited, and wherever I went I would question the older knights and squires who had been present at the engagements I wished to record and who could speak with personal knowledge. I also questioned the most trusted heralds in order to check all my information. In this way I gathered all the noble materials of my chronicle, with the constant help of the Comte de Blois, and as long as I live with God's help I shall continue it, for the longer I work at it the more pleasure I find in it. Just as the true knight or squire loves arms, and by continuing in their service develops and perfects his manhood, so I develop my skill and satisfy my pleasure by working on these chronicles.

queen isabelle enters paris

The marriage of Charles VI with Isabelle (or Isabeau) of Bavaria has already been mentioned. Her entry into her husband's capital and her coronation were delayed for four years, and the ceremonies that accompanied these occasions were such that the parliamentary registers record: 'Never were such elaborate festivities seen in this realm.' Charles had sent his heralds into England and Germany to announce the celebrations to be held in Paris. Isabelle was 19 at this time; she died in Paris nearly fifty years later, deserted by all and having left a sorry record in the history of France.

¶ On Sunday the twenty-second day of August in the year of Our Lord 1389 there were so many people in Paris and round about that it was a most wonderful sight. In the afternoon of that day there were gathered in the town of Saint-Denis all the chief ladies of the nobility who were to accompany the queen, and all the lords who were to escort the litters of the queen and the ladies. There were twelve thousand citizens of Paris, all mounted and ranged in the fields on either side of the route, dressed in tunics of green and scarlet brocade. First came Jeanne the Queen Mother, and her daughter the Duchesse d'Orléans, who were borne in covered litters an hour after nones with a numerous escort of barons; they passed along the wide rue Saint-Denis and came to the palace* where the king was awaiting them. And there, for that day, these two ladies remained.

Then Queen Isabelle of France and her ladies set off—the Duchesse de Bourgogne, the Duchesse de Berry, the Duchesse de Bar, the Comtesse de Nevers, the Dame de Coucy and all the ladies and their daughters in due order. They all had similar litters, so richly ornamented that nothing could have been added; the Duchesse de Touraine, to distinguish herself from the others, had no litter, but

* This is the Palace on the Île de la Cité, of which the Conciergerie is a remaining part.

rode sidesaddle at a slow pace on a richly caparisoned palfrey. All the horses that drew the litters, and those of the escorting barons, went also at a walking pace.

The queen's litter was escorted by the Duc de Touraine* and the Duc de Bourbon at the head, with four other lords behind, first the Duc de Berry and the Duke of Burgundy and then Sir Pierre de Navarre and the Comte d'Ostrevant. The queen's litter was most richly ornamented and was entirely open. After them, riding on a richly caparisoned palfrey, came the Duchesse de Berry, escorted by the Comtes de Nevers and de la Marche, at a walking pace. Next in an open litter came the Duchesse de Bourgogne and the Lady Margaret of Hainault, Comtesse de Nevers, her daughter, led and escorted by Sir Henry de Bar and William the young Comte de Namur.

After them in an open litter came the Duchesse de Bar and her daughter, wife of the Seigneur de Coucy, escorted by Sir Charles d'Albret and the Seigneur de Coucy. No mention can be made of the ladies and maidens who came behind on covered waggons or on palfreys. The sergeant-at-arms and the king's officers were fully occupied in clearing the way and keeping back the people, who were so numerous in the streets that it seemed as if the whole world had been invited.

At the outer gate of Saint-Denis† as one enters the city of Paris, near the place known as La Bastide, there was a representation of the starry firmament, and within it were young children dressed as angels, singing most melodiously. There was, moreover, a living tableau of Our Lady holding in her arms a child playing with a windmill made from a large walnut. The upper part of the firmament was richly emblazoned with the arms of France and Bavaria, and a golden sun in its glory—the king's badge in the jousting tournaments to follow. The Queen of France and her ladies were delighted with all these as they passed, as indeed were all the others who went by.

When they had seen it the queen and her ladies went slowly on to the fountain in the rue Saint-Denis, which was covered all round about with a fine blue cloth powdered with golden fleurs-de-lis; the pillars surrounding the fountain bore the arms of several of the principal lords of the kingdom of France, and from its spouts the fountain gave forth streams of excellent claret and spiced wine. Ranged about the fountain were gaily dressed girls with fine caps of gold, singing

* He took the title of Orléans in 1392.

† On the site of the present Porte Saint-Denis.

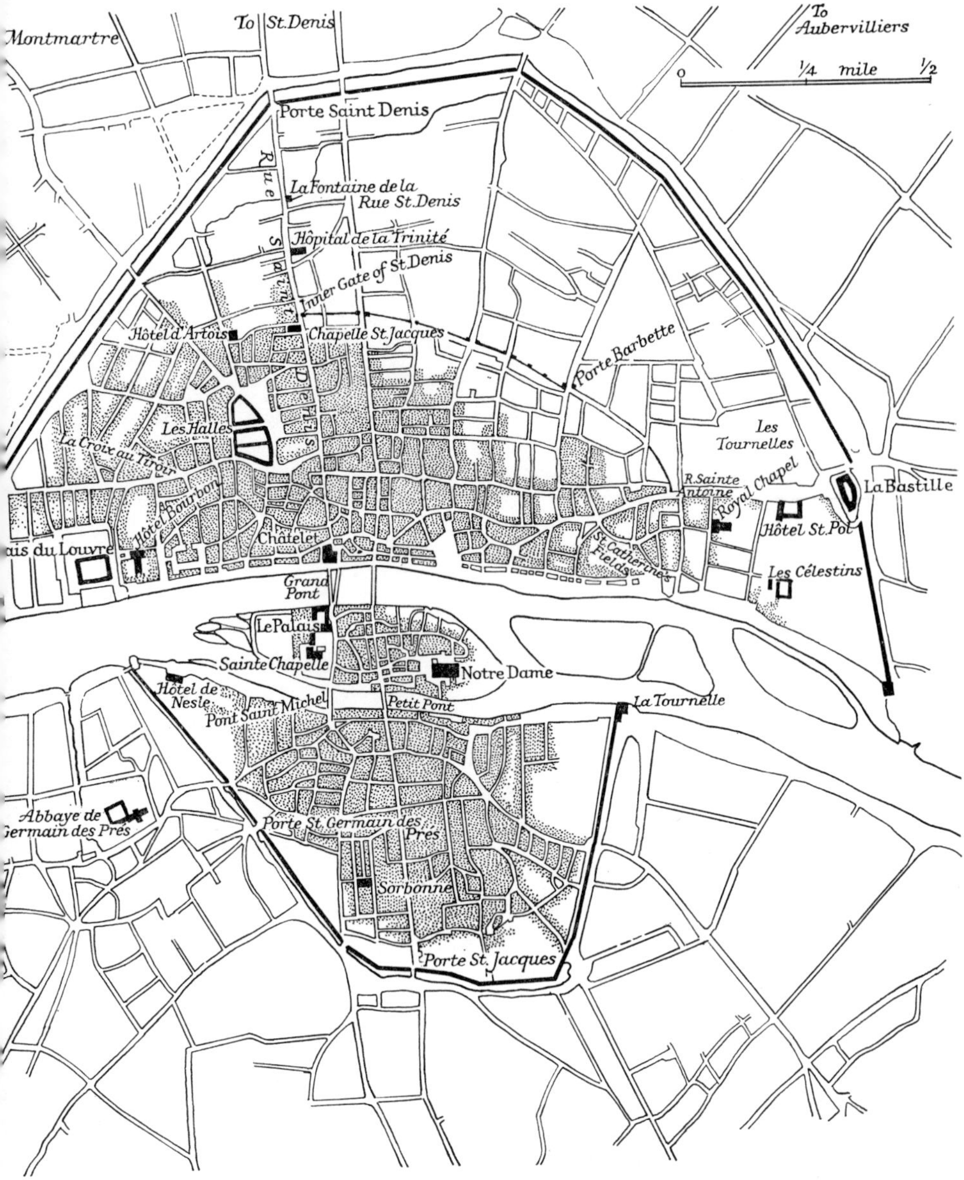

PARIS IN 1389

very tunefully; it was most agreeable to listen to them, and they held in their hands golden cups and goblets, offering drink to all who wanted some. As she passed, the queen halted to enjoy the spectacle and delight in the way it had been arranged; all the ladies and maidens and all the men who passed did likewise.

Farther on, in front of the Hospital of the Trinity, a wooden platform had been set up in the street, and on it a castle in front of which was a representation by living actors of the battle with Saladin, the Christians on one side and the Saracens on the other. All the most famous barons who took part in the battle were shown, each armed in the style of that time.* A little above them was a man who represented the King of France, with the twelve peers of France round him, each wearing his own coat-armour. When the Queen of France in her litter had reached the platform King Richard (Coeur-de-Lion) left his companions in the play and approached the King of France to ask his permission to attack the Saracens. When it was granted to him he returned to his companions and they arrayed themselves and went to attack Saladin and the Saracens. Then followed a mock-battle which was very fierce and lasted some time, affording a most interesting spectacle.

Then the procession passed on and came to the inner gate† of Saint-Denis, where they had built a castle like the one at the outer gate, with a coloured sky sprinkled with stars, in which sat God in His majesty—Father, Son and Holy Spirit—and in the sky were choir-boys dressed as angels singing most sweetly. At the moment the queen passed in her litter under the arch of the gate, the heavens opened and two angels came down, holding in their hands a golden crown richly studded with precious stones which they laid very gently on the queen's head, and as they did this they sang:

O Lady, girt with fleurs-de-lis,
Queen are you now of fair Paris,
Of France, and all this rich country.
—Now back to Paradise we flee.

When they came in front of the Chapelle Saint-Jacques‡ the lords and ladies saw another platform which had been erected on the right-hand side of the street, sumptuously constructed and hung with lofty curtains as if it were a room, and in the room were men playing sweet music on organs. The whole length of the rue Saint-Denis was covered over with camlet or silk in such profusion one would have thought the stuff was to be had for the asking—as if one lived in Alexandria or Damascus. I, the author of this book, was a witness of all these things, and when I saw such a profusion of stuffs I wondered

* The battle took place in the year 1192.

† Situated where the rue Étienne-Marcel crosses the rue St-Denis.

‡ At the corner of the present rue Mauconseil.

how it could all have been obtained. All the houses on both sides of the great rue Saint-Denis as far as the Châtelet, indeed as far as the Grand Pont,* were hung with tall tapestries representing various scenes so that the whole street was a source of pleasure to the eye. And so the concourse of ladies in their litters with their escorting lords reached the gate of the Châtelet at a walking pace, and there they again halted to watch other scenes that had been prepared for them.

In front of this gate a fortress had been constructed in wood and equipped with watch-turrets, strong enough to last for forty years. On each of the turrets was a man fully armed; within the castle was a ceremonial bed, as richly hung as if it were for the king's bed-chamber, and this throne was called the Bed of Justice. On it sat a woman representing Saint Anne. In front of the castle was a large flat space arranged with bushes to look like a warren; among the bushes were large numbers of hares, rabbits and small birds who kept darting out, only to fly back again at once for fear of the vast crowds of people. From the side on which the ladies had approached a white hart came out of the undergrowth and stepped towards the Bed of Justice; then from the bushes on the opposite side came a lion and an eagle, skilfully counterfeited, who went up to the hart before the throne. At this there emerged from the bushes a dozen young maidens, richly clad and wearing golden chaplets, each with a naked sword in her hand, and they placed themselves between the hart and the eagle and lion. With their swords they showed that they would protect the hart and the Bed of Justice, an allegory that appealed greatly to the queen and those about her.

From there they went on towards the Grand Pont, so finely decorated that the work could not have been improved, and covered over with an awning of green and crimson samite in the form of a starry sky. All the streets were decorated as far as the church of Notre-Dame, and when the ladies had crossed the Grand Pont and were nearing the church it was already late, for throughout the length of the journey from Saint-Denis their speed had never been faster than a walking pace . . . But before the Queen of France or her company entered the church of Notre-Dame she had other pageants to watch as she went which gave all of them great pleasure, and these, too, I must tell you about.

A good month before the queen's coming to Paris a skilful man from Geneva had been in Paris, who had attached to the top of the highest tower of Notre-Dame a long rope which stretched above

* Now Pont au Change.

the houses and was attached at the other end to the tallest house on the Pont Saint-Michel.* Just as the queen and her ladies entered the rue Notre-Dame this man, carrying a wax torch in each hand because it was growing dark, stepped from a small platform he had constructed at the top of the tower, and sat on the rope; then, singing as he went, he progressed along the rope—and those below were amazed to think how he could do it. All the while he still carried the candles, which could be seen from one end of Paris to the other and for two or three leagues outside the city. He performed many acrobatic tricks, and his agility and skill were much praised by all.

At the square in front of the Church of Notre-Dame the Bishop of Paris, wearing the badges of Our Lord, and all the college of clergy in great numbers, were waiting for them. There the queen got down from her litter, aided by the four lords who were her escorts, the Dukes of Berry, Burgundy, Touraine and Bourbon. In similar manner all the ladies were helped from their litters or their horses, and entered the church in due order, the bishop and clergy leading and singing loudly in praise of God and the Virgin Mary.

The Queen of France was escorted through the church and the choir to the high altar and there she knelt to say what prayers she wished, and made a present to the Treasure of Notre-Dame of four cloths of gold and the fair crown which the angels had placed on her head at the gate of the city as she entered. Immediately Sir Jean de la Rivière and Sir Jean le Mercier were ready with another and finer crown than this, which was placed on her head by the bishop and the four dukes who were her escorts. After this ceremony they returned down the church, and the queen and her ladies were placed back in their litters, by the light of more than five hundred candles, for it was now late. So they were led in procession to the palace where the king was awaiting them with Jeanne the Queen-Mother and the Duchesse d'Orléans her daughter. There the ladies got out of their litters and were escorted in due order to rooms that had been prepared for them. The lords did not return to their lodgings until after the dancing was over.†

On the following day, Monday, the king gave a dinner in his palace to the ladies, of whom there were a great number. At the hour of High Mass the queen was escorted into the Sainte Chapelle by the four dukes already mentioned, and during the mass she was crowned and anointed according to the rites due to a Queen of France, the

* Even if this should refer to the Petit Pont it was a fair stretch.

† Thus the text. With whom did they dance?

mass being celebrated by the Archbishop of Rouen, who was at that time Guillaume de Vienne. When the solemn mass had been sung the king and queen returned to their apartments in the palace, together with all the ladies, who had rooms there. Soon after their return the king and queen entered the great hall* with all the ladies.

You will know that there is in the palace a great table of marble which cannot be moved,† this was extended by means of a huge oak board four inches thick, and it was here that the dinner was laid. A little distance from the table, against one of the pillars, was the royal sideboard, a particularly fine piece of furniture, laden with gold and silver vessels, and much coveted by many who saw it that day. In front of the king's table there was across the width of the hall a strong wooden barrier, through which there were three entrances, and at these there were many sergeants-at-arms, ushers and mace-bearers of the royal household to guard them so that no one should pass save those who were appointed to serve at table. For it must be told that there were, in fact, so many people there in the hall that there was scarcely room to turn round. Minstrels and other entertainers were there in numbers, each doing his very best according to his particular skill.

When the king, the bishops and the ladies had washed their hands they all sat down to table in order of precedence . . . Apart from the king's table there were other tables round the hall at which five hundred ladies were seated. I am not concerned to give you details of the dishes that were served, fine though they were, but I should wish to add a word about the interludes that were offered by way of entertainment between the courses; these were unusually well prepared and would have provided much pleasure for the king and the ladies if only the actors had had room in which to perform.

In the middle of the banqueting hall a wooden castle had been erected, forty feet high and twenty feet square, with turrets at the four corners and a larger tower in the centre. This castle was to represent the city of Troy, and the central tower its fortress; from it floated pennants with the arms of the Trojans, King Priam, the valiant Hector his son and his other children, as well as those of the kings and princes who were his allies in the city. This castle could be very skilfully moved on four invisible wheels. Then a body of men came to attack this fortress, emerging from a pavilion which could similarly be moved without any of the works being seen; this pavilion bore the

* This hall is now the Salle des Pas-Perdus in the Law Courts (Palais de Justice).

† The marble slab of this great table was reputed to be the largest in the world. Its destruction by fire is recorded in 1618.

arms of the kings of Greece and other parts, who long ago laid siege to Troy. There was also a ship, skilfully simulated, in which were at least a hundred men-at-arms, and this came to their aid, moved by a clever arrangement of wheels. Then followed a fierce attack from the men of the pavilion and the ship against the men of the castle, who put up a great defence. But the pageant could not last long because of the throng of people on all sides; many were stifled by the heat and the crowd. One of the side-tables near the door of the Parliament Chamber, at which many ladies were sitting, was overturned by the pressure of the crowd. The Queen of France was nearly fainting, and a window behind her had to be broken to allow her air; the Dame de Coucy was similarly indisposed. The pageant was called to a halt, and the tables were taken down and removed to give the ladies more space and comfort. Wine and sweetmeats were quickly served, and all left as soon as the king and queen had withdrawn to their own room. Some of the ladies were lodged in the palace; others, including the Dame de Coucy, went to their own houses in the town, for greater ease from the effects of the heat and the crowd.

At five o'clock the queen, accompanied by some of the duchesses, left the palace and went in an open litter through many of the city streets, accompanied by others of the ladies in litters or on horseback; there were more than a thousand riders in the procession. Their journey ended at the king's private residence of Saint-Pol, by the River Seine, to which the king had been taken by boat. This mansion is of considerable size, yet in the courtyard (approached by a gate opening on to the river) a lofty hall had been constructed in wood, covered all over with rough Normandy cloth which had been sent from various places; its walls were hung all round with tall tapestries which represented strange legends and were most attractive to the eye. In this hall the king entertained the ladies to supper, though the queen did not show herself and that evening took her supper in her own room. The other ladies danced with the king and the barons, and they amused themselves throughout the night; the festivities ceased only with the break of day, when each went to his or her own lodging to get some sleep.

I now wish to tell you of the gifts that the people of Paris gave, before dinner on the Tuesday, to the Queen of France and to the Duchesse de Touraine. The latter (called Valentine and the daughter of the Duke of Milan) had only recently come from Lombardy into France when, that same year, she married Duc Louis de Touraine, and she had never been to Paris until she arrived there in the company of the queen. The citizens of Paris therefore owed her a welcome, too.

At noon on the Tuesday some forty of the chief citizens of Paris, all uniformly dressed, brought their present through the streets of Paris to the king's residence of Saint-Pol. The present was a very richly carved litter, carried by two strong men clad as savages, and covered over with a thin silk crêpe through which one could see all the jewels that had been placed inside it. When they reached Saint-Pol they made their way first to the king's own room, which was open and ready to receive them, for their arrival had been notified and bearers of gifts are always welcome. The citizens placed the litter on two trestles which were in the middle of the room, and kneeling before the king spoke thus: 'Most dear and noble king, we citizens of your town of Paris present to you, on the happy occasion of your queen's presence among us, all the jewels which are in this litter.' 'Most grateful thanks, good people,' replied the king; 'they are both fine and costly.' The citizens then stood up and withdrew, having taken their leave of the king. When they had left the king said to Sir Guillaume des Bordes and to Montagu, who were with him, 'Let us go and look more closely and see what these presents are.' Then going up to the litter they looked inside and saw the gifts that had been sent, which included four pots of gold, four golden goblets, four gold salt-cellars, twelve gold cups, twelve gold basins, and six gold dishes; all these weighed more than eighty pounds.

Another body of citizens of Paris, all dressed alike, came in similar manner to the Queen of France and presented to her their gift on a litter which was carried into her room, recommending the city of Paris and its inhabitants to her. This gift consisted of a gold ship, two large golden flagons, two gold comfit-boxes, two gold salt-cellars, six pots of gold, twelve silver lamps, six large silver dishes, two silver bowls—a weight in gold and silver of some one hundred and sixty pounds. This present was carried into the queen's room on a litter by two men who were dressed to represent the one a bear and the other a unicorn.

A third gift was in a similar way carried into the Duchesse de Touraine's room by two men with their faces blacked to look like Moors and very sumptuously dressed, with white cloths wrapped round their heads as if they had been Saracens or Tartars. The litter was particularly fine, covered like the others with a thin silk kerchief, and escorted by twelve citizens of Paris, all richly dressed in identical costumes. They made their gift to the duchess, and this consisted of a gold ship, two gold comfit-boxes, two large golden dishes, two gold salt-cellars, six silver pots, six silver dishes, two dozen silver bowls, two dozen silver sauce-boats, two dozen silver mugs, the whole weighing over a hundred pounds. The duchess was delighted with this gift, and indeed she had reason to be, for it was a particularly sumptuous one, and she expressed her thanks most sincerely and courteously to the givers and to the whole city of Paris, through whose kindness the gift had been made.

Thus on this Tuesday of which I speak these three gifts were presented to the king, the queen and the Duchesse de Touraine. Give a thought to the value of these presents and to the wealth of the men of Paris: for I who write this and saw the gifts was told that they had cost in all more than sixty thousand gold crowns.

After the presentations had been made it was time for dinner, but on that day the king, the ladies and the barons dined in their separate quarters in order to be finished more quickly, for at three o'clock they were due to be in Saint Catherine's Fields,* where great preparations had been made for the joustings, with wooden stands and boxes made for the queen and the ladies . . . There were thirty knights in the lists, who were all Knights of the Golden Sun, for although this was the king's own badge for this tournament, the king himself was of the challenging party, and jousted with the other outsiders to see whether by good fortune he might win the prize for arms. All these knights bearing the Golden Sun on their armour and shields assembled in Saint Catherine's Fields at three o'clock in the afternoon. The ladies had already arrived in great state, led by the Queen of France in a magnificent coach worthy of her station, and had taken their places in the stands erected for them. Soon afterwards the King of France arrived, fully equipped for jousting (a sport of which he was very fond) and escorted as befitted his rank.

Then the tournament began, and, with knights coming from many parts, it was very fiercely contested. Jean de Hainault, Comte d'Ostrevant, jousted especially well, as did those knights who had arrived in his company. Everyone did his best for the honour of the ladies. The Duke of Ireland,† who was then in Paris at the king's request, also performed well, as did a German knight from beyond the Rhine named Sir Gervais of Mirande. The joustings continued to be fiercely and closely contested, but there were so many knights that it was difficult to handle weapons properly, and so much dust was raised by the horses that it was a serious impediment to action.

* On the site of the present Place Baudoyer, near the Église St Gervais.

† Robert de Vere, Earl of Oxford, Marquis of Dublin and Duke of Ireland.

The Seigneur de Coucy bore himself with particular skill, and the jousting continued without relaxation until nightfall, when the knights all left the field and the ladies were conducted to their lodgings. The Queen of France and her own ladies were brought back to Saint-Pol, and were entertained to such a fine dinner that it would be very difficult to describe. The dancing and festivities lasted until daybreak. The prize for the best and most persistent jouster of the challenging party was by common consent of the ladies and the heralds awarded to the King of France, and of the defending party to the Hasle of Flanders, the Duchess of Burgundy's bastard brother.

Many complaints were made by the knights that there was too much dust in the lists and that their feats of arms had gone unseen. The king therefore made arrangements for two hundred water-carriers to sprinkle the whole arena for the next day's sport. But water-carriers or no there was still plenty of dust on the Wednesday. On that day the Comte de Saint-Pol arrived in Paris, having hastened back from England in order to be present at the festivities and having left Sir Jean de Châtelmorant to bring back the treaty confirming peace on land and sea. The comte was warmly welcomed by the king and all the barons, and at this day's festivities his wife, who was very glad to see him, was placed next to the Queen of France.

After dinner on Wednesday thirty squires in attendance went to the lists where the jousting had taken place the previous day, and the ladies followed them in formal procession, as they had on Tuesday, and took their appointed seats. All that day until nightfall the tournament was continued with the same keenness; then everyone returned to his house. A fine supper was offered to the ladies at Saint-Pol, and at this the prize, on the agreement of the ladies and the heralds, was offered for the challengers to a knight from Hainault named Jean de Floyon, of the Comte d'Ostrevant's company, and for the defence to one of the Duke of Burgundy's squires named Jean de Poulvères.

On Thursday knights and squires jousted together, and the fighting was fierce and long, for they all wanted to prove their skill. The ladies' supper was again held at Saint-Pol, and the prizes for the day's jousting were awarded respectively to Sir Charles des Armoies and to one of the queen's squires named Kouk.

On Friday the King of France offered a sumptuous dinner to all the ladies and their daughters. At the end of the meal, while the king and his guests were still seated at table, two knights rode on horseback into the hall (that is the large one constructed specially for these festivities) fully armed and with lances couched; one was Sir Renaud de Roye and the other the younger Boucicault, and their encounter was fiercely fought. They were followed by other knights who continued the jousting for a further two hours' entertainment, and then returned to their lodgings. After this was over those lords and ladies who wished to go back to their own provinces took their leave of the king and queen, who thanked them all warmly for having been present at the festivities.

the madness of charles vi

While the truce continued—and there were parties on each side that wanted it to become a lasting peace—tournaments like those just described became a feature of the time. In 1390 there were held the famous jousts of Saint-Inglevert, near Calais, in March, and another series of jousts in London at Michaelmas, when Richard was consciously rivalling those held for Queen Isabelle's entry into Paris.

In France there was minor trouble in Brittany. Olivier de Clisson, the Constable of France, had survived an attempt at assassination by Pierre de Craon, who had taken refuge with Jean, Duke of Brittany. King Charles took up the constable's cause, against the advice of his uncles, and marched with an army to punish the duke. They delayed for some time in Le Mans while the king urged on his followers the rightness of this action.

¶ When the King of France and his followers had been some three weeks in the city of Le Mans, meeting daily in council, and the four knights had returned from their embassy to the Duke of Brittany with his answer, the king declared that he would wait no longer in that town but ride ahead to the confines of Brittany to see which barons and knights would show themselves to be his enemies by supporting the Duke of Brittany, who was still harbouring the traitor Pierre de Craon. The king's intention was to do everything to drive the Duke of Brittany from his inheritance for all time, and put a governor in his place until his heirs should be of age, when he would restore the duchy to them. No one could move him from this intention.

He left the city of Le Mans between nine and ten, and after hearing mass and taking breakfast all the lords and their men who had been with him in the city or near by also left, taking up positions either ahead of or behind the king. The previous evening he had summoned his marshals to his room in the castle at Le Mans, and had said to them: 'Early tomorrow you must order everyone to leave this town in good order and take the road to Angers, for it has been decided that we shall not turn back until we have entered Brittany and destroyed the traitors who are causing us so much trouble.' The marshals had obeyed this order, and informed the captains of every body of soldiers that this plan was decided on by the king.

The day on which the king left Le Mans [5 August 1392] was one of fierce heat, as is only to be expected in the month of August when the sun is at its greatest power. Here it must be told, if the reader is to make a balanced judgement, that while he had been in Le Mans the King of France had been wearied by the holding of frequent councils; nor did it help that he was unwell at this time and had indeed been so all the summer, eating and drinking little, suffering from fits of giddiness, and in a fever almost every day. Exertion of mind or body was a great strain to him, and the unhappy fate of his constable had deeply affected him, making him melancholy and disturbed. His doctors and his uncles* were aware of this, but could do nothing to help him, for he refused to abandon the expedition to Brittany, and they dared not advise him to do so.

I have been told that as he was riding into the Forest of Le Mans an event of some significance occurred, of which he ought to have informed his council before proceeding farther. There suddenly emerged from between two trees a man wearing neither hat nor shoes, and clad in a smock of homespun cloth; he was quite obviously deranged and taking in his hands the reins of the king's horse he stopped him in his path and said: 'Ride no further, king, turn back for you are betrayed.' These words badly affected the king's already weak mind and made his state much worse, for he was seriously shaken by the incident.

As he spoke the sergeants-at-arms leapt forward and struck the man's hands so fiercely that he let go of the bridle and stepped back. They regarded him as mad and took no notice of what he was saying; many thought this was foolish and that they should at least have detained the man and questioned him to see whether he was sane or mad, who had made him speak those words and whether there was any basis for what he said. Nothing was done to him, for he slipped away and no one knew what became of him, for he was never

* The Dukes of Anjou, Berry and Burgundy, who had been regents until the king was of age to rule. He was 24 when his madness intervened.

seen again by anyone who could recognize him. Yet those who were with the king at the time clearly heard him say the words I have quoted.

The king and his army continued their march, and it was about noon before they left the forest and came out on a fine stretch of flat sandy country. The sun was shining brilliantly from a clear sky, and the heat was so intense that everyone was overwhelmed; the sand was, moreover, so hot that it reflected the sun's heat and there was no one so cheerful or so accustomed to wearing armour that he was not distressed by the heat. The army was riding by companies, the king more or less on his own to avoid the worst of the dust. Some of the barons were chatting among themselves, quite unsuspecting of what happened so suddenly to the chief of all their company, namely the king. How manifest are the works of God, and how hard his punishments—and everyone must be prepared to suffer them.

In both the Old and the New Testaments we have many examples of this. Do we not read how Nebuchadnezzar, King of Assyria, reigned for a time with such power that there was no one greater than him?—and yet at the height of his glory the Lord God, king of heaven and earth and creator of all things, smote him so that he lost both his wits and his kingdom. For seven years he was reduced to living on acorns and wild fruits, with the tastes and appetite of a pig; when he had worked out his term of penitence God restored his memory to him, and then he said to Daniel the prophet that there was no god beside the god of Israel. To put things simply and the better to understand truth, God the Father, Son and Holy Spirit, three in name but one in substance, was, is and ever shall be all-powerful to display His works as in times past. No one should ever be astonished at what He does.

To return, then, to our subject, I repeat that this happening was the result of divine intervention in the life of the king, and many say it was due to the king's own fault. Because of his health at that time, both of body and mind—of which the doctors attending him were well aware—he ought not to have ridden in the heat of the day, but in the cool of the morning or evening. Those therefore who were charged with advising the king, and whose advice he was accustomed to follow, were held to blame and discharged in disgrace.

The king, then, was riding across this sandy plain, with the sun beating down more fiercely than ever before or since; he was wearing a jerkin of black velvet which kept him much too hot, a plain hood of scarlet cloth, and a necklace of large pearls which the queen his wife had given to him when she bade him farewell. Behind him rode one of his pages, wearing a fine Montauban helmet of steel which shone in the sun; behind this page another carried a tall scarlet lance with silken pennants of the king's colours, the point of shining steel. This lance was one of twelve that the Seigneur de la Rivière had had forged for him while he lived in Toulouse and had then given to the king. (The king had given three to the Duc d'Orléans and three to the Duc de Bourbon.) As they rode on in these conditions it happened, as it often does with children and pages who go off the route through negligence or the whim of their horses, that the page who was carrying the king's lance either lost the path or fell asleep without realizing it and allowed his lance to fall against the steel helmet of the page in front. There was a clatter of steel. The king was so close that the pages were riding at his horse's heels, and at the noise he shook all over and his mind became unhinged, for his head was still full of the words that the man—wise or mad—had said to him in the Forest of Le Mans; he imagined a great host of his enemies rushing on him to kill him. With his mind wandering in this delusion he set spurs to his horse and rushed forward, drew his sword and turned on the pages, for he no longer recognized them or anyone else. He thought he was in the midst of a battle surrounded by his enemies; he raised his sword to deal mighty blows no matter where or on whom they fell, and kept shouting: 'Forward! Advance on these traitors!' The pages were frightened—and with good reason—at seeing the king thus possessed, and thinking they must have annoyed him by their disorder they spurred off in different directions.

The Duc d'Orléans was not at that moment far off, and the king rode towards him waving a naked sword, having in his madness lost all recognition of who was his brother or his uncle. When the duke saw him advancing with his sword held high he took fright and wisely decided not to stand his ground, but set spurs to his horse with the king in pursuit. The Duke of Burgundy was riding a little way off, and when he heard the king's pages shouting and saw the horses stampeding, he looked to the scene of the disturbance and saw the king chasing his own brother with a naked sword; then he, too, took fright and shouted: 'Holla there, disaster has befallen us! My lord the king is out of his mind! For God's sake follow after and capture him!' And then: 'Fly, nephew of Orléans, fly! or the king will kill you!' I can tell you the Duc d'Orléans was not at all happy, and he fled as fast as his horse would carry him. Knights and squires began shouting and following in the direction he had gone. Those who were riding on the right and left wings of the party thought a wolf or a hare had been started, until they learned that the king was out of his mind. However, the Duc d'Orléans got away, by turning and counter-turning and with help from the others.

All the knights, squires and men-at-arms then formed a wide hedge around the king, and waited for him to exhaust himself: the more he charged about the weaker he became. When he came upon anyone, be it knight or squire, that person let himself fall under the blow. I never heard that anyone was killed in this sorry affair, but the king felled several of them, for no one offered any resistance. Finally, when he was worn out and his horse was exhausted and both were running with sweat from their exertions, a knight of Normandy, one Guillaume Martel, who was the king's chamberlain and of whom he was very fond, came up and gripped him from behind, holding him tight with his sword arm inactive. Then the other knights came near and removed his sword, lifted him down from his horse and laid him on the ground, then took off his doublet in order to cool him. When his brother and his three uncles came to see him he did not recognize them or show them any sign of friendship. His eyes rolled horribly in their sockets and he spoke to no one.

The lords of the blood royal were amazed and did not know what to say or do. Then the Duc de Berry and the Duke of Burgundy said: 'We must go back to Le Mans; this expedition is finished for the time being.' They did not then say all that was in their thoughts, though they had plenty to say when they were back in Paris to those whom they did not favour. But more of this later.

If we take a reasonable look at all these events, with a due regard for truth, it is indeed pitiful that the King of France at that time—the noblest and most powerful king in the world—should have fallen into such weakness and his mind become suddenly deranged. There was no means of preventing it, for it was God's will. They made the king as comfortable as they could, fanned him to cool him, and laid him in a litter for the journey back to Le Mans. The marshals were sent out to order all those who were continuing the march to return, because the expedition was cancelled for the time being. To some the reason for this was explained, to others it was not.

In the evening, when the king was brought back to Le Mans, the doctors were much puzzled and his close relatives very disturbed, and all manner of explanations were advanced and discussed. Some suggested that in the morning as he left Le Mans the king had been bewitched with a poison in order to bring shame on the kingdom of

France. This rumour gained such force that the Duc d'Orléans, his uncles and others of the blood royal took note of what was being said and discussed the matter together, saying: 'None of us can fail to have heard how folk are whispering in various places against those who had the care of the king's person. They say, indeed common report has it, that someone has poisoned or bewitched the king. We should like to know when and where this could have happened, but how can we find out?' Some replied: 'Certainly we shall discover this—by asking the doctors. They must know, because they are acquainted with his nature and constitution.'

The doctors were sent for and closely examined by the Duke of Burgundy. They explained that the king had long been subject to this kind of malady. 'And we were well aware that this disease of the brain had been coming on, and that it would show itself some time or other.' Then the Duke of Burgundy said to them: 'You stand acquitted of all these reports and rumours, and the truth is that he would not listen to you or us because his mind was so set on this expedition. He was badly advised, for it has dishonoured him. Better that Clisson and all his band had died than that the king should have fallen to this disease, for it will be much talked about, seeing that he is a young man, and we who are his uncles of the blood royal and had the charge of advising him, shall be blamed for this, yet without cause. Now tell us,' he continued, 'were you with him at breakfast before he mounted his horse?' 'Indeed we were,' replied the doctors. 'And with what appetite did he eat and drink?' 'Truly,' replied the doctors, 'so little that it was not worth mentioning. He merely sat and mused.' 'And who were the last to serve him with drink?' asked the duke. 'We do not know,' they replied, 'for as soon as the table was cleared we left to get ready to mount our own horses. You had better ask his brothers or his chamberlains.' So they sent for Robert de Tanques, a squire from Picardy who was the king's Chief Butler, and asked him who had been the last to serve him with drink. He replied: 'In truth, my lords, it was Sir Helion de Lignac.' This knight was then sent for, and when he had come he was asked the same question, and also where he had got the wine which was served in the king's room before he mounted his horse. He replied: 'My lords, it was Robert de Tanques there who served it and we both tasted it in the presence of the king.' 'That is true,' said Robert de Tanques, 'and there can be no doubt or suspicion because we still have some of the same wine in the king's bottles, and we will gladly taste it in front of you now.' Then the Duc de Berry: 'We are arguing and labouring to no purpose. The only poison and sorcery the king has suffered is that of bad advice, and now is not the time to discuss that. Let us hold such matters over for another occasion.' . . .

It was decided that the king should be moved to Creil, some twenty miles north of Paris, where he would be guarded by a body of chosen knights and under the care of his physicians. His state of health, however, showed no immediate improvement.

A council was [shortly] summoned in Paris, composed of the nobles, bishops and representatives of the chief towns to decide what person or persons were to be regents until the king should be restored to health—if he ever was; whether it was to be his brother the Duc d'Orléans, or his two uncles, or one of them alone, and they spent more than a fortnight debating this before they could reach any agreement. Since the Duc d'Orléans was held to be too young to undertake so heavy a task, it was finally agreed that the regency should be held by the Duke of Burgundy, as chief, and the Duc de Berry, while the Duchess of Burgundy should remain with the queen and be the the second lady in the kingdom.

Then the Seigneur de Coucy remembered the reputation of Master Guillaume de Harselly, and mentioned him to the king's uncles, suggesting that his wisdom and skill might serve to cure the king. The Dukes of Berry and Burgundy listened to this suggestion and summoned the man to Paris. When he arrived he presented himself first to the Seigneur de Coucy, with whom he had long been friendly and who then took him to the king's two uncles and said: 'Here is Master Guillaume de Harselly of whom I spoke.' 'He is very welcome,' replied the dukes, who received him most warmly and then instructed him to join the king at Creil and to remain with him until he was cured.

Following these orders, Master Guillaume left Paris handsomely escorted and arrived at Creil, where he remained with the king as instructed and took precedence over all the other doctors in the medical care of the patient. He was convinced that the king's malady could be cured, seeing that it had been incurred by weakness of the brain and the disturbance in the forest, and he worked hard to bring about a remedy.

News of the king's illness spread far and wide, and however much some regretted it, you can imagine that the Duke of Brittany and Sir

Pierre de Craon were not much worried by it and wasted no tears on him. When Pope Boniface and the cardinals in Rome learned the truth, they could not hide their joy and assembled together in consistory, where they said that their vilest enemy (meaning the King of France) was being beaten with cruel rods when God had deprived him of his senses, that this was an influence come down from Heaven to chastise him, that he had given too much support to the anti-pope in Avignon, that this cruel scourge was sent to him to make an example of him to his own people, and that all this would strengthen their own cause.

In Avignon, Pope Clement* and his cardinals, when they had considered all the implications, saw the very real danger which should have been a warning to them, but they were concerned solely for the honour of the king and of France. They considered that this result was only to be expected from a young and headstrong king, who had for long been badly advised and allowed to do too much as he pleased; that he had done too much hard riding by night after unreasonably heavy days of mental and physical exertion, and that account should be required of those who had been his counsellors in the past years, for the fault was theirs alone. If these men had laid down for the king in his youth a reasonable way of life and had kept him to it, this malady would never have befallen him. 'With all this there is one very important matter,' they added, 'for less than a year ago he swore to the pope on his word as king that he would do everything in his power to destroy the anti-pope in Rome with his cardinals, to destroy the schism in the Church and to set things again in happy order. Yet he has done nothing about it and has broken his pledged word. God is angry at this and is punishing him with the rod of madness, which seems to us but justice. If he recovers his reason, as well he may, it will be our duty to send our most skilful advisers to point out how he has come short of his promises. If he still ignores them it will not be through our fault.' These were the conclusions of the pope and cardinals in Avignon, who thought that the king had asked for the malady with which he was afflicted, and placed the blame on him and on his private advisers. Many others in France held the same opinion.

In the town of Haspres, which lies in Hainault between Cambrai and Valenciennes, there is an abbey, dependent on the Abbey of

* During the Great Schism, which lasted from 1378 to 1417, there were two rival popes, one at Rome and one at Avignon, each of whom claimed to be sole head of the Church.

Saint-Vaast in Arras, in which there is a richly decorated shrine in honour of Saint Aquaire, whose body is buried there. Those who are afflicted with madness come from many parts to visit this shrine. A waxen image of the king was prepared and was offered along with a fine, large wax-candle in honour of the saint so that he might pray to God to relieve the king of his madness; news of this offering travelled widely, and a similar offering was made to Saint Hermier in Rouaix, since this saint is reputed to obtain the healing of disorders of the mind. Similar images of the king were offered wherever there was the body of any saint to whom God had given power to cure people of madness.

When the nature of the king's illness became known in England to the king and his council they were very worried; the Duke of Lancaster in particular expressed sorrow, and spoke in these terms to the knights and squires who were in his company: 'This indeed is a great pity. For he looked like being a man of firm resolve and keen to do good. When I took leave of him at Amiens these were his words: "Fair cousin of Lancaster, I beg you to exert every effort to see that a lasting peace is established between us and our nephew of England, and between our realms, so that we may join our powers in common cause against this Bajazet who has overrun Armenia and who is out to destroy all Christendom.* Thus we can exalt our faith, as we are in honour bound to do." But now,' added the duke, 'the good work is retarded, for he will not again receive as much trust as before.' 'True enough,' replied the knights to whom he spoke. 'This kingdom of France looks like falling on bad days.'

In these various ways the news of the king's madness was received and discussed in countries near and far where it was known. Meanwhile the king was kept quiet in the château de Creil, under the guard of the knights already named and of Master Guillaume de Harselly, who was in supreme charge of the medical arrangements. Not a man or woman was allowed to speak to the king, or to enter the castle, other than those who were specially permitted to do so, though from time to time the Duc de Bourbon and the Duc d'Orléans came to see him in order to find out how he was getting on.

¶ In Paris the Dukes of Berry and Burgundy had not yet instituted any changes, but they fully intended to take legal action within a short time against some who were not in their favour and whom they

* Bajazet, ruler of the Ottoman Turks, overran the provinces of the Eastern Empire, and defeated the Hungarians and the French at Nicopoli in 1396.

AN ATTEMPT TO ASSASSINATE OLIVIER DE CLISSON

considered difficult and rebellious in various ways. The Duc de Berry spoke thus: 'Clisson, La Rivière, Le Mercier and Lebègue de Villaines when they were in Languedoc stole from me my faithful servant and treasurer Béthisac* and put him to death most cruelly out of sheer ill will, and nothing I said or did would persuade them to restore him to me. Let them now watch out, for the hour is coming when I shall pay them back in their own coin—aye, struck from the same mint!' The Duke of Burgundy and those about him had no better love for these same nobles who had previously been the king's closest advisers; whenever he had had business at court he and his men had been coldly received and harshly treated and little had been done for them. They had complained bitterly about this in private.

That cruel and haughty lady the Duchess of Burgundy stayed in Paris with the Queen of France, to whom no one was admitted without her authority. The duchess hated Olivier de Clisson with all her heart, because the Duke of Brittany was closely related to her. She often spoke of this to her husband, and pointed out with much vehemence that it was a most evil thing to have so long supported Clisson against such a great prince as her cousin of Brittany.

The Duke of Burgundy was both wise and calculating, and in affairs of this kind he saw several moves ahead. He hoped to avoid internal dissensions and to keep the peace between the various factions in the kingdom, just as he had till now avoided offending King Charles V his brother or King Charles VI his nephew. His reply was sensible and soft: 'My lady, it is very often a good thing to dissemble. It is indeed true that our cousin of Brittany is a powerful nobleman—in lands and men much more powerful than the Seigneur de Clisson. If I were to side with the duke against Clisson, everyone in France would quite rightly be horrified, for it is Clisson's constant argument that he bears all this hatred to our cousin of Brittany in order to maintain the honour of France, in which you and I have such a great part. Most of the French follow the same kind of argument. I have not yet found any valid reason for going over to the duke and abandoning Clisson. I have therefore had to hide my real feelings, if I was to remain in the good books of my king and country to whom I am bound by oath and loyalty much more closely than to the Duke of Brittany. And now it has so happened that my lord the king is a very sick man, as you know, and all this

* He had charge of the finances of Languedoc. Late in 1389 he was arrested; as his accounts were in order, he was sent to the stake as an Albigensian heretic.

goes against Clisson and indeed will work harm for all those, apart from my brother of Berry and myself, who advised him to undertake that expedition he was so keen on. The rod is prepared for their backs, and they will soon be beaten unmercifully, as you will see before long. Just be patient and wait. My dear lady, there is no cloud without its silver lining, no one's luck is always down, there is no sad heart that is not made to rejoice, and no rejoicing that is not the prelude to a fall. Clisson, La Rivière, Le Mercier and Villaines, and others besides, have done evil deeds, and before very long they will be made to pay.' With such words the Duke of Burgundy consoled his wife.

The two dukes soon collaborated in getting rid of those they claimed to have corrupted the king by bad advice. The constable, Olivier de Clisson, was declared incapable of holding his office and banished from the kingdom; he did not attend his trial and continued to wage war on the Duke of Brittany. The Duc d'Orléans refused to attend the trial of Clisson. La Rivière was tried in person and put in prison, all his territories being confiscated.

¶ The whole of the French nation was sadly depressed by the illness which the king contracted on his expedition to Brittany. This indeed was natural, for he was till then high in the love and favour of his subjects, and because he was the head the distress was all the more deeply felt. When the head of a body is sick, all the limbs suffer in proportion. But no one in the kingdom dared to speak openly of his malady; they concealed it as far as they could, and, in fact, it was completely hidden from the queen, who knew nothing at all about it until she had given birth to her child, which was a daughter this time, I think.

Master Guillaume de Harselly, who was in medical charge of the king, continued quietly at Creil with his work for the cure of his patient. He did remarkably well, and won great honour and riches as the king steadily recovered. First he got rid of the heavy fever, by which the king regained his desire to eat and drink, and was able to sleep peacefully. Then he regained his powers of recognition, but still remained very weak. To give him a change of air, Harselly allowed him to ride out hunting, or to go hawking for larks.

As it became known in France that the king was regaining his memory and his health, all sorts of men were very happy, and praised God most humbly and sincerely. In response to the king's request, the queen and the dauphin went to visit him at Creil. The king welcomed them with great pleasure and with his old courtesy, and gradually by the grace of God he regained his former health. When Master Guillaume de Harselly saw the king was now in good state, he was very delighted to have effected so fine a cure, and handed him over to his brother and his three uncles, saying: 'God be praised, the king is restored. I give him over to you in good health. But from now on you must avoid making him angry or melancholic, for he has not yet fully regained his faculties. They will go on improving gradually, and for the moment the most important things for him are pleasures and relaxations. In so far as you can, spare him from councils of state, since for some time his mind will not have gained its full strength and he will easily be upset. Remember that he has been suffering from a very grave illness.'

It was then agreed that Master Guillaume should be retained in the king's service, and paid whatever he should ask—for the chief aim of doctors is to earn as great wealth as possible from the lords and ladies who are their patients. But although he was most pressingly urged to remain with the king, he excused himself on the grounds that he was now weak and ageing and unable to bear the routine of court life. In short, he preferred to return to his own home. When they saw that there was nothing to be done, they did not annoy him with further requests, but gave him leave to go and made him a present of a thousand gold crowns and a written order for four horses whenever it pleased him to attend at the king's palace. I believe, however, that he never once returned, for he continued to live in Laon, where he had chosen to be, and died the same year a very rich man. He left a fortune of thirty thousand francs, and was the most niggardly and avaricious man of his day; his only pleasure in life was to amass great wealth, and he never spent a sou at home, but preferred to eat and drink at others' houses whenever he could. Such punishments are in store for all doctors.*

¶ You will recollect that a three-year truce had been prepared at Leulinghen between France and England, and that the ambassadors of France had gone to England with the Dukes of Lancaster and York to know what was the will of the King and people of England. Much progress had been made towards a solid peace during the conversations at Amiens and many of the clauses drafted, and it now needed only the English consent, which had been reserved by the two English dukes. The ambassadors had then returned to France, having been told that they would have their reply after the English

* The punishment is the moral one, not presumably that of dying rich!

Parliament had met at Westminster around Michaelmas and had been able to discuss the terms.

Now, when news of the king's madness was known in England, the decisions were held up. King Richard of England and the Duke of Lancaster were, however, greatly in favour of peace, and if they alone had had the deciding a truce would quickly have been confirmed; but they had not, for the people of England did not want peace but war, and declared that a war with France was in all ways more to be favoured than peace. One of the king's uncles, Thomas, Duke of Gloucester, Earl of Essex and Buckingham, who was also Constable of England and much beloved in the country, was of this same opinion. He was all in favour of a war, and he had with him the opinion of all the young nobility of the country, who were eager to excel in arms. His brother, the Duke of Lancaster, who was the eldest of them and very powerful throughout the country, overruled him by saying that the war between England and France had lasted long enough, and that a firm and lasting peace was now needed, because Christendom was too weak and feeble. He reminded them of the increasing threat from Bajazet, who was massing his strength on the borders of Hungary. It would therefore, he said, be a good thing to come to terms now, and all the young knights and squires who wished to prove themselves should fight against Bajazet and nowhere else. . . .

The conclusion reached by the bishops, nobles and representatives of the towns who had assembled at Westminster was that a truce should be agreed and signed for peace on land and sea between France and England, their friends and allies, to last from Michaelmas until St John the Baptist's Day in the second year following. The knights who had been sent to England brought back the signed documents, and the truce was faithfully observed by all parties.

the dance of the savages

The king had recovered by September, but the malady recurred at intervals for the remainder of his life, and for longer and more frequent periods as he grew older. His uncles, as we have seen, used the first period of the king's incapacity to advance their own purposes and rid themselves of at least some of the 'Marmosets'.

As soon as the king had recovered he resumed the life of gaiety in the Hôtel

Saint-Pol. The incident that follows is a tragic example of the consequences of this irresponsibility; it is known in French by the title of this chapter (Le Bal des Sauvages) *or as the Dance of the Burning Men* (Le Bal des Ardents).

¶ About this time a marriage was celebrated between a young knight of Vermandois and one of the queen's ladies-in-waiting, both of the royal household. It was a match that was very acceptable to the whole court, and the king arranged to hold the wedding festivities in his own palace of Saint-Pol in Paris, and to them he invited a large number of lords and other notable guests, among them the Dukes of Orléans, Berry and Burgundy with their wives. The wedding-day was spent in dancing and revelry. In the evening the king offered a supper to the guests and their ladies; the queen was there to preside over the banquet and everyone did his best to be merry, because they saw how much the king was enjoying it all. In the king's household (and a near relative of his) was a squire from Normandy called Hugonin de Guisay, who had thought up an entertainment to please the king and the ladies. What this entertainment was I shall now tell you.

On the day of this wedding-feast (which was the Tuesday before Candlemas) he prepared six suits of linen, which were then set aside in a room where he had them covered with fine flax, in colour and appearance like hair. He made the king put on one of these and the Comte de Joigny (a handsome young knight) another, and fitted them both carefully. The others he similarly fitted to Charles de Poitiers, son of the Comte de Valentinois, to Yvain, the bastard of Foix, another to the son of the Seigneur de Nantouillet, and the sixth he put on himself. When they had all been sewn into their suits, which were each made to measure, they looked just like savages, for they were covered with hair from their heads to the soles of their feet.

A piece of fun such as this was just the thing to please the king, and he was full of gratitude to the squire for having thought of it. They had put these suits on so secretly in a back room, that no one knew anything about it, apart from themselves and the servants who had dressed them. Yvain de Foix—one of the six—foresaw the danger they might be in and said to the king: 'My lord, give orders to someone that no torches be brought near us, for if this were to happen and the flame touched the suits we are wearing, the hair would catch fire and we should be burned to death, I warn you.' 'By God, Yvain,' said the king, 'that's a sound warning, and the order shall be given.' He at once gave instructions that no one was to follow after them, and called in a sergeant-at-arms who was standing at the door and said to him: 'Go into the hall where the ladies are assembled and tell them it is the king's order that all the torches should be placed to one side and that no one is to come close to the six savages who are about to enter.'

The sergeant carried out the king's command most faithfully. He saw to it that all the torches and torchbearers were withdrawn to one of the walls, and ordered no one to go near the dancers until the six savages had retired. The room was cleared of all but the ladies and the knights and squires who were dancing with them. Very shortly afterwards the Duc d'Orléans entered the hall accompanied by four knights and six torchbearers; he knew nothing of the orders the king had given nor of the six savages who were about to come in. At least he claimed he knew nothing, though many have since accused him of complicity. After watching the ladies intently while they danced, he then joined energetically in the dancing, though I do not know what was in his mind in doing this.

At this moment in came the King of France with the five others, covered in flax as we have described above, and so well disguised as savages that not a man or woman could recognize them. The other five were fastened to each other, but the king was in front leading them in the dance. When they came in everyone was so intent on watching them that they forgot all about the torches. The king then left his companions—fortunately for him—and went to show himself to the ladies, for such is the way of young men. He passed in front of the queen and came to the Duchesse de Berry, who was his youngest aunt. She entered into the fun of the game and tried to find out who he was, but the king stood his ground and refused to give his name. At this the duchess said: 'You won't escape me until I know who you are.'

In the general disturbance a most terrible disaster befell the others, and all through the fault of the Duc d'Orléans, though it may be that the thoughtlessness of youth made him do it*—for if he had foreseen the awful consequences he would not have done so for anything in the world. In his impatience to identify the five who were dancing he drew the torch his servant was carrying so close to one of the dancers that the heat set fire to the flax. (You must know that with flax there is nothing that can be done to prevent the flames spreading at once.) The flames then began to melt the pitch that had been used to stick the flax to the cloth, and the linen suits were soon burning fiercely;

* The king was 25 years old, the Duc d'Orléans 21, and the Duchesse de Berry 17.

the men who wore them, tight-fitting as they were, were tormented with pain and began to scream most horribly. It was so terrible that no one dared go near them, though certain knights tried to help them by pulling the burning clothes off them, but they had their hands badly burned by the molten pitch and suffered from their burns for some time afterwards. One of the five, Nantouillet, remembered that the buttery was near by, and ran there quickly and leapt into a large tub full of water in which they rinsed the cups and glasses. This saved him—otherwise he would have been burned to death like the rest, and even so he had very serious burns.

When the queen heard the frightful screams of the burning men she had fears that the king might be among them, for the king had told her he was to be one of the six. She was in such distress that she fainted, and several knights rushed to help her and reassure her. There was so much disturbance in the hall and such agonizing screams that no one knew what to do about it. The Duchesse de Berry saved the king from danger by pushing him under her gown and so shielding him from the flames; but since he was struggling to get away from her she said to him: 'Where are you trying to go? You can hear* that your companions are burning. Who are you—it's high time you told me?'—'I am the king,' he replied. 'Oh, my lord,' said the duchess, 'then off you go at once and change your clothes so that the queen can see you, for she's most distressed about you.'

With these words the king left the hall and went to remove his costume as quickly as he could and put on his ordinary clothes to show himself to the queen. The Duchesse de Berry was with her, and had somewhat comforted her by saying: 'Be reassured, my lady, for you will see the king very soon. I've just been talking to him.' As she spoke the king came into the room, and when she saw him she trembled with joy. Then some of the knights took her in their arms and carried her to her room, the king going with them and comforting her all the way. The bastard of Foix, who was covered in flames, was shouting as loud as he could: 'Save the king! Save the king!' The king was indeed saved in the way I've just told you; it was God's will that he should separate himself from his fellows in order to talk to the ladies, for if he had remained with the other five he could not fail to have been burned to death.

Around midnight in the hall of the Hôtel Saint-Pol there was

* Both Berners and Johnes translate *oyés* as 'see'; they cannot have visualized the king's situation.

such a ghastly scene of disaster that no one could see or hear it without pity and horror. Of the four that were burned, two died on the spot; the two others, the bastard of Foix and the Comte de Joigny, were carried to their lodgings and died within two days in great pain and suffering.

The wedding festivities thus broke up in great sadness, though the bride and bridegroom could have done nothing to prevent it. It must be admitted that it was in no way their fault, but that of the Duc d'Orléans, who, as he said himself, had no thought of harm when he brought the torch nearer to the masked men to try and penetrate their disguise. It was his youth that made him do it, and when he saw the unhappy outcome, he said in the presence of all: 'Listen to me, all who can hear me. Let no one be questioned or blamed for this unfortunate happening, for I alone am to blame for what has occurred. It is a great grief to me that this should ever have come about. I never foresaw any such result, and if I had I would certainly have prevented it.' He then went to the king to offer his excuses, which were accepted.

This horrible disaster took place in the Hôtel Saint-Pol in Paris in the year of Our Lord 1393, the Tuesday before Candlemas. It was an event that was much talked about throughout France, and in other countries, too. The Dukes of Burgundy and Berry were not then present, but had taken their leave of the king and queen earlier in the evening and retired to their own houses in order to be more at their ease.

When morning came and the news was spread abroad among the people of Paris, you can imagine how amazed they all were. All over the town people were saying that God had a second time shown favour to the king, who ought to take note of it and give up those youthful follies which had occupied too much of his time and were unbecoming to a King of France; he had played the boy long enough. The common people of Paris murmured thus among themselves and openly declared: 'Look at the great danger the king was in. If he had been burned to death—and very close he came to it—what would have become of his uncles and his brother? They can rest assured that not one of them would have escaped—they would all have been killed, together with every baron and knight to be found in Paris.'

As soon as the Dukes of Berry and Burgundy heard the news in the morning they were much alarmed, and with good cause. They mounted their horses and rode to the Hôtel Saint-Pol, where they saw the king. They found him much in need of consolation, for he was still frightened when he thought of the great danger he had been in, and could not get it out of his mind. He told his uncles that his fair aunt of Berry had saved him from danger, but that he was still much upset at the fate of the Comte de Joigny, Yvain de Foix and Charles de Poitiers. To comfort him, his uncles said: 'My lord, what has happened cannot be undone. You must forget the death of these men and thank God for your own lucky escape. For in this event both your own person and the whole realm of France have been in great danger of destruction, and you can well imagine (for the common folk of Paris are already saying as much) that if any harm had come to you they would have killed the lot of us. You had better put on your royal apparel and ride in state on a pilgrimage to Notre-Dame de Paris—we will go with you—and show yourself to the people, for the whole town is anxious to see you.' The king replied that he would do this, and as he spoke in came his brother the Duc d'Orléans. The king, who loved him as a brother should, welcomed him most graciously, as did his uncles; but they reproved him for the sorry outcome of his childish behaviour. To this he replied that he was grateful for their forgiveness and that he had not thought to do any harm.

Shortly afterwards, on the stroke of nine o'clock,* the king and these other lords all mounted on horseback and made a circuit of the streets of Paris to calm the people, who were very upset. Finally they came to the great church of Notre-Dame, where the king heard mass and made an offering. They then all returned to the Hôtel Saint-Pol for dinner. The funeral rites, prayers and alms were offered for the dead, and the events of that night were gradually forgotten.

A Burgundian chronicler states that it was Louis d'Orléans who conceived the plan of the mummery and prepared the suits of flax, and that he was himself to have been one of the dancers, but found his own suit too tight and immediately offered to carry the torch. It is recorded that a few weeks after the incident he was forced to swear on oath that if the king were to die he would respect the rights of his heirs.

* This is the first time (in the extracts here given) that Froissart uses astronomical instead of canonical hours; the latter still recur occasionally.

Froissart in England

Negotiations concerning the conditions of a peace that might ensue from the truce of 1389 continued for a number of years, and became much more serious on the English side when later in that year Richard dismissed his uncles and declared he no longer needed a regent. A series of meetings was held and continual adjustments made on each side to secure terms that were both realistic and acceptable. Richard was prepared to evacuate the Breton fortresses (with the exception of Brest) and even Cherbourg, and this was, in fact, carried out by 1393. He was also prepared to become the vassal to the King of France for Aquitaine, so long as he paid simple homage; all French conquests under Charles V, however, with the exception of Ponthieu, were to be restored to England, and the French were to pay the balance of King Jean's ransom. They for their part demanded the cession of Calais and that Richard should pay liege homage.

It was at this stage of events that Froissart made his second visit to England in 1395, and in the course of the narrative of his visit we can trace the story of Richard's plans to marry the infant daughter of the King of France. We also get a full insight into the enthusiasm with which Froissart conducted his inquiries to make his chronicles as complete as possible.

¶ The truth is that I, Sir John Froissart, then Canon Treasurer of Chimay, residing in the county of Hainault and the diocese of Liège, had a great desire to visit England; it came upon me when I was at Abbeville and saw that a truce had been concluded . . . between France and England, and various reasons moved me to make this journey. In the first place I had in my younger days been brought up in the court of King Edward (of blessed memory) and Queen Philippa his wife, and treated as a member of their household, mixing freely with their children and with the barons who at that time formed his entourage. With them I received every honour and was surrounded with courtesy and generosity. This made my desire to return there all the stronger, and I somehow felt that I should live the longer if I managed to do it. For twenty-seven years I had refrained from going over, but even if I did not see the barons I had left there I should see their heirs, and that would be a real pleasure, quite apart from the possibilities of checking all that I had written in my chronicles concerning the English.

I therefore broached the matter to those who were my chief masters at that time,* Duke Albert of Bavaria, Comte de Hainault, Earl of Holland and of Zeeland and Lord of Friesland, to his son Guillaume then Comte d'Ostrevant, to my dear and honoured lady, Jeanne, Duchesse de Brabant et Luxembourg, to that great nobleman Enguerrand de Coucy, and to that fine knight the Seigneur de Gommegnies. These last two I had seen in the king's household in London, when we were all three young, and when they with other French barons were working off the ransom of King Jean of France when he was made a hostage after Poitiers, as is told much earlier in this history. All these encouraged me warmly in my project, and, except for the Seigneur de Coucy, who is French and therefore dared write only to his daughter the Duchess of Ireland, gave me letters addressed to the king and his uncles.

For my own part I had had prepared a collection of all the treatises on love and morals that with God's grace I had written over a period of thirty-four years; when these had been copied in a fair hand and illuminated, my desire to go and see King Richard of England was redoubled. I had not seen him since he was baptized in the cathedral at Bordeaux as the infant son of the noble and mighty Prince of Wales and Aquitaine. I was at that time in Bordeaux and had intended to make a journey into Spain with the Prince of Wales, but when we had reached the town of Dax he sent me back into England to his mother the queen. Everything made me most anxious to see King Richard and his uncles, and I had ready with me a fine and heavily ornamented book, bound in velvet, with studs and clasps of silver gilt as a present of introduction to the king. I was keen enough on this trip not to give any thought to the trouble or expense; for if one is set on something its cost seems very small.

Having provided myself with horses and other equipment, I crossed the sea from Calais and arrived at Dover on the twelfth day of July [1395]. In Dover I could find no one I remembered from my former visit; the inns were kept by different folk, and the young boys and girls of those days had become grown men and women and did not recognize me, nor I them. I stayed there the rest of that day and night (it was a Tuesday) in order to rest myself and my horses, and by nine o'clock on the Wednesday I was at St Thomas of Canterbury to see the saint's shrine and relics, and the splendid new tomb of the valiant Prince of Wales. I heard mass at the high altar and made an offering to the shrine, then went back to my inn. There I learned that

* See Introduction for an account of Froissart's relations with his patrons.

the king was just back from Ireland (where he had been for nine months) and was making a pilgrimage to St Thomas of Canterbury on Thursday, in honour of the saint and because his father is buried there. This persuaded me to spend a further day in the town, and on the next day the king did indeed arrive in full state, accompanied by noble lords and ladies and their daughters. I mingled with them, but everything seemed new and I did not recognize a soul; things had changed a lot in England in twenty-seven years. None of the king's uncles was in his company, for the Duke of Lancaster was in Aquitaine, and York and Gloucester were elsewhere.

My first reaction was of astonishment. If I could have spoken to a certain old knight who had been in the personal service of King Edward and was now one of King Richard's closest advisers I should have found some comfort, and should have hailed him with glee. The man I wanted to see was Sir Richard Sturry. When I asked whether he was still alive, they told me he was indeed, but that he was in London and had not come to Canterbury. In view of this I thought it best to approach Sir Thomas Percy, High Steward of England, who was with the party. I therefore made his acquaintance, and found him most courteous and gracious; he offered to present me and my letters to King Richard. I was more than delighted, because I needed some such means of introduction to so great a prince as the King of England. He went to the king's quarters to see whether it was a suitable time, but found that he had retired to bed, and when he informed me of this I went off to my own lodging.

Next morning I returned to the archbishop's palace where the king was staying and found out Sir Thomas, who was preparing the company to ride to Ospringe, where the king intended to spend that night, and where he had stopped before coming to Canterbury. I asked Sir Thomas about my own affair, and he advised me not to make my arrival known just yet, but to join the king's company and he would see me fittingly lodged. I was to accompany them for two days, until the royal party had reached its destination, which was the fine castle of Leeds in the county of Kent.

This advice I followed, and so arrived at Ospringe, where I put up for the night. I happened to stay at an inn in which there was also lodged a gentle English knight of the King's Household. He had stayed on there after the king and his party left for Canterbury, because of a headache which had come upon him during the night. Since this knight, who was called Sir William de Lisle, saw that I was a foreigner and a Frenchman (for in England all who speak the languedoïl* are considered to be French) we made acquaintance with each other, since the English nobility are always courteous and friendly. He asked me who I was and what business I was on, and I told him all that Sir Thomas Percy had bidden me to do. He replied that I could not have made a better plan, that by dinner on Friday the king would be at Leeds and that his uncle the Duke of York would by then be there, too. This was good news for me, since I had letters also to the Duke of York; when we were both younger he had, moreover, met me in the house of his parents the noble King Edward and Queen Philippa. This would give me an even better welcome to the king's household.

On Friday morning I set off in the company of Sir William de Lisle, and as we rode I asked him whether he had been with the king on his expedition to Ireland. 'Yes,' he replied [and he told me much that I wished to know about that country] . . . I did not push the matter further, though I would gladly have heard what else he had to say about that expedition, for other knights rode up wishing to speak to him, and I broke off our conversation and rode on to Leeds, where the king's company arrived soon after.

There I found Edmund, Duke of York, and I introduced myself to him and presented the letters from the Comte de Hainault his cousin and from the Comte d'Ostrevant. The duke soon recognized me and made me very welcome, saying: 'You must stay with us, Sir John. We will show you every sign of friendship and courtesy, as we feel bound to because of old times and because you served my dear mother, as I well remember.' I gratefully thanked him for this welcome. I thus found myself helped by Sir Thomas Percy, by Sir William de Lisle, and by the duke, who himself took me into the king's private apartment, where I was warmly and kindly received. The king took all my letters and when he had read them in front of me he told me that if I had been welcome in his grandfather's house I was equally welcome in his.

I did not that day present the book which I had brought for him, since Sir Thomas Percy suggested it was not the right moment—he was too busy with affairs of state. Firstly, he wanted to send an important embassy to King Charles of France to treat of his projected marriage with Isabelle, the king's eldest daughter, who was at that

* By the twelfth century the vernaculars of southern and northern France were held to be distinct languages, known respectively as Langue d'Oc and Langue d'Oïl from their forms for the word 'yes'. It is interesting that this linguistic basis of the nation was in Froissart's day considered more important in England than in France.

time six years old. For this purpose he had chosen the Earl of Rutland his cousin, Thomas Mowbray Earl Marshal, the Archbishop of Dublin, the Bishop of Ely, Lord Lewis Clifford, Lord Henry Beaumont, Lord Hugh Spenser and several others, who were appropriately escorted for the journey overseas. The second matter concerned the representations made by certain barons of Aquitaine who with the councillors of Bordeaux, Bayonne and Dax had travelled to England to receive an answer to the bitter complaints they had been making to the king since his return from Ireland about the king's gift of the lands, seignories, and baronies of Aquitaine to his uncle the Duke of Lancaster, a gift which the king claimed to be within his right as sovereign.* The party from Aquitaine held that the gift was invalid, since all these lands were directly dependent on the Crown of England, and could not be made over to anyone else. They proposed various reasonable arrangements about which I shall have more to say in due course. To settle these two important matters King Richard had summoned all the chief bishops and barons of England to meet on the feast of St Mary Magdalene in his royal palace at Eltham, half-way between London and Dartford. On the fourth day of my stay at Leeds the king and his council, together with Duke Edmund, left for Eltham, riding by way of Rochester, and I rode with them.

¶ As we travelled to Rochester, I asked Sir William de Lisle and Sir John de Grelly (who was captain of the garrison at Bouteville) why the king was summoning his council to meet at Eltham. They answered my questions, and Sir John in particular gave me a lengthy explanation why these Gascon barons and the city councillors had come to England. I revelled in all he had to say, for he knew the facts and had frequently discussed the problem with them as friends; they were all, moreover, as it were from the same country and fellow subjects of the English crown . . .

'Let us leave this matter now,' said Sir John de Grelly, 'and pass to the second problem, which is to me a pleasanter one. Now, according to my information the King of England is very keen to marry again, and has cast around everywhere but without success. If the Duke of Burgundy or the Comte de Hainault had had marriageable daughters he would gladly have accepted such a match, but they have none that are not already married or betrothed. Some have

* Richard had presented the duchy of Aquitaine to John of Gaunt in 1394, just before leaving for Ireland.

suggested to him that the King of Navarre has sisters and daughters, but he is not interested. His uncle the Duke of Gloucester has a daughter old enough to be married and would be very glad to see her marry the king, but the king objects that she is too closely related, being his first cousin. It is the daughter of the King of France that appeals to King Richard, but all his countrymen are amazed that he wishes to marry his enemy's daughter; his popularity has decreased, but he does not mind, for he has always made it clear that if there is to be a war he would rather it were not against France, and he is known to support the view that there ought now to be a lasting peace between himself and the King of France, and all their allies. The war between them, he says, has lasted too long, too many valiant men on both sides have lost their lives, too many evil deeds have been perpetrated, and too many Christian folk have been destroyed, to the great weakening of Christendom.

'To break the king of this notion, which is so disagreeable to the English people, they have told him that the French princess is too young, and that in five or six years she would still be too young. To which he replies that God willing she would grow older each year, and that he would prefer she were too young than too old. He adds that if he marries her young he can bring her up according to his own desires, and educate her in the manners of the English, and that he is still young enough himself to wait until she reaches the age to be a wife. No one can get this project out of his head. You will see something of this before you leave us, for the king is now riding towards London to bring about a settlement of the matter.'

I was thus entertained with great courtesy on the road from Rochester to Dartford by Sir John de Grelly, Governor of Bouteville, who was the bastard son of that valiant knight the Captal de Buch. I listened with the greatest pleasure to every word he said and kept them all in my memory. From Leeds to Eltham I rode nearly all the way in his company and in that of Sir William de Lisle.

¶ The king reached Eltham on Tuesday; and on Wednesday lords, barons and knights began to arrive from all parts, among them the Duke of Gloucester, the Earls of Arundel, Northumberland, Kent and Rutland, the Earl Marshal, the Archbishops of Canterbury and York, the Bishops of London and Winchester and all the others who had been summoned. By Thursday at the hour of tierce all had arrived, and the council then began in the king's apartment; also present were the Gascon knights and councillors, and a representative of the Duke of Lancaster. I was not there to hear what was said; indeed, I had no right to be, for no bishops or barons were there unless they were members of the king's council.

When it had broken up after dinner (it lasted four hours) I sought out Sir Richard Sturry, that old knight I have mentioned whom I had met in the house of King Edward the Third in my younger days, and who was now a worthy Knight of the King's Bedchamber. It was twenty-four years since he had seen me, yet he recognized me at once; the last time was at Brussels, in the house of Duke Wenceslas of Brabant. Sir Richard made me very welcome and showered me with courtesies, asking for all my news. I gladly told him all I knew. Later as we were walking together in the alleys outside the royal apartments, which were pleasantly shady and covered with vines, I asked him about the council and whether he could tell me of any of its conclusions. He hesitated for a few moments and then said: 'Yes, there is no point in concealing them, for they will very soon be made public . . .'

Sir Richard Sturry's long narrative is excluded here. He tells Froissart that the envoys from Aquitaine have been heard, and that the gist of their arguments, which were very persuasively unfolded, was that they considered the king had no power to alienate from his own person the loyalty of Aquitaine, and produced charters ('clearly understood because they were in both Latin and French') to show that Richard had himself promised to maintain their privileges and to ensure their dependence on the crown of England; they also feared that if the duchy was made over to another this person might intermarry with a daughter of the French royal family and so cause greater trouble for the future.

Sir Richard gave it as his private opinion that they would succeed in their mission, in spite of the fierce opposition of the Duke of Gloucester, who supported Lancaster's claim to Aquitaine to keep him out of the kingdom.

¶ By the following Sunday all the members of the council had gone back to London or wherever they lived, with the exception of the Duke of York, who remained with the king, Sir Richard Sturry and Sir Thomas Percy. These three advanced my private business with the king, who was now anxious to see the book that I had brought for him. I saw him in his bedchamber, and having brought the book with me I placed it on his bed. He opened and studied it, and expressed himself very pleased with it. Indeed, he had good reason to be, for it was handsomely written and illuminated, and bound in crimson velvet with silver-gilt studs having golden roses in the centre;

the clasps were also of silver-gilt, richly worked with golden roses in the centre. Then the king asked me with what it dealt, and I replied: 'With love.' He was delighted with my reply, and he turned the pages and read several passages, for he both read and spoke French very well. Then he handed it to one of his knights, Sir Richard Credon, to take to his study, and entertained me most hospitably.

The same Sunday that King Richard accepted my book with such affection there was in the royal apartments an English squire, one Henry Chrystead, a man of substance and considerable wisdom who spoke French with some fluency. Seeing the welcome that had been given to me by the king and his barons, and with what pleasure the king had accepted my book, he came up to me and said he presumed I was an historian (indeed, he had been told this by Sir Richard Sturry). 'Sir John,' he said, 'have you ever found anyone in this country to tell you about the king's recent expedition to Ireland and how four great kings of that country made their submission to him?' In order to learn all that he had to say I replied that I had not. 'Then let me tell you about it,' said the squire, who must then have been about 50 years old, 'so that you can record it for posterity when you are back in your own country with leisure to write it all down.' I was very pleased with his offer and thanked him warmly . . .

The events in Ireland are irrelevant to the history of the war, but the episode helps us to see the chronicler at work.

I remained in the king's household as long as I wished, and moved with it from place to place, visiting Eltham, Leeds, Kingston, Sheen, Chertsey and Windsor, none very far from London. I was told on good authority that the king and his council had again written to the Duke of Lancaster, for those in Aquitaine were strongly urging that they should have no overlord but the King of England and that the Duke of Lancaster should be recalled. This had now been agreed by the High Council of England, and the Duke of Gloucester, anxious to have his brother out of the kingdom, had no response when he urged that the gift made by the king must be upheld. But the council in England, frightened of what might be the outcome, took heed of the arguments advanced by the deputies of Bayonne and Bordeaux, and were quite ready to believe that if Aquitaine were alienated from its hereditary allegiance to the English crown a situation full of danger for the future would be created, and this they wished to avoid at all costs. Bayonne, Bordeaux and the Gascon marches had always been foremost in preserving the lands and the honour of the Crown of England. The wiser members of the council brought these points to the king's attention in the absence of the Duke of Gloucester, for they would never have dared to speak of them in his presence. And there the matter rested.

Truce by Marriage

Let me now tell you a little about the success of the Earl of Rutland, the earl marshal and the others who had been sent on an embassy to the King of France to treat of the marriage of King Richard and the King of France's young daughter.

¶ When they left Calais the English lords with six hundred horses rode quickly through the towns of Amiens, Clermont-en-Beauvoisis and Creil and so reached Paris. They were well received wherever they passed, in accordance with orders from the King of France. In Paris they were lodged at the Croix-au-Tiroir and near by; the King of France was in the Palace of the Louvre, the queen and her children in the Hôtel Saint-Pol, the Duc de Berry in the Hôtel de Nesle, the Duke of Burgundy in the Hôtel d'Artois, while the Duc d'Orléans, the Comte de Saint-Pol and the Seigneur de Coucy were each in their own houses, for the King of France had summoned his whole council to advise him in making his reply to the English lords.

Orders were given by the King of France that while the English party were in Paris there should be delivered to them two hundred gold crowns a day for their personal expenses and those of their horses. These noble English lords were often found at dinner with the king, who with his brother and uncles offered the best cheer and the best company they could for love of the King of England, who had sent the lords to Paris. The English asked for a reply to their request, but they were put off with fair words, for many of the French nobles in the Royal Council were still amazed at the demands and offers of the English, since the war had for so long been waged with such cruelty between France and England. Some of them argued thus: 'How can the King of France give his daughter in marriage to his enemy the King of England? It is our opinion that before such a treaty is arranged there should be secure peace on all fronts between

France and England and all our allies.' This view and many others were discussed in the king's privy council.

The Chancellor of France at this time was a wise and courageous man called Sir Renaud de Corbie; he was also a far-sighted politician, and judging how the needs of France might evolve, he said to the king and his uncles: 'We must seize this opportunity with open arms. This King Richard of England makes it clear through his offer of alliance by marriage that he bears only love to the king and people of France. We have now had two separate sessions concerning a peace treaty, at Amiens and Leulinghen, and on neither occasion has any agreement been reached, other than on the terms of a temporary truce. We know, too, that the uncle of the King of England—Thomas, Duke of Gloucester—is in complete opposition to the king and the Dukes of Lancaster and York over this whole question of a peace, and that neither the king nor any of those who favour the cause of peace have been able to change his mind, even though in the end his private view will be of little weight against the king. Let us therefore accept their offers in the way they are meant, and do all we can so that the English go away satisfied with our reply.'

The argument here advanced by the Chancellor of France, which was repeated on other occasions, won over the king's uncles, and more particularly the Duke of Burgundy, who said he was so tired of war that he would gladly see peace established between France and England. The chief reason that persuaded him to this was, he said, because of Flanders,* of which country he had become the lord through his wife and which was so close to the power of England. The Flemings were, moreover, as much inclined to the English as to the French, largely because they have a great volume of trade with England both by land and sea. The king's privy council therefore declared that, as they had so far accorded a warm welcome to the English, it would be wise to continue this attitude, and that this was the king's personal desire, and a decision was reached, whether by dissimulation or otherwise, that the ambassadors from the English court should be given soft answers before they left which would lead them to hope that the King of England's wishes would be met.

* Louis de Nevers, Comte de Flandre, who was killed at Crécy, had been a faithful vassal of the French Crown. His son Louis de Mâle saw that his country's woollen interests urged him to keep in with England. It had been consequently something of a diplomatic triumph for Charles V when he secured the marriage of his brother Philippe le hardi, Duke of Burgundy, to Louis's only child Marguerite, who would therefore inherit the province of Flanders.

During this time the Queen of France and her children were staying at the Hôtel Saint-Pol by the Seine. The English lords were granted their request to visit the queen and her children, in particular the one whose hand they had been sent to obtain, for they were very anxious to see her. The French objection was that this child of six years was too young to have reached the age of discretion. Yet for her age she was well brought up and carefully instructed, and indeed the English lords noticed this when they spoke to her. As the earl marshal knelt before her he said: 'Madame, if it please God you shall be queen and mistress of England'—to which the princess replied without any prompting: 'If it pleases God and my lord and father that I should be Queen of England, I shall gladly accept my lot, for they tell me I should then be a great lady.' She then told the Earl Marshal to rise and led him by the hand to the queen her mother, who was as delighted with her daughter's reply as was everyone else who heard it. The bearing and the good sense of this young French princess made a very good impression on King Richard's ambassadors, and they foresaw that from this excellent beginning she would become a lady of great reputation in their country.

The outcome of all these negotiations was as follows. When the English lords had been in Paris for three weeks, all expenses for themselves and their horses having been paid by the King of France, a courteous and reasonable answer was delivered to them from the king and his council which gave them great hope that their mission would be successful, but not at once, for the lady whose hand they were seeking was still very young and there was the further impediment that she had been promised in marriage to the elder son of the Duke of Brittany. Negotiations had therefore to be started for breaking off this engagement before the matter could go any farther, and things should be left in their present state for the winter that was about to begin. When the season of Lent came round and the days became longer, the weather better and the seas calmer, an invitation to return would be sent to England by the King of France, and those same lords, or others that England might choose, would be welcome at the court of France.

The English were satisfied with this reply and they took their leave of the king and queen, their daughter the Princess Isabelle of France, the king's brother and uncles, and of all the others who had welcomed them, and set off from Paris for Calais, following the route by which they had come. They landed at Sandwich [October 1395] and the whole party hastened to carry their news to the King of England, reaching Windsor in less than a day and a half from their landing. The king was very glad to receive them and declared himself satisfied with the answer from the French court. He did not then dismiss the matter from his mind, but spent all his time in pleasurable anticipation of how he might achieve his purpose of having the King of France's daughter as his wife.

While the King of England spent his energies thus, the King of France and his advisers were no less busily employed in contriving night and day how this affair might be concluded to the honour of themselves and of France. There were many whose opinion was something as follows: 'If we were asked for our opinion concerning these negotiations, we would say that the King of England should never take a French princess to wife until a lasting peace had been established between the two kings and all their allies. What is the good of allowing the King of England to marry the daughter of the King of France when all that has been decided is a two-year truce, for when that has run out they'll all be at war and hating each other again? That needs careful consideration.' The Dukes of Orléans and Berry were of this opinion, as were many important nobles and barons of France. The King of France, with the Duke of Burgundy and the Chancellor of France, were well aware of this, but they were inclined to make a peace if the honour of France could be preserved.

¶ . . . In the course of the winter King Richard had sent frequent messages to keep the King of France aware of this matter, and the council of France were not hostile to this, because they were still hoping to put an end to the war. Negotiations continued so favourably, and the two kings wrote each other such conciliatory letters, that an advanced stage had now been reached, and the King of England had given his word that he would exert the necessary influence over the English to ensure that there would be peace.* As a result of all this, the earl marshal, the Earl of Rutland and the greater number of those who had been of the previous party were again sent to France [February 1396] about this marriage. In Paris they occupied the whole of the street called the Croix du Tiroir and part of another, for there were at least five hundred of them. Their expenses

* In December 1395 King Richard signed a treaty for a peace to last twenty-five years, and the following January had promised that his wife would not be held to continue the French line through her children. The truce was extended to twenty-eight years and sealed on the day of the marriage contract.

were paid by the King of France and they stayed more than three weeks in Paris,

¶ . . . where they were lavishly entertained by the king and queen. Negotiations proceeded so well that the marriage they had come to arrange was, in fact, agreed, and the earl marshal, by virtue of the powers he had received from the King of England, declared that Isabelle, eldest daughter of King Charles of France, was betrothed and espoused to the King of England and that she should henceforth be known as Queen of England. I have been told that it was a joy to see her, young as she was, for she knew how to act the queen.

When all this was concluded and the contract signed and sealed [9 March 1396], the ambassadors from England took leave of the King and Queen of France, of their daughter the Queen of England, and of all the lords. From Paris they went to Calais and so to England, where they were received most warmly by the king and the Duke of Lancaster and by those who favoured the king's policy. But however glad some might be in England at this marriage, the Duke of Gloucester was not at all pleased, for he realized that because of this alliance there would again be peace between France and England, and this he did not want unless it were a peace which would be to England's honour, with a return to the *status quo* when war broke out in Gascony. He often made occasion to discuss this with his brother the Duke of York, and tried to win him over to his own way of thinking, because he considered this brother weak of mind and will and easily influenced. To the Duke of Lancaster, however, he scarcely dared to broach the matter, because he was a thorough supporter of the king's policy and was, moreover, delighted with the marriage, largely because of his own two daughters the Queens of Castille and Portugal.

King Richard Abdicates

The terms of the marriage treaty included English opposition to the pope in Rome, her support for French designs in Europe, and French help for Richard 'against any of his subjects' if he should need it. Such terms earned great unpopularity for Richard, and among the nobles only John of Gaunt, Duke of Lancaster, gave him loyal support. In France the treaty seemed less real, for Richard retained the empty title of King of France, no provision was made for delimiting the frontiers of the two kings' territories, and sporadic warfare of a sort was still waged by the routiers*; her mad king, however, was secure on his throne, and the gaiety continued in the Hôtel Saint-Pol.*

King Richard's hold on his throne began to weaken with every step he now took. In 1397 he had Gloucester murdered in Calais; Warwick and Arundel were put in prison; Arundel's brother, the Archbishop of Canterbury, was banished for life, and Arundel when tried was sentenced to execution. The king was acting, perhaps, in imitation of Charles VI, whom he much admired. Having got rid of his critics, he then rewarded his friends, among them Henry Bolingbroke, son of the Duke of Lancaster, whom he made Duke of Hereford, and Thomas Mowbray, whom he made Duke of Norfolk.

Shortly afterwards the famous dispute between Hereford and Norfolk was brought before the king; a duel was arranged to take place at Coventry on 16 September 1397, and when it was about to begin the king ordered them to lay down their arms, and gave sentence of banishment, to Norfolk for life and to Hereford for ten years.

Richard then developed a policy of claiming large sums for pardons from those who had crossed his will, and his unpopularity became more widely voiced. He was now ruling without a Parliament, and spending lavishly on court life and entertainments. Early in 1399 the Duke of Lancaster died; constantly loyal to the crown, he made no recorded protest at his son's banishment. With his strongest supporter dead, Richard, through fear of Bolingbroke, took the foolish step of extending his banishment for life and divided a great part of his lands among three royalist supporters. A threat of rebellion arose in Ireland, and as Richard set out for Leinster, news reached him that Henry Bolingbroke, Duke of Hereford, had landed in England. He gathered an army in Pontefract and met little opposition. By August, Bolingbroke and his cousin the king had met in Chester, and the king had been forced to summon a Parliament in Westminster for the end of September; the ostensible reason was to secure the restoration of the Lancaster inheritance.

When they returned to London, Richard was placed in the tower. The people of London were united in support of Bolingbroke, but if Richard were to be deposed it was easier and wiser to see that he made a voluntary act of abdication. It seems fairly clear that Froissart received his information from sources friendly to Bolingbroke and that Richard did not willingly resign his crown, though there is no record in the Parliamentary Rolls of the request which he almost certainly made for a hearing before Parliament. Bolingbroke is now referred to as the Duke of Lancaster.

¶ . . . The Duke of Lancaster received word that King Richard was very anxious to speak to him and was asking to see him. He therefore left his house at once, though it was late in the day, and went down the Thames in a barge in the company of his knights. When he reached the Tower he entered by a postern gate and went to the king, who received him courteously and very humbly, in the manner of one who feels his life is in great danger. He then said: 'Cousin, I have been considering my fortunes, which are now in a poor state, God be praised, and I no longer have any desire to prolong my reign, or to govern my people, or to wear the crown. As God may save my soul, I would I had died a natural death and that the King of France had his daughter again, for we have had no great happiness together nor since I brought her hither have I felt myself beloved of my people as I was before. When I reflect on all this, cousin, I recognize that I have behaved ill towards you and towards several nobles of my own blood in this land. For this reason I know that I shall never live in peace and forgiveness. I therefore resign to you, of my own free will, the heritage of the crown of England, and beg you to accept my abdication and this gift in love.'

When the Duke of Lancaster heard these words he replied: 'It is fitting that an assembly of the three estates of England be called to approve your declaration. Indeed, I have already summoned the nobles and the prelates of this realm, together with the representatives of the chief cities, and within three days there will be a sufficient body of them to make due acceptance of your abdication, by which you will do much to soften the hatred and discontent of many persons within this realm. It is in order to circumvent all the evils that have arisen in England through the suspension of justice, which for some time now has ceased to be practised, that I have been summoned from over the seas because the people wish to crown me and because it is widely held throughout England that I have and always have had a better right to the crown than you. When our grandfather King Edward of blessed memory destined you for the throne, he was reproved for it on these same grounds, but he so loved his son the Prince of Wales that no one could break him of his purpose to make you king. If you had followed in the ways of the Prince of Wales and taken good advice, as a good son should always loyally follow in the good steps of his father, you would have remained a worthy king. But you have always done the contrary, so that the rumour has spread in England and elsewhere that you were never the son of the Prince of Wales, but of some clerk or canon, for I have heard it said, by some knights of the household of my uncle the Prince of Wales, that the prince considered his marriage had been dishonoured. Your mother was first cousin to King Edward, who nursed a hatred for her because she had not given his son any children. Twice she had been godparent with him of the children of Sir Thomas Holland. Well she knew how to keep the prince ensnared, having won him in marriage by subtle cunning, but she always feared that the prince might divorce her and so got herself pregnant with the result that you were born and another before you. We need not bother about the earlier one, but since all have seen your behaviour and bearing to be so far removed from that of the noble prince, it is commonly said here and elsewhere that you were the son of a clerk or a canon, for when you were conceived and born in Bordeaux there were plenty of handsome young priests in the prince's household. Such is the report among the people of this realm, and your conduct has served but to support it, for you have always been in favour of pleasing the French and of making peace with them, to the confusion and dishonour of the realm of England. Because my uncle the Duke of Gloucester and the earl marshal in their loyalty rebuked you gently for this, wishing to maintain the honour of the kingdom and to follow in the virtuous works of their fathers, you treacherously put them to death. For my part I have assumed your protection, and I shall out of pity defend you and preserve your life so long as I can, and I shall speak on your behalf to the people of London and the heirs of those you have unjustly killed.'*

'Cousin, I thank you much,' said King Richard, 'and I put greater trust in you than in anyone else in England.' To which the Duke of Lancaster replied: 'You act wisely, for if I had not come between you and the people they would have seized you and treated you shamefully, and would then have killed you for those evil deeds which have put you in jeopardy.'

King Richard considered all the duke had to say and did not know what to say in reply, for it was clear to him that neither force nor arguments were any use and that he would have to rely on meekness and resignation. He therefore showed great humility to the duke and begged that his life might be spared. When the duke had spent two hours with the king in the Tower of London, pointing out all the abuses and evils of which he was accused and which were

* Henry was not content to be king by usurpation and popular acclaim. He did his best to prove Richard's illegitimacy, and (though this is not mentioned by Froissart) he went further by suggesting that Edmund (Crouchback) of Lancaster was really the elder son of Henry III, but had been displaced in the succession because of his deformity. It is doubtful whether these were accepted as more than specious aids to a *fait accompli.*

abundantly proved, he took his leave and returned by the river to his own house.

The next day he sent further orders into the distant parts of England, and soon after there arrived in London the Duke of York his uncle with his son the Earl of Rutland, the Earl of Northumberland with his son Sir Henry Percy, all of whom the Duke of Lancaster received most cordially. There came also a great number of bishops, archbishops and abbots. On the day appointed for the council [29 September 1399] Duke Henry of Lancaster, accompanied by the lords bishop, dukes, earls, barons and knights and by many of the most notable citizens of London, rode to the Tower,* where they dismounted and entered the Hall. King Richard was then brought from his room, robed in his royal robes, carrying his sceptre and wearing his crown. He stood alone, with no one beside him, and addressed the assembly in these words: 'I have been King of England, Duke of Aquitaine and Lord of Ireland for some twenty-two years, and the heritage of this realm, this sceptre and this crown I now freely and fully resign to my cousin Henry, Duke of Lancaster. In the presence of you all I beg him to take this sceptre as a sign of his entering into possession.' Thereupon he gave the sceptre to the duke, who took it and immediately handed it to the Archbishop of Canterbury, who then kept it in his hand. Next King Richard took the gold crown off his head and holding it before him in both his hands, he said: 'Fair cousin, Henry of Lancaster, I give and entrust into your hands this crown with which I was crowned King of England, and with all the rights pertaining to it.' The Duke of Lancaster took it, and immediately gave it over to the Archbishop of Canterbury, who was at hand to receive it.

When the form of resignation had thus been pronounced by Richard of Bordeaux and these two acts had been completed, Duke Henry of Lancaster called a public notary and asked him to prepare a deed which would be witnessed by all the prelates and princes, barons and knights who were present. Soon after Richard of Bordeaux returned to the room in the Tower from which he had been brought, and the Duke of Lancaster with all the lords who had attended the council mounted their horses and left. The two precious objects were placed in coffers and carried to the treasury of Westminster Abbey. The lords returned each to his house to await the day for the Council of Parliament which was

* The Latin act of abdication says this took place 'apud Westmonasterium in loco consueto consilii', though Froissart continues to say that it was in the Tower.

to be held at Westminster concerning the coronation of King Henry.

¶ In the year of Our Lord 1399, on the last day of September, a Tuesday, Duke Henry of Lancaster held a Parliament in the Palace of Westminster outside London, at which there were present the greater part of the bishops and clergy of England, the dukes, earls and barons of the said realm, and representatives of the towns according to their size. There, the Duke of Lancaster laid his claim to the kingdom of England, basing his right to be king on three reasons: firstly, by conquest; secondly, because he claimed to be the direct heir; and thirdly because King Richard of Bordeaux had of his own free will resigned his crown to him in the presence of bishops, dukes, earls and knights in the Great Hall of the Tower of London.

These three reasons having been advanced, Duke Henry demanded of all those assembled that they should declare their will. This they did at once, saying it was indeed their desire that he should be their king and that they would have no one else. Twice more the duke demanded whether this were truly their will, and they all replied: 'Yes!' Whereupon Henry of Lancaster took his seat on the throne, which was raised on a platform in the centre of the Hall so that everyone could see him, and covered over with a canopy of cloth of gold. As soon as he was seated all the people joyfully raised their right arms and promised him their allegiance. At the conclusion of this session the coronation was fixed for St Edward's Day the thirteenth of October, which was a Monday.

¶ On the Saturday before his coronation the Duke of Lancaster left Westminster for the Tower of London with a large body of his men, and those squires who were to be made knights spent the whole night in a vigil. There were forty-six of them and each had his own room and his own bath in which he bathed that night. Next morning the duke made them knights during mass, and gave to each of them a long green robe, with narrow sleeves trimmed with miniver, and large hoods also trimmed with miniver after the style of bishops; on the left shoulder they had a double cord of white silk with white tufts hanging down. When the duke left the Tower to go to Westminster after dinner he went bare-headed and wore round his neck the badge of the King of France. With him went his son, six dukes, six earls and eighteen barons, and in all eight or nine hundred knights. The king* had put on a short jacket of cloth of gold in the German style;

* Froissart's synonymous use of king and duke has been retained in this passage.

he rode a white horse and on his left leg he was wearing the Blue Garter. The duke rode thus through London with a great body of lords, each with his men wearing his own livery and badge, and all the burgesses, both Lombards and Londoners, and the members of the guilds likewise wearing their proper livery and emblems; there were in all six thousand horse who accompanied the duke to Westminster. The streets that day were hung with various kinds of stuffs, and that day and the next there were nine conduits in Cheapside, running with white or red wine in the manner of fountains.

That night the Duke of Lancaster bathed himself and on the next day [13 October 1399]* as soon as he was up he confessed himself (and the need was great) and heard three masses according to his custom. All the bishops and a large body of other clergy who were assembled in Westminster then went in procession from the Abbey to conduct the king from the Tower in company with all the lords, who were wearing scarlet capes and long mantles trimmed with miniver and large hoods similarly trimmed; the dukes and earls had three rows of fur, about a quarter of a yard long, on the left shoulder, and the barons had two rows; the knights and squires had scarlet capes with livery badges. As he rode from the Tower to the Abbey a canopy of blue silk was borne over the king's head, supported on four silver poles with four golden bells, and this was carried by four burgesses of Dover according to their right.† On either side of him were carried the swords of mercy and of justice, the former by his eldest son the Prince of Wales, the latter by Henry Percy, Earl of Northumberland. The Earl of Westmorland, Marshal of England, carried the sceptre.

The duke and all the nobles entered the Abbey about nine o'clock, and approached the platform which had been prepared, covered with crimson cloth. In the centre of this platform was a throne covered with cloth of gold, and here the duke took his seat. The duke was clad in royal state, except that he had neither crown nor hat on his head. From the four corners of the platform the Archbishop of Canterbury proclaimed that here was the man whom God had sent to be their lord and king. Then he asked whether it was the will of the people that this man should be crowned as their king, and they all replied with one voice: 'Yes', raising their right arms and making profession of allegiance and loyalty.

* This was significantly the Feast of St Edward the Confessor, whose crown was to be placed on the head of the new sovereign.

† Actually it was the right of all the Cinque Ports.

After this declaration, the duke stepped down from the platform and went to the altar for the ceremony of coronation, for which there were two archbishops and ten bishops. There before the altar King Henry was divested of his royal state except for his shirt, and was anointed in six places—on the head, on the breast, on the shoulders and between his shoulders and hands. A cap was placed on his head, and while he was being anointed the clergy sang the litany and the office that is used for the dedication of a font. Then he was clad in the vestments of a deacon of the Church, and shoes of crimson velvet like those of a bishop were put on his feet, together with sharp spurs without rowels. Then the sword of justice was drawn from its scabbard to be blessed, after which it was handed to the king, who replaced it in the scabbard and the Archbishop of Canterbury himself girt it on him. St Edward's crown—arched over in the form of a cross—was then brought and blessed, and placed on the king's head by the archbishop. When mass had been sung the king left the Abbey in his royal state, being met outside by the Constable and the Marshal of England, with the constable's lieutenant, who prepared the way for the king to proceed to the palace, in the middle of which was set a fountain from which red and white wine flowed from various jets. The king entered the Hall and visited his cabinet before returning to the dinner that was prepared. The first table was for the king, who had with him the two archbishops and seventeen bishops, the second for the four dukes of England, the third for the burgesses of London and the fourth for the knights and squires who had been invited. The king was accompanied on one side by the Prince of Wales bearing the sword of mercy, and on the other by the constable, who was bearing the sword of justice. Behind came the marshal with the sceptre.

In the middle of the dinner there entered into the Hall a knight of the name of Dymock, mounted on a charger and both horse and rider covered in chain-mail and crimson as if ready for a challenge to arms. A knight came before him, carrying his lance, and with a naked sword and a dagger at either side. The knight presented to the king a parchment which was read aloud, saying that if there were any knight, squire or nobleman who wished to claim that King Henry was not the lawful sovereign, he was ready to offer him combat in the presence of the king or whenever the king should be ready to appoint a time. The king had this challenge cried aloud in the Hall by a herald, but no one accepted it. When the king had dined he took wine and sweetmeats in the Hall, and then retired to his apartments.

All the guests also left for their homes or wherever they were staying.

Thus passed the day of King Henry's coronation, and he spent that night and the following in the Palace of Westminster.

¶ Not long after this the rumour was abroad in London that Richard of Bordeaux was dead. How he died and by what means I could not discover on the day I write these chronicles.*

After his death King Richard of Bordeaux was laid on a litter which was borne on a cart covered with a black cloth and drawn by four black horses which were led by two men clad also in black; behind the cart walked four knights in black. Thus they left the Tower and went slowly through the streets of London until they reached Cheapside, which is the chief throughfare of that city, and there they halted for more than two hours while over twenty thousand people, men and women, came to see King Richard lying there, with his face uncovered on a black pillow. Some who saw this sight felt pity for him, while others said that he had long deserved death.

Reflect upon this, you lords, kings, dukes, earls, bishops and all men of birth and power, and consider how astonishing are the changing fortunes of this world. King Richard reigned over England for twenty-two years in great pomp and power. Never did any King of England keep such state, spending as much as a hundred thousand florins a year to maintain his household. For I, Jean Froissart, Canon of Lille and Chimay and treasurer of the Abbey of Chimay, had experience of this when I was his guest for more than a quarter of a year, during which time he showed me warm hospitality because in my younger days I had been a clerk in the royal household and on terms of friendship with his grandfather King Edward the Third, of blessed memory, and of his wife the lady Philippa of Hainault, Queen of England. When I took leave of him at Windsor he made me a present, through one of his knights called Sir John Golofre, of a silver-gilt goblet weighing over a pound and containing a hundred gold nobles, which I have since valued the more and shall continue to treasure. It is therefore my bounden duty to pray for him, and only

* Many manuscripts of the Fourth Book of Froissart add a long note at this point, written by a commentator who reproaches the author with passing over the truth concerning the death of Richard. He gives an account of how Sir Piers of Exton visited him in the Tower of London with four followers. In a fight that ensued Richard showed extraordinary courage and killed the four men, but was then himself killed by Sir Piers. He adds that some believed that Richard had allowed himself to die of starvation. After his recent visit to Richard it is odd that Froissart refrains from mentioning this account.

unwillingly do I write of his death. But since I have undertaken to write these present chronicles to the best of my ability, I must write down what I know at this present time in order to give information of his fate.

In my time I have heard two prophecies, which turned out very differently yet which were both true. I was in the city of Bordeaux and sitting at table when King Richard was born; it was on a Wednesday on the stroke of ten.* And at that hour exactly I was visited by Sir Richard de Pontchardon, at that time Marshal of Aquitaine, who said: 'Froissart, write down that it may be recorded—the princess has given birth to a fine son on Twelfth Day, the Feast of Kings, and he is a king's son, for his father is King of Galicia, which land had been given to him by the King Don Pedro, and he is about to set off to make good his claim. Thus the child is of royal lineage and he, too, will be a king.' The knight of Pontchardon did not lie, for he was King of England for twenty-two years, but on the day he said this to me he knew nothing of how the young prince's life would turn out, and I have often since then thought about his words. For on my first visit to England in the household of Queen Philippa, she and King Edward and all their children were at Berkhamsted, a manor belonging to the Prince of Wales some thirty miles outside London, where they had gone to say farewell to the prince and princess before they left for Aquitaine. It was there that I heard an old knight named Sir Barthélemy de Burghersh, who said, in conversation with some of the queen's ladies who came from Hainault: 'We have in this country a book known as "Brut",† in which it is written that neither the king's eldest son the Prince of Wales, nor the Duke of Clarence, nor the Duke of Lancaster, nor the Duke of York, nor the Duke of Gloucester will be king of England, but the crown will revert to the House of Lancaster.'

Now I, Jean Froissart, author of these chronicles, can say on mature reflection that both these knights spoke truth, for like everyone else I have seen Richard of Bordeaux reign for twenty-two years over England, only for the crown to return in his lifetime to the House of Lancaster; this was when Henry was crowned King of England in the circumstances that have just been narrated, though he had not before aspired to the throne, and never would have done if Richard of Bordeaux had behaved decently towards him, since it

* Almost certainly an anachronism. See Introduction, pp. 22–23.

† A Middle English poem by Layamon, written in about 1200. It contains a strange mixture of legend and history.

was out of pity for his wrongs that the Londoners made him king.

When the cart bearing King Richard of Bordeaux had stayed for more than two hours in Cheapside, they moved off again, with the four knights following. When they were outside the city the four knights found their servants waiting for them with horses; they mounted and rode on to a village about thirty miles from London called Langley, where the king and queen have a manor. There King Richard of Bordeaux lies buried. May God have mercy on his soul!

KING RICHARD RESIGNS THE CROWN

THE CHRONICLES OF
ENGUERRAND DE MONSTRELET

Orléans and Burgundy

The reign of Henry IV was something of an interlude in the history of the war, not by his desire, but because of the circumstances to be found in the two kingdoms. Henry was too busy consolidating his throne, and in making it clear that he held it by election (and if necessary by conquest) rather than by usurpation. His enemies were numerous, but scattered, and he established his ascendancy at the battle of Shrewsbury in 1403, though the Welsh opposition under Owen Glendower persisted after that date.

The war, in fact, had come to the close of its first phase with Richard II's marriage settlement and the meeting of the two kings at Calais. To sum up briefly this first phase, we may say that no real attempt had been made at a conquest of France, and the chief aim of the English had been to keep Aquitaine under control of the English crown, which appointed the 'French' barons who effectively governed the duchy. The English nobility had, of course, found the war profitable, and victories had provided the means for continuing it. If peace had nominally existed, the French had not always found this easy to believe in view of the activities of the routiers, *whose activities were invariably blamed on the English. Henry's intention was to pursue a warlike policy towards France, and in this he was strengthened by his desire to make a break with Richard's policy; but his domestic troubles and poor health prevented him from putting his intention into practice. He even allowed the French to ratify the Treaty of Leulinghen, a treaty he had never intended to keep.*

Charles VI, in spite of the ratification, toyed with two ideas: support for the Welsh insurrection and fostering a revolt of the barons in Aquitaine. The former never got much beyond the stage of money and promises of help; the latter was launched with the capture of a number of border fortresses, but the campaign, led by Louis d'Orléans, petered out, as did another in which the Duke of Burgundy was to besiege Calais. The weakness of the monarchy at this time saw the rise of important provincial lords, who reigned as sovereigns over their territories. From among them two soon rose to prominence, and their ambitions led to frequent clashes between them, each trying to secure the chief favours of the demented king. The details of the struggle are outside the scope of this book, but the consequences are of great importance. When Philippe, Duke of Burgundy, died in 1404 he was succeeded by his ruthless son Jean sans Peur, who three years later decided on murder to advance his cause. The chronicling of events is now taken up by Monstrelet.

¶ At this time there happened in the city of Paris an event which was more pitiful than any that had occurred for a very long time in the Christian kingdom of France, and that event was the death of one man. Because of it the king and all the princes of his blood and indeed nearly all his people suffered greatly; the kingdom was for a long time divided against itself and much weakened by this strife, as will become very evident from the story that is to be unfolded in this present book. I am speaking of the death of the Duc d'Orléans, only brother of the king of France, Charles the well-beloved and sixth of his name.

This duke was in Paris on a Wednesday which was the Feast of the Pope Saint Clement [23 November 1407], and after dinner on that day, at about seven o'clock, he was treacherously murdered. The agents of this crime were some eighteen men who, as it was afterwards discovered, had for several days lodged at an hotel bearing the sign of Our Lady near the Porte Barbette* with the intention of carrying out this crime. On the Wednesday, it seems, they sent a man named Thomas de Courteheuse, one of the king's servants and their accomplice in this, to seek out the Duc d'Orléans, who had gone to visit the Queen of France in the house she had recently purchased from Montagu, Grand Master of the King's Household. This house was very close to the Porte Barbette, and the queen was then recovering from the birth of a child which had not long survived† and she had not yet completed the time of her purification.

The man Thomas approached the duke and falsely declared: 'My lord, the king bids you to come to him without delay, because he has something concerning himself and you which he must discuss at once.' When the duke heard this alleged order from the king he immediately leaped on his mule to answer the summons. In his company there were two squires on one horse‡ and four or five foot-servants in front and behind carrying torches; his other followers were in no hurry and he was poorly attended that day, though he maintained in Paris a staff of quite six hundred knights and squires. At the Porte Barbette the eighteen men were waiting for him in the shadow of a house with their weapons concealed from view. The night was dark. As the duke approached the gate they leapt upon him in a wild fury, and one of them shouted: 'Kill him!' dealing

* A gate in the fortifications of Philippe-Auguste (which date from the end of the twelfth century), near the present rue Vieille du Temple.

† Philippe de France, who was born and died on the 11th of November 1407.

‡ A normal custom of the times.

him a blow with his axe which severed his hand clean at the wrist.

The duke, seeing such a cruel attack made upon him, shouted out loud: 'I am the Duc d'Orléans', to which some of those who were striking at him answered: 'That's just what we wanted to know.' At this the rest of the men joined in, and shortly the duke was knocked off his mule and his head so smashed with blows that the brains ran out on the roadway. Even then they turned him over and over, so hacking at him that he was very soon completely dead. With him was also killed a squire who had been his page; when he saw his master on the ground he lay upon him to protect him, but to no avail. As for the horse which was carrying the two squires, it began to neigh when it felt the murderers close at hand, but they let it pass on, and when it had passed them it started to run and the squires were unable to stop it for quite some distance. When they were able to do so they found that the duke's mule had followed after them without its rider. They thought he must have fallen off, and took the beast by the bridle in order to lead it back to the duke, but when they came up with the murderers the men threatened them that if they didn't go away they would be dealt with in the same way as their master. Seeing that their lord had been killed where he lay, they rushed off to the queen's lodging shouting: 'Murder'. The men who had killed the duke started to shout out: 'Fire', for they had so organized things that while the slaughter was taking place one of their number entered the house where they had been staying and set fire to it. Then on horse or on foot they went off with all possible speed, throwing down caltrops behind them so that they could not be followed.

As the news spread, some of them entered the Hôtel d'Artois* by a back door to see their master, Duke Jean of Burgundy, who had given orders for this deed, as he has since publicly confessed. There they told him how it had been carried out, and then hastened away to put their persons in safety. The leader in this cruel murder was one Raoulet d'Auquetonville, a Norman, whom in the past the Duc d'Orléans had removed from his post of counsellor-general, which the king had bestowed on him at the request of Philippe, the late Duke of Burgundy. Because of this humiliation Raoulet had been reflecting how he could revenge himself on the Duc d'Orléans. His accomplices were Guillaume and Thomas de Courteheuse, who were natives of the county of Guines, Jean de la Motte and others to the number beforementioned.

About half an hour later the household of the Duc d'Orléans

* In the present rue Mauconseil.

received news of the pitiful death of their lord and lamented bitterly; nobles and people of his household ran to the spot and found him dead on the cobbles. There was much weeping and sadness among his knights and squires and all his servants when they saw his body so terribly mutilated. Then they lifted him up and carried him sadly to the house of the Seigneur de Rieux,* Marshal of France, which was near by. Shortly afterwards the body was covered with a white shroud and decorously removed to the Church of Saint-Guillaume,† which was the nearest church to where he had died. A little later the King of Sicily, who was at that time in Paris, and several princes, knights and squires who had heard of the cruel death of the only brother of the King of France, came to the church to weep over the body, which had been placed in a lead coffin. Throughout the night the monks of that church kept watch, reciting vigils and psalms, and the members of his house watched with them.

Early next morning the duke's men found his severed hand and a part of his brains on the roadway; these were gathered up and placed alongside the body in the coffin. Soon all the princes in Paris had come to the church, with the exception of the king and his children; there were present King Louis of Sicily, the Duc de Berry, the Duke of Burgundy, the Duc de Bourbon, the Marquis du Pont, the Comte de Nevers, the Comte de Clermont, the Comte de Vendôme, the Comte de Saint-Pol, the Comte de Dammartin, the Constable of France and many others who assembled with the clergy and a multitude of the people of Paris in the Church of Saint-Guillaume. Then the chiefs of the house of Orléans took the coffin bearing his body and carried it out of the church with a procession formed of the dead duke's squires carrying lighted torches. The nobles took their places in order beside the coffin, King Louis and the Dukes of Berry, Burgundy and Bourbon, weeping and holding each a corner of the shroud which covered the coffin. After them in order came the princes, the clergy and the barons saying prayers for his soul to his Creator, and thus he was carried into the Church of the Célestins. After his funeral service had been solemnly chanted he was buried with due pomp in an elegant chapel which he had himself built and endowed; the princes and all the others went off to their own homes.

Everyone was most anxious to know who was the author of this crime against the Duc d'Orléans. It was at first thought that Sir Aubert de Canny had been responsible, since he was known to have

* In the present rue Vieille du Temple.

† Now the Église des Blancs-Manteaux, rue des Blancs-Manteaux.

nursed great hatred towards the duke, who had gone off with his wife and had a child by her, of whom more will be told later.* However, it was not long before the true facts of the murder were known and that Sir Aubert was in no way guilty. When Queen Isabella heard of this murder committed so close to her house she was so angry and so frightened that even though she was not sufficiently recovered from childbirth, she had herself carried in a litter that same day, by her brother Ludwig of Bavaria and his men, to the Hôtel Saint-Pol, where for greater safety she took up residence in the room next to the king's. On the night of the murder several nobles, including the Comte de Saint-Pol, armed themselves and entered the king's palace, not knowing where this affair might end.

After the duke's funeral, the king summoned the princes and all the members of the council, together with the Provost of Paris and other men of law, who received an order from the council to make every possible effort to discover who was the author of this crime and who were his accomplices. It was ordered that all the gates of Paris should be closed, except two which were to be closely guarded so that anyone leaving the city could be identified. When these and certain other orders had been promulgated the council broke up in miserable uncertainty and reassembled at the Hôtel Saint-Pol on the the next day, a Friday. With the king were King Louis, the Dukes of Berry, Burgundy and Bourbon and many other lords. The Provost of Paris was immediately called in and the Duc de Berry asked him what steps he had taken to discover the murderer of so important a person as the king's only brother; the provost replied that he had pursued his inquiries with the greatest possible diligence, but had not yet discovered his identity, and added that, if he were given permission to search the homes of the king's counsellors and of the other princes, he thought he might discover who was the murderer or at least his accomplices. King Louis with the Dukes of Berry and Bourbon gave him authority to enter wherever they chose.

When Duke Jean of Burgundy saw this permission being given to the Provost of Paris he began to be alarmed, and drawing aside King Louis and his uncle the Duc de Berry he confessed to them that by the temptation of the devil he had done this murder through the agency of Raoulet d'Auquetonville and his accomplices. The two royal princes were dumbfounded and could scarcely reply, pointing out only that they disapproved of the cruel method by which this murder of a cousin had been carried out. When they had

* Jean, Comte de Dunois.

received the duke's confession they returned to the council, but made no allusion to the matter; shortly after their return the session was concluded, and the members departed.

On Saturday the council reassembled at ten in the morning in the Hôtel de Nesle,* where the Duc de Berry was lodging. When the Duke of Burgundy arrived, in company with Comte Waleran de Saint-Pol, his uncle the Duc de Berry said to him: 'Fair nephew, don't go into the council today—not everyone will be pleased to see you.' And with these words the Duc de Berry entered the council chamber and had the doors shut, as had been ordered by the council. The Duke of Burgundy was upset by this act, and turned hesitantly to the earl, saying: 'You see that, cousin? What do we do now?' The earl replied: 'You have merely to return home, my lord, since the members of the council do not wish you to sit with them.' 'Come back with me, then,' said the duke. But the earl replied: 'Forgive me, my lord, I have been summoned to the council, and to the council I shall go.'

The Duke of Burgundy was by now in a state of considerable fear as he returned to the Hôtel d'Artois, where he lived; to avoid the threat of arrest or capture, he mounted his horse with only six of his men to accompany him and rode swiftly out of Paris by the Porte Sainte-Denis. Stopping only to change horses, he reached his castle at Bapaume; there he slept for a short time, and then immediately rode on to Lille in Flanders, where his men whom he had left in Paris rejoined him as soon as possible, for they, too, were afraid of being arrested. As for Raoulet d'Auquetonville and his accomplices, they changed their clothes and disguised themselves, and on the orders of their master the duke rode by different routes to the Château de Lens, in Artois. Thus poorly accompanied did the Duke of Burgundy leave Paris after the murder of the Duc d'Orléans, leaving the nobility of France in that same city in a state of great confusion and distress.

When the members of the Duc d'Orléans' household heard that the Duke of Burgundy had secretly left Paris, some six score of their armed men, under the leadership of Sir Clugnet de Brabant, rode out of the city in pursuit, with the intention of killing the duke if they could find him. But King Louis sent word forbidding this, and they returned very annoyed to their homes. By now it was common knowledge in Paris that the duke was responsible for the murder; the Parisians, who had been told that the Duc d'Orléans was the

* On the site of the present Institut, opposite the Louvre.

instigator of their heavy taxes and subsidies, whispered among themselves that he had met his deserts.*

This sorry event occurred during the fierce winter of 1407, when the frost lasted for sixty-six days with the greatest severity. With the thaw the Pont-Neuf collapsed into the Seine, and great damage was done throughout France by frost and flood. As for telling of all the hatred that had grown up between the Dukes of Orléans and Burgundy before this murder, there is no room for all that in this chapter, since it will be dealt with in full in the account of the proceedings that were instituted shortly afterwards, including the public justification that was pronounced for the Duke of Burgundy, in the presence of the lords temporal and spiritual, to show why it was necessary to kill the Duc d'Orléans, and also the reasons that were put forward in his excuse by the dowager duchess and her children. These will be recorded in this volume exactly as they were delivered in the presence of the king's council and of many others of different ranks.

Monstrelet deals at wearisome length with the manoeuvres that followed the murder. With the aid of Jean Petit, doctor of theology in the University of Paris, the Duke of Burgundy prepared a lengthy 'Justification' of his action, and this was read by Petit to a large gathering of the court and people, the king being not present, on the 8th of March 1408. In it the duke proclaimed his catholic faith, and catalogued the sins of the murdered Duc d'Orléans—defrauding of the Treasury, debauchery, his evil influence over the queen, attempting to procure the death of the king by sorcery and witchcraft, and other lesser charges. In spite of appeals by the widowed duchess and of the queen's suspicious departure from the capital, the Duke of Burgundy was soon reconciled with the king and pardoned for his crime. Just a year later the king arranged a ceremony at Chartres at which the duke was publicly reconciled to the nobility of France.

The rift between the two houses nevertheless grew into civil war, and the whole course of hostilities was changed. The Duke of Burgundy set himself persistently at the head of all movements for reform of the administration, and won the support of the University, led by Cauchon, who was to become Bishop of Beauvais, and the burgesses of Paris, led by Simon Caboche, a skinner in the Guild of Butchers. The new duke, Charles d'Orléans, issued a defiance to Burgundy in 1411, but was answered by a manifesto. Burgundy endeavoured to win Henry of England to his cause, by promising support in Flanders and

* Literally—'The knotty stick is made smooth.' Louis d'Orléans' badge was a knotty stick; Jean sans Peur had a carpenter's plane for his badge.

Normandy; indeed, one of Henry's rare interventions in the war was to send a small force to help Burgundy to raise the siege of Paris being conducted by the Orleanists, known as the Armagnacs. In 1413 the people of Paris were led in insurrection by Caboche, and many Armagnacs were murdered. A long list of demands for reform was presented to the king and most were granted; they chiefly concerned the administration of the royal finances.

After a fruitless attempt to kidnap the king, Burgundy left Paris (his absence was to last five years), and the Armagnacs returned to power and cancelled the concessions forced on the king a few months earlier.

death of henry iv and henry v's invasion of france

¶ Henry of Lancaster, King of England, died towards the end of this year [1413]. In his time he had been a most valiant knight, zealous and cunning against his enemies. It was he who, as is explained in other histories, used improper and dishonourable means to obtain the crown from his first cousin Richard, who had then been King of England for twenty-two years. His death was due to leprosy, which had pitifully oppressed his last years, and he was buried with his predecessors in Westminster Abbey. He left four sons: the eldest was Henry, Prince of Wales, who succeeded to the crown; the second was named Thomas, Duke of Clarence; the third was John, Duke of Bedford; and the fourth was Humphrey, Duke of Gloucester. He had one daughter,* who had married the wily Duke of Bavaria. All four brothers were handsome men, and well educated; they went on to play important roles which we shall describe in their proper place, but we must not fail to record some words that passed (just before his death) between the late king and his son.

In the last few days of his illness he was quite helpless. One day those who were looking after him, seeing that he had stopped breathing, thought he had indeed died and covered his face with a cloth. Now it is the custom in that country, when the king is ill, to place his crown on a couch near the bed so that his eldest son and heir can take it as soon as he is dead. This had been done and the eldest son readily took it when the attendants gave him to understand that his father was dead. But soon after this the king sighed deeply,

* Monstrelet omits Philippa of Lancaster, who married the King of Denmark.

uncovering his face, and his mind suddenly became clear. He looked to where the crown had been, and not seeing it asked where it was. His attendants replied: 'Sir, my lord the prince your son has taken it away.' The king asked for him to be sent for, and he came. Then the king asked him why he had taken away the crown, and the prince replied: 'My lord, those here present had given me to understand that you had departed this life, and since I am your eldest son and your crown and kingdom will belong to me when you have gone from this world to the next, I took it.' Then with a sigh the king said to him: 'Fair son, what right have you to it?—for I never had any as you well know.' 'My lord,' replied the prince, 'as you won and kept it by the sword, so shall I keep and defend it all my days.' 'Do as seems good to you,' said the king. 'I leave everything else to God and pray him to have mercy on my soul.' Soon afterwards, without speaking again, he died.*

After he had been buried (as we have stated) the Prince of Wales was crowned in great state in the presence of all the princes and bishops of the realm of England, and no one of any degree appeared to challenge his right. As soon as they heard of their sovereign's death the Duke of Clarence and the other English nobles who were still over in the duchy of Aquitaine came back to England as quickly as they could, because at that time there was a truce between the two kingdoms. In spite of the truce, however, the English around Calais began to harass the Boulonnais as soon as the king was dead, to such effect that the Constable of France had to reinforce the garrisons at Ardres, Gravelines and at other places held by the French.

Prince Hal was 25 when he succeeded to his father's throne. He had proved his military ability in the Welsh campaigns, and he had also played a large part in the councils of his ailing father. By the reputation thus acquired, and by the immediate steps he took to enlist the Church and the nobles in support of a campaign in France, he ensured that the throne would be his without fear of opposition, in spite of a Lollard 'rebellion' soon after his accession.

Interminable parleyings took place with France during the years 1413 to 1415, ostensibly concerning the nature of the truce, but much concerned also with a proposed marriage between Henry and Catherine, daughter of Charles VI; the terms of the dowry were the apparent stumbling-block in the negotiations. Henry demanded the crown of France, the completion of King

* 'The story of the crown-wearing which occurs in Shakespeare's *Henry IV Part II* . . . is an invention of Monstrelet from whom it passed to Holinshed and so to Hall' (E. F. Jacob in *The Fifteenth Century*).

Jean's ransom, the boundaries of Aquitaine to be as defined by the Treaty of Calais; as negotiations proceeded he claimed also the whole of the Angevin empire. At the same time he was negotiating with the Duke of Burgundy, with whom he would make war, not on King Charles, but on the Armagnac princes who were controlling the king, and they would divide their lands between them; Henry would also receive in marriage another Catherine, daughter of the duke. Burgundy saw in all this a threat to his own ambitions and held back; news of the proposals reached the French king's ear and the Armagnac attitude hardened.

Henry may never have expected the truce talks to succeed; he certainly cannot have been surprised that they failed. From early summer in 1414 he had been accumulating arms and siege equipment, and in 1415 an invasion army was being gathered in the Portsmouth-Southampton area. On the 6th of July the king left Winchester for Southampton. The plans had been laid with extraordinary thoroughness, equal no doubt for their time to those prepared in exactly the same area over 500 years later; for the first time there is mention of surgeons commissioned to accompany the army. Over fifteen hundred ships were there to transport the troops and equipment to France.

¶ It is now time to return to the affairs of King Henry of England, who was (as we have said) preparing a great army and vast quantities of equipment for his expedition to France, which was to embark at Southampton. The truce between the countries expired on the second day of August, and after that date the English in Calais and other places began to overrun the country of the Boulonnais and to lay it waste. The King of France sent the Seigneur de Rambures, master of the crossbowmen, and the Seigneur de Louroy with five hundred fighting men to offer resistance and to defend the country. A few days later King Henry's preparations for the crossing to France were almost complete, and he sent one of his heralds named Gloucester to present a letter to the King of France in Paris. The terms there set forth were as follows:

'To the very noble prince, Charles, our cousin and adversary, of France—Henry, by the grace of God, King of England and of France. To give to each his due is, dear prince our cousin and adversary, a work of inspiration and wise council; in former days the noble kingdoms of France and England were united and now they are divided. It was then the custom of both to fulfil their duty by glorious victories over the infidel, and for them it was sufficient virtue to embellish the house of God, to whom alone belongs holiness, and to give peace to the various parts of His Church by together overcoming in battle her common enemies. But alas! this ancient loyalty has perverted such fraternal aims, and Lot now persecutes Abraham for worldly reasons, the glory of brotherly love is departed, and the old sin of Dissension, mother of Wrath, has been raised from the dead. We, however, call to witness the wisdom of the Sovereign Judge, who is swayed neither by prayers nor by gifts, that we out of pure affection have done everything in our power to procure the means of peace. We shall therefore regain by the sword and by negotiation the just titles of our inheritance, with all our former rights. In the book of Deuteronomy we are taught this law, that if a man is preparing to attack a city he must first offer terms of peace. And although violence which is the enemy of justice has for long deprived us of the rightful inheritance of our crown, yet charity on our part has done little more to restore it to us. As there is no justice to be had, we must therefore consider recourse to arms, yet in order that our conscience may be clear in this matter of war we hereby make personal request to you at this cross-roads of our interests, and in the denial of justice to us we beseech you in the bowels of Jesus Christ to act in accordance with the pure teaching of His gospel. Friend, repay what thou owest, and the will of almighty God shall be done. So shall we avoid spilling the blood of men who were created in God's image. The restitution of our rightful inheritance, or at least of that part which we have so often requested through our ambassadors, will be pleasing in the sight of God and will favour the cause of peace. Because of our alliance by marriage we recently were inclined to forgo the offer made to us of fifty thousand gold crowns,* because we desire peace more than wealth and wished to share the patrimony left to us by our venerable ancestors with our very dear cousin Catherine your beloved daughter, rather than to pile up ill-gotten gains and so dishonour the crown of our realm, which God forbid.

'Given under our privy seal in our castle of Southampton the fifth day of the month of August [1415].'

This letter was presented to the King of France by the herald, and he received answer that the king and his council had read what was written by his master the King of England and that a decision would be conveyed when they chose to make it. Meanwhile he could return to the king his master when he pleased.

* Negotiations had been proceeding for many months about terms of a possible agreement, and in particular about which provinces of France Henry could be allowed to claim. The reference here is to an embassy from the King of France which, at Winchester in July 1415, had offered to Henry the hand of Catherine, together with the sum mentioned here.

¶ While the King of England was in Southampton with all his army ready to sail for the invasion of France he was informed that some of the chief lords of his household had conspired against him to place the Earl of March on the throne of England as the rightful heir to the late King Richard. It was a fact that the Earl of Cambridge with some others had plotted to seize the king and his brothers with that aim in view. They revealed their intentions to the Earl of March, who immediately told the king, advising him to be on his guard or he would be betrayed, and gave the names of the conspirators. The king had these men taken, and shortly afterwards he executed the three leaders, who were the Earl of Cambridge, brother of the Duke of York, Lord Scroop of Masham, who slept each night in the king's room, and Sir Thomas Grey. Others were executed later.

A few days after this matter had been dealt with the king and all his army set sail, and making good speed arrived late on the eve of the Assumption of Our Lady at a harbour* between Harfleur and Honfleur where the River Seine enters the sea. They had about sixteen hundred ships heavily laden with men and equipment, and they landed without any bloodshed. When all had landed the king established his quarters in a Priory at Graville, the other lords going where they could near by. They then proceeded in force to the assault of the town of Harfleur, which by sea holds the key to all Normandy. With the king were about six thousand men-at-arms, twenty-four thousand archers, without counting the cannoneers and those in charge of slings and other engines of war, of which they had great numbers. Within the walls of Harfleur, apart from the citizens, there were four hundred men-at-arms appointed to defend the town and the town gallantly resisted the English. But their efforts were of little force against such large numbers, and after their sallies they could scarcely get back within the walls. As the English landed the French had taken up the roadway between Montivilliers and Harfleur to make things difficult for the enemy and carried the stores into the town.

The English nevertheless were able to roam the countryside, taking prisoners and capturing booty, while outside the town they set up their heavy engines of war in suitable positions, and had soon done considerable damage to the walls. The men of Harfleur defended themselves with energy and killed a number of English with their

* Johnes suggests Quillebeuf, but this is the wrong side of the river and much too far upstream. As they lodged at Graville, which is four kilometres from Le Havre in the direction of Harfleur, perhaps it was Le Havre itself.

crossbows and other weapons. The town has only two gates, the Porte Caltinant and the Porte Montivilliers, and from these they made several well-manned sorties against the English, who defended themselves vigorously. The walls of the town were particularly strong and thick, making a complete circuit, and protected on the outside by wide, deep ditches. An unfortunate loss befell them when a supply of arms and gunpowder that had been sent by the king was captured by the English before it reached the town.

Meanwhile a large body of men-at-arms had been sent to oppose the English at Rouen and those parts, under the charge of the constable and other barons. They protected the country so effectively that the English, with the siege of Harfleur on their hands, were unable to capture any other towns or fortresses, though they did not spare their efforts to do so. They often rode over the plain in search of food supplies and also to seek encounters with their enemies. In the course of these sallies they did great damage and often returned with much plunder; but because the constable and his men protected the land so effectively the English were often short of food, since what they had brought from their own country had for the most part been spoiled by the sea air. Added to this, an outbreak of dysentery had killed two thousand or more in the English camp, among them some of their leaders, the Earl of Stafford, the Bishop of Norwich, and several other nobles.*

In spite of everything the King of England persevered most diligently in maintaining the siege. He had three mines dug beneath the walls so that they were on the point of collapsing; with his engines he battered down a great part of the walls and gates. In the end the inhabitants, knowing that they were every day in danger of being captured, gave themselves up to the King of England provided that they did not receive help within three days. Hostages were handed over, and terms agreed that their lives should be spared for a payment of money. The Seigneur de Bacqueville and some others were then sent to the King of France, who with the Duc d'Aquitaine was at Vernon-sur-Seine, to tell him of their dire straits, and to beg him to send help within three days, for otherwise he would lose the town and all its inhabitants. To sum up the conclusions, the reply was given that the king's forces were not ready in sufficient strength to lend the support that was requested. At this the Seigneur de Bacqueville went

* The number of dead appears to be grossly exaggerated, and the figure given probably includes those invalided home. The bishop was Richard Courtenay of Powderham, a personal friend of the king.

back to Harfleur, which was surrendered to the King of England on Saint Maurice's Day [22 September 1415], to the great misery of the inhabitants and indeed of all the French, for it was the chief port in all the duchy of Normandy.

¶ As soon as the King of France and his council had been told how the town of Harfleur had surrendered to their enemy the King of England, they feared that he would from there make further attacks upon their country. As a means of organizing resistance, the king sent orders to his bailiffs and seneschals in every part of the kingdom to raise the greatest force of men-at-arms that they could. He explained how he had earlier sent his ambassadors to the King of England to offer his daughter in marriage with a handsome gift of land and money in order to secure peace, but with so little success that the King of England had come and invaded their country and taken the town of Harfleur by siege, which greatly displeased him. Because of this he required all his vassals and subjects to respond to his call at once. He similarly sent messengers with sealed letters to various lords in Picardy, bidding them to rally to him at once with all their armed followers, on pain of his extreme displeasure. They were to report to his son the Duc d'Aquitaine,* whom he had appointed leader and captain-general of the kingdom. But the barons of Picardy delayed obeying, because the Duke of Burgundy had sent them along with all his other subjects written orders to be ready to go with him, as soon as he should send them a summons to do so, and not to obey any orders from another lord of whatever rank he might be. Because these men were too slow in reporting for service to the king, fresh orders were issued . . . The king also sent ambassadors to the Dukes of Orléans and of Burgundy requiring them to send him without fail five hundred armed men each. The Duc d'Orléans was at first satisfied to send this number, but later followed in person with all his armed followers; the Duke of Burgundy replied that he would not merely send his men, but would come in person to serve the king, with all his subjects. However, some reason for delay arose between them, and in the end he did not go himself, but sent large numbers of his followers.

* This is the king's son Louis. The title was conferred by Charles VI on his brother Louis Duc d'Orléans in 1407, shortly before the latter was murdered. It was then transferred, first to the king's eldest son Louis, who predeceased his father, and later to his third son Charles. It was presumably bestowed in support of his own pretensions and as an insult to the English.

¶ When the three days had expired the men of Harfleur opened their gates in accordance with the treaty they had made. The King of England first sent his commissioners into the town, but when he himself reached the gates he dismounted from his horse, ordered his shoes to be removed and in that state went on foot to the parish church of Saint Martin, where he offered devout prayers to God and gave thanks for the success of his enterprise [23 September]. He then had all the nobles and men-at-arms who were in the town made prisoner, and shortly afterwards turned most of them out of the town dressed only in their doublets, but not before he had had a list prepared in writing of their full names and they had sworn on oath to surrender as prisoners in the town of Calais before next Martinmas; this done they departed. Next the greater part of the townsmen were made prisoner and forced to ransom themselves for large sums, then driven from the town with most of the women and children, each as they left being given five sous and part of their clothing. It was a pitiful sight to see the misery of these people as they left their town and their belongings behind. The priests and clergy were likewise dismissed. As for the wealth that was found in the town, this was immense; it was all taken over by the king, who shared it out as he chose. Two towers on the sea side of the town, which were particularly strong, held out for ten days after the surrender, and then they, too, yielded.

When all this had been completed the King of England sent the greater part of his army home from Calais, the ships being laden with prisoners and weapons of war. At the head of this section he placed his brother, the Duke of Clarence, who was accompanied by the Earl of Warwick. He then ordered the repair of the walls and ditches of Harfleur, and established a garrison there of five hundred men-at-arms and a thousand archers, under the captaincy of Sir John le Blond, knight.* He also left ample provision of victuals and equipment of war. After a fortnight the king left Harfleur with the intention of marching to Calais, taking with him two thousand men-at-arms and about thirteen thousand archers and large numbers of followers. They camped the first night at Fauville and the surrounding parts; then proceeding through Caux came to the Comté d'Eu. The English vanguard reached the town of Eu, where a body of French men-at-arms advanced to attack them. One of them was a valiant man named Lancelot Pierres, who in the onslaught received a

* According to Holinshed, the governor was the Duke of Exeter, and his lieutenant was Sir John Fastolf.

wound in the belly from an English lance which pierced his plate armour, a wound from which he later died; but while mortally wounded he had killed the English lancer. The Comte d'Eu and the other French were very grieved at Lancelot's death.

The King of England pushed on through the Vimeu, intending to cross the Somme at Blanchetaque, where his ancestor King Edward the Third of England had crossed before winning the battle of Crécy against King Philippe of Valois. But his scouts warned him that the French were holding the passage in great force, and he changed his course to head for Airaines, burning several towns and taking many prisoners and much booty. On Sunday the 13th of October he camped at Bailleul in the Vimeu. Marching across country from there, he sent a body of men ahead to take the crossing

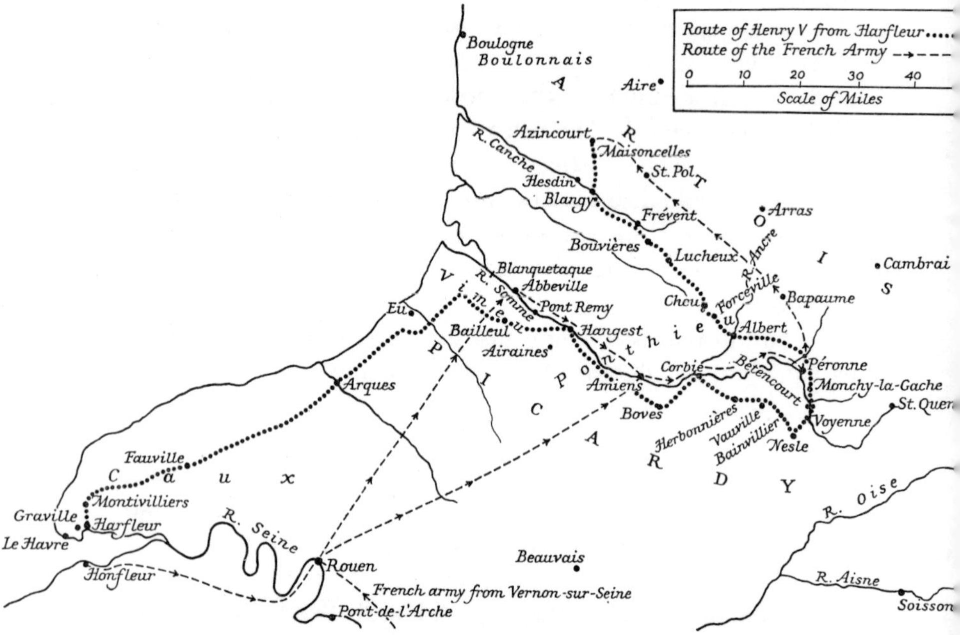

AGINCOURT: ROUTES OF THE OPPOSING ARMIES

of the Somme at the Pont de Remy, but they found the bridge vigorously defended by the Seigneur de Vaucourt et Pont de Remy, with his sons and a large force of armed men. The King of England, unable to effect a crossing, therefore decided to camp at Hangest-sur-Somme and in the neighbouring villages.

The Seigneur Charles d'Albret, Constable of France, Marshal Boucicault, the Comte de Vendôme, Grand Master of the King's household, the Seigneur de Dampierre, who styled himself Admiral of France, and other lords were at this time at Abbeville with a strong force of knights. When they heard which way the King of England had taken they moved off to Corbie and from there to Péronne, with their army in close attendance to guard all the passages of the River Somme against the English. Meanwhile the King of England left Hangest for Ponthieu, and from there, skirting round Amiens, marched to Boves, where he camped, and on to Herbonnières, Vauville, Bainvillier, with the French all the time following them on the other side of the river. The English finally made a crossing the day after Saint Luke's day [19 October] by the ford between Voyenne and Betencourt, where the crossing had not been staked by the men of Saint Quentin as they had been instructed to do by the orders of the King of France. The King of England camped that night at Monchy-la-Gache, near the River Ancre, while the French lords and all their army withdrew to Bapaume and the surrounding villages.

the battle of agincourt

¶ During these operations the King of France and the Duc d'Aquitaine came to Rouen, where a council was summoned for the twentieth day of October to decide what action was to be taken against the King of England. Also present were King Louis,* the Dukes of Berry and Brittany, the Comte de Ponthieu, younger son of the king, the Chancellors of France and of Aquitaine, and many other notable counsellors to the number of thirty-five. After various points of view had been discussed in the king's presence, it was decided by thirty of the council that they should oppose the King of England and his army. The other five advanced various reasons why they thought that no opposition should be offered just yet. In the end the majority view prevailed, and the king gave immediate orders in writing to his constable and his other officers to assemble the greatest army they could gather together to fight the King of England and his men without delay. They quickly spread the order through the whole country, instructing all noblemen who were accustomed to bear arms and who desired to preserve their honour, to set off at once to join

* King Louis II of Sicily, whose daughter Marie was the wife of the future Charles VII, over whom Louis's widow, Yolanda of Aragon, had considerable influence.

the constable's army wherever it might be, marching all night if necessary. Duc Louis d'Aquitaine was most eager to join the army, even though he had been forbidden to do so by his father the king. In the end King Louis and the Duc de Berry prevailed upon him to abandon the idea.

The various nobles now set off in great haste to join the constable, who was marching towards Artois. He had sent ahead the Seigneur de Montgaugier to inform the Comte de Charolais of the decision to fight the English and to request him respectfully on behalf of the king and the constable to be with them for the battle. Montgaugier found the count at Arras and was most honourably received by him and his barons. When he had explained the reason for his visit to the count and his whole council, the reply was given by his chief advisers, the Seigneurs de Roubaix and de Viefville, to the effect that preparations would be hastened so that he might join them on the day, and with this Montgaugier left. Now, it so happened that the Comte de Charolais was himself most anxious to fight the English, but, although his advisers gave him to understand he would be doing so, they had been expressly forbidden to allow this by his father, Duke Jean of Burgundy. In obedience to this order they conducted the count from Arras to Aire. Here the constable again sent envoys to him, this time Montjoye, king of arms, and other nobles. By various means the advisers we have mentioned above always contrived to effect a delay, and even kept the count shut up in the castle so that he could not receive any news or know when the battle was likely to take place. Meanwhile the majority of his men, who knew that there was certain to be one soon, left the place secretly and went to join the French for this fight against the English. For his only company the count had the young Seigneur d'Antoing and his close advisers, who were in the end obliged to tell their master that they had received orders not to allow him to go off to battle. He did not receive this well, and according to my information he went away to his room in floods of tears.

To return to the King of England. From Monchy-la-Gache he went to Albert and made his camp at Forceville, while his men camped at Cheu and round about. On the next day, Wednesday, he rode to Lucheux and camped at Bouvières-l'Escaillon; the Duke of York, who was leading the advance guard, camped at Frévent on the River Canche. The English were, in fact, spread over seven or eight villages, but they met no opposition here, for the French were rushing towards Saint-Pol and the River Aunun to cut off the English advance. On Thursday the English moved from Bouvières and riding in splendid array reached Blangy, where they crossed the river and climbed the hill beyond. Their scouts could here see large companies of French men-at-arms converging from all sides on Ruissauville and Azincourt* in order to offer battle to the English on the next day.

That Thursday evening Philippe, Comte de Nevers, was knighted by Boucicault the Marshal of France for his work on a scouting party, together with several other nobles. Shortly afterwards the constable arrived close to the village of Azincourt, and the whole French army gathered together to camp there, each near his own banner, except for some of the lesser folk who went to the nearest villages. The King of England and his men were quartered in and around Maisoncelles, about three bowshots from the enemy. The French had with them all the royal officers—the constable, the marshal, Boucicault, the Seigneur de Dampierre and Sir Clugnet de Brabant, who both called themselves Admiral of France,† the Seigneur de Rambures, master of the crossbowmen, and many other princes, barons and knights. They all planted their banners around the royal banner of the constable with every sign of rejoicing; the field they had chosen lay across the path the English must take the next day to go to Calais, and was situated near Azincourt in the county of Saint-Pol.

That night they lighted great fires near the banner under which they were to fight on the morrow. Yet although the French numbered easily a hundred and fifty thousand horsemen,‡ with large quantities of carts, waggons, cannons, ribaudekins and other equipment, they had few musical instruments for their amusement, and scarcely any of their horses neighed all night—which many took to be an omen of evil to come. The English played music on their trumpets and other instruments throughout the night, and the whole neighbourhood re-echoed with the sound of it. Although they were weary, and suffered from cold and hunger and other discomforts, they did not neglect to make their peace with God and tearfully to confess their sins; many of them received the body of Our Lord, for, as many prisoners afterwards revealed, they thought they faced certain death on the next day.

* So the text; but the word had been Englished to Agincourt long before Shakespeare's day.

† Sir Clugnet is again styled admiral on p. 276; so is Dampierre in the list of the dead at Agincourt.

‡ Considered estimates of the two armies are 25,000 French and 5,700 English.

During the night the Duc d'Orléans sent for the Comte de Richemont, who was leading the Bretons and the Duc d'Aquitaine's men; together they formed a body of two thousand men-at-arms and archers and their march took them close to the quarters of the English, who, thinking the French were about to attack, drew themselves up in battle order. A sharp skirmish followed, after which the Duc d'Orléans was made knight* along with several others, but the French soon returned to their quarters and there was no further engagement between the two sides that night. At this same time the Duke of Brittany was marching from Rouen to Amiens with more than six thousand men to help the French—if only they could have waited till Saturday. Similarly the Seigneur de Loigny, Marshal of France, was marching to their help with six hundred men-at-arms and camped that night only six leagues from the French army, leaving very early next morning in the hope of reaching them.

¶ The day that followed was Friday the 25th of October in the year 1415. On that morning all the French, under the direction of the constable, put on their armour and came out from their quarters and drew themselves up in three divisions according to the plan decided on by the royal council—vanguard, main army and rearguard. The first consisted of about eight thousand men-at-arms, knights or squires, four thousand archers and fifteen hundred crossbowmen, and was placed under the command of the constable, who had with him the Dukes of Orléans and Bourbon, and many other nobles and officers of the king. The Comte de Vendôme with sixteen hundred men was to command one wing which was to fall on and enclose the English; the other wing was to be led by Sir Clugnet de Brabant, Admiral of France, Sir Louis Bourdon, and some eight hundred picked horsemen, whose aim was to crush the English archers. The main body consisted of the same number of knights, squires and archers as the vanguard; the commanders were the Dukes of Bar and Alençon and a number of counts. In the rearguard were all the remainder of the men-at-arms under the command of Comtes de Marle, Dammartin, and Fauquembergue, together with those men that had been brought from the Boulonnais by the Seigneur de Louroy.

When all these men were drawn up in formation it was indeed a

* An hereditary peer had still to win his spurs as a knight. The duke was about 21 at this time. He was made prisoner at Agincourt and remained in England for twenty-five years.

wonderful sight to behold. A rapid calculation would put their number at six times that of the English. When their positions had been settled the French sat down by companies, as near as possible to the banner under which they served, to eat some food while awaiting the English attack. They also took this opportunity to settle any private feuds there might have been between them in the past. They waited thus until somewhere between nine and ten o'clock, certain among themselves that the English could not escape before their superior numbers, though there were some wiser heads on the French side who were not a little afraid of the outcome of an open battle.

The English similarly, seeing that the enemy were not launching an attack, sat down to eat and drink. After calling for God's help against these French who showed such scorn for them, they left their quarters at Maisoncelles, and sent some of their scouts ahead to the village of Azincourt, where they found no armed Frenchmen. To scare the enemy they set fire to a barn and a house belonging to the Priory of Saint George at Hesdin. The King of England sent some two hundred archers behind his army, so that they should not be seen by the French; these men went unnoticed to Tramecourt, where they took up their position in a meadow not far from the French vanguard, and waited there until it was time for action. All the remainder of the English stayed with their king, on whose orders a grey-haired old knight, Sir Thomas Erpingham, gave them their stations, placing the archers in front and men-at-arms behind. He then drew up as it were two wings of men-at-arms and archers, and collected the horses and baggage trains behind the army. Each archer planted a stake, sharpened at both ends, in the ground in front of himself.*

Sir Thomas exhorted everyone in the name of the King of England to fight vigorously in defence of their lives. He was riding in front of the army with two others, and when he was ready he threw his baton high into the air with a shout of 'Nestrocque!'† then dismounted as the king and all the others had done. As the baton was thrown all the English suddenly gave a great shout, to the amazement of the French. Since the French made no move to advance, the English

* This must have been done by the front rank of archers only.

† This clearly represents what the French thought they heard, at some distance, from the mouth of Sir Thomas Erpingham; the word also occurs in an account of the battle by the French squire, Jean de Wavrin. Archers have interpreted it as 'Knee stretch', an order for stringing the bow, or 'Now stretch', an order for drawing up the first arrow. More likely, perhaps, being closer to the French, are the words: 'Now strike'.

marched firmly towards them in close order, stopping only to get their breath for another shout. At this the archers hidden in the field loosed their arrows on the French and themselves, too, gave a great shout. At once the English archers (at least thirteen thousand of them) who were in the van of the advancing army, started to shoot volleys of arrows into the ranks of the French, who were a full bow-shot away. Most of these archers had no armour, but wore doublets and loose hose, and carried swords or axes on their belts. Some were bare-footed and had nothing on their heads.

When the French saw the English advancing upon them they ranged themselves each under his banner and placed their helmets on their heads. They were encouraged by the constable and by the sons of the princes to confess their sins with true contrition and to fight bravely against the enemy. As they drew closer the English sounded their trumpets, and the French bent down to avoid receiving the arrows in their visors, retreating a little before the English advance. Before the two armies engaged there were many French wounded and put out of action through the work of the English archers, and when the two armies were close to each other the French were so tightly packed that they could not raise their arms to strike the enemy, except for some of those in the front, who had cut their lances in half in order to make them more manageable in close combat.

The company under Sir Clugnet de Brabant who were detailed to break the line of the English archers were reduced from eight hundred to seven score before the attempt was made. Sir Guillaume de Saveuses, who was also in this company, rushed ahead of his own men, thinking they would follow him, but before he had dealt many blows among the archers he was pulled from his horse and killed. Most of the others and all their horses were driven back among the vanguard by fear of the English archers, and there they did much damage, breaking the line in several places; so many of the horses were wounded by the English arrows that their riders could not control them, and they caused many more knights to fall and so disordered their ranks that some fled behind the enemy in fear of their lives and others were forced to withdraw into some newly sown land. Their example caused many more French from the main body to flee.

As soon as the English saw this disorder in the vanguard they all entered the fray, and throwing down bows and arrows, they took their swords, axes, mallets, billhooks and staves and struck out at the French, many of whom they killed, until they came up with the main army. The King of England and his bodyguard followed close behind the archers. Then Duc Antoine de Brabant came up with a small body of men, having been ordered there by the King of France and having had to leave his main company behind because of the

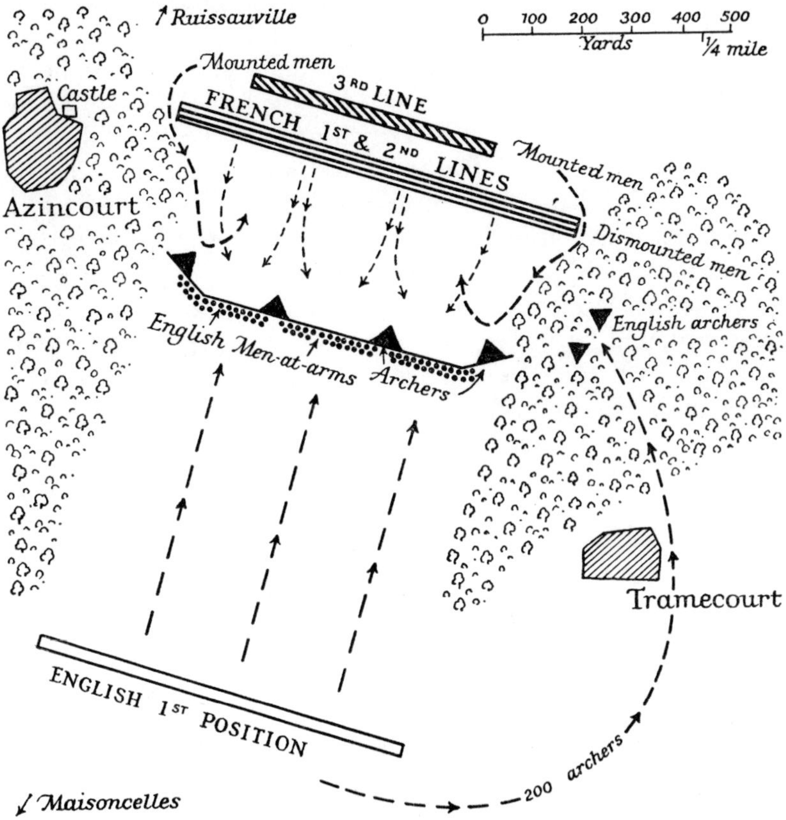

THE BATTLE OF AGINCOURT

need for haste; he was to give necessary support between the van and the main army, but he was very soon killed by the English, who were now advancing decisively on the main body to break that as they had the vanguard. As they advanced they killed cruelly and without mercy; if a man who was down could be got on his feet by his servant he might escape, because the English were so single-mindedly killing and taking prisoners as they advanced that they had no time to pursue those who fled. When all the rearguard, who had remained on horseback, saw the first two divisions getting the worst of it, they all took to flight with the exception of some of their leaders.

When in the heat of the battle the English had gained the upper hand and taken several prisoners among the French, news reached the King of England that the French were making an attack in the rear and had already taken some of the baggage and beasts of burden. This was indeed true, for Robinet de Bournonville, Rifflart de Clamasse and Isembart d'Azincourt with some other men-at-arms and six hundred peasants had fallen upon the English baggage camp and had taken the baggage and a great number of the English horses while the camp guards were engaged in the battle. Because of this report, and seeing also that the French who had fled from the fight were re-forming by companies on the open land, the King of England feared that a fresh attack was being prepared, and had it announced with a trumpet call that every Englishman on pain of death should kill his prisoners so that they could not possibly rejoin their own side. All the French prisoners were then immediately massacred, and for having been the cause of this massacre Robinet de Bournonville and Isembart d'Azincourt were later punished with a long imprisonment by Jean, Duke of Burgundy, in spite of the fact that they had made a gift to his son the Comte de Charolais of a very valuable sword ornamented with jewels and precious stones which had belonged to the King of England. They had taken this with the other booty, and made a present of it so that the count could speak in their favour if there were any trouble over what they had done.

The Comtes de Marle and Fauquembergue, with other barons and six hundred men-at-arms whom they had with difficulty collected together, made a brave attack on the English lines, but without success, for they were all very soon killed or taken prisoner. There were other small groups of Frenchmen in various parts who were captured or slain by the English without offering any serious resistance. In the end the King of England gained the victory over his enemies, and on the field sixteen hundred English of all ranks lay dead;* among them was the Duke of York, the king's uncle. On the morning of this battle and on the evening before, four hundred or more Frenchmen were made knights.

When the King of England found himself master of the field, and all the French who were not dead or captured had fled in various directions, he made a circuit of the battlefield with some of the princes. While his men were engaged in stripping the dead of their armour, he sent for the French herald, Montjoye, and several other English and French heralds, and said: 'It is not we but God Almighty who has ordered this great slaughter, to punish the French

* Sixteen hundred is much more probable than the usual contemporary English estimate of forty.

for their sins.' He then asked them whether the battle was to be awarded to him or the King of France. Montjoye replied that the victory was his and not to the King of France. Then the king asked them the name of the fortress he could see not far off, and they replied that it was called Azincourt. 'Every battle,' said the king, 'must bear the name of the fortress nearest to which it was fought, and this battle shall now and for all time be known as the battle of Azincourt.'

When the English had remained on the field for some time and saw that their enemies were now gone, they returned together as night fell to the town of Maisoncelles, where they had camped the previous day. There they again camped, bringing with them some of their wounded. When they had left the field of battle some of the French who had been left for dead dragged themselves as best they could to a wood near by, where many of them died. Others dragged themselves to any village or settlement they could find.

On the next day they left Maisoncelles very early and returned to the battlefield with all their prisoners. Any French they found there still alive they either killed or made prisoner. Then they continued on the route they had been taking, at least three-quarters of them on foot, and all of them worn out with fighting, hunger and disease. Thus the King of England returned to Calais after his victory, without meeting any obstruction on his journey. They left the French lamenting bitterly the loss and destruction of their men.

the burgundian rise to power

Henry V's attitude after Agincourt became that of negotiating from strength, and he set about systematically preparing for a further invasion of France, in which the building up of the navy was a strong element. His peace-making was done for him by an unexpected agent, the new Emperor Sigismund of Luxembourg, who took his title of King of the Romans seriously enough to regard himself as the obvious intermediary. Little welcome in France, he came to England in the early summer of 1416 and protracted negotiations ensued. By August he and Henry had signed a pact of eternal friendship at Canterbury, and undertook to support each other in any war that might occur. North of the royal domain round Paris only the Burgundian territory of Flanders remained uncommitted. In October the two met in Calais, in the presence of the Duke of Burgundy; no written treaty came from these talks, but Henry received a verbal assurance that Burgundy would help him when the need arose.

Armagnac support of King Charles was now greatly weakened: Charles, Duc d'Orléans was a prisoner in England, Berry and the dauphin were dead; the new dauphin, Charles, had quarrelled with his mother, who was banished to Tours. Henry was now ready to invade Normandy; he landed at what is now Trouville on the 1st of August 1417. By the following spring he had conquered the Cotentin, Caen, Cherbourg, Rouen, and virtually the whole of Normandy was in his hands.

Late in 1417 Queen Isabelle had escaped from Tours and had joined the Duke of Burgundy in Troyes, where a shadow Government was set up. Their aim was now to take possession of Paris, and events in the city played into their hands.

¶ You will already have read how the Parisians were not very fond of the Comte d'Armagnac, now Constable of France, or of the king's other advisers, because these men were not prepared to carry out the treaty of peace that had recently been signed with the Duke of Burgundy, for the Parisians were very much afraid of the duke and his army and realized that if he was not reconciled to the king and the dauphin they would long remain in their present state of uneasiness. There was a large party who liked the duke and wanted him to govern the kingdom, but could not conceive how to bring it about, for they were very closely watched and could not by any means meet to discuss their projects; the king's ministers always had plenty of armed men to deal with any semblance of revolt.

There were, however, certain hot-headed young men of the people, who had in the past been punished for some misdemeanour or other, and who now took the risk of paying a secret visit to the Seigneur de l'Isle-Adam, who was in the garrison at Pontoise. The leaders of these young men were Perrinet le Clerc, son of Jean le Clerc, a blacksmith, Jean Thiebert, son of Michel Thiebert, a butcher, Perrin Bourdechon and three or four others. After some discussion de l'Isle-Adam promised them that he would assemble as many fighting men as he could and on the twenty-ninth of May [1418] would bring them outside the Porte Saint Germain-des-Prés in order to enter Paris. They promised to open and deliver this gate to him, and on this they parted.

The Seigneur de l'Isle-Adam gathered as secretly as he knew how a band of about eight hundred combatants, including some others of the nobility, and led them on the appointed day to Paris. Outside the gate they found Perrinet le Clerc, who had extracted the keys of the Porte Saint-Germain from under his father's pillow (his father was keeper of the gate), and with him were the others. They opened the gate and went out to have a word with the Seigneur de l'Isle-Adam, and told him he could now enter safely and that they would conduct him through the town. The eight hundred then came into the city, fully armed as if they were about to engage in battle and yet in fear and trembling; it was now about two hours past midnight. When he saw that they were all in, Perrinet le Clerc locked the gate and threw the keys over the wall.

Now they rode silently towards the Châtelet, where they joined up with some four hundred combatants from within the city who were ready armed. They agreed together to make attacks on the houses of the king's chief ministers. They sorted themselves into two companies, who went through the streets shouting out loud that all who wished for peace should join them in arms. As a result they were joined by great numbers of the people, and thus reinforced they went off to attack the houses that had been designated. One of the companies went to the king's house of Saint-Pol, where they broke in the gates and doors, and managed to speak with the king himself, who was perfectly ready to grant them all their requests. They soon persuaded him to mount his horse and accompanied by the brother of the King of Cyprus* to ride with them through the streets of Paris. The other company went to attack the constable's house, but he had been warned and had escaped in disguise to the house of a poor man near to his own, and then on to the houses of the chancellor and of Raymounet de la Guerre, whom they arrested. It was not long before Tanguy du Chastel, Provost of Paris, heard the uproar; he then rushed to the dauphin's house and wrapping him only in a blanket carried him to the Bastille Saint-Antoine; with him went several of his men who had heard the hue and cry in the streets.

All that day and the two days following the Burgundian lords and their men, with great numbers of the Paris mob, raided many of the houses of the ministers and of their supporters. They robbed them of everything and took countless prisoners whom they shut up in the Palace, the Louvre, the Châtelet and various other places. Among them were the bishops of Senlis, Bayeux and Coutances and many nobles. The Seigneur de l'Isle-Adam went during the night to the Hôtel Bourbon, where he sought out Charles de Bourbon, who was then about 15 years old. When he had roused him he asked him which party he supported. Receiving the reply: 'My lord, the king's

* The kingdom of Cyprus was held by the de Lusignan family; it is not clear which of his several brothers is referred to here.

party', he took him off to the king's house, and there he stayed.

During these confused days many of the constable's and Tanguy's men-at-arms escaped into the Bastille Saint-Antoine, along with certain highly placed persons. Among others who were captured were the Cardinals de Bar and de Saint-Marc, the Archbishop of Reims, and all their horses. At the personal request of the Bishop of Paris, however, and because they had favoured the cause of peace, they were set free and all their property was restored. On Monday morning at eight o'clock a royal trumpeter declared that Tanguy du Chastel had been dismissed from the post of Provost of Paris by the king's command; in his place le Veau de Bar, Bailiff of Auxois, was appointed. In fact, every one of the king's counsellors in the Parliament or the courts, and all the notable citizens who were attached to the party of the Comte d'Armagnac were either robbed and made prisoner or cruelly murdered. It was, moreover, announced by trumpeters and a town-crier at every cross-roads, on pain of confiscation of person and chattels, that any man or woman who knew the whereabouts of any Armagnac supporter who was in hiding should at once give information to the new Provost of Paris or one of his captains. For this reason the poor man in whose house the Comte d'Armagnac had taken refuge at once went to reveal this to the provost, who came and found the count as the man had stated. He told him to mount his own horse behind him, and took him to the palace with the other prisoners.

As soon as things had quietened a little Tanguy du Chastel dispatched the dauphin, Charles, Duc de Touraine, to Montargis by way of the bridge at Charenton, Corbeil and Melun. He also sent word among all his supporters to send men-at-arms to join him in the Bastille Saint-Antoine in Paris. But the Seigneur de l'Isle-Adam had sent similar instructions to all the Burgundian party as far away as Picardy to send men-at-arms to Paris, and in a few days they were arriving in large numbers. Thus it happened that on the Wednesday following this dawn seizure of Paris the Marshal de Rieux, the Seigneur de Barbasan and Tanguy du Chastel entered Paris by the Porte Saint-Antoine with at least sixteen hundred chosen men, intending to reconquer the city of Paris. One company went to the king's house of Saint-Pol, and approached it from the back in the hope of finding him and carrying him off with them. But only the previous day he and his court had been taken to the Château du Louvre. The rest of them rode fiercely through the streets, with banners unfurled, as far as the Hôtel de l'Ours, where they shouted:

'Long live the king, and the dauphin, and our constable, the Comte d'Armagnac!' At this cry the Parisians gathered together armed and in great numbers, with the new provost, the Seigneur de l'Isle-Adam, and all the other men-at-arms who were in the city, and made a determined advance from several directions on the Armagnac supporters. Then followed a fierce battle, in which finally, because of the numbers of the Parisians, who were coming in on all sides, the Marshal de Rieux and his men were forced to retreat to the Bastille, but not without loss, for there were three or four hundred of his best men left dead on the ground. Of the Parisians and their allies there were only forty killed. Barbasan and Tanguy, seeing their losses increase every minute, sent some of their men into the Bastille, and let others go their ways, some to Meaux in Brie, others to Corbeil, Melun and other places held by their party.

On Thursday Hector and Philippe de Saveuses, with two hundred combatants, reached Paris, to the great delight of the Burgundian nobles in the city. They were lodged at the Tournelles and in other houses near the Bastille Saint-Antoine, in which there were still some men of the Comte d'Armagnac. On Friday, Saturday, Sunday and for another week thereafter most of the captains from Picardy arrived with their men-at-arms, among them Sir Jean de Luxembourg, the Seigneur de Fosseux and his brothers, Sir Jennet de Poix and many others, hoping to find much gain in the city. But they found the opposite of what they expected, and had to pay their own expenses. Those of the constable's party who had been killed were carted out of the city by the public executioner, and buried in the fields. Those of the Parisians' party were honourably buried in consecrated ground.*

All Paris now wore the badge of the Duke of Burgundy—a Saint Antony's cross—which had for so long been an object of contempt in the city. On the Saturday following these events those in the Bastille realized they were wasting their time trying to hold it and offered terms to the Seigneur de l'Isle-Adam and the other barons in Paris: they would surrender up the Bastille if their persons and goods were unharmed. This was agreed, and they left under promise of safe-conduct. The Seigneur de Cany was appointed Governor of the Bastille by the king and the Duke of Burgundy; he had been a prisoner there since his return from an embassy he had made to the Duke of Burgundy in Amiens.

* There were nearly two thousand dead in all.

the treaty of troyes

When the shadow Government was set up in Paris, King Charles weakly retreated (though there was no need for him to do so) to his province of Berry, south of the Loire, while the new Government was forced to reduce taxes in order to retain its apparent popularity. In view of the threat from Henry's operations in Normandy, Armagnacs and Burgundians resolved to attempt a compromise; after some negotiatory overtures, a meeting of representatives of the two factions met on the bridge at Montereau in September 1419. The reception accorded to the Duke of Burgundy was one of calculated hostility, and when in kneeling to the dauphin he happened to touch the hilt of his sword the royal guards fell upon him and killed him. The murder of Jean sans Peur avenged that of the Duc d'Orléans twelve years previously.

The kingdom of France was now in a hopelessly divided state. Popular feeling in Paris was against the Armagnacs, and Charles again retired south of the Loire. The new Duke of Burgundy was Philippe, Comte de Charolais, an indolent man by comparison with his father, but no less ambitious to govern. At Rouen he had promised Henry to make war with him on the dauphin, whose sister Michelle he had married. The ground was ready for Henry to make an advantageous peace, and after protracted negotiations on a tripartite basis, a treaty was signed at Troyes on the 21st May 1420—a diplomatic triumph for Henry, who had successfully played the rival French factions against each other.

The two kings met in Troyes on the 20th May and Charles's daughter, Catherine, was promised in marriage to Henry. Next day the treaty was signed, King Charles being represented by Queen Isabelle. The principal conditions are given by Monstrelet in the following terms:

¶ CHARLES by the grace of God, King of France. To all our Bailiffs, Provosts, Seneschals, and to all our chief officers of justice, greetings. Be it known that in sign of lasting agreement and perpetual peace we have, in this our town of Troyes, just concluded and sworn a treaty between us and our most dear and well-beloved son Henry, King of England, heir and regent of France, in his name and our own on behalf of the crowns of France and England, in token of his marriage to our dearly-beloved daughter Catherine and of other articles made and agreed between us for the welfare and

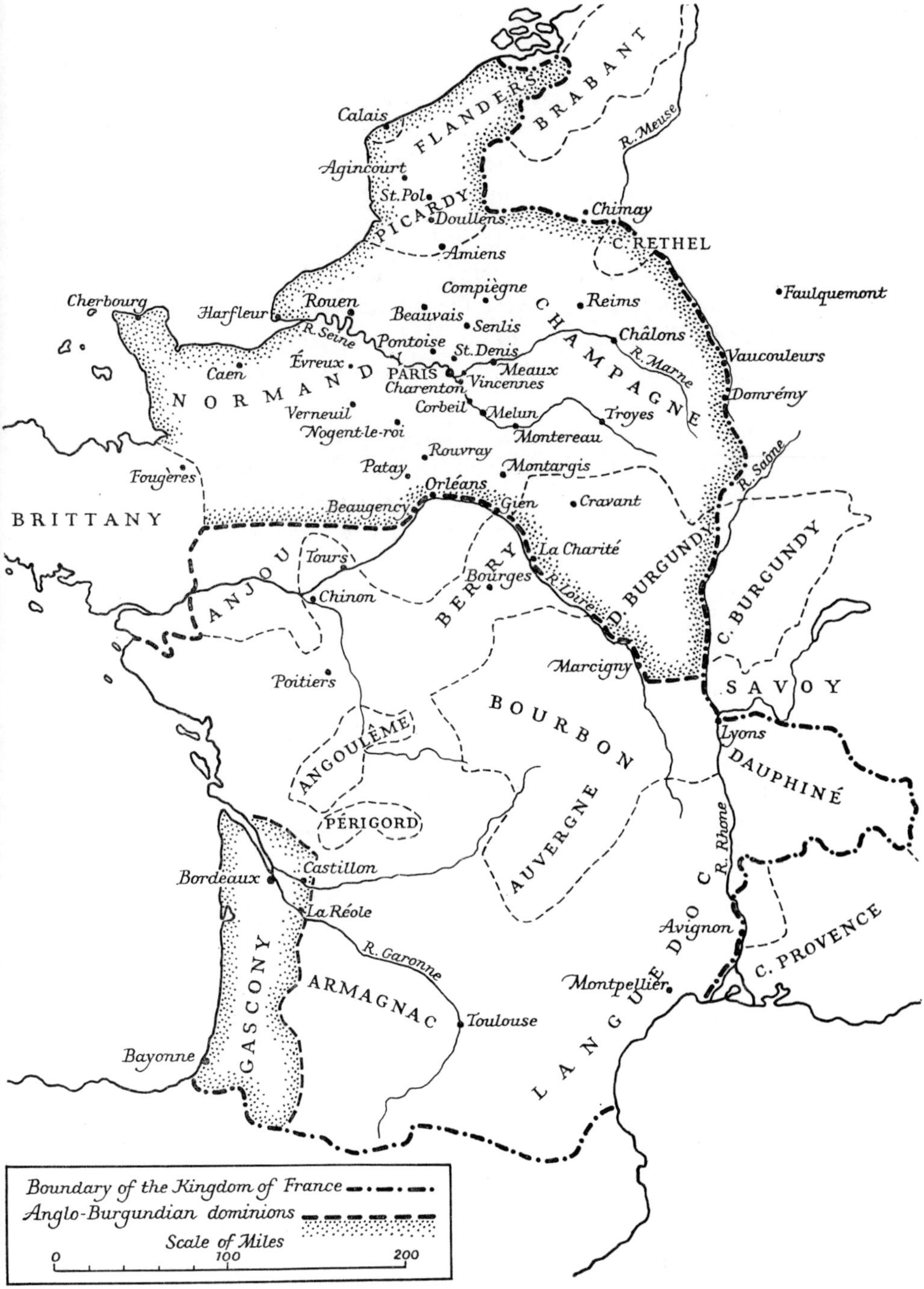

FRANCE AFTER THE TREATY OF TROYES 1420

good of ourselves and our subjects and for the security of this country . . .

ITEM it is agreed that immediately upon our decease and for all time thereafter the crown and sovereignty of France with all rights and appurtenances thereunto belonging shall be transferred in perpetuity to our said son Henry and his heirs.

ITEM since we are for the most part prevented from attending to the cares and government of our kingdom, the practice and exercise of governing and ordering the public weal shall for the duration of our life be given over to our said son Henry, with the Council of Nobles and wise men who are in our obedience.

Among the other clauses the following are worth noting: Henry was to be responsible for the administration of justice in the kingdom and for its defence; he was to have the appointing to vacant places in the national and local government; he was authorized to reduce to the king's obedience all places rebelliously held by the Armagnacs; he was to be known in France as 'our very dear son Henry, King of England and heir to France'; only French-born citizens were to be appointed to King Charles's personal entourage; neither Henry nor Burgundy was to enter into any treaty with the man Charles 'calling himself dauphin' and whom the king does not even here call 'son'.

Perpetual peace was thus to be ensured between the two kingdoms. On 1st December the two kings riding side by side made their ceremonial entry into the city of Paris. They both remained in Paris until Christmas and Monstrelet gives us an interesting comparison of the state maintained by the two kings.

¶ At this time [1420] there gathered in Paris many representatives of the three estates of the kingdom of France according to instructions previously issued, and many councils were held, either with or without their presence, concerning the government and welfare of the kingdom. As a result, the gabelle,* quarter-taxes and other levies were renewed, with the exception of the tax on grain.

At the season of Christmas the two kings and their queens held open court in the city of Paris, the King of France in his Hôtel de Saint-Pol, the King of England in the Louvre. But there was a vast difference between the state they kept, for the King of France was

* The gabelle, or salt-tax, was first levied on the whole of France by an ordinance of 1341; by it salt could only be bought at royal stores which were set up in the chief towns. As salt was a necessity for all classes, this became a useful means of universal taxation, and lasted, in fact, till the French Revolution.

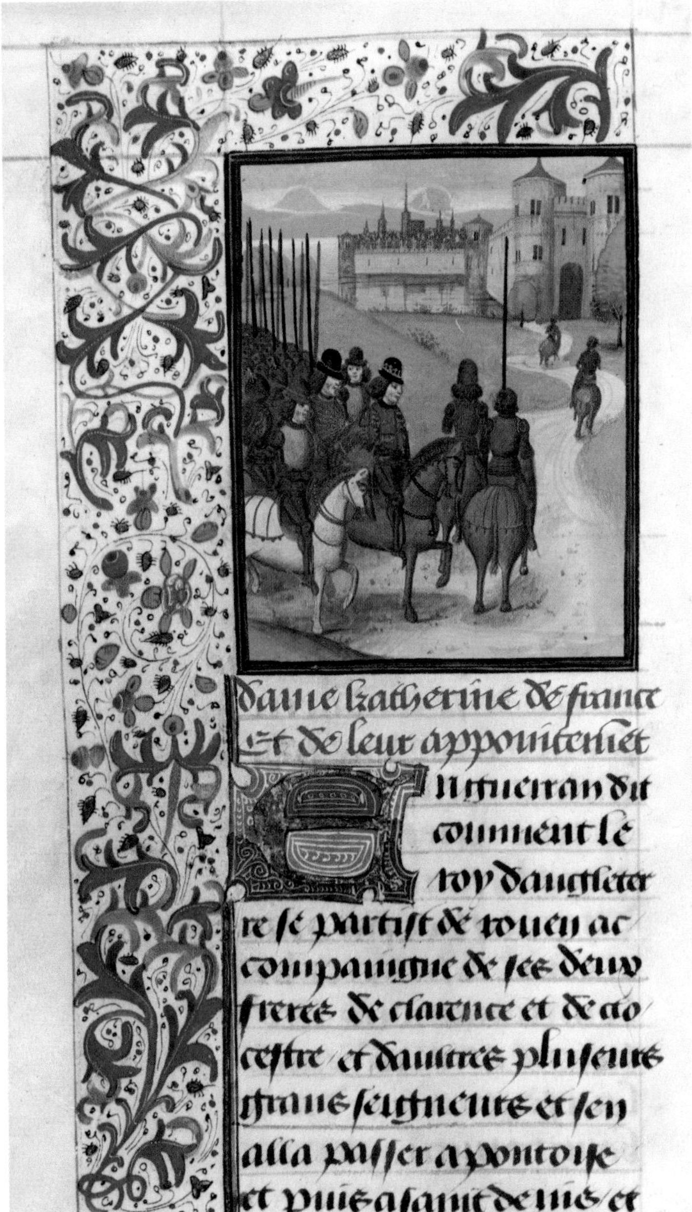
dame katherine de france
et de leur appointement
nguerran dit
comment le
roy dangleter
re se partist de rouen ac
compaignie de ses deux
freres de clarence et de glo
cestre et daultres plusieurs
grans seigneurs et sen
alla passer a pontoise
et puis a saint denis et

KING HENRY V ARRIVES AT TROYES

poorly served and attended by comparison with the great and mighty state he used to maintain, and on that day he received few visits apart from a small number of old servants and persons of low degree. How painful it must have been to the hearts of all true Frenchmen who were there to see this noble kingdom under the government of their old enemies through the misfortunes of war, and that for the present they were forced to live under foreign dominion.

As for the King and Queen of England, it is scarcely possible to tell in detail of the state they kept that day, of the feasts and ceremony and luxury of their court or in that of the princes. Subjects of the noble kingdom of France came from all parts in the greatest humility to do the king honour. From that time King Henry began to undertake the government and administration of the affairs of the kingdom of France, and to appoint officers at his pleasure in the place of those who had been appointed to the posts many years ago by the King of France and the late Duke of Burgundy. He gave to the Earl of Kent the position of captain-general of the town of Melun, with an adequate garrison of men-at-arms and of archers; his cousin the Earl of Huntingdon was made captain of the Bois de Vincennes; while the Duke of Exeter was ordered to remain in Paris with five hundred fighting men.

After these orders had been made and the feast of the nativity was passed, King Henry left Paris with his queen, the Duke of Clarence, the Duke of Bedford and other nobles and princes, and went to Rouen, where he held further councils concerning the government of France, and remained there some time before returning to England. Duke Philip of Burgundy also left Paris, and went to Beauvais for the ceremony of the enthronement of Pierre Cauchon, doctor of theology, as the bishop of that city.

The Deaths of Henry V and Charles VI

The kingdom of France was now fatally divided—and ill will was so fostered between the two parts that the division could have been a model for that effected by Hitler in 1940. In spite of the treaty, Henry controlled only Burgundian France.

In January 1421 Henry returned to England: the Government was clamouring for his presence, his queen had to be crowned, and he needed to re-establish his personal authority. As soon as he returned he set out on a triumphal tour of the country; he was acclaimed everywhere and lost no chance of securing loans for the continuation of the new campaigns that would now be necessary. His actions leave us in no doubt that he realized two truths: that the success of Agincourt had never been turned into a conquest, and that the Treaty of Troyes, and the marriage alliance that went with it, were not enough to convert into a reality his ambition to unite the two kingdoms.

During his progress through England he learned that the dauphin's troops had defeated an English force at Baugé (22 March 1421) and killed the Duke of Clarence, the king's brother and heir-presumptive. Henry now hurried back to France, though his military preparations were incomplete; the royalist element was obviously not so insignificant as he had supposed, and their troops, with Scottish reinforcements, were moving towards Paris. When Henry landed at Calais he had first to satisfy Burgundy by confirming his power in Picardy and east of Normandy; this took longer than expected, and the key towns of Meaux and Compiègne had not fallen until June 1422. His troops were seriously affected by dysentery in the siege of the first of these two towns. Henry himself contracted the disease, and on 31 August he died at Vincennes.

¶ Then King Henry, knowing that he was suffering from a mortal illness, sent for his brother the Duke of Bedford, his uncle the Earl of Warwick, Sir Lewis Robsart and three or four others whom he trusted most of all those about him, and told them most pitifully that he knew it was his Creator's pleasure that he should now leave this world. He then addressed the Duke of Bedford saying: 'Dear brother John, I beseech you on the loyalty and love you have always shown me, to show the same loyalty and consideration to my fair son Henry your nephew. And I further charge you that, whatever errors you may make, you do not so long as you live suffer any treaty to be made with our enemy Charles de Valois, and in no circumstances allow the duchy of Normandy to be restored to him. If our fair brother of Burgundy should wish to undertake the regency of this realm of France, I advise you to grant it to him, but if he refuses it then take it on yourself. To you, fair uncle of Exeter, I hand the sole regency of the kingdom of England, for I know you can govern it well, and I beseech you not to return to France on any pretext whatever. I further require you to be guardian in all respects of my fair son your nephew, and ask you on the love you have always borne me to pay frequent visits to see him. You dear cousin of Warwick I wish to act as his tutor, remaining always with him to bring him up according to the rank for which he is destined—for I know no one I would more readily ask.

'I further entreat you as earnestly as I know how that you should not for any reason enter into disagreement with our fair brother of Burgundy—and this you must expressly recommend to our brother Humphrey—for if there were any ill will between you (which God forbid) the affairs of this realm, which are at present in a very healthy state, would soon worsen. Take care not to set at liberty our fair cousin of Orléans, the Comte d'Eu, the Seigneur de Gaucourt or Guichard de Sisay until such time as our fair son has come of age. In other things do what seems best to you.'

After he had spoken these words and others in the same vein, the lords who were present, their hearts full of grief, replied on their honour that they would carry out everything that he had ordered, and anything else that they knew would please him, and to the best of their ability they would never do otherwise. They were all overcome with sorrow to see to what straits he was reduced, and shortly afterwards some of them left the room. Sir Hugh de Launay, who had been sent to the king's presence by the Duke of Burgundy, when he had spoken with the king, also left and returned to the duke.

Shortly afterwards the king sent for his physicians and earnestly begged them to tell him what they thought of his condition and how long he might expect to live. They hesitated before replying and then, to give him some hope, they told him that it depended on God whether or not he would be restored to health. He was not satisfied with this answer and again asked them to tell him the truth. The doctors then discussed the matter among themselves and then one of them, kneeling by the king's bed, said to him: 'My lord, think now of your soul, for it is our opinion that unless God wills it otherwise you cannot live more than two hours.' The king then sent for his confessor, for other members of his family, and for priests whom he ordered to recite the seven penitential psalms. When they got to the *Benigne fac, Domine* and reached the words *muri Hierusalem* he stopped them, and said that he had always intended before he died, and as soon as he had established order in the kingdom of France, to set out on the conquest of Jerusalem, if it had been his Creator's pleasure to allow him to live long enough. When he had said this he made them finish the psalms, and shortly afterwards, in the time allowed by his physicians, he gave up the ghost on the last day of August . . .

Thus ended the life of King Henry in the flower of his days, for when he passed from life into death he was only about 40* years old. He was very wise and capable in everything he undertook, and he had an iron will. In the seven or eight years during which he ruled in France he made greater conquests than any before him for many years past. He was so feared by his princes and captains that there was no one, however close or dear to him, who was not afraid to go against his orders, especially those of his own kingdom of England. Everyone under his rule, in France and England alike, whatever his rank, was reduced to this same state of obedience. The chief reason for this was that anyone who thwarted his will and disobeyed his orders was most cruelly punished and received no mercy.

When the [funeral] ceremonies were duly completed, the three estates of the realm of England met together in full assembly, to decide on the succession to the throne. In the end they elected the only son of the late King Henry as king, although he was only sixteen† months old, and submitted themselves to his obedience in spite of his tender age. They granted him immediately a royal establishment, the Earl of Warwick with some others agreeing to accept guardianship of the young king.

Henry therefore never survived to inherit the crown of France by the terms of the Treaty of Troyes. Had he lived two months longer it would have been his, for Charles VI died (at the age of 54) on 22nd October. His funeral was delayed until the Duke of Bedford, regent for the infant King Henry VI, had returned from Normandy; it was attended by neither the queen nor any of the princes, nor even the Duke of Burgundy. After his burial in the abbey church of Saint-Denis the succession was ceremonially proclaimed.

¶ . . . Then Berry, king-of-arms, attended by several heralds and pursuivants, cried over the grave: 'May God have pity and mercy on the soul of this most noble and excellent prince, Charles, King of France, and the sixth of his name, our natural sovereign lord!' Then immediately he shouted again: 'May God grant long life to Henry, by the grace of God King of France and of England, our sovereign lord!' Then the king-of-arms repeated the same cry again. This done, the sergeants-at-arms raised again their maces with the fleurs-de-lis upon them, and shouted with one voice: 'Long live the king! Long live the king!'

* He was 34 when he died.

† He was, in fact, 9 months old.

South of the Loire another succession was proclaimed with rather less ceremony.

¶ After the death of King Charles of France, his only son Charles the dauphin, Duc de Touraine, on the advice of the princes had himself crowned and made King of France in the city of Poitiers. From that day he was called King of France, as was his father before him, by all those of his party.

the siege of orléans

England had many problems to face with her king a mere infant and rival interests competing for positions of power. These problems were ultimately resolved by the appointment of Bedford as regent in France—Burgundy being unwilling to accept the office—of Gloucestor as protector of England (when Bedford could not be in the country) and of the young Henry, to whom Exeter was appointed tutor. There were two dangers inherent in this set-up: Gloucester was a notoriously unreliable person, and the alliance with Burgundy would need to be very carefully fostered.

Bedford proved an able administrator and an excellent general, almost the equal, it is said, of Henry V. He cemented the Burgundian alliance—a wise move—by marrying the duke's sister Anne, though this did not prevent the duke from negotiating sporadically with the dauphin, who became known as the King of Bourges. (Monstrelet, though a Burgundian, calls him King Charles of France; he also tells us that Bedford 'styled himself Regent of France'.) Bedford's chief work was in fulfilment of the Treaty of Troyes—to win France to the allegiance of Henry her king. For nearly ten years he was successful in clearing up pockets of territory held by the dauphin. In 1424, at Verneuil, he achieved a victory, over greatly superior forces, almost a second Agincourt.

About this time Gloucester embarked on a marital project the details of which it would be tedious to record: it is enough to say that it involved him in a visit to Hainault with an army, his flight when the Burgundian forces threatened him, complications in England which Bedford was called home to sort out, and the worsening of Anglo-Burgundian relations. Bedford, in fact, was needed in France if the campaign was to prosper, and fifteen months' absence was unfortunate. If he had then made an advance on Bourges the dauphin's cause could have been seriously damaged, ruined perhaps. Before leaving for home he chose rather to conquer the remaining pockets of resistance north of the Loire—at consolidating 'occupied France'.

When he returned to France early in 1427 he brought with him Lord John Talbot, who had proved himself in the Welsh campaigns and who was to become a legendary figure in the fighting in France. Next year reinforcements were sent out from England, and the plan to capture Orléans was accepted by Bedford.

¶ In May of that year [1428] King Henry gave orders in his council for the gathering of an army of six thousand chosen men, well tried in war, the greater part of whom were to be sent to France to the assistance of the Duke of Bedford, who styled himself Regent of France. The king placed all these arrangements under the command of the Earl of Salisbury, a veteran soldier with a great reputation in war. Three thousand of these were first sent to Calais, from where they went to Paris to maintain the war against the French. Around Midsummer Day the earl followed with the remainder of his men; from Calais they went by way of Saint-Pol, Doullens and Amiens to Paris, where he was warmly welcomed by the Duke of Bedford and all the members of the council of France which supported King Henry's cause.

Immediately after their arrival several days were spent in important councils on the conduct of the war. The conclusion was that, as he had reduced to obedience certain towns which were held by the enemy, the earl should lay siege to the city of Orléans, which was something of a thorn in their side. As soon as the council was over orders were issued for the Normans and their supporters to assemble, and they responded with such alacrity that the Earl of Salisbury very soon had ten thousand fighting-men under his command, including the Earl of Suffolk and many brave and well-tried leaders. They were given a splendid send-off in Paris, with much feasting, before leaving to besiege Nogent-le-Roi, which was held by the French. This town was soon captured; many of its defenders were executed, and others were set free if they could pay a sufficient ransom.

¶ When the Earl of Salisbury had conquered Jargeau, Janville, Meung and other fortresses in that part of the country, he made serious preparations for the siege of Orléans, where he arrived with his army during October. The town had been long expecting him, and had had time to prepare fortifications, engines of war, stores of food and equipment, and to bring in experienced men-at-arms in order to defend themselves against the earl. To prevent him from using the buildings outside the city proper as quarters or fortifications, they had completely demolished several fine large buildings, among them twelve churches, including the priories of the four mendicant orders, and many stately country houses of the leading citizens. They had done this work so thoroughly that there was a clear view in every direction, so that they could easily fire their cannons and other engines of war.

This did not prevent the Earl of Salisbury and the English army from taking up their quarters close to the walls of the town, even though the garrison was vigorous in defence, making several sallies on the enemy and discharging cannons, culverins and other artillery to kill and wound a fair number of the earl's men. The English, however, repulsed these attacks with great courage, coming so close to the walls that the defenders greatly admired their bravery. The Earl of Salisbury then ordered an attack to be made on the tower which commanded the bridge over the Loire, and before long it had been captured, along with a small bulwark near by, in spite of French resistance. He garrisoned the tower with his own men, so that the defenders could not come out to attack them by that route. He also took over some ruined houses near the tower and there quartered himself and his captains, with his men near the town, and constructed earthworks, covered siege-engines and other protections against the heavy rain of arrows from the town.

On the third day after his arrival before the city the earl went into the tower where his men were, and posted himself at a window on the third floor to study the approaches to the town and see by what means he might capture it. While he was at the window a stone shot from a small bombard on the walls struck the frame, and though he immediately drew back he was mortally wounded and a great part of his face was shot clean off, while a knight standing behind him was killed outright. All his men were very grieved to see his wound, for he was both feared and loved by them, and they considered him the most experienced and skilful as well as the most fortunate of all the princes and captains in England . . . Having summoned all his chief officers to him, he exhorted them in the name of the King of England to continue the fight to subjugate this town of Orléans and not to give up on any pretence; he then had himself carried to Meung, where he died a week later.

The Earl of Suffolk was appointed captain-general of the English in his place, with some notable captains under him. In spite of the loss of their beloved constable, they all recovered their vigour and exerted themselves to the utmost in every way to continue the siege and finish off what they had undertaken. They engaged in several skirmishes and erected new fortifications, and posted themselves behind them so that they could not be surprised by enemy attack.

King Charles of France now realized that the English intention was to conquer the great city of Orléans and to place it under their control; he therefore secured from his council an agreement that this town should be defended with every available resource, since he knew that if this town fell to his enemies it would mean the complete destruction of himself and his kingdom. For this purpose he had sent to Orléans some of his best and most trusted captains; they commanded twelve to fourteen hundred thoroughly experienced fighting-men, the number varying because the siege was at that time not so complete as to prevent them from procuring reinforcements of men and provisions, or from going about their business outside the city if they so wished. While the siege was on there were many skirmishes between the two parties, but to recount each of them and to sort out who lost and who won would be both boring and unnecessarily long. From reports I have received, however, from some of the chief men on each side, I do not gather that in these sallies the besieged inflicted much harm on their enemy, though they did do a certain amount of damage with the cannon and other engines they fired from the walls . . .

¶ Meanwhile in Paris the Duke of Bedford had collected from the borders of Normandy some four or five hundred carts and waggons, and by arrangement with certain of the local merchants these were laden with provisions and artillery and other necessaries to be taken to the English at the siege of Orléans. When everything was ready the convoy was placed under the command of Sir John Fastolf, grand master of the household to the Duke of Bedford, who had with him several officers from the region of the Ile de France, sixteen hundred combatants and easily a thousand unskilled men. They left Paris on Ash Wednesday, and proceeded in good order by short marches till they reached the village of Rouvray in Beauce, between Janville and Orléans.

At this spot a number of French captains who had known for some time of their coming had gathered a body of armed men to oppose them; among these were Charles, Duc de Bourbon, the two Marshals of France, the Constable of Scotland* and his son and a large number of other influential noblemen, and they had altogether

* Sir John Stewart of Darnley.

three or four thousand fighting-men. The English were well aware that this force had been gathered together from some of their own men garrisoned in that region, and quickly set about forming their convoy of carts into a large enclosure, big enough to take them all and leaving only two openings which were covered by the archers. On the better-protected side they placed the merchants, carters, pages and other non-combatant persons, with all the horses.

Thus drawn up the English waited two hours for the enemy, who then arrived with much noise and formed in battle array out of bow-shot from the enclosure. They thought that in view of the threat represented by their superior numbers they would soon have conquered their enemy, whose escapes were blocked and who were composed of men of various nations, only six hundred of them being true-born Englishmen. There were, however, some who were much less confident, for the reason that their various officers could not agree on the line of attack; some, particularly the Scots, wanted to fight on foot, while others preferred to fight on horseback . . . Meanwhile the Constable of Scotland and his son and all their men dismounted, and shortly after, with some on foot and some mounted, a general attack was made on the enemy, who withstood them with great courage.

Then the English archers began to shoot their arrows thick and fast from the cover of their waggons, and the accuracy was such that both riders and foot-soldiers were driven back. At one of the entrances to the enclosure there was a fight with the Constable of Scotland and his men, but they were soon repulsed and most of them killed on the spot; among the dead were six score knights and five or six hundred other combatants, mostly Scots. The remaining captains with their men went back where they had come from.

The English then took some refreshment and marched off as speedily as they could to their town of Rouvray, where they spent the night. Next day they set off again in good order with all their equipment in the convoy—coats of mail, helmets, crossbows, fire-sticks and other necessary weapons and in a few days they arrived before the fair city of Orléans, rejoicing because of the success they had had and because of the provisions they had brought to the besiegers. This battle was always afterwards known as the Battle of Herrings, because the greater part of the food carts were laden with herrings and other Lenten provisions.

King Charles was sick at heart to learn of this further disaster to his fortunes, for he saw things going from bad to worse. This battle of Rouvray was fought on the night of the first Sunday in Lent [12 February 1429], about three hours after midnight, and in it the English lost only one man, named Bresanteau, nephew of Sir Simon Morbier, Provost of Paris. Three men were knighted by the English that day; their numbers in the battle were seventeen hundred fighting-men of tried courage, without counting the non-combatants, while the French had three or four thousand. The Seigneur de Chateaubrun was knighted, as was Charles de Bourbon. Only one prisoner was taken that day, and he was a Scotsman.

Charles might well have been sick at heart, for this battle of Rouvray had a disastrous influence on the morale of his captains, and their weakness had for some time been in morale rather than military potential. With the arrival of armaments and provisions English confidence was assured, and negotiations were opened for the surrender of Orléans. Joan of Arc could have come at no more opportune moment.

¶ In the same year a young maiden about 20 years old* whose name was Joan came to King Charles at Chinon, where he was then living. She was dressed just like a man, and had been born where Lorraine and Burgundy meet, in a village called Domremy, not far from Vaucouleurs. This Joan, the Maid, had for some time been chambermaid in an inn; she was also thoroughly used to riding horses and taking them to water, and could do other feats which girls do not usually do. She was sent on her way by a knight called Sir Robert de Baudricourt, who commanded the garrison at Vaucouleurs for the king and had encouraged her by giving her horses and half a dozen men to escort her. She described herself as a maiden inspired by divine grace, and said she was sent to restore his rights to King Charles, who had been wrongfully driven from his kingdom and reduced to so pitiable a state.

She remained in the king's household for about two months, and made frequent petitions to him to grant her men and support, with which she would repulse his enemies and restore his royal prerogatives. At this time the king and his counsellors did not put much faith in her or her promises, and considered her to be out of her right mind. To princes and barons of such importance it is very risky to believe the sort of words she spoke, as much for fear of God's wrath as for the blasphemies her claims might arouse among the ordinary people.

* There is doubt about her age, but it is probable that she was 17 years old.

However that might be, she was given support after a certain time, by the grant of men and equipment, and she had a standard made with a representation of Our Lord. She constantly spoke of God, so that great numbers of those who saw and heard her were convinced that she was truly inspired by God as she claimed to be. She was examined on more than one occasion by learned clerks and other wise men of some repute, so that her real intentions could be discovered. But she held throughout to her original claim, that if the king would believe her she would restore his kingdom to him. Since then she has done many deeds which secured for her great fame, and these will now be told.

When the king now sent for her he had with him the Duc d'Alençon, the king's marshal, and several other captains, for he had summoned an important council to discuss the siege of Orléans. From there he went to Poitiers, and the Maid went with him. Shortly afterwards orders were given to the marshal to take provisions and other necessities to Orléans, with a strong escorting force. Joan the Maid asked to go with him and to be given arms and armour, which was granted. Soon afterwards she raised her standard and went to Blois, where the force was to be assembled, and thence to Orléans with the others, all the time dressed in full armour. During this expedition many tried soldiers served under her, and when she reached the city of Orléans there was much feasting in her honour, and all the people were delighted that she had come . . .

¶ The English had now maintained the siege of Orléans for about seven months, and had caused considerable distress and damage within the town by their artillery and from the siege-towers and other fortifications, of which they had constructed about sixty. The besieged, in fact, began to see themselves being reduced to submission, and knew that their only hope lay in united action with all the power at their disposal. They sent to King Charles for reinforcements of men and provisions, and four or five hundred combatants were sent at once, followed by seven thousand more, with provisions, who arrived by boat up the River Loire. With them came the Maid Joan; up to this time she had done little that was worth telling. The English army tried to capture the provisions, but they were well defended by the Maid and those who were with her and got through to safety. The people of Orléans were very relieved to have more food supplies, and also that the Maid had come among them.

On the next day, a Thursday, Joan the Maid rose early and spoke to several captains and other men-at-arms, persuading them in the end to arm and follow her, because she wanted (as she put it) to get at the enemy, adding that she knew they would be defeated. The captains and the soldiers were amazed at what she said, but they nevertheless armed and went with her to that part of the English fortifications known as the Bastille Saint-Loup, which was particularly strong. It was held by three or four hundred English, but they were soon beaten, all of them either killed or wounded or captured, and the tower demolished and burned. Then the Maid Joan returned to Orléans with all the knights and men she had led, and there she was feasted and acclaimed with joy by all ranks of men.

On Friday the Maid Joan again left the city with a body of men-at-arms to attack another of the enemy fortifications, and this like the first was captured and its defenders put to the sword. After she had ordered it to be destroyed by fire, she returned to Orléans, where she was more than ever honoured by all the inhabitants. On Saturday they made a determined and courageous attack on the strongly fortified tower at the other end of the bridge; this tower was of very solid construction and defended by the flower of England's most experienced men-at-arms. For a long time they held their own with skill, but to no avail, for they were finally defeated by the sheer strength and courage of the attack, and the greater part were put to the sword. Among these was a brave and renowned English captain known as Glasdale, and with him the Seigneur de Moulins, the Bailiff of Évreux and several other rich noblemen of great importance. After this victory, Joan the Maid returned to Orléans with her noble and renowned Frenchmen, having suffered but few losses.

In these three assaults it was commonly held that the Maid Joan had been the leader, but it must not be forgotten that she had with her all or most of the noble knights and captains who had been in the city throughout the siege, and of whom mention has already been made. They had all conducted themselves with such exemplary courage as is expected of men-at-arms that in these three battles between six and eight thousand of the enemy were killed while the French lost only one hundred men of all ranks [5–7 May 1429].

On Sunday the chief captains of the English—the Earls of Suffolk, Talbot, Lord Scales and others—seeing that some of their fortifications had been captured and destroyed with much loss of men, decided to move their remaining forces out of the fortifications and assemble them into one body, to see whether the French would offer battle. If not, they would march off to some of the towns which were in English hands. During that Sunday morning therefore they abandoned the fortifications which were still standing, setting fire to several of them, and drew up in battle order, waiting for the French to come out and attack. But the French, on the advice of Joan the Maid, had no intention of doing so, and after some time the English, realizing that their forces were sadly depleted and that worse might befall them if they stayed, took the decision to move off and went to various towns and strongholds which they still held.

There was great rejoicing throughout the city of Orléans when this was known, for they were now delivered from their treacherous enemies who had kept them for so long in great danger, and could see the survivors marching away to make their peace with God. A number of experienced men-at-arms were dispatched to examine the towers and fortifications; here they found provisions and considerable supplies of various kinds, which they brought back to the town and with which they prepared a feast all the more enjoyable in that it had cost them nothing. All the remaining fortifications were burned to the ground, so that they might never again be of use to any army of any nation.

Joan of Arc: the Coronation Campaign

¶ The French in Orléans, that is the captains with Joan the Maid, now agreed together to send messengers to the King of France to let him know of their successes and of the departure of the English to their own garrisons, and to request that he should without delay send them such reinforcements of fighting-men as he could procure from the great nobles, so that they could follow and attack the enemy while they were still smarting under their recent losses; they begged him, moreover, to come in person, and to place himself at the head of his men.

This news was most welcome to the king and his council. He immediately summoned to his presence his constable, the Duc d'Alençon, Charles, Seigneur d'Albret, and several other noble lords of renown; the greater part of these he sent to Orléans. Shortly afterwards the king moved to Gien with a large army. The captains who had been in the siege of Orléans, together with the princes and barons who had recently arrived in the city, met frequently in council together to decide whether to pursue their enemies the English. The first to be heard in these deliberations was Joan the Maid, who was now held in the highest repute.

On the fourth day of May (the siege having been raised at the turn of the month)* the French took the field with five or six thousand fighting-men and every equipment of war, and marched to Jargeau, which was held by the Earl of Suffolk and his brothers. The English had from there sent messengers to the Duke of Bedford in Paris to tell him of their reverses at Orléans, and to say that if he did not send reinforcements they were in danger of being driven back and of losing a number of their strongholds in Beauce and along the Loire. The Duke of Bedford was greatly depressed at the news, but seeing that he had to do something he hastily collected men of various nations under his control, and sent about four or five thousand of them to the Orléanais under the command of Sir Thomas Rampstone and the bastard of Thian among others. He sent a promise that he would himself follow shortly afterwards with the reinforcements he had sent for from England.

¶ When the French under the constable, Joan the Maid and the other captains . . . reached Jargeau, the Earl of Suffolk hastily organized the defence of that town with the three or four hundred men of his own and the townsfolk themselves. It was not long, however, before they were surrounded on all sides by the French, who launched simultaneous assaults of great ferocity at various points round the town. The attack was maintained with bitter fighting for some time and the persistence of the French was so great that in spite of the enemy they forced their way into the town and captured it. Three hundred English were killed in the fighting, one of them being a brother of the Earl of Suffolk. The earl himself, with another brother, the Baron de la Pole, were taken prisoner, a fate which befell at least sixty of his men. Thus the town and fortress of Jargeau were conquered by the French, who ate and rested after the battle [12 June 1429].

From there they went to Meung, which soon fell to their attack; the English in La Ferté-Hubert fled on their approach, and went to Beaugency, where they were hotly pursued by the French, who camped in various spots near by. All the time Joan the Maid was at their head with her standard. Never had such fame been granted to

* The dates are inaccurate.

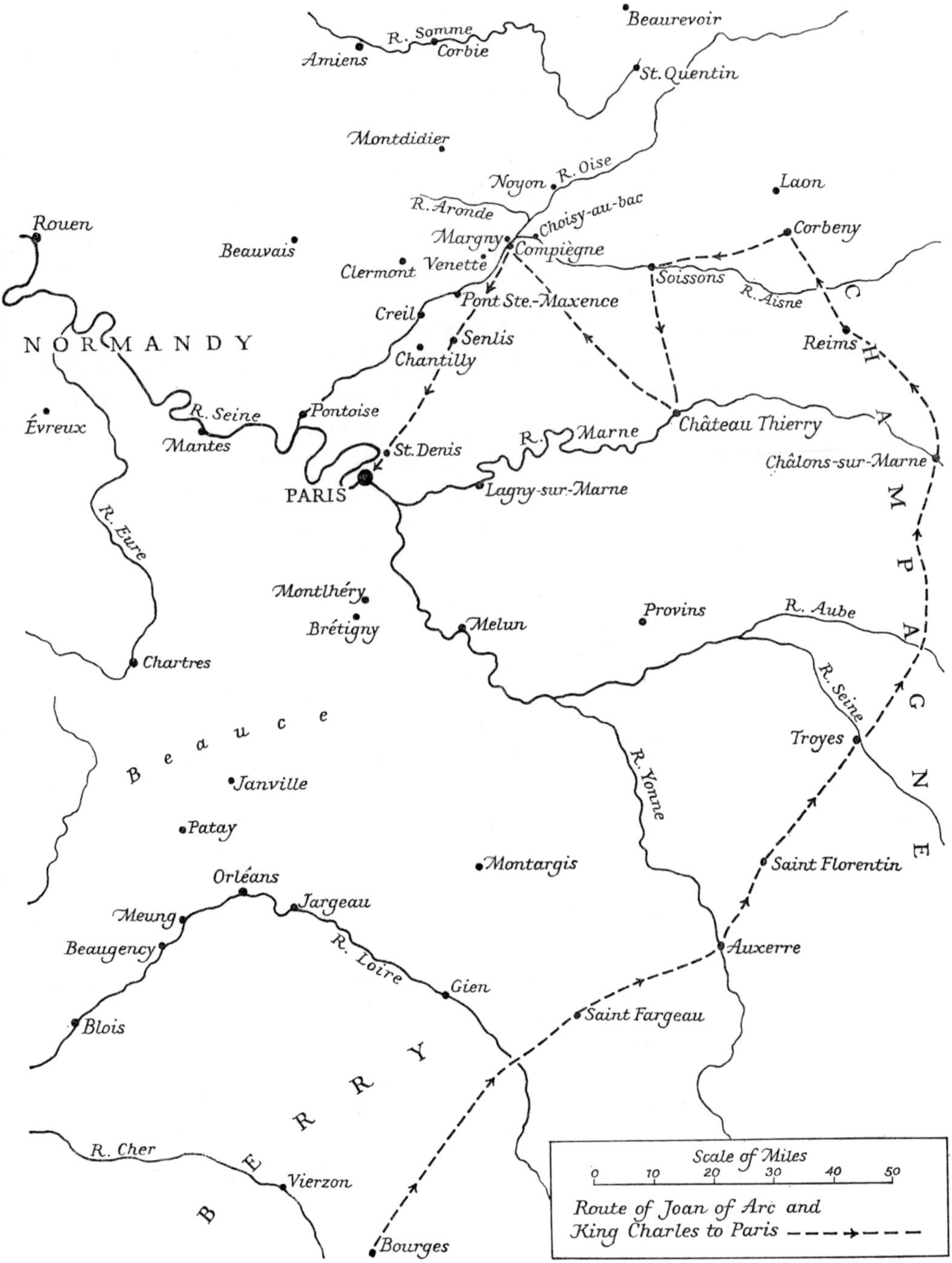
Beaurevoir
R. Somme
Amiens
Corbie
St. Quentin
Montdidier
Noyon
R. Oise
Laon
R. Aronde
Choisy-au-bac
Rouen
Margny
Corbeny
Beauvais
Compiègne
Clermont
Venette
Soissons
R. Aisne
Creil
Pont Ste.-Maxence
NORMANDY
Senlis
Reims
Chantilly
CHAMPAGNE
Pontoise
Évreux
R. Seine
Château Thierry
Mantes
R. Marne
St. Denis
Châlons-sur-Marne
PARIS
Lagny-sur-Marne
R. Eure
Montlhéry
Brétigny
Melun
Provins
R. Aube
Chartres
R. Seine
Beauce
Troyes
R. Yonne
Janville
Patay
Montargis
Saint Florentin
Orléans
Jargeau
Meung
Beaugency
Auxerre
R. Loire
Gien
Blois
Saint Fargeau
BERRY
R. Cher
Vierzon
Bourges
Scale of Miles
0 10 20 30 40 50
Route of Joan of Arc and King Charles to Paris

JOAN OF ARC'S ROUTE 1429–30

anyone in all the country thereabouts; no other military commander was ever mentioned. The chief English captains in Beaugency saw that this maiden's fame had completely turned their own fortune, causing them to lose several towns and fortresses which had gone over to the enemy, some by attack and conquest, others by private agreement. Moreover, their men were mostly in a sorry state of fear, and seemed to have lost their usual prudence in action; they wanted to withdraw into Normandy, and their leaders did not know what to advise or to do, since they did not even know when or whether their reinforcements were likely to arrive.

In this state of things they negotiated with the French to be allowed to leave the town in safety with all their goods on condition that it was handed over to the supporters of King Charles of France, and these terms were accepted [18 June]. The English went off through Beauce towards Paris, and the French entered Beaugency with much rejoicing. There they were advised by Joan the Maid to advance for an encounter with some English who, they had heard, were coming from the direction of Paris to do battle. They again set off on the march, and each day they received reinforcements from different quarters.

It was decided that the constable, the Marshal de Boussac, la Hire, Pothon and some other captains should go to form the vanguard, the remainder under the command of the Duc d'Alençon, the bastard of Orléans and the Seigneur de Retz should form the main army of eight thousand or nine thousand fighting-men following fairly closely on the vanguard. Some of the princes asked Joan the Maid what should be done and what orders she thought they ought to give. She replied that she was certain their old enemies the English were coming to offer battle, and that in God's name they should go and oppose them bravely; they could not fail thus to conquer the enemy. When someone asked her where they were to be found, she said: 'Ride forward boldly, we shall be guided to them.'

Then the army was drawn up in marching order and started to advance, while some three or four score of their most experienced warriors were sent ahead on the best horses to find where the enemy were. They rode for some days,* and on a Saturday came to within a mile or so of a large village called Patay, when their scouts started a stag which ran straight towards the English army just then being formed up of those coming from Paris and those who had left

* This should probably read 'some hours', for the battle of Patay took place on the same day as the capture of Beaugency, Saturday, 18 June.

Beaugency and other places around Orléans. When they saw this stag come dashing through the midst of the armed camp, the English set up a shout, not knowing their enemies were so close. But the noise revealed their whereabouts to the French, who shortly moved up within sight of them. Some riders were sent back to the captains to tell them to march straight ahead in battle order, because now was the time to be ready. Final preparations were hurriedly made, and they rode forward till they came within sight of their old enemies.

The English now knew that the French were at hand, and made their own preparations for battle. Some wanted to take up their positions on foot near a hedge in order to prevent a surprise attack from the rear. Others, however, were not satisfied with this kind of strategy, and said they would find more advantageous ground; they turned round and retreated six or seven hundred yards from their former position, which was full of hedges and undergrowth. The French, who preferred to fight on open ground, nearly all dismounted from their horses and continued on foot, their vanguard impatient to attack the English, because they had lately found them to be ill prepared in defence. With a sudden bold onslaught they caught them before they could form up in any order, while Sir John Fastolf and the bastard of Thian, both knights, and their men, who had not dismounted, took flight across the open country to save their lives.

Meanwhile those English who were fighting on foot were soon surrounded on all sides, since they had no time to make their customary defences of sharp stakes stuck in the ground. They were unable to inflict much damage on the French and were soon completely beaten. Some eighteen hundred English were left dead on the field, and a hundred or more taken prisoner, among them the Lords Scales, Talbot and Hungerford, Sir Thomas Rempstone and several more. Among the dead were a certain number of the leaders, the rest were men of middling or low degree—the sort who are always brought from their own country to die in France.

The battle was over by two o'clock in the afternoon. All the French captains gathered together to give humble and devout thanks to their Creator, and all the army celebrated their victory. That night they lodged in the town of Patay, a couple of leagues from Anville in Beauce, and it is by the name of Patay that this battle is known. On the next day they and other French from round about returned to Orléans with all their prisoners and the booty they had taken from the English dead. They were welcomed with open arms by the people of that town, and special acclaim was given to Joan the Maid, because of whom, it seemed, their enemies had lost their will to resist and King Charles would be restored to his kingdom. She accompanied the princes and captains to the king, who was delighted at their return and received them with great honour. A council was held shortly afterwards, at which it was decided to summon as many fighting men as possible from the lands Charles held, so that they could pursue their enemies and drive them out of the country.

On the morning of the battle of Patay, before the English knew that the enemy was so close, Sir John Fastolf, one of their chief captains, who had fled without striking a blow, had assembled a hasty council at which he had spoken of the great losses they had suffered at Orléans and Jargeau and elsewhere, of the frightened state of their troops, and of the supreme confidence of the enemy, advising that they should retire to their own strongholds and not engage in further battle until they had re-established their strength with the coming of the reinforcements from England promised by the regent. But these views were not well received by the other captains, especially Lord John Talbot, who said that if the enemy arrived he would fight. When Sir John Fastolf came before the Duke of Bedford he was bitterly reproached for having fled from the battle, and in the end he was deprived of the Order of the Garter which he wore round his leg. Since then, however, partly because of the explanations already reported and partly for others that he advanced later, which were considered reasonable, it was decreed that the garter should be restored to him, although dissension was renewed between him and Lord Talbot when the latter returned from captivity . . .*

¶ While these matters were being settled King Charles of France assembled in Bourges a large force of men-at-arms and archers, under a notable group of lords and barons from Aquitaine, Gascony, Poitou, Berry and other parts. From Bourges they marched to Gien on the Loire, the king accompanied always by Joan the Maid, and also by a preaching friar of the Augustinian order named Brother Richard, who had recently been driven out of Paris and other towns because in his preaching he had shown himself to be a strong partisan of the French cause. From Gien the king marched towards Auxerre, though a detachment of men-at-arms under the constable went to

* John Talbot, Earl of Shrewsbury, was taken prisoner in this battle. When released he continued to be one of the greatest of the English captains at this period. He was finally killed at the battle of Castillon, near Bordeaux, in 1453 when leading the English forces at the age of over 80 (see p. 340).

Évreux in Normandy to prevent the garrisons of that province from assembling under the command of the Duke of Bedford; the Cadet d'Armagnac was sent south to protect the duchy of Aquitaine and the Bordelais.

In the course of his march the king reduced two small towns to his obedience, Saint-Fargeau* and Saint-Florentin, whose citizens promised henceforth to King Charles and his allies the loyalty they owed to their rightful sovereign, while the king promised to govern them with justice according to their ancient customs. When he came near to Auxerre he sent a summons to them to receive him as their true lord. At first they would not agree to this, but when ambassadors had been exchanged between the two sides a settlement was reached, and the citizens of Auxerre agreed to accept whatever terms should be accepted by the towns of Troyes, Châlons and Reims; they then sent provisions and other supplies to the king on payment, while remaining neutral, a fact for which the king forgave them this time.

The king then marched to Troyes in Champagne, where he remained in camp round the city for three days before they consented to receive him as their sovereign. When certain promises were made to them the men of Troyes agreed to open their city to him. The king and his men then entered the city and heard mass; after an exchange of oaths the king returned to his camp outside the town. He published a decree in several places in his camp and inside the town that no one on pain of death should harm the citizens of Troyes or those others who had come over to his obedience. During the march the vanguard was led by the two Marshals of France, Boussac and the Seigneur de Retz, and with them were La Hire, Pothon de Xaintrailles and other captains. They secured the submission of many large towns and strongholds in the country through which they passed, but for the sake of brevity I shall refrain from mentioning them by name.

¶ While King Charles was at Troyes in Champagne representatives came to him from Châlons, bringing him the keys of their city as evidence that they were ready to submit to his rule. He accordingly continued his march to that town, where he was received with warmth and humility. The keys of Reims were similarly brought to him with a promise to receive him as their sovereign, in spite of the fact that the Seigneur de Saveuses had been there only recently on

* Monstrelet says 'Jargeau', but this had already been conquered, and is not on the route, while Saint-Fargeau is. Auxerre, however, is between the two towns.

the part of the Duke of Burgundy with a force of men-at-arms and had secured from the governor of the city and many of its inhabitants a promise to remain loyal till death to the cause of King Henry and the Duke of Burgundy. Nevertheless they submitted to King Charles through fear of the Maid, whose marvellous doings had been reported to them. The Seigneurs de Châtillon and Saveuses, their captains, had done everything to persuade them not to submit, but seeing that the people of Reims would not listen to them and had used threatening words towards them they left the town and made for Château-Thierry.

The citizens of Reims agreed to open their city to King Charles, and were encouraged in so doing by their archbishop, who was the king's chancellor, and by certain others. The king marched into the city on the sixteenth day of July [1429] with a large concourse of knights, and on the following Sunday he was there crowned and consecrated king by the archbishop in the presence of his princes and bishops, and all the barons and knights who were there. Among their number were the Duc d'Alençon, the Comte de Clermont, the Seigneur de la Trémouille his chief minister, the Seigneur de Beaumanoir in Brittany and the Seigneur de Mailly in Touraine, who were dressed in coronation robes to represent the noble peers of France who could not be present at this great coronation ceremony, though their names were all called at the foot of the high altar by the king of arms of France according to custom.

When the consecration was completed the king went to dine in the archbishop's palace, in company with the lords and prelates. At the king's table was the Archbishop of Reims, and they were served by the Duc d'Alençon, the Comte de Clermont and other great lords. On this coronation day the king made three men knights in the cathedral. Next day he left the city and went as a pilgrim to Corbeny, to pay homage to Saint Marcou. While he was here he received deputies from Laon who had come to submit themselves to his obedience as other towns had done.

From Corbeny he made for Provins and Soissons, who immediately opened their gates to him. He appointed La Hire bailiff of Vermandois, in the place of Sir Collart de Mailly, who had held the post from King Henry of England. He then proceeded to Château-Thierry, which was held by the Seigneur de Châtillon and other barons of the Burgundian party with some four hundred men-at-arms. The defenders, feeling that the townsfolk were inclined to support King Charles and seeing little hope of immediate reinforcements, considered they were ill equipped for a siege and surrendered the town and its fortress to King Charles. They were allowed to leave the town and departed with their baggage unharmed to Paris, where they joined the Duke of Bedford, who was preparing a strong force to fight King Charles.

the capture and death of joan

In a few months the whole fortunes of the war had been changed by a girl of seventeen. France now had a king who had been traditionally anointed in the cathedral at Reims, the doubts concerning his legitimacy were no longer relevant, the relief of Orléans and the coronation campaign had restored French morale. England had only the boy king aged seven, set on the throne by the Treaty of Troyes, but not yet crowned in France; her power was obviously going to depend on continuing support from the Burgundians—and Duke Philippe was already negotiating a truce with Charles. Joan kept pushing Charles to attack Paris, but for the time being he seemed content to accept the submission of towns without military action, among them Compiègne, where he set up temporary headquarters.

¶ While King Charles was at Compiègne news reached him that the Duke of Bedford, Regent of France, was marching into Normandy with his whole army to fight the constable, who was in the region of Évreux and harassing all the countryside. After a stay of twelve days the king left Compiègne, leaving Guillaume de Flavy in command of the town, and marched with his army to Senlis, where the inhabitants came to an agreement to surrender to the king. He lodged the greater part of his army in the town, the remainder being accommodated in the surrounding villages. About the same time other towns surrendered to his cause—Creil, Beauvais, Pont-Sainte-Maxence, Choisy, Gournay-sur-Aronde, Remy-la-Neuville, Moignay, Chantilly and several more. The seigneurs de Montmorency and Moy also made oaths of loyalty to him, and indeed if he had then marched with his army to Saint-Quentin, Corbie, Amiens, Abbeville and other such towns he would have found them ready to acknowledge him as their lord and desiring nothing better than to open their gates to him. He was advised, however, not to advance so far into the Duke of Burgundy's territory, as much because of the strength of the opposition as from the expectation that an amicable treaty would shortly be signed between them.

After some days in Senlis, the king marched to Saint-Denis, where he found that the chief inhabitants had fled to Paris; his men were lodged in Aubervilliers and Montmartre and other villages round Paris. With him was Joan the Maid, whose reputation was at its height, and she tried daily to persuade the king and the princes to attack the city of Paris. Eventually it was agreed that on Monday the eighth [of September] an attack would be made. The army was therefore prepared for battle and on the appointed day the king, with his princes and lords, drew up his army between Montmartre and the city; the Maid was also with him. With her standard unfurled, the vanguard, which was very large, marched to the Porte Saint-Honoré, taking with them scaling-ladders, bundles of wood to fill the moat and other siege weapons. There she told some of the men to go into the moat on foot. At about ten o'clock the assault began in earnest, and it lasted for four or five hours. Inside the city were some four hundred men-at-arms under Louis de Luxembourg, the Bishop of Thérouanne, Chancellor of France for King Henry, and other lords sent by the Duke of Burgundy; they defended themselves vigorously and with courage, having carefully distributed their forces at different points, each under a separate captain.

In the course of the attack many of the French were driven back into the moat, and many were killed or wounded by the cannons, culverins and other weapons fired from the walls of Paris. Among them was Joan the Maid, who was seriously wounded; all day she had remained behind a small mound until the time of vespers, when Guichard de Thiembronne and others went to look for her. Some of the defenders also were wounded. When the French captains saw that they were in considerable danger and realized that it was not possible to take the city by storm in view of the united will of the defenders, they immediately gave orders for the retreat to be sounded. They gathered their dead and wounded and returned to their quarters. Next day King Charles marched to Senlis to care for his wounded, much downcast at the loss of his men.

The Parisians were more than ever united now, and swore to resist King Charles with all their might, for the king wished to destroy them all. But it could be that they were frightened of him, as men who had it on their consciences that they had turned him out of the city and killed some of his most loyal supporters.

The Duc d'Alençon had been covering the approaches to the Porte Saint-Denis, but did not intervene in the fight; the king never left his quarters at

Saint-Denis. It would seem that the Maid's first failure had been intended.

Charles now retreated south of the Loire, reaching Gien on 21 September, and disbanded his army. Joan was kept idle all the winter, except for a fruitless attack on La Charité-sur-Loire. In the spring she was allowed to accompany small marauding armies that attacked Melun, Lagny, Senlis and Soissons with varying success. Only the second of these assaults is described by Monstrelet.

¶ At the beginning of May [1430] a valiant man-at-arms named Franquet d'Arras, a Burgundian, was overcome and captured. He had conducted a small expedition with some three hundred combatants into enemy territory in the direction of Lagny-sur-Marne. On his return he was met by Joan the Maid with a force of four hundred French. He and his men launched several courageous attacks against the French, and indeed the skill of their archers was such that the Maid and her men gained no ground at all in the first two attacks. She, however, contrived to summon the garrisons of Lagny and other strongholds that were loyal to King Charles, and reinforcements arrived in large numbers with culverins, crossbows and other weapons, with the result that the Burgundians, after their horsemen had done much damage among the French, were overcome and most of them put to the sword. The Maid finally ordered Franquet's head to be cut off; his death was much lamented by his followers, because he was a most courageous man in battle.

One of the terms of the treaty that Burgundy had signed with King Charles was that Compiègne should be handed over to the duke. As this had not been done, he ordered Jean de Luxembourg to reconquer the town. When Joan heard of this she gathered a small band of armed men and marched with them to Compiègne, where she arrived on 13 May.

¶ While the Duke of Burgundy was camped at Coudun, and his men either there or in other villages near Compiègne, it happened at five o'clock in the afternoon on Ascension Day [24 May 1430] that Joan the Maid, Pothon and other valiant French captains with some five or six hundred combatants made a sally out of Compiègne by the bridge leading to Montdidier, intending to storm the position held by Sir Bando de Noielle at Margny on the far side of the River Oise. Sir Bando had with him Jean de Luxembourg and the Seigneur de Crequy, who had ridden over with eight or ten knights, but few other attendants to confer on the best means of attacking Compiègne.

This company of Frenchmen then approached close to Margny

while the defenders of that place were still unarmed, and a sharp skirmish soon began, with the cry of 'To arms!' being shouted by Burgundians and English alike. Then they drew up in battle order on the meadow outside Venette where they were camped, some five hundred combatants in number. The French under Jean de Luxembourg, who were camped at Clairoix on the other side of Margny, heard the clash and hastened to the help of their lord in his efforts to withstand the enemy. In this engagement the Seigneur de Crequy was seriously wounded in the face.

When the fighting had been going on for some time the French saw their enemies increasing in number and withdrew towards Compiègne, leaving the Maid with the rearguard and doing her best to encourage her men and bring them back without loss. But the Burgundians, knowing that help was quickly available on all sides, made a sudden attack on the French rear, at the conclusion of which (as I have been informed) the Maid was dragged from her horse by an archer. To the bastard of Wandomme, who was near by, she gave her oath of surrender, and he took her at once to Margny, where she was held as a prisoner under a strong guard. At the same time Pothon the Burgundian was also taken prisoner, but very few others. The French went back to Compiègne, wretched and angry at their defeat and particularly at the loss of the Maid. The Burgundians and the English, however, were more excited than if they had captured five hundred fighting men, for they had never been so much afraid of any captain or commander in war as they had been of the Maid until the day of her capture [24 May 1430].

Shortly after this the Duke of Burgundy came up with all his army from Coudun, where his camp was in the meadow opposite Compiègne. There he and his men and all the English assembled together, shouting with joy because the Maid had been captured. The duke went to visit her at Margny and had some words with her; what they were I do not now remember, although I was present. The duke and his men then withdrew to their quarters, leaving the Maid under the guard of Jean de Luxembourg, who soon afterwards sent her with a strong escort to the Castle of Beaulieu, and from there to Beaurevoir, where she remained a prisoner for some considerable time.

With Joan out of the way, the situation improved for England, and in June the young Henry VI was brought to Rouen, awaiting the moment when it would be expedient to have him crowned.

In November, on the advice of Pierre Cauchon, Bishop of Beauvais, the English paid 10,000 pounds (gathered from the Estates of Normandy) to Jean de Luxembourg; Joan was handed over to them, and taken to the prison in Rouen. Her trial was delayed until the 21st of February 1431; she was burned at the stake on the 30th of May. None of these events concerning Joan is directly recorded by Monstrelet; we have to rely on his transcription of a letter from King Henry.

¶ The sentence against Joan the Maid was pronounced in the city of Rouen; here follows a copy of the letter about her trial sent by the King of England to the Duke of Burgundy.

'Most dear and well-beloved uncle, the very warm love we know that you as a true Catholic bear to our holy mother the Church and our zeal for the faith have given us good reason to send you an account of what has recently been performed in this our city of Rouen for the honour of holy mother Church, the strengthening of our faith and the extirpation of pestilential errors. It is already common knowledge that the woman Joan, who caused herself falsely to be known as the Maid, had for two years and more gone about in man's dress, a thing that is against divine law and the condition of her sex, and abominable in the sight of God. In this state she joined with our common enemy and frequently told him and his followers—churchmen, nobles and people—that she was sent by God, and presumptuously boasted that she had had personal and visible communication with Saint Michael and a great host of angels and saints in Paradise, such as Saint Catherine and Saint Margaret. By such false representations and the hope she gave of future victories, she turned the hearts of men and women from the truth, and caused them to believe in lies and fairy stories. She also wore armour appropriate to knights and squires, and raised her own banner, on which in her presumptuous pride she asked leave to bear the excellent and noble arms of France, and this was in part granted, for in many attacks and engagements she bore a banner with two fleurs-de-lis or on a field azure, and a sword surmounted by a crown. Thus equipped she led men-at-arms and archers into battle in large companies and practised inhuman cruelties in shedding human blood and arousing sedition and disloyalty among the people whom she led into perjury, rebellion, superstition and false doctrine; in disturbing the established peace and renewing war to the death, and in allowing herself to be honoured and revered as a holy woman; and generally in other damnable works that there is not room to detail, but which are widely known and which have brought scandal to almost the whole of Christendom.

'Yet the divine mercy has taken pity on her loyal servants and would not leave them long in such danger of strange and perilous beliefs, but has allowed in her all-embracing pity that this woman should be taken prisoner by your army when you were laying siege to Compiègne and by you transferred to our safe custody. When this was done it was required of us by the bishop in whose diocese she was captured that this Joan, accused of crimes against the Divine Majesty, should be handed over to him as her rightful judge in matters ecclesiastical. We accordingly delivered the said Joan to be tried by him, as much out of respect for our holy Mother the Church, whose wishes we have always rightly considered before our own desires, as for the honour and exaltation of our own faith. We were unwilling that any punishment should be exercised by the officers of our own secular justice, although to have allowed this would have been perfectly within our rights, seeing the great harm, the horrible murders, the ghastly cruelties and other countless evils she inflicted on our sovereignty and on our loyal and obedient people.

'The bishop, having called also the vicar-general of the Inquisitor of the Faith and a large number of masters and doctors of theology and canon law, began the trial of Joan with due and solemn gravity. After he and the Inquisitor, her chief judges in this court, had interrogated her for many days, they asked the masters and doctors to examine carefully all her confessions and claims, and sent them also to be studied in all the faculties of our well-beloved daughter the University of Paris. As a result of the learned opinions thus received the judges declared that Joan was superstitious, a trafficker with devils, a blasphemer of God and his saints, a schismatic, and guilty of many errors against the faith of Jesus Christ. In order to bring her back into the only true faith of our holy mother the Church, to purge her of her horrible crimes and deadly sins, and to save her soul from everlasting damnation, she was given long and frequent admonitions, delivered with great clarity, so that she might renounce all her errors and humbly return to the way of Truth, for she would otherwise imperil both body and soul. But that dangerous and factious spirit of pride and obstinate presumption, which is constantly trying to damage the unity and steadfastness of Christians, held this same Joan so fast in its grip that no holy doctrine or advice or gentle exhortations were able to soften or humble her hard and obstinate heart; indeed, she boasted often that all she had done was well done and done, moreover, at the commandment of God and of the holy virgins who had visibly appeared to her. What was worse, she refused to recognize any power on earth save that of God and His holy saints in paradise, rejecting the judgement of our holy father the Pope, of the council general and of the church catholic and militant.

'The ecclesiastical judges, seeing that she continued in this wilfulness and hardness of heart, had her brought before the clergy and people there assembled in great numbers, and in their presence a famous master of theology preached to her on the exaltation of the faith, the removal of errors, and the edification of Christian peoples. She was once more gently admonished to return to the bosom of holy Church and to renounce the errors in which she so obstinately persisted. Having considered her case, the judges prepared to pronounce the sentence against her which they had reached by due conclusion.

'But before it was spoken she gave signs of a change of heart and said she was willing to return to the bosom of the Church. This the judges and the clergy heard with great pleasure, receiving her kindly because they hoped by this means that her soul and body would be redeemed from everlasting torment. She now submitted herself to the ordinances of holy Church, and made a public renunciation of her errors and her horrible crimes, signing with her own hand the schedule of her recantation. Thus did our merciful mother Church rejoice over the sinner doing penance, anxious to bring back into the fold the sheep wandering in the wilderness that was found again; Joan was ordered to perform her penance in close confinement.

'This state of affairs did not last long before the fire of her pride, which seemed to have been extinguished, burst into pestilential flames again with the breath of the Tempter, and the wretched woman soon fell back into the old errors and wilfulness which she seemed to have renounced. In accordance therefore with the judgements and institutions of holy Church she was again preached to in public so that in future she might not corrupt the other members of Christ's body; and since she had relapsed into her old errors and evil crimes, she was handed over to the secular justice, which immediately condemned her to be burned. When she saw her end approaching she made full acknowledgement that the spirits which she said had appeared to her were often evil and lying spirits, and that the promises they had made to deliver her were false, confessing by these words that her spirits had deceived and mocked her. Then she was taken by the civil authorities to the old market-place in Rouen and there publicly burned in the sight of all the people.'

This done, the King of England sent letters to the Duke of Burgundy so that the execution of justice could be published in various places by him and the other princes, and so that in future their subjects and followers might have strength to place no faith in such errors as had governed the Maid.

Burgundy and Orléans reunited

¶ On the seventeenth day of December [1431] King Henry left the palace with a large concourse of lords spiritual and temporal and entered the church of Notre-Dame de Paris to be crowned. In the nave of the church there had been erected a large platform eighty feet long and in height reaching to the rood; it was approached by some steps from the nave, and extended as far as the choir. The coronation was performed by the Cardinal of Winchester, who also sang the mass, which displeased the Bishop of Paris, who claimed that this office was by right his. At the offertory, the king made the customary offering of bread and wine, the wine being contained in a large silver-gilt chalice which was afterwards removed from the church by the king's officers, and this greatly displeased the canons of Notre-Dame, who said that it rightly belonged to them. They later went to law against the king and his council, and finally after they had spent much on legal proceedings the chalice was restored to them. All the ceremonies proper to a coronation were performed on this day, more in accordance with the customs of England than of France, and the lords of England and France who were with the king in church served him each according to his special office.

When mass was concluded, the king returned to the palace, where he dined at the marble table which was placed in the middle of the hall. On one side of the table sat the Cardinal of Winchester and Pierre Cauchon, Bishop of Beauvais, and Jean de Mailly, Bishop of Noyon, as representing the peers of France; on the other side were the earls of Stafford, Mortimer and Salisbury.

With two prelates (and one of them Cauchon!) to represent the whole French peerage, with offence given to the bishop and canons in Notre-Dame, and with the coronation performed by an English cardinal, the ceremony was far from propitious. People in France, whichever loyalty happened to bind them, were tiring of English pretensions and English overlordship in their country. Though England's military success, under Bedford and then Talbot, was renewed after Joan's death, the beginnings are now to be seen of the great upsurge in France which was to throw the English out of France in twenty years.

Bedford—faithful to Henry V's dying commands—knew that the two essentials for England, if Henry's son was to retain the crown of France, were to have the support of Burgundy and to hold on to Normandy. Duke Philippe now started a series of negotiations and discussions, in which he secretly reviewed his whole position: Charles would let events take their course, and probably represented no great threat; England was a different matter, for he had promised her his support in the Treaty of Troyes, and with his support she would engulf both him and Charles. In 1432 Bedford's wife died; she was Anne of Burgundy and with her went a great part of her brother the duke's support for the English cause.

Burgundian lawyers now told the duke that the treaty he had signed at Troyes allowed Henry V to inherit the crown, and so to hand it down, but not for his son to inherit it directly from Charles VI. Finally a tripartite conference was convened for Arras in July 1435, to see whether a general peace might be possible. After seven weeks of talking, in which the French consistently asked that Henry should renounce the crown of France, the English party left with nothing concluded. Philippe of Burgundy then lost no time in signing a fresh agreement with Charles; since England did not want peace he would make his own peace with France, and Charles would pay dearly in land and money for this priceless support against the English. A preamble to the treaty, drawn up by the two cardinals representing the now unified papacy, declared that Burgundy's oaths to the English were no longer binding.*

Thus the Treaty of Troyes became a dead letter. As Professor Perroy says, it disappeared at the same time as its chief architect, Queen Isabelle, who died deserted in the Hôtel Saint-Pol a few weeks after its chief executant, the Duke of Bedford.

¶ When the peace of Arras [1435] had been concluded the Duke of Burgundy sent his king-of-arms of the order of the Golden Fleece, with one of his heralds known as Franche-Comté, to visit King Henry in England. They carried letters to the king and his council

* The Great Schism had been ended by the Council of Constance in 1415 with the deposition of the anti-pope John XXIII.

in which the duke tried to persuade the king to conclude a peace with the crown of France, and explained how he had been reconciled by a treaty with his sovereign lord King Charles and had abandoned his previous alliance with the late King Henry of England at the exhortation of the legates from the holy father, of the council of Basle and of the three estates of both dominions. Accompanying them was a mendicant friar, a doctor in theology, who had been charged by the two cardinals present at the negotiations in Arras to point out in the presence of the king and his council the terrible cruelties and countless acts of tyranny which were occasioned by the present war, to the great shame of Christendom, and the good that would come if peace were concluded between the two kings.

The three ambassadors travelled to Calais and took ship to Dover, where a message was delivered to them from King Henry forbidding them to leave their lodgings. They were asked to hand over their letters of credence, and these were taken to the king in London, after which they were conducted with suitable halts to the capital. They were met on the road by a herald and a clerk from the king's treasury, who conducted them to their lodgings in the city, at the house of a shoemaker, where they remained for several days. They could not attend mass unless they were accompanied by heralds and pursuivants who made them frequent visits. They were, in fact, forbidden to leave their lodgings without express permission, and lived in constant fear that they might personally suffer for the content of the message they carried.

Although the three of them made frequent requests to the heralds who attended them to be allowed to speak to the king and council so that they could deliver the charge they had received from their masters, they were unable to gain any such audience. However, the Lord Treasurer of England, to whom the letters had been delivered, called to an assembly in the king's presence the Cardinal of Winchester, the Duke of Gloucester and many other princes, bishops and members of the royal council, and there he made known what the Duke of Burgundy had written to the king—but the form of address and superscription were not in the same style as the many letters he had sent in the past, for he now addressed him as 'King of England, high and mighty prince, dear lord and cousin' and no longer recognized him as his 'sovereign lord' as he used to.

Before any reply was formulated everyone expressed the greatest astonishment on hearing these letters. Young King Henry was so displeased that tears ran down his cheeks, and he said to some of his privy counsellors that it was evident that, since the Duke of Burgundy had shown such disloyalty to him in reconciling himself with his enemy the King of France his possessions in France would suffer. The cardinal and the Duke of Gloucester left the council much concerned and annoyed, and several others followed their example before any conclusion was reached. These men gathered together in groups to curse the Duke of Burgundy and all his works. It was not long before the news had spread through the city of London, and there was not a self-respecting man in the town who had a good word to say for the duke. Some of the common people formed into a band and went through various parts of the town looking for Flemings, Hollanders, Brabanters, Picards and men from Hainault and other parts of the duke's dominions who had come to London as merchants; in the heat of anger some of these were caught and murdered. King Henry soon put a stop to these activities and the ringleaders were brought to justice.

In a short time the king and his council assembled to decide what reply should be sent, and there proved to be a divergence of opinion. Some were for an immediate declaration of war on the Duke of Burgundy, others wanted to send letters asking him to explain his action. While this council was still in session news was brought to the king that in his peace treaty with King Charles he had required the surrender to himself of the towns, fortresses, lands and belongings of the towns of Saint-Quentin, Corbie, Amiens, Saint-Riquier, Abbeville, Doullens and Montreuil, which had previously given their oath of loyalty to King Henry, whose officers were in command of their government. This naturally made the council all the more furious, and their final decision was that no answer of any kind should be sent. The lord treasurer was sent to the three ambassadors in their lodging and told the heralds of the Golden Fleece and Franche-Comté how the king, the royal princes and the lords in council had seen and examined the letters they had brought and had been astonished both at their content and at the behaviour of the duke towards the king, and that he would deal with the matter in God's good time. Although the Duke of Burgundy's heralds several times repeated their request for an answer in writing they were unable to procure one, but were told to return home. When they saw that there was no alternative they recrossed the sea and reported by word of mouth what had transpired. The doctor of theology also returned to those who had sent him, without having achieved anything. During their return they were much afraid of being maltreated, for in several places before they left England they heard cursings and murmurings against the Duke of Burgundy and they did not receive the sort of welcome they had previously been used to.

¶ At the beginning of this year [1436] the Comte de Richemont, Constable of France, the bastard of Orléans, the Seigneurs de la Roche, l'Isle-Adam and Ternant, with Sir Simon de Lalaing, Sausse his brother, and other French and Burgundian leaders assembled a force of five or six thousand combatants and marched from Ponthieu towards Paris, hoping to gain entry to the city by means of overtures that had been made by the Seigneur de l'Isle-Adam to the Burgundian faction in Paris. After a halt of four or five hours, it became obvious that they would not achieve this aim, so they took up quarters in Aubervilliers, Montmartre and other villages. Next day they attacked the town of Saint-Denis, which was held by four or five hundred English, and took it by storm; some two hundred were killed and the rest fled to the Abbey of Le Velin, where they were besieged, but soon surrendered on the sparing of their lives, with the exception of certain local men who were to remain at the disposal of the conquerors.

The next day, Thursday, Sir Thomas Beaumont, who had recently come to Paris from Normandy with a force of six hundred English, marched from Paris to Saint-Denis to discover the disposition of the French forces. As soon as they saw him coming they made an attack in considerable strength, and very soon had the better of his troop; there were three hundred dead, and eighty were taken prisoner, including Sir Thomas. The remainder saved themselves by fleeing to Paris, and were pursued to the gates of the city. Meanwhile those Parisians who were the keenest supporters of the Duke of Burgundy, namely those in the district of Les Halles, certain members of the University, Michaut Lallier and other important citizens, seeing the losses the English had just sustained and the strength of the French and Burgundian forces outside the city, gathered together in groups and agreed among themselves to drive the English out of Paris and invite the French and Burgundians to take over. They sent word of this to the Seigneur de l'Isle-Adam, so that he could bring the others with him, and he in his turn informed the Constable of France and the other lords, who quickly agreed to march on Paris; early on Friday morning [13 April] they left Saint-Denis in fine array. Meanwhile Louis de Luxembourg, the Bishop of Thérouanne, with the bishops of Lisieux and Meaux and Lord Willoughby and others of

JOAN OF ARC AT THE SIEGE OF ORLÉANS

the English party began to fear that the common people might turn against them; they therefore posted their men in the Rue Saint-Antoine near the Bastille, furnished the Bastille itself with provisions and weapons of war, and kept their men armed and on the watch, ready to retreat to the Bastille if need arose.

When the French and Burgundians arrived outside Paris, near the Porte Saint-Jacques, on the other side of the river towards Montlhéry, they sent the Seigneur de l'Isle-Adam to parley with the men on the walls of the city. He showed them a general amnesty from King Charles of France, sealed with his great seal, and begged them earnestly to submit to the same King Charles at the request of the Duke of Burgundy, who was now reconciled to him, adding that in view of their constant loyalty to the duke they would remain under his governance. The Parisians listened to the gentle words of the Seigneur de l'Isle-Adam and others, and it was not long before they had accepted their offer and agreed together to admit them into the city. Ladders were quickly placed against the walls, and the Seigneur de l'Isle-Adam climbed up into the city, followed by the bastard of Orléans and numbers of their men. A large body of the Burgundian faction and the common people gathered with them and went through the streets shouting: 'Peace! Long live the king and the Duke of Burgundy!'

Shortly after this they opened the gates to admit the constable and other lords with all their armed followers, who at once marched towards the Bastille, where the English—the bishops and lords who had hoped to resist from that stronghold—had retreated. But their resistance was in vain, because their enemies were too numerous for them and they were soon driven back, and a few killed or taken prisoner. Barriers of heavy timber were then put up in front of the Bastille and armed men stationed in the Tournelles and other parts near by, to prevent the English from making a sally. Everything they had left in their houses was taken and shared out, and some of their chief supporters were put in prison and their goods confiscated. New officers were appointed to govern the town in the name of King Charles.

The Bishop of Thérouanne, Lord Willoughby and others in the Bastille held a parley with the Seigneur de Ternant and Sir Simon Lalaing in the name of the French, and it was concluded that if they were prepared to surrender the Bastille they could depart in safety with all their effects. The Constable of France gave them a safe-conduct, and they went by land and water to Rouen. As they left the

Parisians made great sport, shouting after them: 'À la queue!'* Thus the city of Paris resumed its loyalty to King Charles, and the English left by the gate leading to the country and came round about to their boats behind the Louvre. During all this the Bishop of Thérouanne lost all his communion plate, and most of his jewellery and rings, which fell into the constable's possession. However, he was well in favour with the Seigneur de Ternant and Sir Simon de Lalaing, and some of his property was collected from various parts of the town and secretly restored to him.

The Duke of Burgundy's standard was displayed at the gates of the city, to persuade the inhabitants to support his cause. The constable created some new knights—Sausse de Lalaing and Robert de Neuville from Picardy, with others of the French party. The constable remained in Paris for some time, and with him the Seigneur de Ternant, who was made provost of the city. Sir Sausse de Lalaing, the bastard of Orléans, and the others from Picardy returned to their various homes.

Bedford was replaced, as regent in France, by Richard, Duke of York; he and Talbot fought effectively to keep the French out of upper Normandy, though elsewhere in France the English were losing one town after another to the now united French forces.

In both England and France there was rapidly increasing poverty and a growing hatred of the war; bands of soldiers were leading a lawless life of private plunder; and in both countries there were treasonable plots against the crown—in France the Dauphin Louis's first attempt to get the better of his father, and in England perpetual squabbles in the council of regency.

¶ In this year 1437 wheat and other grains were so dear in France, and indeed throughout Christendom, that what had previously cost four sous of French money was now being sold for forty or even more. The result was widespread famine, and many of the poor people died of want: it was a pitiful sight to see them dying in large numbers on the dunghills of the great towns. There were some towns that turned these folk out of their gates, and others that welcomed them and ministered to their needs as long as they could do so through works of

* '*A le queue leu leu*' (*leu* is a Picard variant of *loup*, wolf) is a children's game in which the players hold on to each other in single file, the leader having to wheel round and catch hold of the player at the tail. In his poem *L'Espinette Amoureuse*, Froissart tells us that he played the game himself while at school. (In modern French the phrase has come to mean 'helter-skelter'.)

charity. Foremost among the welcoming cities was Cambrai. The famine lasted into the year 1439, and was the cause of many edicts by princes, lords and municipalities which forbade the removal of any corn crop from the area under their control. An order was published in Ghent that no beer or other liquor should be brewed, that all the poor people should kill their dogs, and that no one should keep a bitch unless it was spayed. These and similar decrees were issued in various parts, so that the poor and beggars might be able to subsist.

¶ At the beginning of this year [1438] the widespread famine that we have already mentioned increased greatly in severity, and great numbers of the poor continued to die pitifully each day. There were also fatal epidemics in many parts of France, particularly in Flanders, and the cities of Bruges and Paris suffered more than any others. The war, too, continued in great severity and was waged in various parts of the country.

Because of these three misfortunes many of the nobility and common people alike, in France and the surrounding countries, were reduced to a state of doubt and misery. Those bands of Frenchmen known as the skinners were operating on the borders of Burgundy, where they were causing considerable damage by taking castles, seizing prisoners, killing men and ravishing women of all classes, just as if they had been the enemies of France. When this was reported to the Duke of Burgundy he was extremely annoyed because of the suffering that was already widespread in this time of famine and epidemic.

It is not surprising that negotiations for peace should have continued, and they were maintained intermittently after Arras. Neither side had a stable government or the financial resources to set up an army that could achieve worthwhile results. France had probably the greater urge to fight, for her people were becoming more resolute and united in the desire to drive the English from their land, while England had only her diminishing imperial conquests to maintain, and her will to do so was weakened by dissension at home. Since Joan of Arc, and the reconciliation with Burgundy that was the logical result of her crowning of Charles VII, we can speak almost for the first time of France as one country.

Fighting had continued sporadically after the treaty of Arras, but to no conclusion; a few fortresses changed hands and Talbot had some successes in Normandy. In England the domestic quarrels, grouping themselves into a struggle between Gloucester and Cardinal Henry Beaufort of Winchester, saw the former party becoming the party of war and the latter that of negotiation with the Valois monarchy. In all the parleyings for peace that occurred the price to be paid for the release of Charles d'Orléans, a prisoner in England since Agincourt, was one of the first questions to be settled. He had been taken over to Arras by Beaufort, but when the ransom offered was too low and the negotiations had broken down he was brought back again to London.

Finally in 1440 he was released for a sum of 240,000 crowns, and the English hoped that he would be an advocate of the cause of peace in the French camp.

¶ Several attempts had been made, by ambassadors of the kings of France and England and the Duke of Burgundy, to obtain peace between the two kingdoms and to treat for the liberation of Charles, Duc d'Orléans, but they had had little success, for the English replies gave no hope of a treaty that would not be against the interests of the King of France; they were not ready to consider terms unless all their conquests in France, and in particular the duchies of Guyenne and Normandy, should be theirs without any reference to the sovereignty of France, and this the French king and his council would never grant.

As far as the Duc d'Orléans was concerned the English did not much wish to set him free, because several of them received large sums to cover his expenses; according to some who professed to know the secrets of the King of England this was one of the reasons why he was so long kept a prisoner. It would seem that if the King of France and those who were controlling the duke's affairs had decided not to send the sums in question his freedom would have been granted much sooner. However, I believe that all this was done honourably and with good intentions.

From the beginning of the negotiations the Duke of Burgundy had had a genuine desire to obtain the freedom of the Duc d'Orléans, partly because of their near relationship and partly so that on his return to France they might remain loyal friends and all the past dissensions due to their now dead fathers might be forgotten and never brought up again. He therefore frequently sent men to discuss with the duke and his advisers how he might most conveniently be set at liberty by the King of England. He moreover made inquiries whether the duke would be prepared to marry his niece the Duchess of Cleves, who was at that time a member of his household. He also asked whether, if his freedom could be obtained, he would be ready to sign a treaty of alliance with him and to undertake never to take any action against him or his family because of past quarrels, the King of France and the dauphin always excepted. The Duc d'Orléans, in consideration of his long imprisonment and the danger in which he had been and might remain, signified his agreement and gave his word as a prince that if the Duke of Burgundy could secure his release he would be glad to marry his niece and to agree to his further requests. Measures for his release were now actively pursued with the King of England and his council, and an agreement was reached that he should be freed if the Duke of Burgundy would give his sealed authority for the ransom agreed between them.

When this treaty had been duly concluded the Duc d'Orléans was given his full liberty. He gave his solemn promise that he would do all that lay in his power to secure a lasting peace between the two countries, and took his leave of the King of England and some of the nobility and left London, arriving with a safe-conduct a few days later at Calais, whence he was escorted to Gravelines by Sir John of Cornwall, Sir Robert Roos and other English knights. Here he was received by the Duchess of Burgundy and other great lords and knights. They all expressed great joy at this reunion, the duke for his deliverance and the duchess for his safe arrival. A few days later the Duke of Burgundy arrived to see him and as before great joy was expressed by all at seeing these two princes together. They embraced each other heartily several times, and for some time could find no words to express their pleasure.

The Duc d'Orléans first broke the silence and said: 'Upon my faith, dear cousin and brother, I owe more to you and my fair cousin your wife than to all the other princes of this realm, for if it had not been for you and her I should have remained in the hands of my enemies, and I have no better friends than you.' To this the Duke of Burgundy replied that it had weighed much on his mind that he had not done this sooner, and that he had long desired to ransom him. These and similar words were exchanged several times by the two princes, and the various nobles of each party who were present were overjoyed at this reunion, and particularly at the safe return of the Duc d'Orléans, who had for so long been a prisoner in the hands of his enemies the English, where he had been, in fact, from the Friday before All Saints in the year fourteen hundred and fifteen till the month of November in the year fourteen hundred and forty.

the english lose normandy

King Charles was now stirred into action by a fear that the union of Burgundy and Orléans might turn into a threat. In 1441 he took personal command of his army against Talbot and captured Pontoise and other towns near by, thus removing the English threat to Paris. In 1442 he led a six months' campaign in the south-west, taking Saint-Sever and Dax and threatening Bordeaux. Aquitaine was, in fact, becoming less well disposed towards the English, another sign of the remarkable unification of the French that had followed the life of Joan of Arc.

In 1443 the Duke of Somerset was sent to Normandy with an army and Richard, Duke of York, was asked to strengthen the defences of Rouen. Somerset proved a poor leader and his campaign was a failure. In 1444 it was proposed that William de la Pole, Earl (later Duke) of Suffolk, should lead a peace delegation to France, with Charles d'Orléans to join them as mediator. They met at Tours, the terms agreed being a two-year truce and the marriage of Henry VI to Marguerite, niece of the French king and daughter of René, Duc d'Anjou and King of Sicily; her dowry was the islands of Majorca and Minorca. The English claims to the French crown and to Normandy and Aquitaine were quietly ignored, yet Suffolk returned home to an enthusiastic welcome. Was England tired of the war and of the unrealistic claims of the Treaty of Troyes?

It is here that the second book of Monstrelet ends, and with it probably his own part in the rest of the work which usually bears his name. Suffolk's reputation slowly waned, especially when he arrested Gloucester, who died mysteriously in prison in 1447; his other rival, Richard of York, was sent out of the way as Lieutenant of Ireland. In France, Charles VII, under the strangely inspiring influence of his mistress, Agnès Sorel, was reforming his administration, his currency and above all his army. Only his son the Dauphin Louis showed opposition, and in 1445 Louis took refuge in Dauphiné. In the same year a French embassy was sent to England to negotiate a 'final peace'; this resulted in a renewal of the truce, on condition that the two kings met shortly and that Maine was ceded to René d'Anjou, Henry's father-in-law. When delays occurred in carrying out both conditions, Charles attacked Le Mans, chief city of Maine, and the English promptly withdrew their forces into Normandy. Somerset was then sent to Normandy, and he chose to initiate an offensive against Brittany; the attack on Fougères was made with his connivance.

¶ In this same year [1449], on the eve of the Feast of the Annunciation, the town and fortress of Fougères was taken and pillaged by Sir Francis de Surienne, called the Aragonian knight of the Order of the Garter, and a renowned leader of those parts of France which were under the dominion of the English, in open defiance of the truce between the two kings. Fougères is a very rich town, inhabited by many influential people and of great antiquity, situated in the duchy of Brittany on the borders of Normandy. Sir Francis was accompanied by six or seven hundred men-at-arms, some French-speaking and some English, who did all possible damage in the city, killing many, taking some prisoner, destroying churches, raping women, and seizing all the wealth they could lay their hands on. Not content with this, they overran the duchy, where they killed or took prisoners, ravaged the countryside and generally did every exploit that is customary in war.

When all this was reported to the Duke of Brittany he was most indignant at the capture of this town and sent the Bishop of Rennes and others to the king at Chinon to complain that in spite of the truce in which he had placed his trust, the English had taken his town and fortress of Fougères, and to beg him (as his humble servant and nephew) to grant help and support by declaring war on the English, since for his part he was ready to do so without sparing himself. The king sent a reply that he would not abandon the duke and would make common cause with him, as was only just; but to ensure that God was with them and to transfer the blame to his enemies, he would first summon the King of England to make reparation for these wrongs, through the Duke of Somerset, who was his deputy on this side of the sea, and who had full power to make such reparation for any infringement of the truce. Indeed, he hoped reparation would be made to avoid the trouble that would follow from a renewal of the war.

To this purpose he dispatched to the King of England his esquire-trenchant, Jean Hovart, and Jean Cousinot, one of the Masters of Requests in his household; to the Duke of Somerset he sent Pierre de Fontaines, the equerry of his stables. The replies from each were the same—that they disavowed what had been done by Sir Francis de Surienne, even though common report held that the assault had been made at the express orders of the king and the Duke of Somerset.

The Duke of Brittany, who had a more personal interest in the taking of Fougères, sent his own king-of-arms to the duke, requesting him to restore and repair the town of Fougères, and to make restitution for all the money, movable goods, jewellery and other effects which had there been seized, the whole being estimated at a price of sixteen hundred crowns. The reply he received was that the duke took no responsibility for the affair. When the herald and the other ambassadors had left, the Duke of Somerset, who had some desire to make amends for the action of Sir Francis in those parts, sent messengers to the king to offer excuses for what Sir Francis had done, while continuing to disclaim any responsibility and added that he was annoyed at the taking of the town. All this was so much empty talk, for when it came to offering to repair the damage of this treacherous act he would not make any firm suggestion, but merely asked that things should remain as they were for both parties, which was to his own advantage.

The King of France replied to this that if the Duke of Somerset was so displeased by the capture he should do his duty in accordance with the powers he possessed and make full reparation of the town and restore the property that had been unjustly seized, so that the truce might be maintained. If he would not do this, they could be sure that he would support his nephew of Brittany. As to guaranteeing the security of certain places held by the English, he would do no such thing. The Duke of Brittany had in his dominion great lords of his own blood and leaders and captains among the Bretons who were indignant at the capture of Fougères, and it was natural to expect that they would wish to take their revenge and to reconquer such places from the English. Let them therefore attend to the protection of their own towns, if they so wished. For his part he would protect his own.

When the English received this reply they asked the king to send ambassadors plenipotentiary to Louviers, for they knew that when they had returned to Rouen the Duke of Somerset would send some of his men to confer with them with a view to reaching some agreement. The king always preferred to employ gentle measures and avoid bloodshed, and therefore granted their request by appointing representatives. The English then left his court and returned to the Duke of Somerset, to whom they related all that had occurred between them and the King of France, and what agreement had been reached. The duke shortly afterwards sent some of his own men to Louviers to treat with those of the King of France, as it had been agreed.

While Charles was negotiating he allowed his captains to continue hostilities which resulted in the capture of some towns on the borders of Normandy and others in the Bordelais. In July a council was held at Chinon—Charles still hesitated to set up his Government in Paris—and here it was decided to break off all further negotiations and resume the war. Dunois was placed in command and set out from Beauvais, while other armies were to converge on Normandy from the south and west; this movement was to bring the end of English power in Normandy. Town after town was taken, either by capitulation or by the artillery of John Bureau, whom Charles had commissioned to modernize his equipment of war. In early October they camped by the Seine a few miles above Rouen, the king having now joined his army.

¶ On the tenth day of October [1449] the people of the city of Rouen gathered together in the palace of the archbishop, because of their great fear that the city would be attacked and destroyed by the French and also to avoid further bloodshed, having seen some of their own men killed in the recent assault. If at that moment they had come across Lord Talbot they would have murdered him as he had done their own kith and kin. But it was Lord Somerset they saw, and they told him it was high time to make a treaty with the King of France, for otherwise they would be ruined by starvation, as no corn, wood, meat or wine had been brought into the city for more than six weeks. These words were not very welcome to the duke, but when he looked round and saw that he had with him only fifty or sixty English and that there were present eight hundred or a thousand men of Rouen (not counting the rest of the inhabitants who were in armed groups in the streets) he was considerably alarmed and made a humble reply to the archbishop and people who were there, saying he was ready to fall in with the wishes of the townsfolk. To appease the populace, he then went to the Hôtel de Ville, where such assemblies are normally held, and there after some discussion it was agreed that the archbishop with certain English knights and citizens of the town should go to Port-Saint-Ouen to talk with the king or some members of his Council concerning the welfare of the city and its inhabitants.

An official of the town was first sent to the king at Pont-de-l'Arche to procure a safe-conduct for members of the Church, the army and the merchant corporations to come and discuss a settlement of their problems. This was granted, and the official returned with it to the archbishop and the duke. A party was then drawn up consisting of the archbishop and some notable citizens, together with some knights and squires representing the Duke of Somerset, and they left for Port-Saint-Ouen, about a league short of Pont-de-l'Arche, where they conferred with the Comte de Dunois, lieutenant-general to the king, the Chancellor of France, the Seneschal of Poitou, Sir Guillaume Cousinot and others who were representing the King of France. Their deliberations lasted some time, and an

BRITTANY AND NORMANDY

urgent plea was made for a general amnesty, so that those who wished to leave the town on the departure of the English could leave, and those who wished to stay could do so without molestation or loss of property. The English should be granted a safe-conduct for themselves and their possessions when they left. All these requests were accepted by the Comte de Dunois and other members of the king's council, as well as by the archbishop and his colleagues, who then promised to deliver the town to the king's obedience.

The archbishop and the other delegates left to make their report to the English and to the people of Rouen, but since they arrived there late in the evening they could not do so that night. On the next day, Saturday the eleventh, the archbishop and the others went early in the morning to the town hall to report to the English and to the townsfolk what had been discussed and what decisions had been reached between them and the king's representatives. The decisions were very welcome to the townsfolk, and most disagreeable to the English, who were astonished to find how anxious the people were to support the King of France—above all the duke and Lord Talbot. They left the Hôtel de Ville in an evil mood, and immediately armed themselves and withdrew to the palace, the bridges, the gates and the castle. When the citizens realized their intentions, they took alarm and they, too, armed themselves and established guards to keep watch all that Saturday and the night following, as did the English. During the night those citizens who were anxious to expel the English for not being ready to accept the terms of the treaty sent a messenger to Pont-de-l'Arche, who arrived at dawn on Sunday to tell the king that if he would send a party to their aid they would open their gates to his men.

On Sunday the twelfth of October, at eight o'clock in the morning, the townsmen who formed the guards attacked all the English they found armed in the streets and set upon them with such ferocity that they had difficulty in joining their comrades at the bridge, in the palace and the castle; the English lost seven or eight in the fighting, but the townsmen gained possession of the walls, the gates and the towers. The Comte de Dunois now set off in great haste to bring speedy help to the townsfolk, with a large company of men-at-arms. Among them was Floquet, the Bailiff of Évreux, but having had no time to put on his greaves he was so badly kicked by one of the horses in the troop that he had to be carried back to Pont-de-l'Arche to recover, after handing over the command of his men to the Seigneur de Maulny.

When this company reached the outskirts of Rouen they called on the military in the Faubourg Sainte-Catherine* to surrender that place to the king. While this was proceeding the king had set out for Rouen from Pont-de-l'Arche with a large company of men-at-arms and archers. He ordered his artillery to be charged for an attack on Sainte-Catherine, but this proved an unnecessary precaution. The captain of that place had no more than six score English with him and could see the numbers of the relieving force; he knew, moreover, that the king was also on his way and was anxious to do nothing to offend him. He therefore surrendered the place to the Comte de Dunois, and the English were allowed to leave and go wherever they wished. Until the king's arrival the men of the Bailiff of Évreux were set to guard the place. For the protection of the English, a herald was delegated to conduct them in safety as far as Port-Saint-Ouen. On their way they met the king, who ordered them to take nothing from the countryfolk as they passed without paying for it; when they replied that they had no money or other means of making payment,

* This occupied the north-western end, nearest the city, of the chalky outcrop now known as Bon-Secours.

he gave them a hundred francs to defray their expenses. They then went off unmolested, and with what few possessions they had brought, to Honfleur or other places of their choice. The king went ahead, and camped that night at Sainte-Catherine.

In pursuance of the plan to take Rouen, the Comte de Dunois and the other lords, with the companies under their command, came to the gate known as Martainville, on the Paris side of the city, with the king's banners unfurled, and drew up in battle order as close as possible to the fortifications of that gate. Here the citizens came and presented the keys of the city to the Comte de Dunois, and asked him to send in as many armed men as he could. He told them he would obey their wishes. After further exchange of words concerning the welfare of the city, Sir Pierre de Bresé, Seneschal of Poitou, was ordered to enter the city with archers and a hundred lance, followed by the Seigneur de Maulny with a hundred lance, a body of archers most of whom were the men of Robert de Floques, and archers and a hundred lance from the Comte de Dunois' own men. They took up stations as close as possible to the English: the Comte de Dunois' men in front of the palace, in which were the Duke of Somerset and Lord Talbot with twelve hundred English; the Seigneur de Maulny between the palace and the castle; the Seneschal of Poitou in front of the castle; all the other captains went and camped in the fields of the faubourgs Cauchoise and Beauvoisine. This army of the King of France was a wonderful sight to see; never within memory had there been so fine a king's army, with so many lords, barons, knights, squires and men assembled at one time.

In the evening of the same day the English surrendered the bridge, and the Seigneur de Herainvillier was appointed to guard it. On the following day the gates of Rouen were opened, and any man who wished could come in or out at leisure. When the Duke of Somerset saw the strength of the forces under the royal command he was heavy-hearted and asked to be allowed to speak to the king, who was very glad to receive the request. On the fifth day following the duke set out from the palace, with a small body of his own men and escorted by some of the king's heralds, who took him to Saint Catherine's Hill to see the king, with the King of Sicily, the Comte de Dunois, and others of the council and princes of the blood royal. Also present were the Patriarch of Antioch, the Archbishop of Rouen and several other bishops. When the duke had made his reverence to the king he requested that he and Lord Talbot, and the remainder of the English should be allowed to leave the city unmolested, as others of the town had done, in accordance with the amnesty which had been agreed by him and the members of his council. After careful thought the king replied that this request was unreasonable, seeing that he had not been prepared to accept the terms of the amnesty, but had in contempt of the treaty occupied, and was still occupying, the palace and castle of the city of Rouen against all his wishes. Nor had he allowed the citizens of Rouen to surrender their city, but had done everything by his resistance to prevent such a surrender, thus making himself ineligible for the benefits of the amnesty. Before they could be allowed to leave the palace, they must now surrender to him the towns of Honfleur, Harfleur and all other strongholds in the Pays de Caux now held by the King of England. On hearing this the duke took his leave of the king and was escorted back to the palace by the Comte d'Eu and the Comte de Clermont, and on his way he observed everyone in the streets wearing the white cross,* and was not much cheered by the sight.

¶ On Wednesday the twenty-second of October the king gave orders for the palace and castle of Rouen to be besieged by a company of eight hundred lance accompanied by archers; he also ordered deep trenches to be dug around the palace, both in the town and in the fields, and had bombards and cannons immediately placed on these two sides opposite the gates of the palace. When the Duke of Somerset saw all these preparations he was not a little alarmed, for he knew that they had scanty provisions in the palace for so many men. He therefore sent to ask the king for permission to go and speak with him on Thursday the twenty-third, an interview which the king was very ready to grant. The duke left the palace accompanied by some forty of his principal knights and squires. He was dressed in a long robe of blue figured velvet lined with sable fur, wearing a hat of crimson velvet trimmed with sable, and he was escorted through the town by the French king's heralds to the barbican of the city gate, where he was met by the Comte de Clermont, elder son of the Duc de Bourbon, and other barons, knights and squires, who conducted him to the hill of Sainte-Catherine, where the king received him very warmly in a richly decorated apartment, having in his company the King of Sicily, the Comtes du Maine, de Dunois, de Nevers, de Clermont, de Saint-Pol, de Castres, de Tancarville, the Vicomte de

* French soldiers at this time wore a white Greek cross on a red ground, the English a red cross on white, while the Burgundians wore a red Saint Antony's cross or tau.

Loumaigne, and other lords, knights and squires whom it would be tedious to enumerate.

When the duke had made his greetings to the king he requested his majesty to grant to him and to the English who were in the castle and the palace the same amnesty that he had granted to the townsfolk. To this the king again replied in fair words that by the treaty made at Port-Saint-Ouen the same terms for an amnesty had indeed been offered to them as to the town, but that he and the rest of the English had been sufficiently ill advised to refuse them. His request was therefore unreasonable and could not be entertained. The duke then took leave of the king and returned to the palace with his men, escorted for their safety by the Comtes de Clermont, d'Eu and de Castres.

The king now renewed his orders to the Comte de Dunois, his lieutenant-general, to have trenches and ditches dug all round the palace—on the side of the fields as well as the town—so as to facilitate their means of attack. Dunois carried out these orders with such skill and knightly courage that the English were completely unable to leave the palace or the castle on any side. On the twenty-fourth day of October the English demanded a parley with the Comte de Dunois, and a truce was granted by both sides for this purpose. When the Bailiff of Évreux, the Maréchal de la Fayette and other members of the king's council had been summoned to join the lieutenant-general, the conversations were begun. The truce had to be prolonged from day to day for a period of twelve days, all because the English were not prepared to accept a treaty requiring Lord Talbot to be left behind as a hostage. After long discussion between the two sides, however, it was agreed that the Duke of Somerset, who was governor for the King of England, with his wife and children and the remainder of the English in the castle and the palace, should be allowed to leave and go where they chose and take their belongings with them, exception being made only for the prisoners and the heavy artillery. Within a year they were to pay to the king the sum of fifty thousand crowns, and six thousand to those with whom the treaty had been made. They further promised to make a faithful settlement of all that they owed to the innkeepers, townsfolk, merchants and anyone else in the city.

The Duke of Somerset and his companions also gave assurances that they would deliver to the King of France or his representatives the castle of Arques, the town of Caudebec, the castles of Tancarville and Lillebonne and the towns of Honfleur and Montivilliers. Apart from his written assurances, the Duke of Somerset left as hostages for their fulfilment Lord Talbot and seven other English noblemen.

When this treaty had been concluded the Duke of Somerset and the other English left the palace on Tuesday the fourth of November, making straight for Harfleur, either by boat or on land. The hostages were left in the hands of the king's men in Rouen. In accordance with the agreement the duke ordered Sir Thomas Hoo and Fulk Hoo to restore to the king all those towns that were named; this they did with the exception of Honfleur, where the governor Thomas Curzon refused to surrender the place, with the result that Lord Talbot remained a prisoner of the French. On Monday the tenth of November, the eve of the Feast of Saint Martin, the Comte de Dunois and the bailiff of Rouen had the king's banner hoisted on the palace, the castle and the gates of the city by one of the king's heralds, in the presence of all the most notable citizens of the town.

By the end of the winter the English held only the country around Caen and Bayeux, and most of the Cotentin. The prospect of losing Normandy aroused the English Parliament, and an army (of something under 3,000 men) was sent out under Sir Thomas Kyriell. They landed at Cherbourg on 15 March 1450 and advanced on Bayeux, but not without waiting to collect reinforcements and recapture Valognes, a delay which allowed the French forces to collect near Caen. On the 15th of April a battle was fought at Formigny which sealed the fate of Normandy. Kyriell's troops were successfully engaging those of the Comte de Clermont, when the constable, Richemont, arrived in the rear of the English and routed them almost to a man.

Before England could carry out Sir John Fastolf's project to raise another army the French had taken Bayeux, Caen and Falaise; in this last siege Talbot was released as a condition of the town's capitulation, but he had to promise never again to wear armour against the French. Only Cherbourg remained.

¶ The siege of Cherbourg was begun under the direction of the Comte de Richemont, the Constable of France, who commanded a large force of lords, knights and squires, and was carried on with great valour on the part of all the French. The besieged were severely harried by the trenches, mines and other methods of attack, though the French lost a knight and a squire from Brittany; they were Sir Pregent de Coëtivy, Seigneur de Retz, who was killed by a cannon shot—a great loss to the king, for he was one of the most renowned and valiant knights in France, rich in wisdom and experience—and

Tuddual le Bourgeois, Bailiff of Troyes, of great courage on foot or on horseback and highly reputed for his skill in the arts of war, who was killed by a shot from a culverin.

The town received such a heavy battering from cannons and bombards that the like had never been seen before. There were even bombards situated on the sea shore between high and low tide, which were loaded with boulders; although they were under water when the tide was in, they were covered over with greased skins so that the sea did no harm to their powder, and as soon as the tide went out the cannoneers removed the coverings and continued firing into the town, to the great astonishment of the English, who had never seen anything like it. Four bombards and one cannon burst while firing at the town, and great deeds of bravery were performed on sea and land, but more to the detriment of the English than in their cause.

Because of all this the English governor, Thomas Gonville, esquire, who had a thousand fighting men under his command, asked for a treaty with the constable and it was granted. The terms were that Gonville should hand over the town and castle to the King of France, on condition that one of his sons, who was held as a hostage for the payment of the sums due to the king and the town of Rouen, should be restored to him. As soon as his son was freed, he surrendered the town and castle of Cherbourg to the king's representatives on the twelfth day of August [1450]. He then left the town with his son and his soldiers and their baggage, and sailed to England. The king appointed the Seigneur de Bueil as governor and gave him eighty lance and a body of archers.

Thus was completed the conquest of the duchy of Normandy; all her cities, towns and fortresses had been won over to the king within the space of a year and six days, which was a wonderful achievement, for never had so large a province been conquered in so short a time or with so little destruction of life and property. This was greatly to the honour of the King of France, the princes and all the lords and others who had been with him, and a matter for thanks to God to whom praise and glory are due. . . .

¶ If I were to mention all the valiant men and all the gallant actions of this reconquest of Normandy, there would be no end to my writing. But I must nevertheless make some mention of the chief features of the campaign for the benefit of those who in future times will wish to read of them.

In the first place the King of France organized his army campaign, and in particular his men-at-arms, in most admirable fashion. He equipped his fighting-men and archers with good, sound clothing and armour—the men-at-arms in cuirasses, greaves, light helmets called salades, silver-hilted swords, and a lance for their pages; each also had three horses, one for himself, one for his page and one for his servant, who was equipped with a salade, a brigandine or corslet, a jacket or haubergeon, a battle-axe or a halberd. Each man-at-arms had two archers on horseback, also equipped with brigandines, greaves and salades, mostly decorated with silver, though some had stout jackets and haubergeons. All these soldiers were paid regularly each month, and during the campaign none of them would dare to make any prisoners or ransom any horse or other beast, unless they belonged to the English or their allies, nor to seize provisions anywhere without paying for them, again unless they were in the possession of the English engaged in warfare, for they could lawfully seize only these latter . . .

The king had similarly made provision concerning artillery for his defence and for attacking towns and fortresses. Never in living memory had there been such an assemblage of large bombards, heavy cannon, veuglaires, serpentines, mortars, culverins and ribaudekins and these were amply provisioned with powder, protective coverings known as cats, a great number of carts to transport them, and everything else necessary for the capture of towns and castles, and well provided with men to operate them all. They all received their pay daily, and were placed under the command of master Jean Bureau, treasurer of France, and Jasper Bureau, his brother, master of the artillery. These two men endured great dangers and hardships throughout the campaign, for they were very attentive to their duty. It was an inspiring sight to see how they organized the bulwarks, trenches, ditches and mines at every siege that was laid during the campaign. Indeed, there was not a single besieged town or fortress that surrendered which would not have fallen to the skill of these assailants, if it had not been for the clemency of the king, who insisted on a treaty of surrender to avoid the spilling of blood and the destruction of his towns . . .

Thus King Charles of France, the seventh of his name, had by the grace of God chiefly, and also by the skill and wisdom of his knights and counsellors and soldiers of all ranks, regained his duchy of Normandy which had been occupied for thirty years by his ancient enemies the English. He had placed the whole province under his power, and made provision for new government, and for police and military garrisons in each city, town and fortress, all the while trusting in the grace and mercy of the King of Kings, who wills that every man should have his own, as it is written in a passage in Saint Matthew, addressed to the Pharisees: 'Render unto Caesar the things which are Caesar's; and unto God the things that are God's', which means that we should give to every man his own. Because of this he resolved to march into Guyenne and Bordeaux, which had been occupied by the English since time immemorial, against all reason and against the gospel passage just quoted. The nobles and people of that land have always been rebellious against the crown of France—or at least for two hundred years, which is a considerable time—although it forms part of the kingdom of France.

the end of the war

Aquitaine was now more or less emptied of English troops, and it seemed that Charles had only to assemble his forces and his artillery to win back the duchy after 300 years of occupation, and this he set about doing. In June 1451, however, some French entered Bordeaux and took possession of the city; the citizens sent some of their number to England to beg Henry to liberate them. England was at that time torn with internal worries—the banishment and death of Suffolk, Jack Cade's rebellion, and the sudden return from Ireland of Richard, Duke of York—but an army was nevertheless raised and sent out under John Talbot, Earl of Shrewsbury. Soon after they landed in October 1452 the French garrison was thrown out of Bordeaux.

Meanwhile Charles was completing his preparations, and by late spring 1453 he had initiated a three-pronged attack on the duchy, in the manner that had been so successful in Normandy.

¶ In the year 1453 the King of France left the city of Tours and took up residence in his castle at Lusignan. Meanwhile John Talbot, Earl of Shrewsbury, laid siege to the castle of Fronsac, which was governed for the King of France by Joachim Rouault; the French were forced to surrender to the English before the king's army was ready to help them, and they marched away with arms and baggage . . .

On the thirteenth of July the French laid siege to Castillon-sur-Dordogne in Périgord, which was held by the English. The Seigneurs de Lohéac and Jalogne, Marshals of France, were sent to conduct the siege, along with many other lords, barons, knights, squires, captains and combatants, to the number of sixteen to eighteen hundred men-at-arms and archers. The king's artillery, both heavy and light, was also sent there under the charge of Jean Bureau, and his brother Jasper Bureau, master of the royal artillery; their company consisted of seven hundred gunners, whom the brothers instructed to dig trenches round the field containing the artillery, before the siege was begun.

When Talbot heard of this he immediately left Bordeaux in haste with eight hundred to a thousand English horse, attended by some of the most valiant lords and knights in the whole realm of England and from the Bordelais, and followed by from four to six thousand English on foot. Talbot and his men arrived before Castillon soon after dawn on Wednesday the seventeenth of July. When the French heard that he had come they withdrew into the field surrounded by ditches, but Talbot caught up with some of the foot-archers before they could enter it; these they attacked, killing some five or six score. At this stage the French made increased efforts to get into the enclosure as the English marched towards them, fully expecting them to flee and abandon the siege. While waiting for the rest of his foot-soldiers to come on, Talbot had a cask of wine set up for the refreshment of his men; meanwhile the French were able to enter the enclosure from various sides and re-establish their ranks, and the gunners set up their culverins and ribaudekins on the dykes facing the English.

The besieged within Castillon had found means to inform Talbot that if he marched quickly to their relief the French would flee. On his arrival, however, he was astonished to find that the French had prepared an entrenched artillery camp.

Talbot and his men now marched right up to the barrier, expecting to make an entry into the field; but they found themselves courageously opposed by a body of valiant men, well tried in war, which was surprising after the information they had received. Talbot was riding a small hackney, and remained in the saddle because of his age,* but he ordered all the other riders to dismount. As they arrived the English marched under eight banners, those of England, Saint George, the Trinity, Lord Talbot and four others skilfully executed.

The attack then began, with great show of valour and hard fighting on each side, and lasted for a full hour. At this point the Duke

* He was 86 or 87, and wore no armour, in accordance with the promise he had given at Falaise.

of Brittany's men, who had been sent to the king under the chief command of the Comte d'Étampes, were sent for to relieve the French who had laboured to defend the barriers. When they arrived with the Seigneur de Montauban and the Seigneur de la Hunodaie in command, the French, who had fought all day and with renewed courage at the sight of these reinforcements, were able with the help of God and their own skill to turn the English back, and the Bretons fell upon them and trampled all their banners underfoot. In the camp there was such a noise of culverins and ribaudekins being loaded that the English were forced to flee. Many, however, were killed in the field, and Lord Talbot's hackney was struck down by a shot from a culverin and he was killed where he lay beneath the horse.* Also among the slain was his son, Lord de Lisle . . .

Since the French were on foot and so exhausted by their labours that they could not engage in pursuit, many of the English and Gascons escaped; between eight hundred and a thousand took refuge in the fortified town of Castillon. Those who could not reach the town made off where they could by land or water, though the latter were for the most part drowned. The Comte de Penthièvre, the Bailiff of Touraine and others of the French mounted their horses, pursued and killed the English as far as Saint-Émilion. Some four or five hundred English were buried by the French. Next day the commanders ordered all the cannon, veuglaires and bombards to be ranged before the walls of Castillon to cheer the inhabitants.† When they saw all these preparations being made they became more humble and abandoned the pride that had filled them by surrendering themselves as prisoners, to the number of fifteen hundred. The chief lords among them were made the personal prisoners of the king.

¶ . . . On the seventeenth of July the king marched from the city of Angoulême into the Bordelais, to bring reinforcements to his army, and reached the town of Libourne with a great company of nobles and knights. At this time his army was before Fronsac, which had been held by the English, but they surrendered and were allowed to leave for England with nothing but a stave in their hands. This done, the king crossed the Dordogne with his army, in order to reduce to his obedience the lands between that river and the Gironde. Here they took many small towns and castles from the English, and passed

* In his honour a chapel, known as Notre-Dame de Talbot, was erected on the battlefield of the victorious French captains.

† As opposed to the English garrison.

on to Montferrant, where the king gave orders for part of his army to erect a blockhouse at Lormont, which is not far from Bordeaux, while the remainder were to lay siege to the fortified town of Cadillac. The Comte de Clermont, at that time lieutenant-general in Guyenne and the Bordelais, with certain other lords and a company of a thousand lance and attendant archers, were posted near Bordeaux in the direction of the Landes to destroy all the hay, corn and other provisions so that those within the city might not be able to use them.

On the eighteenth the king in person led his army against Cadillac and the town was taken by storm; the first to enter the town was a squire named Geoffroy de Saint-Belin, Bailiff of Chaumont-en-Bassigny. The English then withdrew into the castle, which was particularly well fortified. But in spite of their security, they could see the strength and good discipline of the French army, amounting as we have said to a thousand lance apart from the archers, and in the month of October they gave themselves up as prisoners to the king, their captain, named Gaillard, being beheaded. In the blockhouse at Lormont was the Seigneur de Lohéac, Marshal of France, with other nobles, fifteen or sixteen hundred lance, and a body of archers and artillery men with their weapons. Anchored near by in the Gironde was the king's fleet of armed provision ships, from Brittany, Poitou, Spain, Holland, Zeeland and Flanders, and there they remained until the surrender of Bordeaux.

Similarly there were the provision ships sent by the English, and as soon as they arrived Sir Roger de Camoys had their sailing gear impounded in the city, so that they could not leave *hospite insaluto*, that is to say, without taking leave of their hosts. The English also constructed a blockhouse opposite to the French one, but loftier, though it was not much use to them, in spite of the distinguished company of English in the town, which included Sir Roger Camoys, Lord Clinton, the bastard of Somerset, the Seigneur de l'Esparre, a Gascon, the Seigneur de Rosem, with three or four thousand Englishmen, and as many of their party from Gascony, of whom half were quartered in the town and the other half in the blockhouse to guard the ships.

These two forces in the blockhouses opposite each other were engaged in the protection of their respective ships from the first day of August to the seventeenth of October, and in doing as much damage or annoyance each day as they could manage to do. When the English found themselves being seriously affected by lack of provisions they began to take alarm, particularly since reports were reaching them of the loss of one place after another to the King of France, and they sent a request for reasonable terms of capitulation. The king was ready to listen for two reasons, firstly because he was always prepared to render good for evil, and secondly because he could envisage the slaughter that might follow and he wanted to improve relationships. He was therefore glad to make an agreement with the English on the following terms: the city of Bordeaux was to be made over to him; all its inhabitants were to remain his loyal and obedient subjects and take an oath never to rebel against the French crown, in recognition that the King of France was their sovereign lord. The English were to be allowed to leave by sea for England, or for Calais if they preferred. Since some of the barons in the city and surrounding lands had treacherously visited England to seek help against the oath of loyalty they had made to the king the previous year, so that he had to expend great labour and expense in re-conquering the territory, some twenty of these persons were banished from the Bordelais. This treaty was signed on the seventeenth day of October.

The king had worked for this conclusion with all his strength and all his resources, as well as his intelligence. For after the help of God, it was his own skill in leadership, the gentle welcome he gave to those who returned to his obedience and the encouragement he gave to his men as he went about that enabled him to regain peacefully the mastery of his lands. All his vassals and all his allies served him in the same spirit and with the same vigour, behaving always as though the king's cause was their personal interest, and they and their heirs deserved the utmost praise.

With the capture of Bordeaux in October 1453 hostilities came to an end. No treaty was signed, and England did not renounce her claim to the throne of France; indeed, the fleur-de-lis remained on her royal arms until 1801. If the real cause of the war had been the nature of the homage to be paid for the fief of Aquitaine, then the war lapsed because there was now no fief for which homage could be paid or refused.

This same year saw the capture of Constantinople by the Turks and the decline into madness of Henry VI. France was utterly exhausted by war and civil war; England was about to succumb to a civil war which would make it impossible to think of reconquering Aquitaine. She retained only Calais and the tiny county of Guines near by. Charles d'Orléans, the French poet who had been a prisoner in England for twenty-five years after Agincourt, tells in his Ballade CI how God punished the English for their pride in thinking to control a part of France and struck Henry with madness because they had so often betrayed their king—

De sa verge Dieu les pugnist et bat
Et t'a rendu Guyenne et Normandie.

It could be argued that Henry inherited his madness through his mother, the daughter of Charles le fou.

When Charles VII died eight years later the chronicler records his achievements without any mention of what he owed to Joan of Arc, whose rehabilitation had been proclaimed in 1456.

¶ On the twenty-second day of July in the year 1461 King Charles the Seventh of France departed this life in the fifty-eighth year of his life and the thirty-ninth of his reign. In the beginning of his reign fortune was so much against him that he lost all that part of his kingdom which extended from Flanders and the English Channel to the Loire, and which was taken from him by the efforts of King Henry the Fifth of England, who had married his sister and who laid claim to the crown of France with the support of the Duke of Burgundy. King Charles had ordered or consented to the murder of this duke's father, Jean, in the town of Montereau-sur-Yonne, in spite of the fact that they had shortly beforehand sworn a pact of friendship, sealing it on the true body of Christ by receiving the wafer divided between them: to have gone back on such a promise of friendship—held to be inviolate—was a heinous and dishonourable crime which cannot be too strongly condemned. In time, however, the noble Duke Philippe of Burgundy, in loyalty to the crown of France, would not see the destruction of so noble a kingdom and the crown falling into the hands of her ancient enemies the English, and at the earnest request of King Charles made a treaty of reconciliation with him at Arras in the thirty-fifth year of the king's reign.

From this moment King Charles's fortunes so prospered that he regained all his kingdom from the English, with the exception of Calais, Guines and Hammes, which are situated in the Comté du Boulonnais. After these conquests, he always kept on foot an army of fifteen hundred lance and five or six thousand archers, who received regular wages as follows—for men-at-arms with three horses, fifteen florins a month from the Royal Mint, and for archers seven florins a month. These sums were raised by taxes on the good towns and villages, and so regularly collected that the payments were never in arrears.

The men-at-arms conducted themselves so honourably throughout the kingdom that no robbers or brigands dared to infest the roads for fear of being found and caught by the military, who helped the officers of justice to hunt them out wherever they gathered. These men-at-arms also guided and escorted merchants and other travellers, so that they could now go from place to place in safety. Everyone was pleased with this admirable change in the state of affairs, for previously all travellers had been subject to the Skinners, who robbed and pillaged everybody.

It was this King Charles who established in his kingdom the tax known as the Fourth, which was levied for the royal purse on all retail sales of wine. When this tax was first instituted it was said that only one-hundredth would be taken for the king. From a hundredth it became a fiftieth, then a twentieth, then an eighth, and finally a quarter, which is a great burden to those who sell and even greater to those that must pay it.

Before his reconciliation with Duke Philippe of Burgundy, King Charles led a very devout life, but after he had regained his kingdom he changed his ways, keeping women of evil reputation in his household and abandoning the company of his lawful wife; he required that his court should pay greater honour to them than to the queen, and they were more richly clothed than she, which was a very bad example from so noble a person. As for his kingdom, however, he governed that nobly and wisely, and showed many virtues in the maintenance of justice throughout the land.

appendix

[1]

FROISSART ON THE ENGLISH

IN THE ROME MANUSCRIPT*

The English are men of a haughty disposition, hot-tempered and quickly moved to anger, difficult to pacify and to bring to sweet reasonableness. They take delight in battles and slaughter. They are extremely covetous of the possessions of others, and are incapable by nature of joining in friendship or alliance with a foreign nation. They are underhand and proud. There are no more untrustworthy people under the sun than the middle classes in England.

There is in England a very great difference between the outlook of the nobles on one hand and that of the middle classes and the common people on the other, for the gentlefolk are upright and loyal by nature, while the ordinary people are cruel, perfidious and disloyal. Yet when the people wish to show their animosity and their own power the nobles offer no resistance. For a long time they have been in complete agreement, for the nobles only ask that the people should be reasonable; they will not allow them to have anything—even an egg or a chicken—without paying for it. The craftsmen and peasants in England live by the work of their hands; the nobles by the income from their lands. If the king requires their services they are paid, but the king cannot tax his people, nor would they put up with being taxed. There are certain agreed taxes on the wool trade, and these are an additional revenue for the king above that of his lands. When he is at war this tax is doubled.

England is the best-protected country in the world; otherwise its people could not continue to exist. Any man who is king of that country must conform to the will of the people and bow to many of their wishes. If he fails to do this, and misfortune comes to the country, he will be thrown over, as happened to this King Edward [II] of whom I have been speaking, the son of that other Edward who was so full of valour that he overcame the Scots in many battles.

* Ed. Luce, t.I, 2e partie, p. 214.

appendix

[2]

BIBLIOGRAPHY

JEAN LE BEL

Chroniques
ed. J. Viard and E. Déprez, Société de l'Histoire de France, Paris, 2 volumes, 1904–5

JEAN FROISSART

Chroniques
Volumes I–VIII, ed. S. Luce, 1869–88
Volumes IX–XI, ed. G. Raynaud, 1889–99
Volume XII, ed. L. Mirot, 1931
Volume XIII, ed. L. Mirot and A. Mirot, 1957
Société de l'Histoire de France, Paris.
This edition is in course of publication, and at present ends at Book III, §176.

Œuvres
Volumes I–XVI: Text of the 'Chroniques'
Volumes XIX–XXV: Glossary and analytical tables
ed. Kervyn de Lettenhove, Brussels, 1867–77

L'Espinette Amoureuse
ed. A. Fourrier, Klincksieck, Paris, 1963.

Chronicles
translated by John Bourchier, Lord Berners (1523–5), ed. W. P. Ker, Tudor Translations, 8 volumes, 1927–8
translated by Thomas Johnes (1802–5), Routledge, 2 volumes, 1874

ENGUERRAND DE MONSTRELET

Chroniques
'A Paris, chez Marc Orry', 1603, 3 volumes

La Chronique
ed. L. Douët-d'Arcq, Société de l'Histoire de France, 6 volumes, Paris, 1857–62

Chronicles
translated by Thomas Johnes (1810), William Smith, London, 2 volumes, 1840

E. PERROY
The Hundred Years War trans. W. B. Wells, Eyre & Spottiswoode, London 1951

M. MCKISACK
The Fourteenth Century The Oxford History of England, 1959
E. F. JACOB
The Fifteenth Century The Oxford History of England, 1961
A. H. BURNE
The Crecy War Eyre and Spottiswoode, 1955
The Agincourt War Eyre and Spottiswoode, 1956
W. ROTHWELL
The hours of the day in medieval French article in French Studies, July 1959
G. G. COULTON
The Chronicler of European Chivalry Studio Publications, 1930
H. S. BENNETT
Chaucer and the Fifteenth Century O.U.P., 1947

appendix

[3]

INDEX OF SOURCE REFERENCES

The beginning of a new section in the original text is marked by the sign ¶.

I JEAN LE BEL

(Edition of the Société de l'Histoire de France)

page	
25	Prologuc
27	XIV
29	XVII
31	XX
33	XIX
35	XXV
39	XXVII
41	XXVIII
44	XXIX
44	XXX
48	XXXI
49	XXXII
53	Froiss., t.1 §88
58	LXX
62	LXXI
68	LXXII
74	LXXIII
75	LXXVI
76	LXXX
81	LXXXI

II FROISSART

The extent of insertions from variant MSS is indicated by the sign ||.

(Edition of the Société de l'Histoire de France)

page	§
	Livre Premier
87	t.1 Prologue
91	t.5 § 371
92	372
95	373
96	374
98	375
99	376
100	377
102	MS d'Amiens
102	t.5 § 378
104	379
105	MS B 6
105	t.5 § 380
107	MS d'Amiens
107	t.5 § 381
108	382

page	§
109	383
109	384
112	385
112	386
113	387
115	388
116	389
117	391
117	392
119	393
120	394
121	395
122	396
123	397
124	398
126	399

page	§
128	403
136	t.7 § 662
136	663
137	665
138	666
139	MS d'Amiens
140	t.7 § 667
141	668
142	t.8 § 669
144	670
145	672
147	694
147	695
148	696
151	697
152	698
153	699
154	700
155	705
157	706
158	707
159	708
160	709
161	710
162	711
162	712

page	§
164	713
166	714
167	715
168	716
170	773
170	774
171	775
171	776
172	777
173	778
174	779
176	780
177	781
	Livre Troisième
180	t.12 § 57
181	58
182	t.13 § 102
182	103
184	104
185	105
188	116
190	117
191	118
192	120
198	121

(Edition of Kervyn de Lettenhove; the sections are not numbered)

page	§
199	t.13 p.105
200	273
201	297
202	315
	Livre Quatrième
204	t.14 p.1
205	5
216	t.15 p.35
224	53
226	76
227	79

page	§
229	84
234	140
238	148
239	156
240	167
242	182
245	232
245	237
247	t.16 p.198
251	203
251	204
254	233

III MONSTRELET

(Edition of 1603; the chapters are numbered in the first book only)

page	chapter	page	chapter
	Livre premier	294	38b
258	ch. 36	296	41b
264	101	298	42b
266	141	299	43b
268	142	301	44b
270	144	302	45a
271	145	306	47b
273	146	307	48a
276	147	309	51b
282	188	311	58b
286	223	311	59a
288	233	313	72a
290	265	316	78a
292	267	317	120b
		320	127a
	Livre deuxième	322	151a
293	p. 1b	323	155b
294	37b	324	176b

(Anonymous continuer of Monstrelet)

page	chapter	page	chapter
	Livre troisième		
327	p. 6b	336	32a
329	19a	338	56b
333	20b	340	58a
335	31b	343	86a

appendix

[4]

GENEALOGICAL TABLE

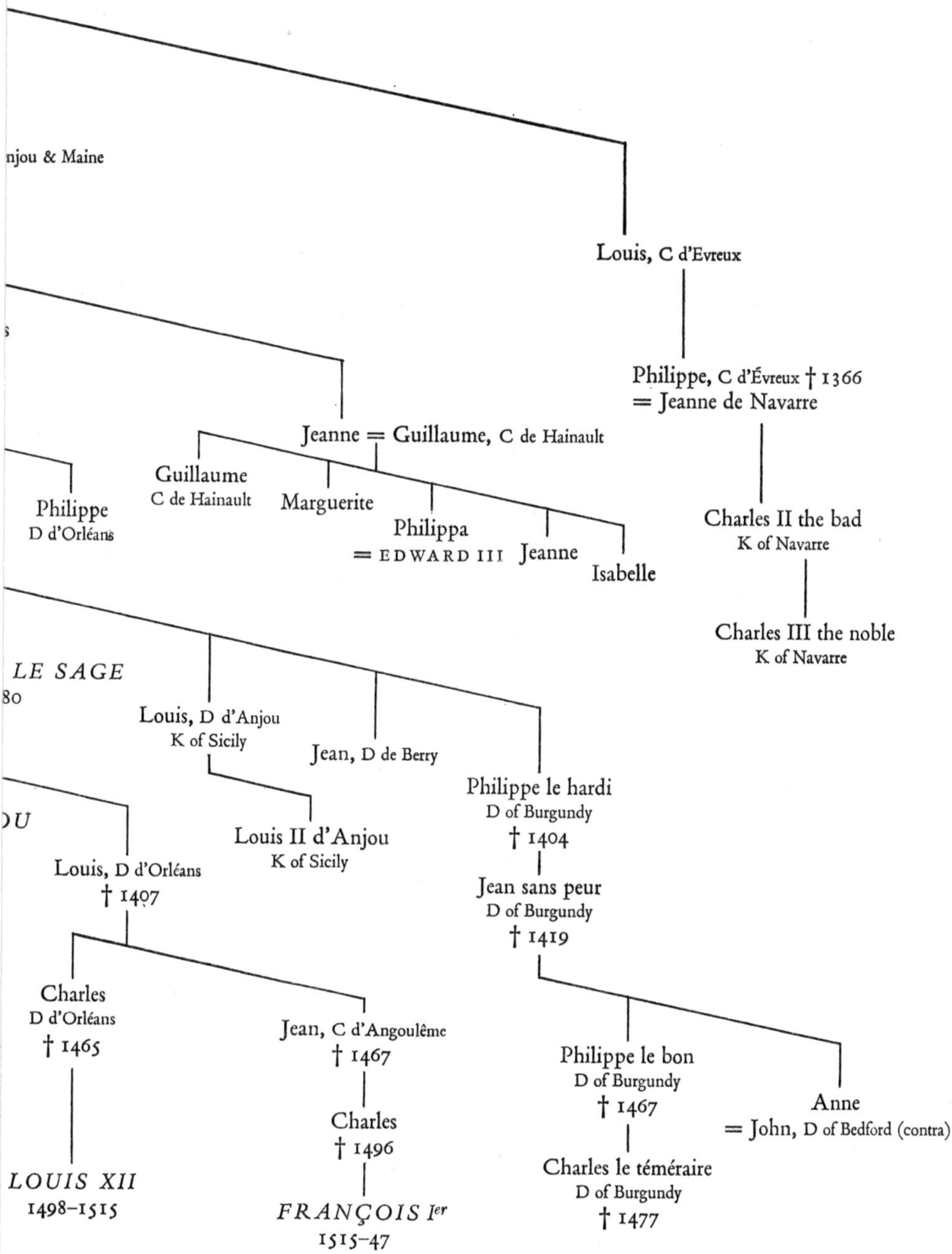

njou & Maine
Louis, C d'Evreux
Philippe, C d'Évreux † 1366
= Jeanne de Navarre
Jeanne = Guillaume, C de Hainault
Philippe
D d'Orléans
Guillaume
C de Hainault
Marguerite
Philippa
= EDWARD III
Jeanne
Isabelle
Charles II the bad
K of Navarre
Charles III the noble
K of Navarre
LE SAGE
80
Louis, D d'Anjou
K of Sicily
Jean, D de Berry
Philippe le hardi
D of Burgundy
† 1404
U
Louis II d'Anjou
K of Sicily
Louis, D d'Orléans
† 1407
Jean sans peur
D of Burgundy
† 1419
Charles
D d'Orléans
† 1465
Jean, C d'Angoulême
† 1467
Philippe le bon
D of Burgundy
† 1467
Anne
= John, D of Bedford (contra)
Charles
† 1496
Charles le téméraire
D of Burgundy
† 1477
LOUIS XII
1498–1515
FRANÇOIS Ier
1515–47

index